Jill T. Freeze

with
Dorothy Burke
Jane Calabria
Galen Grimes
Shelley O'Hara
Joe Lowery
Sue Plumley

SAMS
Teach Yourself
Computer Basics

in 24 Hours

SAMS

A Division of Macmillan Computer Publishing
201 West 103rd St., Indianapolis, Indiana, 46290 USA

Copyright © 1998 by Sams Publishing

Trademarks

EXECUTIVE EDITOR
Karen Reinisch

AQUISITIONS EDITOR
Don Essig

DEVELOPMENT EDITOR
Melanie Palasia

TECHNICAL EDITOR
Bill Bruns

MANAGING EDITOR
Thomas F. Hayes

PROJECT EDITOR
Lori A. Lyons

COPY EDITORS
Julie McNamee
Tom Stevens

INDEXER
Becky Hornyak

PRODUCTION
Lisa England
Chris Livengood

COVER DESIGNER
Aren Howell

BOOK DESIGNER
Gary Adair

Overview

Contents

Dedication

To Christopher James and Samantha Ashley, the joys of my life (in addition to Daddy, of course).
Mommy loves you very, very much!

Acknowledgments

Only one word can describe how I feel as I key in the last few sentences of this book: "Whew!" It was a frenzied schedule, but we made it against all odds. I want to thank my friends at Macmillan—Karen, Don, and Melanie—for having faith in me yet again, and for tolerating my twisted sense of humor. And to the countless people in production whom I've never had the opportunity to meet or even talk to—thanks for turning these grungy files into a polished product! And to my Tech Editor, Bill…you're the best (and your sense of humor cracks me up, too)!

About the Author

Jill T. Freeze is a freelance management consultant who has worked with such organizations as the John F. Kennedy Center for the Performing Arts, the National Endowment for the Arts, The Smithsonian, and the White House. Having used computers extensively over the past decade for work and play, Jill finally decided to put her experience to good use writing computer books. She authored *Using Microsoft Office 97* (Que, 1997) and *Introducing WebTV* (Microsoft Press, 1997). In addition, Jill has assisted her husband, Wayne, in writing several advanced computer programming books. Her formal education includes a bachelor's degree magna cum laude from the University of Massachusetts at Amherst (in Arts Administration and Writing) and a master's degree from George Washington University (in Nonprofit Administration). For fun, Jill likes listening to music, writing fiction, surfing the Net, playing her flute, cheering for her favorite NASCAR driver, Terry Labonte, and playing with her two children, Christopher and Samantha. Jill can be reached at Jfreeze@JustPC.com.

Tell Us What You Think!

As a reader, you are the most important critic and commentator of our books. We value your opinion and want to know what we're doing right, what we could do better, what areas you'd like to see us publish in, and any other words of wisdom you're willing to pass our way. You can help us make strong books that meet your needs and give you the computer guidance you require.

If you have access to the World Wide Web, check out our site at http://www.mcp.com. If you have a technical question about this book, call the technical support line at (317) 581-3833 or send email to support@mcp.com.

Your comments will help us to continue publishing the best books available on computer topics in today's market. You can contact us at

Publisher
Sams Publishing
201 West 103rd Street
Indianapolis, Indiana 46290
USA

Introduction

Congratulations, you finally did it; you joined the ranks of millions of happy PC owners from across the globe! In fact, more than 80 million people throughout the world each year are getting a new PC just like you. So what do you do with the big hunk of machinery now that you've got it?

Sams Teach Yourself Computer Basics in 24 Hours gives you the answers. Whether you decide you can't live without the Internet and want to install a modem after all, or you simply want to know how to use all that cool software that came with your system, you will find the information you need in the pages that follow.

We've also done our homework and have researched just which software is being put on the most popular computer systems today. As a result, you won't be bombarded with complex garbage you could care less about.

Who Should Read This Book?

Obviously new computer owners will find this book extremely useful, but even those contemplating buying a PC will find the hardware suggestions helpful in researching their purchase.

We've done our best to compress everything you need to know about the most popular hardware and software into one affordable volume so that you can save your hard-earned cash for fun stuff like computer games. (I highly recommend Civilization, SimCity 2000, Boggle, Microsoft Flight Simulator...anyway, back to business.) If you find you want to learn more about a certain subject, you won't be left in the dark—I will point you in the direction of some great books.

How This Book Is Organized

This book is divided into four parts:

- Part I, "What To Do First." Whether you want to learn one part of a PC from another, or you need help deciding which computer configuration to buy, this section is for you.

- Part II, "Working with Windows." An operating system can be intimidating, or it can be a powerful tool to enhance your productivity. This section of the book shows you how to "do Windows" with ease, even if your previous experience with Windows has only been a bottle of Windex.

- Part III, "The Internet and World Wide Web." We've all heard about life on the Internet. Maybe you're itching to give it a try yourself. From setting up your modem and choosing an Internet service provider to finding the information you want on the Web, it's all here in a series of quick, easy lessons.
- Part IV, "Home Essentials—What Can You Do With It?" Many new PCs come pre-installed with Microsoft's Home Essentials suite of applications. I recognize that you want to get the most for your money, so I've shown you how to get the most out of the software you already have in this section. And wait until the last chapter!

I've also included an appendix about installing and uninstalling Windows software. Each part is made up of chapters, or hours as we call them in the *Sams Teach Yourself* series.

At the beginning of each hour, you learn what's in store for you during that particular hour. You are then presented with what may seem like massive quantities of information. I've sprinkled tips and notes throughout to guide you, and have used concise steps to lead you through more complicated processes.

At the end of the hour is a quiz with multiple choice questions to test what you've learned. The answers are printed immediately following the questions, so you can check your answers quickly. And the very last thing you see in an hour is a recommended activity—an exercise that will help you put what you've learned to practice. You obviously don't have to take the quiz or complete the suggested activity to learn the material, but it sure couldn't hurt. And you may even get a laugh or two out of some of the quiz questions.

Obviously we don't intend for you to stay up 24 hours straight to get through the book (that was my job while writing it). The "in 24 Hours" part of the title is merely there to show you just how little time it will take you to get up to speed with your new computer and its software.

Finally, I feel as if I should warn you about my warped sense of humor. I behave myself a majority of the time, but every once in a while the humor escapes—usually when I'm writing questions for the end of an hour at 5:30 in the morning after being up all night fueled by Diet Coke. Don't say I didn't warn you!

Special Highlighted Elements

Because there are relatively few differences between the Windows 95 and Windows 98 operating systems, you'll often see me refer to Windows without the 95 or 98. This generic term is used only in instances where the programs behave identically. Where there are differences, I take special care to clarify it by specifying Windows 95 or Windows 98.

You'll also see a variety of special element boxes, including the following:

A **Note** presents interesting information related to the discussion.

A **Tip** offers advice or shows you an easier way of doing something.

A **Caution** alerts you to a possible problem and gives you advice on how to avoid it.

Text that you type and text that you see onscreen appear in monospace type:

```
It will look like this.
```

NEW TERM New terms are introduced using the New Term icon.

Okay, are you ready to put that new PC to work for you? Turn to Hour 1 and start your journey to becoming a confident and productive PC user. But most of all, have fun with it; you won't be receiving a report card at the end of the 24th hour.

PART I
What to Do First

Hour

Hour 1

Basic PC Hardware Defined

Whether you recently purchased a new PC or are merely contemplating taking the big plunge, this hour introduces you to all the hardware you'll find on a PC. In this hour, you learn the answers to a number of questions including

- What parts make up a computer?
- Would a smaller computer cost less money?
- How do I use the mouse?
- Can I tell how large my hard drive is?
- How much memory should my PC have?

Defining a PC

A computer is an electronic appliance—such as a TV or VCR—that you use to do some task. The amazing thing about a computer is that you can use it to do so many things. You can write letters to your favorite aunt, draw a map to include in a party invitation, play a game, create a professional-looking newsletter for your daughter's nursery school—the list goes on and on.

You don't really have to know a lot about how a computer works to use it. Think about your car. Your car works because of the different elements that make up the car: the engine, the transmission, the wheels, and so on. A PC is the same. It is actually a group of components working together.

Basically, a PC consists of hardware and software.

What Is Hardware?

The items that you unpack and actually touch are the hardware components. The hardware consists of the system box, display, keyboard, mouse, and other physical components.

What Is Software?

Software is the program instructions that turn your PC into anything you want it to be. With the applicable software, you can use your PC to write letters, create reports, draw illustrations, make a presentation, balance your check book, get on the Internet, and more. You can find many different types of software. Hour 2, "Getting Your PC Up and Running," describes some basic types of applications.

Types of PCs

Basically, you can purchase two types of computers: a PC or a Macintosh. Around 80% of the computers sold are PCs, so this book will focus on their use. You can find companies like Dell, Gateway 2000, Hewlett-Packard, and others that manufacture best-selling PCs.

Most new PCs use either Windows 98 (more about this topic in Part II, "Windows 98," of this book), Windows 95 (Windows 98's predecessor), or Windows NT (a networking version of Windows) as the operating system.

NEW TERM An *operating system* is the software that enables your computer to work. You use the operating system to run and install programs, to manage files, and more.

System Box Types

When discussing types of PCs, you may hear the term *tower model* or *desktop model*. This description refers to the style of the system box. A tower model sits upright on your floor (see Figure 1.1). A desktop model sits horizontally on your desk. The orientation of the system box is the only thing that is different; the components and how they work are the same.

FIGURE 1.1.

System boxes come in different styles: tower and desktop models.

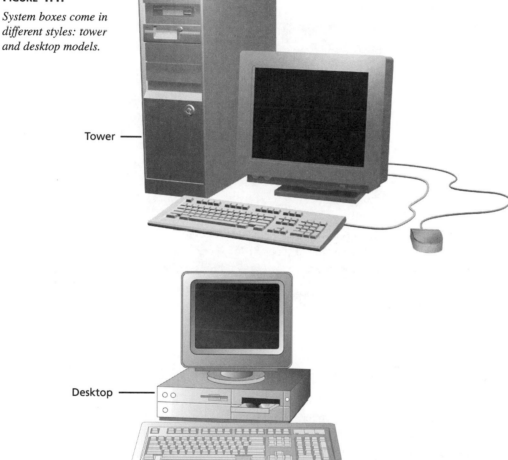

Tower

Desktop

Laptop and Notebook Computers

If you want to use your PC in one spot like your home or office, you most likely have a desktop or tower model. If, on the other hand, you travel and want to take your PC with you, you may decide to purchase a portable PC.

With a portable PC, all the elements are compacted and combined into one unit so that it's easy to carry. Portable models differ in size and weight.

A *notebook* computer is about the size of a school notebook (10 inches by 12 inches) and can weigh as little as 4–6 pounds (see Figure 1.2). You could fit a notebook PC in your briefcase. A *laptop* computer is similar to a notebook computer, but is slightly bigger. It's usually thicker and weighs more.

FIGURE 1.2.

With a notebook PC, all the components are compacted into one small case.

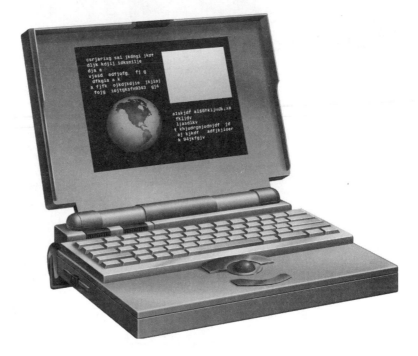

If you're thinking that smaller is less expensive, think again. Because a lot of complex technology is required to create a thin, lightweight display, laptop machines are much more expensive than their desktop counterparts. A basic laptop display costs between $1,000 and $2,000, which is a far cry from the $200 you might pay for a 15-inch monitor for your desktop system. If you *need* a notebook PC, then certainly get one. But if you don't really need one, you'll get more power and performance from a similarly priced desktop model.

A Typical PC

When you purchase a PC, whether desktop or laptop, these components are included:

- System unit
- Display (a physical monitor on a desktop system or an LCD display panel in the case of a laptop)

- Keyboard
- Mouse (or a pointing device like a trackball or touchpad in the case of a laptop)

The next sections describe these key elements as well as printers. Your PC may also include other elements like a modem or sound card.

What's Inside the System Box?

Probably the biggest element of your computer is the system box. This box houses all the electronic wizardry that makes up a PC. If you opened up the box and took a look inside, you would find the following (see Figure 1.3):

- *Microprocessor.* The most important part of the computer is the microprocessor. You can think of this chip as the computer's "brain." The microprocessor is part of the system board (the main electronic board inside the system unit) and determines the speed and features of a PC. Most everything hooks up to the system board.

- *Memory.* When you run a program or create a document, the information is stored in memory, a temporary holding area. Your computer has memory chips inside, housed on the motherboard.

- *Disk drives.* You need a more permanent storage place for your data and programs, and this place is your hard drive. In addition to a hard drive, your system has a floppy drive and a CD-ROM drive.

- *Power supply.* To power all the elements inside the system box, you need a power supply. This box is housed inside the system unit.

- *Expansion slots.* Expansion slots are used for adding features to your PC. You can insert electronic cards (sometimes called expansion cards) into these slots. Some slots may already be taken with such features as an internal modem or a sound card.

Looking at the Monitor

The monitor is the TV-like screen that you use to see what you are working on. The monitor displays programs onscreen. What you type also appears in the program window on the monitor. To use the monitor, flip the power switch. You may also make some adjustments to the display using the control knobs on the front of the monitor.

FIGURE 1.3.

The system unit houses all the important electronic components of the PC.

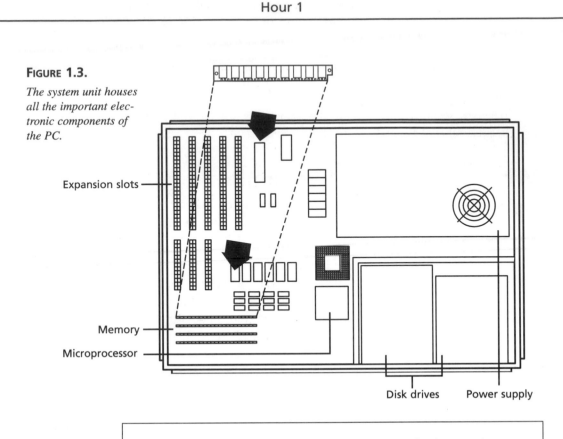

Expansion slots

Memory

Microprocessor

Disk drives   Power supply

Help, my control knobs are gone! Don't panic; many of today's monitor manufacturers conceal the knobs behind small doors near the bottom of the monitor. Look closely for what appear to be cracks in the monitor's frame, then gently try to open the door.

A monitor is actually two hardware components working together. You have the box that sits on your desk (or is the display connected to your laptop), and you have a video card inside the PC's system unit. The video card and system board are connected directly through an expansion slot; and the video card and the monitor are connected via a plug on the back of the PC. In the case of notebook and laptop computers, this connection is usually made through the computer's hinges.

Monitors differ in a few key ways: size, quality of the image (or resolution), and the standard. The easiest thing to understand is the size. Monitors are measured diagonally like TVs. Most new monitors are usually 14 inches or larger. (The larger the monitor, generally the more you can see onscreen.)

Resolution, or the quality of the displayed image, is a little trickier to understand. Computer monitors measure the number of pixels, or dots per inch, a monitor can

1

display horizontally and vertically. You may see this as 640×480 or 1,024×768. With some monitors, you can select which resolution is used. The higher the number, the more dots per inch, thus the sharper the image.

New Term A *pixel* is a dot that, when viewed in groups, makes up a larger picture. If you get close enough to your TV, you'll notice that its picture, too, is made up of tiny dots (or pixels). The more pixels, the sharper the image.

Typing on the Keyboard

To enter information—type text, select commands—you use the keyboard. Most keyboards look about the same and have about the same number of keys. The most popular keyboard is the 104-key keyboard.

You use the keyboard like a typewriter: simply press the keys. In addition to alphanumeric characters, the keyboard also includes special keys you can use for shortcuts in programs. Different keys do different things depending on the program. For instance, pressing the F1 key in most programs displays the Help contents.

To avoid repetitive stress injuries sometimes associated with typing (such as carpal tunnel syndrome), you can buy a special type of keyboard designed to support your wrists while you type. Microsoft, for instance, sells this type of ergonomic keyboard. You can also purchase special mousepads with gel-filled wrist supports to protect your wrists from injury.

Using a Mouse

Windows, because it is a graphical user interface, provides an additional way to make choices. Windows enables you to point to and select what you want with an input device called a *mouse*.

New Term Commands can be given by pointing to or clicking on certain pictures known as icons. In the past, computer users had to use text made up of sometimes cryptic abbreviations to tell the computer what to do. Thanks to *Graphical User Interfaces,* or *GUIs* (pronounced "gooey"), all we have to do now is point and click.

The mouse is standard equipment on a PC. You can use the mouse to select menu commands, start programs, open windows, manipulate windows, and more.

Instead of mice, laptops may have a touch pad that allows you to control the cursor with your fingertip, or it may have something called a *trackball* which you roll to move the cursor. In both cases, you still have access to two buttons that act as counterparts to the left and right mouse buttons.

Many beginners have trouble getting the hang of the mouse, but after you get some practice, you'll find that it comes natural. The following are the basic mouse moves:

- *Point*. To point to something onscreen, move the mouse on the desk until the pointer (it looks like an arrow) is in the spot you want.
- *Click*. To click, press the left mouse button once. Most mice have more than one button. The left button is used most often.
- *Right-click*. You may find some shortcut menus that you can access by using the right mouse button.
- *Double-click*. To double-click, press the left mouse button twice in rapid succession.
- *Drag*. To drag, click and hold down the left mouse button and then drag the mouse. You use this dragging motion to select text, to move items, and to perform other tasks.

Many different companies manufacture mice, including Microsoft. The newest Microsoft mouse is called the Intellimouse and includes a roller between the left and right mouse buttons that allows you to scroll through Microsoft Office documents quickly without having to position the cursor on the vertical scrollbar.

Printing with the Printer

When you purchase a new PC, you can expect that PC to include the system unit and all its contents, the display, the keyboard, and the mouse. This is a typical PC setup. In addition to these elements, you may also purchase a printer. Most likely you'll use your PC to create some type of document that you will want to print.

You can expect to find the following types of printers: inkjet printers and laser printers.

Inkjet Printers

You can think of inkjet printers as middle of the road. This type of printer doesn't offer the same quality as a laser printer, but it is far better than a dot-matrix. They are usually between the two in cost also.

An inkjet printer works by spraying tiny dots on a page through a tiny nozzle. The quality of the printout is usually pretty good, and the price is often reasonable. If you want a color printer, inkjet color printers are especially worth considering.

Laser Printers

A laser printer offers the fastest printing and better quality than any other type of printer. On the downside, it is usually a bit more expensive than other printer types. The price range and feature list of laser printers can vary greatly.

What Drives Do You Have?

Computers need a place to store information (files and programs) and that place is called the disk drive. When you save a file, the information is recorded magnetically onto the drive's surface. When you want to use that information again, the disk reads the information from the drive. On most new PCs, you can expect to have the following drive types:

- *Floppy drive.* If you take a close look at your system unit, you'll notice a slot (like a little mail slot) on the front. This is the door to your floppy drive. To get data onto and off of your hard drive, you can use a floppy disk and drive.
- *Hard drive.* A hard drive is housed inside your system unit and is your main "cabinet" for storing files.
- *Zip drive.* A removable drive similar to a floppy disk, but stores about 80 times as much data. This drive can be integrated into the system unit or attached as an external drive to your system's parallel port.
- *CD-ROM drive.* Newer PCs usually come with a CD-ROM drive as standard equipment; older computers may not have this type of drive.

Learn What Kinds of Drives You Have

Which drives do you have? A quick way to find out is to open My Computer. Don't worry, you won't need a screwdriver for this. You should see drive icons for each of the drives on your system.

To Do: Checking the Drives on Your PC

1. Double-click the My Computer icon on the desktop. You see the contents of your system, including icons for each drive (see Figure 1.4). You also see some system folders.
2. Click the Close (X) button to close the window.

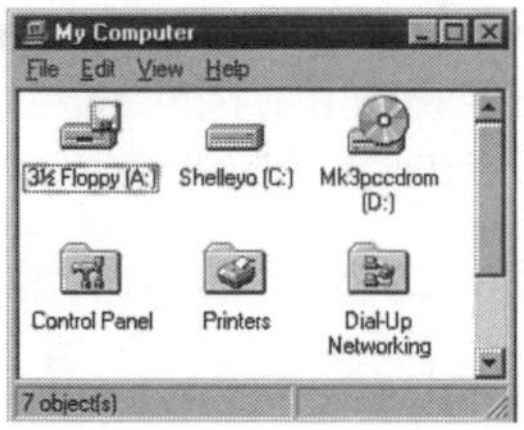

FIGURE 1.4.

Check out the drives on your PC by clicking the My Computer icon.

What Is a Floppy Drive?

Your hard disk is the primary storage space for programs or files; therefore, you need a way to get programs onto the hard disk. Also, you may want to take a file with you—for example, take a file from your office PC to your home PC. A floppy disk drive provides the medium for moving information onto and off of your hard drive. This type of disk is 3 1/2 inches in size and is encased in hard plastic.

Disks vary in the amount of information they can store (called the *capacity*). The capacity is measured in megabytes (MB) or kilobytes (KB). A typical 3 1/2-inch floppy disk can contain about 1.44MB of data. Some older 3 1/2-inch floppy disks may contain only 720KB of data.

Although Windows allows you to have up to two floppy disk drives, most likely you'll have only one. This drive is known as Drive A.

To insert a floppy disk into the drive, slide it label up into the drive until you hear a click. If you don't hear a click, turn the floppy over and slide it into the drive again. Do not force the floppy into the drive or you could damage the drive. To eject a disk, press the disk drive button.

What Is a Hard Drive?

All PCs come with a hard disk, and you store your programs and data files on this hard disk. The hard disk is housed inside the system unit. Most systems have just one hard disk, but you can always add another—either another internal drive housed in the system unit or an external drive that is connected to the PC via a cable.

Like the floppy drive, the hard drive has a name, and it is called Drive C. In some systems, you may have more than one hard drive. In this case, the additional drives will be called Drive D, Drive E, and so on. The last drive in your system will typically be the CD-ROM drive. In a system with only one hard drive, the CD-ROM will be called Drive D. In a system with two hard drives, it will be called Drive E.

How Drives Differ

Drives differ in a few key ways. The most important distinction is size (again, called the capacity). Hard drives are measured in megabytes (MB) or gigabytes (GB). The bigger the drive, the better. You will be surprised how fast your drive fills up with programs and files.

The microprocessor and hard drive communicate to each other via a controller, and drives differ in the type of controller they use. Table 1.1 gives you a quick breakdown of the different controller types.

TABLE 1.1. DISK DRIVE CONTROLLERS.

Name	Description
IDE	Stands for Integrated Device Electronics. This older controller has been replaced by EIDE.
SCSI	Stands for Small Computer Systems Interface. A controller that enables you to chain different devices together. Typically used when speed is most important.
EIDE	Stands for Enhanced Integrated Device Electronics. A newer version of the IDE controller.

To Do: Figure Out the Size of Your Hard Disk

When you first purchased your PC, you probably knew the size of the hard drive off the top of your head; but after you've had your PC awhile, you may not remember the size. You also may want to review how much space is taken and how much space is free. You can quickly review this and other hard drive information using Windows 95 or 98. Follow these steps:

1. Double-click the My Computer icon on the desktop.
2. Right-click the icon for your hard drive.
3. From the submenu that appears, select Properties. You see the Properties dialog box, shown in Figure 1.5. You can see the capacity of the drive, the space used, and the space free.
4. Review the information and then click the OK button.

In addition to a hard drive, you may also have a CD-ROM drive, which is covered in the next section.

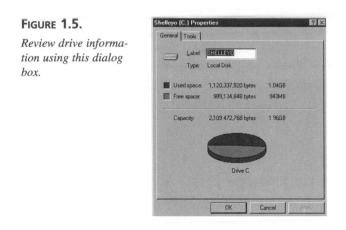

FIGURE 1.5.

Review drive informa-tion using this dialog box.

What Is a CD-ROM Drive?

Floppy disks can only store so much information; therefore, a newer method for distrib-uting information emerged: CD-ROMs. These discs can store much more information than a regular floppy disk; they can store over 600M of data. You can both read and write information to a floppy disk, however, you can only read the data from a CD-ROM. (ROM stands for Read-Only Memory.)

If you have a newer PC, you most likely have a CD-ROM drive as part of your system. Usually this drive is housed inside the system unit, and like other drives has a name. If you have just one hard drive, your CD-ROM drive is most likely Drive D.

CD-ROM drives differ in their speed. You often see the speed advertised as 12X; that's twelve times as fast as the original drive's speed. Speed measurements like 12X can be arbitrary. If you really want to know the speed, you'll have to find out its access time and transfer time.

To insert a disc into the drive, press the Eject button and then lay the disc inside the drive. Press the drive door to insert the disc. Some drives have a cartridge. Insert the disc into the cartridge and then insert the cartridge into the drive.

Other Drives

If you use your PC for business, you'll want to be sure to set up a backup routine. A backup makes an extra copy of your data so if something happens to the original, you can use the backup copy. To save time backing up, you may have purchased a special type of tape backup unit.

A floppy disk can store only so much information. If you work with large documents—graphics, sound, and video documents are usually huge—you may want to try the new

1

Zip drives by Iomega. These drives are similar to floppy drives, but the disks can store much more information. Many new PCs offer a Zip drive as an optional upgrade.

New CD-R (CD Recordable) drives are becoming available. With this type of drive, you not only can read information from a CD, but you can also write data to the disc. However you can only write to a CD-R once. A newer technology called CD-RW (CD ReWritable) is also available, which will allow you to change the contents of the disk after it's been written.

What Is the Microprocessor?

The most important part of a computer is the microprocessor chip, sometimes called the CPU (central processing unit) or simply processor. This chip determines the power of a computer. The two most important distinctions of the microprocessor are the name, or type, of chip and the speed.

The Type of Chip

Originally, processor chips were named with numbers—the higher the number, the more powerful the chip. The following is a breakdown of the recent history of the microprocessor used in PCs:

Pentium	The fastest computer chip available four years ago. Today it is the slowest.
Pentium MMX	A Pentium chip with enhanced multimedia capabilities. This chip effectively made the Pentium obsolete.
Pentium Pro	Faster than the Pentium chip, but does not include MMX capabilities.
Pentium II	A Pentium Pro chip with MMX capabilities.

If you recently purchased a PC, you probably have a Pentium MMX or Pentium II. If you have an older PC or a used PC, you may have a PC that uses an older chip. How can you tell? Look at the system box. Usually, you can find the processor type and speed (covered next) somewhere on the system box.

How Fast Is Your PC?

The speed of the chip is rated in megahertz (MHz). One megahertz equals one million clock ticks per second. The higher the megahertz, the faster the computer.

Most chips are available in different speeds, and you pay more for the faster computer. If you went shopping for a PC today, you could expect to find PCs at 200MHz (slowest) to 333MHz or more (fastest). Again, the system box or the model name of your PC usually includes the speed. For instance, if you see P6-200, you have a 200 MHz Pentium II processor.

Who Makes the Microprocessor?

You may see advertisements for Intel and even see an Intel logo on your PC. Intel does not make PCs. They only make the microprocessors. For a long time, Intel dominated the PC chip market, but you can now find a few other companies such as AMD and Cyrix that also manufacture microprocessor chips. These chips are compatible with the Intel chips and will run Windows applications without any problems.

What Is Memory?

After the microprocessor, the next most important component of the computer is the amount of memory, or RAM, it has. RAM stands for *random access memory* and is the working area of the computer where the computer stores instructions and data. The more memory, the better.

RAM is measured in bytes. One kilobyte (abbreviated K or KB) equals roughly 1,000 bytes. (One kilobyte actually equals 1,024 bytes, but the numbers are rounded.) One megabyte (abbreviated M or MB) equals roughly 1,000,000 bytes. One gigabyte (abbreviated G or GB) equals roughly one 1,000,000,000 bytes. If you bought a new PC today, you could expect to find PCs with anywhere from 16MB to 64MB or more of RAM, although some PCs can have as much as 1GB of memory.

How Much Memory Do You Have?

It's easy to forget just how much memory your system has. If you aren't sure, you can display the amount of memory (as well as the processor type) by following these steps:

1. On the Windows desktop, right-click the My Computer icon.
2. From the shortcut menu that appears, select Properties.

   You see the System Properties dialog box which displays some information about your system (see Figure 1.6).
3. Click the Cancel button to close the dialog box.

FIGURE 1.6.

You can tell the processor type and amount of memory from this dialog box.

Adding Memory

You can add memory to upgrade your PC. Doing so can improve the performance of your PC dramatically. Adding memory is a fairly simple upgrade. The hardest part is figuring out what type and size of memory chips your system takes. Sometimes, you may have to remove your current memory to increase the total size. You can usually find out this information by reviewing your system documentation or by calling the PC manufacturer.

> Although Windows can run with 16MB of memory, upgrading to 32MB of memory is worth the extra expense.

Modems

Your PC may also include a modem. Why have a modem? Because you can use a modem (and a phone line) to hook up to online services such as America Online and to connect to the Internet. You can send and receive email messages, visit Web pages, participate in online discussion groups, and more. (You can learn more about the Internet in Part III, "The Internet and World Wide Web.")

You may have either an internal modem that is housed inside the system unit, or an external modem that sits on your desk and is connected to your PC via a cable.

How a Modem Works

The computer creates and works with digital information (on and off switches, or 0s and 1s). A phone line, on the other hand, transmits information using analog signals (or sound waves). That's where the modem comes in. *Modem* stands for *MO*dulator-*DEM*odulator, which means it translates the digital information to analog and sends the analog information over the phone lines. The receiving modem then translates the analog information back to digital.

How Fast Is Your Modem?

Time is money, even if you're merely linking up to the Internet to scan the latest NASCAR rumors. The speed of your modem can radically affect your surfing speed. Modem speed is measured in bits per second (bps) or kilobits per second (Kbps). (You may hear the term *baud* which is often used to mean bps.) Common speeds for today's modems are 33,600 (or 33.6Kbps) and 56,000 (or 56Kbps). Many new computers come with 56Kbps modems.

> Your existing phone line may not be able to handle the full speed of your modem. This may be due to the amount of noise on your telephone line or the type of modems used by your Internet provider.

A Combination Fax Modem

In addition to a plain modem, you can also purchase a fax modem. Using your computer and a fax modem, you can send and receive faxes over the phone line.

With a fax modem, you create the document you want to fax on the computer. Then using the fax modem, you can send this document over the phone lines to any type of fax machine (not just computer fax modems). Your computer can also receive faxes. You can view them onscreen or have them printed directly to your printer.

> Keep in mind that you can't fax paper copies using a fax modem; you can send only documents created using the computer. So much for faxing your ad sketch to a client, unless, of course you scan it (see upcoming section on scanners).

Sound Cards and Speakers

Another hardware component you may have (or consider adding) is a sound card. A sound card is an electronic card housed inside the system unit; it is inserted in an expansion slot inside your PC. You then hook up speakers to the sound card.

With a sound card, you can play and hear sounds. Where do you find these sounds? Many multimedia programs include sounds. For instance, if you have a multimedia encyclopedia (like Microsoft Encarta, which is packaged with Microsoft Home Essentials 98), you can look up entries for, say, Martin Luther King and play back his famous "I Have a Dream" speech.

Many games also include sound effects. You can even record and include a sound message in a document. Also, as you explore the Internet, you will find sound files, such as interviews, new music clips, and other audio information.

And yes, you can play your audio CDs on your computer's CD-ROM drive. To do so, you can use the CD Player program included with Windows 98. Hour 7, "Using Windows 98 Applications," describes this and other sound features of Windows 98. Some audio CDs, such as James Taylor's Hourglass, include photos and interviews that are displayed on your computer while you listen to the music.

Scanners

If you are an artist or have an interest in creating artwork, you may consider adding a scanner to your PC. A scanner converts a printed image into an electronic image so you can manipulate the image on the PC. For example, you can scan in photographs, illustrations, and documents and email them to others, or use them to design a personal Web page.

A flat-bed scanner works like a photocopier. A hand-held scanner works by moving the scanner over the image. Much like a monitor, the resolution of a scanner is expressed in terms of dots per inch. The greater the number, the higher the image quality.

Scanners can also be used to convert typed text into a computer file. Remember that terrific creative writing project you did in college? Using special OCR (Optical Character Recognition) software that often comes with a scanner, you can quickly convert the document into a computer file for easy manipulation.

Joysticks

Play a lot of games? If so, a joystick might be on your PC upgrade list. Some games, especially arcade-style games, are easier to play with a joystick. You plug a joystick into one of the ports at the back of your PC. You can then use the joystick controls to jump, punch, shoot, dodge, and so on, depending on your game of choice. Microsoft even manufactures a force feedback joystick that moves according to the action onscreen. You can actually feel that fighter jet's resistance! You can also purchase a variety of steering wheels, gas pedals, and rudder pedals.

Digital Cameras

Tired of wasting film only to get one or two good pictures per roll? Consider investing in a digital camera. Although the quality of a standard 35mm camera is still quite pricey in its digital counterpart, that's bound to change in the foreseeable future. With digital cameras, you can take your pictures, then accept or reject your shots using your computer without having to purchase all the shots on the developed film.

Frame-Grabbers

For around one hundred dollars, you can hook a device called a Snappy up to your computer. When the second end is attached to your television, you can grab pictures of your favorite TV stars. Likewise, you can connect your camcorder to your computer via the Snappy to grab still pictures or even video of your friends and family.

Summary

In this hour, you learned the basics of all the hardware you're likely to encounter when dealing with your PC. You now know how all the hardware works together to perform the tasks you desire. Although it's far from in-depth coverage, it's more than enough to give you a sound foundation for getting the most out of your PC.

In the next hour, we'll get you up and running on your PC, and introduce you to the software that makes a computer "do its thing."

Workshop

The following workshop helps you solidify the skills you learned in this hour.

Quiz

Take the following quiz to see how much you've learned.

Questions

1. The speed of a modem is measured in:

    a. MHz (megahertz)

    b. MB (megabytes)

    c. bps (bits per second)

2. What is resolution?

    a. The number of dots (pixels) per inch

    b. Something you make on New Year's Eve

    c. A powerful computer monitor cleaning solution

3. How much RAM should your computer have?

    a. What do sheep have to do with computers?

    b. As much as you can possibly afford!

    c. 8MB is just fine

Answers

1. c. bps.

2. a. Although a and b are perfectly legitimate answers, a is the correct choice given the context of the question.

3. b. Of course sheep have nothing to do with computers. And if you think 8MB will cover you, I have some swamp land…

Activity

Use the steps presented in this hour to learn the following about your PC:

- How much disk space is free on your system

- How much memory your PC has

Hour 2

Getting Your PC Up and Running

Your new PC just arrived at your home, so what should you do next? This hour gives you everything you need to prepare for the big event. From choosing a workspace to installing new software, it's all here. In this whirlwind tour, you'll learn the answers to the following questions, among others:

- How do I hook up my new computer?
- What happens when I turn the PC on?
- Can I just shut it off when I'm done with it?
- What kinds of computer programs are available?
- How do I install a new program?

Setting Up Your PC

Although PCs have become easier to set up over time, there are still plenty of things to consider before you can rip open that box and begin playing around. First, be sure you've chosen an appropriate workspace:

- *Choosing the right workspace*. You need a flat surface (usually a desk, although a banquet table is a good, sturdy alternative in a pinch) for the system unit, monitor, keyboard, and mouse. You can stack the monitor on top of the system unit if you want. If you have other hardware components, such as speakers, or a printer, be sure you have room to accommodate these items, too. All these components must be located close enough to your PC to allow you to plug them into the back of your PC. You'll also want to have enough space to be able to lay papers and office supplies as you work.

Before you rush out and buy that neat computer desk you saw at the local wholesale club, here are some things to consider. If you've got a 17-inch or larger monitor, not just any desk will do. Some value-priced furniture will warp quickly under the enormous weight. Check out the furniture by placing your palms on the surface in between the legs, then shifting your weight to your hands. If the furniture moves or wiggles a bit, it's unlikely to hold up well long-term.

- *Power supply*. The system unit, monitor, and printer need to be plugged into a three-pronged outlet, so you need a power source close by. (If your house has only two-prong outlets, you can use one of the three-to-two prong adapters, but please make sure that you use it properly to ensure your own safety and the safety of your system.) You would be wise to purchase a surge protector. Not only can you plug all the components into this power strip, but the surge protector can protect against power surges, which can damage data and your PC. Also, don't confuse a surge protector with a regular power strip. They often look the same, but a power strip offers no protection against power surges.

Surge protectors cannot protect from lightning. In severe weather, unplug the entire system from the power and the telephone lines to avoid damage to your PC. A surge protector outlet strip has a specific rating for surges. Also these types usually have a guarantee from the manufacturer that if your equipment is damaged, they will reimburse a "flat" monetary rate. Surge protectors also can provide protection for a telephone line.

- *Phone jack*. If you plan to use your modem to connect to the Internet or other online services, you need a phone line connection.
- *Typing comfortably*. When deciding where to place your keyboard, keep in mind that you want your wrists flat as you type. If you bend them up or down, you run

the risk of injury. You can purchase computer desks that have a separate, pull-out shelf for the keyboard.

- *Viewing the monitor.* You don't want the monitor too close or too far away. Check the height of the monitor; it should be directly in front of you at eye level to avoid neck and eye strain. If you place the computer in a room with windows, check for glare on the monitor. Remember to check during different times of the day to avoid early morning or late afternoon glare from the sun.

Unpacking the PC

After you have picked out the location for your new PC, you can unpack your system unit. Be sure to save all the documentation and paperwork included with the PC. Keep all this information in one place.

You should also save your boxes and molded foam in case you need to ship your system. If a problem occurs with your PC, you may need to ship it back to the manufacturer in the original packing. The boxes are also handy if you move or need to ship your PC for some other reason.

Making All the Connections

Your computer should come with complete instructions on what connections you need to make. On all PCs, you make some basic connections (the monitor, keyboard, and mouse). Depending on the equipment you have, you may need to make other connections. For instance, if you have a sound card, you need to hook up your speakers.

All the connections are made to the back of the PC which, as you can see in Figure 2.1, has various types of connectors. You have to match up each connector to the appropriate cable. If you are lucky, each connector is labeled or color-coded. If not, you can refer to your system documentation for help.

The basic connections you need to make include

- Connect the video cable from the monitor to the monitor connector on the back of the PC.
- Connect the keyboard cable to the keyboard connector on the back of the PC.
- Connect the mouse cable to the mouse connector on the back of the PC.
- Connect the printer to the printer port on the back of the PC. Most printers connect to the parallel or LPT1 port. If you have a serial printer, you connect to one of the serial ports.
- Connect the power cord for the monitor to the back of the monitor. The other end will plug into the power source.

- Connect the power cord for the PC to the back of the PC. The other end will plug into the power source.

FIGURE 2.1.

The back of the PC has connectors for each hardware component you need to hook up.

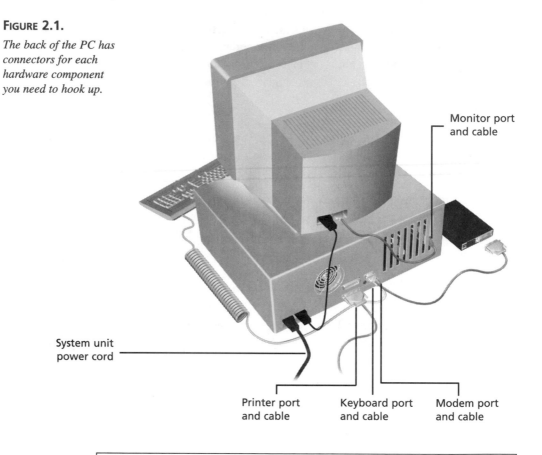

Monitor port and cable

System unit power cord

Printer port and cable

Keyboard port and cable

Modem port and cable

> If you can't figure out what goes where, you can count the pins. A printer port has 25 pins. A standard serial port on current retail computers has 9 pins, and a VGA monitor port has 15 pins. Also, use care when hooking up the keyboard and mouse because they usually have similar connectors. Look on the back of your system for matching icons or colors to ensure that you have the correct device plugged into the proper port. (See your system's documentation for more information.)

You may also need to hook up speakers to the sound card. The speakers may also have a separate power connection. Check your manual.

If you have an internal modem, the back of the PC also contains jacks for plugging in your phone line. Make any other connections.

> You should keep all the paperwork together—invoice, warranties, software certificates, receipts, and so on. Keep all the system documentation in one place. You may need to refer to the documentation for setup and to troubleshoot any problems that pop up.

Turning On the PC

Now that everything's hooked together, you're all set to go. Flip the power switches to start the PC. You should see some information flash across the screen as your system goes through its startup routine. For instance, you may see the results of a memory check, or you may see setup commands for your hardware. After the system starts up, you should see Windows 98 (or whatever operating system you have on your PC). Windows 98 starts automatically each time you turn on your PC.

If nothing happens when you turn on your PC, check the following:

- Do both the PC and the monitor have power?
- Are all the components connected?
- Did you turn on both the monitor and the PC? They each have separate power buttons.
- If you are using a surge protector/power strip, is it turned on as well?
- Do you need to adjust the monitor? The monitor includes buttons for controlling the brightness of the display. It's easy to think the monitor isn't working when in fact you just can't see anything because of the brightness or other settings. Check these controls.

Try These Things Before Restarting Your PC

Using a PC isn't error-proof. Sometimes things happen that make the PC freeze up. For instance, a program may crash. When this happens, pressing the keys does nothing. First, check to see if the disk activity light is blinking. You can find this light on the front of the PC. If the light is blinking or you hear sounds from the hard drive, the PC may be busy saving a file or handling some other activity. Wait a few minutes. Second, be sure you know where you are. It's easy to switch to a different program, say back to the Windows desktop, without intending to. You think you are typing in your word processing program, but you are really back at the desktop, and Windows 98 doesn't understand all that typing. Try clicking in the area you were working in to make sure you are in the program you think you are.

Third, check the screen. As another example, you may have opened a menu or dialog box without realizing it. Again, if you try typing, all you may hear are beeps. Try pressing Esc (the Escape key) to close any open menus or dialog boxes.

To Do: Restarting the PC

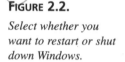

If all else fails, you can restart your PC. First, try the menu command:

1. Click the Start button and select Shut Down. You see the Shut Down Windows dialog box (see Figure 2.2).

2. Select Restart the Computer.

3. Click the Yes button.

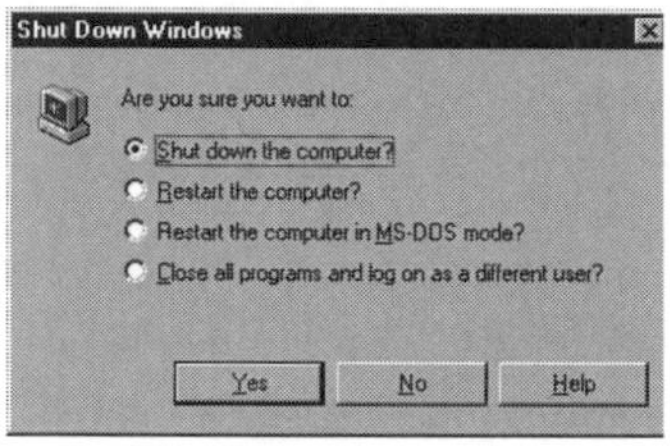

FIGURE 2.2.

Select whether you want to restart or shut down Windows.

Shut Down Windows	✕

Are you sure you want to:

- ⦿ Shut down the computer?
- ○ Restart the computer?
- ○ Restart the computer in MS-DOS mode?
- ○ Close all programs and log on as a different user?

| Yes | No | Help |

If you can't click to get the Start menu to open, you have to use a different method. Try the keyboard method: Press and hold down the Ctrl key. Then press Alt and Delete. You often see this abbreviated as Ctrl+Alt+Delete.

If the keyboard method doesn't work, press the Reset button on the front of the PC. Finally if that doesn't work, or if you don't have a Reset button, try turning the PC off, count to ten, and then turning the PC back on. Note that although this will physically stop Windows, you may encounter problems when you start your system next time.

> If you need to install a DOS program, you can restart your PC in MS-DOS mode by selecting Restart in MS-DOS mode. Many games, for instance, are DOS programs and are installed and run from MS-DOS mode. Learn more about installing software later in this hour.

Shutting Down the PC

Windows 98 takes care of all the background details of using your PC—things like storing files, handling the printer, and so on. Because it is often busy in the background, you shouldn't just turn off your PC. Instead, use the proper shutdown procedure so Windows can take care of any housekeeping tasks before turning off the power.

To Do: Shutting Off Your PC

Follow these steps to shut off your PC properly:

1. Click the Start button and select Shut Down. You see the Shut Down Windows dialog box (refer to Figure 2.2).

2. Select Shut Down the Computer.

3. Click the Yes button.

▲ When you see a message saying that it is safe to turn off your PC, you can turn it off.

So What, Exactly, Is This Thing Called Windows?

To handle the communication between the different hardware components, you need a system program. This program is called the operating system, and it handles such things as starting programs, storing files, printing documents, and so on.

All computers come with an operating system, and the most popular operating system is Windows 95 or Windows 98. Windows NT is another operating system that may be running on your machine if you are using a high-end workstation. To determine which operating system you are using, click the Start button. The name of the operating system will appear in a vertical bar on the left side of the menu choices.

To use your computer, you do need to know a few things about Windows, and you can find some of the key Windows tasks and concepts in Part II, "Windows 98." Most of your time using your computer won't be spent actually in Windows, although Windows will be busy in the background handling all the behind-the-scenes type of work.

Most of your time using a PC will be spent using some type of application. The next section discusses the most popular types of applications.

Other Types of Applications

To perform a certain type of task using your computer—for instance, typing a letter—you need an application or program for that task. When you purchase a new PC, you may receive some applications as part of the purchase. (Many of the most reasonably priced systems today are shipped with Microsoft Home Essentials 98, which we'll look at in-depth in Part IV, "Home Essentials—What You Can Do With It.") Windows 95/98 also includes some mini-applications, for instance a paint program, an audio CD player, and the ever-popular solitaire card game. These applications will get you started. You may later want to purchase additional applications as you learn to do more and more with your PC.

> You will hear the terms program, application, or some combination (application program) used interchangeably. They all mean the same thing.

Word Processors

The most common type of application is word processing. You can use this type of program to create documents such as letters, memos, reports, manuscripts, and so on. If there was something you would have once done on a typewriter, you now use a word processing program for the task. The following is a quick list of some of the things you can do with this type of program:

- *Easily edit text.* You can move text from one page to another, even one document to another. You can also copy or delete text with just a few keystrokes.
- *Format text.* Formatting means changing the appearance of text. You can make text bold, change the font, use a different color, and so on. Later in this hour you learn how to make some formatting changes.
- *Format paragraphs and pages.* In addition to simple text changes, you can also format paragraphs (indent, add bullets, add a border) and pages (change the margins, add page numbers, insert a header).
- *Check accuracy.* Most programs include a spell-check program for checking the spelling. Some programs also include programs for checking grammar.

If you have Home Essentials and Windows 95 or 98 installed on your computer, you have three word processor programs available to you. These programs are described in the following list:

- *WordPad*. This is a basic word processor that includes the capability to edit and format text.

- *Works Word Processor*. A more advanced word processor than WordPad. It includes features such as spell checking and table formatting that are not included in WordPad.

- *Word for Windows*. This is Microsoft's premiere word processing program, which offers many features like IntelliSense AutoCompletion and AutoCorrection, grammatical analysis, and other advanced features beyond those available in the Works Word Processor.

Spreadsheets

If numbers are your game, you'll probably work with a spreadsheet application. This type of program enables you to enter and manipulate all kinds of financial information: budgets, sales statistics, income, expenses, and so on. The benefit of a spreadsheet program is that you have so many options for working with the data you enter. You can do any of the following:

- *Perform simple to complex calculations*. You can total a row of numbers, calculate a percentage, figure the amortization of a loan, and more.

- *Format the data*. You can make changes to how text and numbers appear in the worksheet. You can also adjust the column width, add borders, change the alignment of entries, and more.

- *Chart the data*. You can create different types of charts to visually represent the data. For instance, add a line chart to a report to illustrate a sales trend.

- *Manage data lists*. Most spreadsheets also include features for managing simple data lists. You can enter, sort, and query simple data lists using the grid structure of a worksheet.

Home Essentials comes with a spreadsheet tool called *Works Spreadsheet Tool* (which is discussed in Hour 20, "Using the Works Spreadsheet Tool") that has all the features mentioned previously. If you need a more powerful spreadsheet program, you might want to purchase Microsoft Excel, Lotus 1-2-3, or Quattro Pro, which are all popular spreadsheet programs.

In addition to spreadsheet programs, you can also use other types of financial programs. For example, you can purchase a program to keep track of your check register. One of the most popular check management programs is Money 98, which you'll see in detail in Hours 22, "Getting Started with Microsoft Money 98" and 23, "Using Money 98" of this book. You can also find programs for calculating your income tax (TurboTax), managing your small business (QuickBooks), handling major accounting tasks (PeachTree Accounting), and so on.

Databases

If word processing and spreadsheets are the first two in application popularity, then databases round out the Big Three. You can use a database program to track and manage any set of data: addresses and phone numbers of friends and clients, business and home inventories, orders, events, and so on. Database programs vary from simple list managers to complex programs you can use to manage linked systems of information.

Databases offer a lot of advantages when you are working with large amounts of information. First, you can easily search for and find a particular piece of information. Second, you can sort the data into different orders as needed. Sort a client list alphabetically for a phone list. Sort by ZIP code for a mailing. Third, you can work with subsets of the data: all clients in South Dakota, all clients that ordered more than $1,000 worth of products, and so on.

Home Essentials includes a database program called Works Database Tool, which offers all these features. In addition to this tool, some other popular database applications include Microsoft Access, Lotus Approach, and Borland Paradox. Each of these applications offer more power and flexibility than the Works Database Tool. If your needs are not complex, however, you may want to try building a simple spreadsheet using the Works Spreadsheet Tool.

Graphics and Presentation Programs

Even if you aren't artistic, you can use your PC and the right software program to create graphics. Depending on your needs (and skill levels), you can consider any of the four types of programs in this category:

- *Simple drawing programs*. You can use a simple drawing program, such as Paint, which is included with Windows, to create simple illustrations. Larger applications, like Microsoft Word, include applets (small applications) such as WordArt and AutoShapes that let you dabble in the visual arts whether you have artistic talent or not.

- *Complex drawing programs*. You can also find more sophisticated programs for drawing and working with images. For instance, Adobe Illustrator and Adobe Photoshop are two such packages.

- *Special purpose drawing programs.* There are special purpose drawing programs like Microsoft Greetings Workshop and Microsoft Publisher that let you perform specific tasks such as creating your own greeting cards or developing a newsletter. Many children's games also include ways for them to create and print their own artwork.

- *Presentation programs.* If you ever have to give a presentation, you may want to use a program designed just for creating presentations. You can use this program to create slides, handouts, and notes. Microsoft PowerPoint, Corel Presentations, and Freelance Graphics are popular presentation programs.

Suites or Bundles

Microsoft Home Essentials 98 includes everything from a word processor to an encyclopedia to a greeting card designer and more. Part 4 of this book is dedicated to this useful collection of software. Microsoft offers several versions of Office 97, its suite of applications. The standard Office suite includes Word, Excel, PowerPoint, and Outlook. The professional edition adds Access. Corel and Lotus offer similar suites that include their most popular word processing, spreadsheet, database, and presentation programs.

Personal Information Managers

Most people have several things to keep track of: people, events, appointments, places, and so on. Personal information managers (or PIMs) are just the program for storing names and addresses, keeping track of your schedule, jotting down notes, and so on. You can think of this type of program as your "electronic" day planner. Microsoft Outlook acts as a PIM in addition to being an email program.

Games and Educational Software

Two other broad categories of software are games and educational software. Here you will find a wealth and variety of programs. Learn how to cook, chart your family tree, play a card game, conquer another planet, speak French. The list goes on and on. See Hour 24, "Having Fun with Home Essentials," for more information about this type of software.

Internet Programs

If you want to use your computer to hook up to the Internet, you need a Web browser. The two most popular are Netscape Communicator and Microsoft Internet Explorer. These programs also act as email applications. Netscape has Messenger, and Microsoft has Outlook Express. You can even buy easy-to-use Web authoring tools like Microsoft FrontPage, although Microsoft's word processor and desktop publishing programs also have Web page design capabilities. You'll learn to use Internet Explorer 4 in this book, starting with Hour 11, "Using Microsoft Internet Explorer."

Utility Programs

When you want to fine-tune your computer, check out some of the utility programs available. These programs may add capabilities to your system such as virus checking, backing up, and so on. Norton Utilities is an example of this type of application.

Purchasing a New Program

Although your computer probably came with a number of preinstalled applications, at some point you'll want to make some changes. You may want to upgrade an existing program to the newest version, or you may want to purchase an entirely new program.

You can find software in some retail stores, computer stores, and through mail order outlets. Computer magazines list available programs as well as the cost. You can also use the Internet as a resource for researching and finding programs.

> You can find freeware and shareware at many Internet sites. Freeware programs are provided free to you. Shareware programs are provided to you to try without cost. If you like the program, you must pay a small fee to register and continue using the program. www.shareware.com is one of my favorite places to go shopping for shareware online.

When you are looking for new programs to purchase, be sure that you can run that program on your system. Each program has system requirements—the type of microprocessor, amount of memory, hard disk space, video card, and any other required equipment. You can usually find these requirements printed on the side of the software box. Check the requirements to be sure your PC is capable of running the software.

> Often times you'll see a reference to "minimum system requirements" on a program's box. Although technically the application can function with those specs, it may be painfully slow. The reduced performance may not be noticeable in a word processor, but in a driving game, your vehicle might be nearly uncontrollable because of the jerky system performance. Just keep in mind that minimum requirements are just that—minimum. Exceeding the minimum hardware requirements usually leads to a more enjoyable game.

Be sure that you get the right program for your system. If the package says it requires Windows 98, don't expect it to work on a system with Windows 3.1. Likewise, if the package requires Windows 3.1 or greater, it should work fine with Windows 95 and Windows 98. Programs designed to run under DOS may or may not work properly under Windows, so use extreme caution when purchasing these programs. To be absolutely sure the program will work on your system, check that your operating system is listed on the box.

As a final precaution, check to see how the software is distributed—on floppy disks or on a CD-ROM. If you have both a floppy disk and CD-ROM drive, you don't have to worry. But if you don't have a CD-ROM drive, be sure to get the version on floppy disks. CDs have become the most popular method for distributing programs, especially large programs.

Installing a New Program

When you install a new program, the installation program will copy the necessary program files from the disk(s) to your hard disk and also set up program icon(s) for the program. You need to specify which folder to use for the program files, where to place the program icons in the Start menu, and what program options you want to set. The options will vary depending on the program; but you don't have to worry too much because the installation program will guide you step-by-step through the process, usually by asking simple, nontechnical questions. You only have to get the installation program started.

You can use one of two methods to run the installation program. You can use the Add/Remove Programs icon or the Run command. This section gives you the basic procedure for both. Be sure to check the documentation that came with your software for any specific instructions. (See Appendix A, "Installing Windows Applications," for a detailed discussion of how to install Internet Explorer 4.)

To Do: Using the Add/Remove Programs Icon to Install Software

Windows provides an Add/Remove Programs icon which you can use to install new programs and remove (or uninstall programs). Follow these steps to install a program:

1. Insert the installation disk in the drive.

> If you are installing from a CD, that disc may have an AutoRun feature. If so, when you insert the disc, the installation program starts automatically.

▼   2. Click the Start button, select Settings, and then select Control Panel. You see the program icons in the Control Panel.

3. Double-click the Add/Remove Programs icon.

4. If necessary, click the Install/Uninstall tab. You see the options for installing and uninstalling programs (see Figure 2.3).

FIGURE 2.3.

Use this dialog box to install new programs.

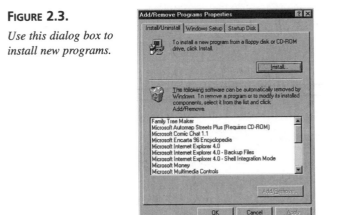

5. Click the Install button. Windows looks on the floppy drive and CD-ROM disc for an installation program. It then displays the name of this program in the dialog box.

6. Click the Finish button to run this program. Windows starts the program's installation program.

7. Follow the onscreen instructions for installing that particular program.

Try this method first; and if it doesn't work, then try using the Run command, which is
▲   covered next.

Using the Run Command

You can also install a program by using the Run command to run the installation program. To use this method, you need to know the exact name of the program's installation file. It's usually named something like INSTALL.EXE or SETUP.EXE.

To Do: Using the Run Command to Install a Program

Follow these steps to use the Run command:

1. Insert the program disk into the drive.

2. Click the Start button.

3. Select the Run command. The Run dialog box appears.

4. In the Open text box, type the program name. Remember to type the drive letter. Your floppy drive is usually Drive A. Your CD-ROM drive is usually Drive D (see Figure 2.4).

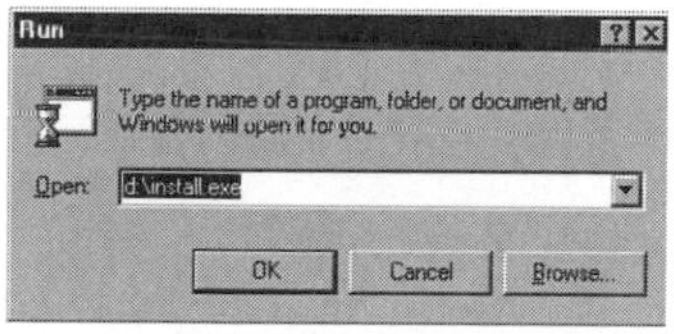

FIGURE 2.4.

Type the installation program name.

> If you aren't sure of the name of the installation program, type the drive name and then use the Browse button to look through the files on that drive. Select the installation file.

5. Click the OK button.

6. Follow the onscreen instructions for installing the program.

Uninstalling a Program

If you have a program you no longer need, or if you upgrade a program and want to get rid of the previous version, you can uninstall it. You could simply delete the program folder; but keep in mind that the original program installation may have put files in other folders and also changed some system settings. The best way is to uninstall the program using the Add/Remove Program icon.

To Do: Using the Add/Remove Program to Uninstall a Program

Follow these steps to uninstall a program:

1. Click the Start button, select Settings, and then select Control Panel. You see the program icons in the Control Panel.

2. Double-click the Add/Remove Programs icon.

▼   3. If necessary, click the Install/Uninstall tab. You see the options for installing and uninstalling programs (refer to Figure 2.3).

4. Select the program you want to uninstall.

> If the program is not listed in this dialog box, you cannot use this method. Check the program documentation for information on uninstalling the program.

▲   5. Click the Add/Remove button. Windows 95 removes the program files and any shortcuts to the program.

Summary

This hour covered a ton of ground toward introducing you to your new PC. You were given some pointers for selecting a workspace; you learned about the different types of software; and you even learned how to install and uninstall your software. Now you're ready to cut to the chase and have some fun.

In the next hour, you learn all the basics of working in the Windows environment. In fact, all of Part II is devoted to using Windows 98 and its applets.

Workshop

The following workshop helps you solidify the skills you learned in this hour.

Quiz

Take the following quiz to see how much you've learned.

Questions

1. Where is the best place to put your computer monitor?

    a. In direct sunlight to enhance the monitor's illumination.

    b. In a location that does not get direct sunlight.

    c. In your basement because monitors are too heavy to remain on an upper level.

2. What is a surge protector?

   a. A device that protects your computer from sudden power spikes.

   b. A device that, when attached, gives your PC a power boost.

   c. A tarp-like cover to place over your computer to protect it from floods.

3. If you needed to calculate and report on the profits of your school fundraiser, what type of application would you use?

   a. A spreadsheet

   b. A word processor

   c. A database

Answers

1. b. Remember the direction of the sun changes as the day goes on, so you'll want to look at the monitor throughout the day before settling on a permanent location.

2. a. This device will protect your equipment from sudden bursts of power.

3. a. A spreadsheet will give you accurate, professional-looking results.

Activity

Think about some things you'd like to do, or skills you'd like to learn. Make a list of five things. Now scan the ads in the Sunday paper, a software catalogue, or wander through a computer store in search of software to help you with your list. Whether you want to learn how to play guitar or plan your upcoming trip to the Orient, you'll find helpful software packages to fit the bill.

Part II
Windows 98

Hour

HOUR 3

Windows Desktop Basics

If you purchased a new computer in May 1998 or later, chances are that you received Windows 98 as your operating system, or at least a coupon entitling you to a free upgrade to it when it comes out. If your computer is older than that, Windows 95 is most likely installed on your system. Luckily, because Windows 95 and Windows 98 have very few differences, you're able to use the information in this hour no matter which system you have. Where they have differences, I make special note of them.

In addition to getting acquainted with the Windows desktop, you find the answers to the following questions in this hour:

- How does mouse use differ between the classic desktop and the active desktop?
- What does the Start button do?
- How do I use the new Windows 98 toolbars?
- If I need help with something not covered in this book, where can I find it?
- How do I print documents in Windows?

Starting Windows

To start Windows, you simply turn on your computer as mentioned in Hour 2. Windows prepares your computer for use—a process called booting the computer.

In a few moments, you see the Windows Desktop, which appears similar (although perhaps not identical) to Figure 3.1. The term Desktop is used metaphorically here; it symbolizes how the objects you work with in Windows are arranged and managed, just as you arrange the everyday papers and other objects on your desk.

FIGURE 3.1.

The Classic Windows 98 Desktop.

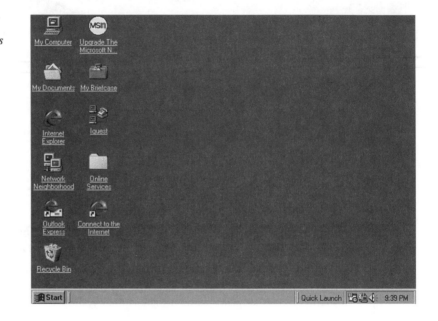

 The Classic Windows 98 desktop and the Windows 95 desktop have very few differences.

 Windows 98 offers you a choice of two different Desktops: the Classic Desktop and the Active Desktop. (You learn more about the Active Desktop and how to switch between it and the Classic Desktop later in this hour.)

Using the Mouse

A mouse is a device that you use to manipulate objects in Windows. The mouse pointer, or simply pointer, is the small symbol (such as an arrow) that moves on the screen when you move the mouse. As you move the mouse on its pad, the mouse pointer onscreen moves in tandem.

Because the mouse is such a simple device, mechanically speaking, you need to perform only a few gestures with it:

- To point to an object on the screen, move the mouse pointer so that it is directly over that object. Point to an object when you are preparing to do something to it.

- To click an object to which your mouse pointer is currently pointing, press the left mouse button once and quickly release it. Generally, you click an object to issue a command, open a program, or select an object.

- To right-click an object, point to it and then press and release the right mouse button. When you right-click an object, Windows and many applications display a menu called a context menu, which lists commands that pertain to that object.

- To drag an object from place to place, first point to it and then click and hold down the mouse button—don't release it yet. Next, move the pointer in the direction that you want to drag the object. When the pointer is in the position in which you want the object to appear, release the mouse button. (If you want to drag a word or paragraph, you have to select it first.) This process is called drag and drop. You might use drag and drop to move a file from one directory to another or to move a paragraph within a word processing document. Normally, a drag operation involves the left mouse button; however, Windows 98 and some Windows programs do employ so-called right-drags that open a context menu after the button is released.

- To double-click an object, point to it and then press and release the left mouse button twice rapidly without moving the mouse between or during the clicks. Double-clicking is the standard method in Windows for starting an application or selecting an object from a dialog box and immediately dismissing it.

If you're having trouble clicking and double-clicking with the mouse, you might want to adjust its speed. (See Hour 5, "Customizing Windows" for help.)

3

How Using the Mouse Is Different in Web Style

When you activate Windows 98's new Web Style option, your mouse operation changes dramatically. For instance, to select an object, instead of clicking once on that object with the left mouse button, you point to it, stop the mouse completely, and wait for Windows to recognize that the pointer has stopped (about a third of a second by default). Windows then highlights the object you selected.

Double-clicking is replaced entirely with single-clicking, thus treating each object as though it were a hyperlink. For example, unlike prior versions of Windows, with the Web Style option activated you can simply click a file to open it. (The optional Web Style setting is covered in greater detail in Hour 5, "Customizing Windows.")

As you see later in this hour, you can access the Active Desktop and its Web-Style option with Windows 95 as well, so keep this mouse information handy.

Using the IntelliMouse

Because Microsoft is the manufacturer of both Windows and the IntelliMouse pointer device, Microsoft has provided extra support for the IntelliMouse. This Microsoft-brand pointer has a small gray vertical wheel between its two buttons. The wheel is used for scrolling, and it can also be clicked—to act as a third button of sorts.

Windows applications that can work with the IntelliMouse driver (especially Microsoft-brand software) can make use of the IntelliMouse wheel. The following are the basics:

- To scroll slowly, simply rotate the wheel up or down.
- To scroll more quickly, click the wheel once and then move the mouse in the direction in which you want to scroll. Click the wheel again to turn off the automatic scrolling.
- To zoom in or out, press the Ctrl key as you rotate the wheel up (to zoom in) or down (to zoom out).

For instance, with Microsoft Word 97, you can use the wheel to pan through a long document the way that a camera pans a scene by simply rotating the wheel. Using the wheel more like a button, you can hold it down and then move the mouse in the direction that you want to scroll. Alternatively, you can press the Ctrl key while rotating the wheel up or down to increase or decrease, respectively, the zoom factor of the active worksheet.

Using the Start Button

Almost every operation that you initiate in Windows begins with the Start button, located in the lower-left corner of the screen. You can start programs, change Windows features, locate files, shut down Windows, and perform other operations with the commands you find on the Start menu (shown in Figure 3.2).

FIGURE 3.2.

The Start menu, which is displayed when you click the Start button.

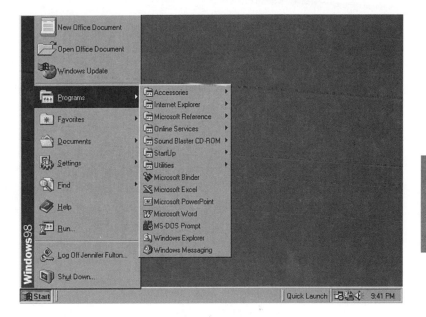

When you click the Start button, the Start menu appears. The following are brief descriptions of the commands that are displayed:

- *Windows Update*. If you have a connection to the Internet, you can use the Windows Update command to update your version of Windows periodically. This command, available only in Windows 98, connects you to the Microsoft Web site.

- *Programs*. Displays a categorized listing of the applications (programs) available on your system. Simply navigate through the various categories or submenus that appear until you find the program that you intend to start.

- *Favorites*. Opens a list of the documents, channels, and Internet links that you most frequently access, either on your local system or on the World Wide Web.

- *Documents*. Displays a list of documents that have recently been accessed or created with your applications. Click one of these entries to open the document in the associated application.

- *Settings*. Opens a short list in which you can access, among other things, the Control Panel, which enables you to change the major characteristics of the operating system, such as display properties, printer status, and computer setup.

- *Find*. Helps you locate files, folders, or computers on your system or on your company's network. You can also use Find to locate Web pages on the Internet, or people's email addresses.

- *Help*. Opens the Windows Help system, which provides information on the various aspects of Windows, including quick pointers on using the operating system.

- *Run*. Enables you to manually enter a program's executable filename, along with its path and any switches that the program might require. For example, you might use the Run command to initiate the setup command for a new software program.

- *Log Off*. Enables you to log off your company's network so that you can log back on as a different user. You might use this command when you share your computer with a coworker.

- *Shut Down*. Provides the means for shutting down Windows safely. You can also use this command to restart (reboot) your computer when needed.

As you select commands from some parts of the Start menu, additional menus are displayed. For example, when you select Programs, a listing of your favorite programs, along with your program groups, is displayed.

Shutting Down Windows

In Hour 2, you learned how to shut your computer down safely from the Shut Down menu. This same menu also enables you to do the following:

- *Restart*. You might need to restart your computer after making a system configuration change (such as changing the screen resolution) or simply to refresh Windows' internal resources. Because of the way Windows works, you find that running multiple applications at once often causes a severe drain on your system's resources. By restarting your PC, you can remove all programs from memory and refresh your system.

> It used to be that you restarted your PC by pressing Ctrl+Alt+Delete. This "three-finger salute" is used in Windows to open a dialog box that enables you to terminate a faulty application (end a task) without shutting down the entire system, or to initiate an emergency shutdown when your system locks up. For instance, if Word freezes your system, you can execute these keystrokes to free up your system and restart your Word session without going through a complete system shutdown.

- *Restart in MS-DOS mode.* You can most likely run programs written for the MS-DOS operating system in Windows 98 without switching to the MS-DOS mode. Many DOS programs are displayed in their own windows and won't interfere with other Windows functions or applications. Some older DOS applications, however, especially graphically intense games, require you to shut down Windows mode in order to eliminate the constraints that Windows places on running programs.

- *Close all programs and log in as a new user.* Although this option occupies the last line on your shutdown menu, you most likely never use it as a beginner.

Conserve Resources by Suspending Your System

Suppose that you're in the middle of reconciling your checking account, designing a birthday card for Grandma, writing a letter, and entering names into your personal address book. You look at your watch and suddenly realize that you're running late to pick up your daughter from gymnastics. Wouldn't it be great if you could just suspend your system rather than shut it down? In many cases, you can.

Some computers enable you to suspend their operations, which means to switch them into low-power mode, maintaining just the central processor without the peripherals, hard drive, or display. The Power Management options in Windows enable you to maintain what you're currently doing on your computer with the minimum amount of power necessary. This is an alternative to shutting down your computer and loading everything from scratch when you want to work again. If your computer supports standby or suspend mode, the Stand By or Suspend command appears just above Shut Down on the Start menu.

Understanding the Windows Desktop

The Windows Desktop appears when you start Windows. The Desktop holds objects, called icons, that you use to start applications; copy, move, and delete files; connect to the Internet; and perform other functions. (The Classic Windows Desktop is shown in Figure 3.3.) You learn how to use the Desktop components later in this lesson, but to give you a running start, the following are the vital components along with a brief description of what they do:

- *Desktop.* The basic Windows work area

- *Taskbar.* Provides a means for organizing your applications and files and navigating between them

- *Icons*. Represent files, folders, programs, and other objects that you use
- *Start button*. Displays a menu of commands for starting programs, changing system settings, and more
- *Mouse pointer*. Indicates the current position of your mouse

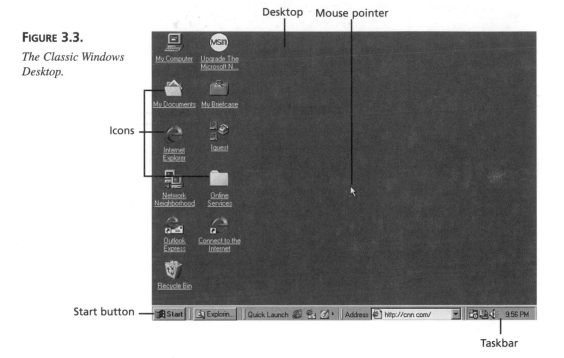

FIGURE 3.3.

The Classic Windows Desktop.

Web Integration and the Active Desktop

One of the most important new features of Windows 98 is the Active Desktop (see Figure 3.4). The Active Desktop combines the features of the Classic Desktop with some of the features of a Web browser.

NEW TERM A *Web browser* is a program used to view Web pages on the World Wide Web. Web pages often contain graphics, text, animations, and other special elements, and a Web browser is designed to display these elements properly.

With the Active Desktop, you can have up-to-date Web content at your fingertips without the hassle of constantly logging onto the Internet, starting your Web browser, and selecting a Web page to view. For example, you might want to display current stock prices, news, weather, or even updates from your company's local intranet. Having this up-to-date content, however, requires a full-time connection to the Internet that few of us can afford to have. So what else does the Active Desktop have to offer?

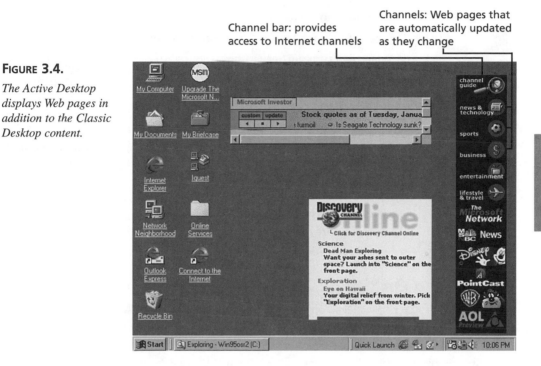

Channel bar: provides
access to Internet channels

Channels: Web pages that
are automatically updated
as they change

FIGURE 3.4.

The Active Desktop displays Web pages in addition to the Classic Desktop content.

The Active Desktop can also affect how you browse your files and folders. Unlike the Classic Desktop, in which you usually double-click to open a folder or file, the Active Desktop enables you to single-click instead. This feature (called Web Style) enables you to open files and folders more quickly.

Windows 98 even comes with special toolbars you can use to access Web pages that you visit frequently. (You learn how to use the Windows 98 toolbars later in this lesson.)

Getting the Active Desktop in Windows 95

Just because you have Windows 95 doesn't mean that you're out of luck when it comes to having an Active Desktop. First, you need to install the Windows Desktop Update from the Web.

To Do: Installing the Active Desktop for Windows 95

To install the Desktop Update, follow these easy steps:

1. On the Start menu, point to Settings, and then click Control Panel.
2. Double-click Add/Remove Programs.
3. Click Microsoft Internet Explorer 4.0, and then click Add/Remove.
4. Click Add Windows Desktop Update from Web site.

If you do not see this option, then the Windows Desktop Update is already installed. To activate the Active Desktop in Windows 95, just follow the directions in the next section, "Turning On the Active Desktop."

> Don't have Internet Explorer 4.0+ on your system? You need both Internet Explorer 4.0 and the Windows update in order to access the Active Desktop. You can get Internet Explorer 4.0 for free if you download it from the Internet at www.microsoft.com/ie4, or you can purchase it from your favorite software retailer.

Turning On the Active Desktop

By default, the Classic Desktop is displayed when you first start Windows. You can switch to the Active Desktop at any time. Remember that the two Desktops offer all the same features, except that the Active Desktop enables you to display and access Web content more easily. Also, the Web Style option, with which you can single-click to open files and folders, is turned on initially, although you can turn it off if you like. You can use the Web Style option with the Classic Desktop as well.

To Do: Switching to the Active Desktop

To turn on the Active Desktop, follow these steps:

1. Right-click an open area of the Desktop. A shortcut menu appears.
2. Click Active Desktop. A cascading menu appears with more options.
3. From the cascading menu, select View as a Web Page. The Active Desktop is displayed.

That's it! When the Active Desktop option is initially turned on, you won't see much of a change. The Channel bar appears, and with it, you can subscribe to the channels that you want to display. (You learn more about channels in Hour 12.) Also, the Web Style option is turned on, meaning that you now point to objects to select them and click objects to open or activate them. If you don't want to use the Web Style option with Active Desktop, right-click the Desktop, select Active Desktop, select Customize My Desktop, click Folder Options, click Yes, select Classic style, and click OK.

> Because the Active Desktop's main duty is to display Web content, your computer has to be connected to the Internet—if not all the time, then at least when you initially turn on the option. If you haven't yet established an Internet connection for your PC, the Connection Wizard appears. (See Hour 10, "Choosing an Internet Service Provider and Getting Connected," for help in completing the wizard and making your first connection.)

Switching Back to the Classic Desktop

After using the Active Desktop for a while, you might want to switch back to the Classic Desktop. Switching back and forth between the two Desktops doesn't remove any customization or channel selections that you have made.

To Do: Switching to Classic Desktop

To switch back to the Classic Desktop, follow these steps:

1. Right-click an open area of the Desktop. A shortcut menu appears.
2. Select Active Desktop. A cascading menu appears.
3. Select View as a Web Page. This removes the check mark in front of the command, turning the option off. The Classic Desktop appears.

If the Web Style option is turned on in Active Desktop, it remains on when you switch to Classic Desktop. To turn it off, right-click the Desktop, select Active Desktop, and select Customize my desktop. Click Folder Options, click Yes, select Classic style, and click OK. If you switch back to Active Desktop, the Web Style option won't be turned on, because you turned it off while using Classic Desktop. Repeat these steps to turn it back on, but select the Web style option instead.

Using the Taskbar

At the bottom of the Desktop is the taskbar. In addition to the Start button, the taskbar contains many elements (see Figure 3.5).

The elements of the Windows taskbar are described in the following list:

- *Start button*. With the Start button, you can select commands to open programs, customize Windows, locate files, and search the Internet.

- *Active programs and open windows.* Your currently running programs and any open windows, such as folder windows, appear as buttons on the taskbar. To switch to an open program or window, simply click its button.

- *Toolbars.* Windows contains several toolbars that provide quick access to popular programs and functions, such as Web addressing. These toolbars include Address, Links, Desktop, and Quick Launch. In addition, you can create your own toolbars. (See Hour 4, "Working with Menus, Toolbars, and Dialog Boxes," for help.)

- *Status area.* At the right end of the taskbar, icons occasionally appear to update you on the status of various things such as the current time, your Internet connection status, whether you have new email messages in your inbox, and so on.

FIGURE 3.5.

The Windows taskbar.

Start button

This icon enables you to adjust the volume

This icon shows that you're connected to the Internet

| Start | Exploring - Win95osr2 (C:) | Quick Launch | 10:36 PM |

Buttons for active programs and open windows

Windows toolbars provide quick access to your programs and the Internet

Current time

The taskbar initially appears at the bottom of the Desktop; however, you can move it to the top, left, or right side by simply clicking it, holding down the left mouse button, and dragging it to where you want it.

You can also hide the taskbar to have it appear only when needed. Hiding the taskbar gives you more room on your Desktop for viewing your programs.

To Do: Hiding the Taskbar

To hide the taskbar, follow these steps:

1. Click the Start button. The Start menu appears.

2. Select Settings. A cascading menu appears.

3. Select Taskbar & Start Menu. The Taskbar Properties dialog box appears (see Figure 3.6). You can also right-click the taskbar and select Properties to display the Taskbar Properties dialog box.

4. Click the Auto Hide option.

5. Click OK. The taskbar disappears. To make it reappear, move the mouse pointer toward the taskbar's former location. The taskbar reappears.

FIGURE 3.6.

The Taskbar Properties dialog box.

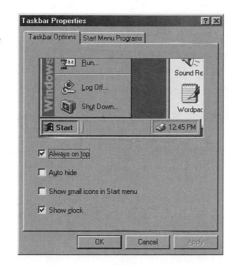

Using the Windows 98 Toolbars

Windows 98 comes with several new toolbars that you can use to access the Internet and your programs more quickly. These toolbars initially appear on the taskbar, but you can remove them and place them on the Desktop when needed for more convenient access.

A toolbar, by the way, is a bar of buttons that represent various commands. When you click the appropriate button, the associated command is carried out. Just like the toolbars you often find in Windows programs, a Windows 98 toolbar might contain text boxes in which you can type a command, or list boxes from which you can make a selection.

The following are the Windows 98 toolbars:

- *Address.* When you type an Internet address here, such as the address of a Web page, Internet Explorer opens to display the location you entered.

- *Links.* This toolbar provides access to your favorite Internet Explorer links (Web sites).

- *Desktop.* Displays the icons that appear on your Desktop. This enables you to access those programs when the Desktop is covered with open windows.

- *Quick Launch.* Provides easy access to the programs that you use most, such as Internet Explorer, Outlook Express, your Desktop, and the Active Channel Viewer.

- *New Toolbar.* You can create your own toolbars as well.

To Do: Displaying a Windows Toolbar

To display a toolbar, follow these steps:

1. Right-click the taskbar and select Toolbars from the shortcut menu that appears.
2. Click the toolbar that you want to display. The toolbar appears on the taskbar.

To use a toolbar, simply click one of its buttons. If the toolbar has a text box (such as the one on the Address toolbar), click inside the text box and type your information (in this case, the address of the Web page that you want to display).

To remove a toolbar from the taskbar, right-click the taskbar, select Toolbars, and select the toolbar that you want to remove.

You can adjust the amount of space that the toolbar takes up on the taskbar by dragging its handle—the ridges that appear on the toolbar's left edge. Alternatively, you can drag a toolbar off the taskbar and onto the Desktop. Simply click anywhere on the toolbar, press and hold down the left mouse button, and then drag the toolbar onto the Desktop, releasing the mouse button when the toolbar is in position. After the toolbar appears on the Desktop, you can resize it just like any other window. (See Hour 4, "Working with Menus, Toolbars, and Dialog Boxes," for help.)

Getting Help in Windows

Help is always close at hand in Windows. When you press F1, the Help system is activated. The Help window that appears usually coincides with whatever action that you were performing. You can also activate Help by clicking the Start button and selecting the Help command.

The Help window appears with two panes. The left one is used to navigate Help, and the right one displays information on a help topic. Also included are five buttons:

- *Hide/Show*. Hides, or redisplays, the left Help pane (the Table of Contents).
- *Back*. Returns you to a previously viewed Help page.
- *Forward*. After you've used Back, this button redisplays a previously viewed Help page.
- *Options*. Displays a list of Help options.
- *Web Help*. Provides a link to Microsoft help on the World Wide Web.

In addition to pressing F1 to activate Help, most dialog boxes feature a Help button that you can click to get help in choosing the options in that dialog box.

In Windows 95, the Help screen consists of a dialog box with three tabs—one for Contents, one for Index, and one for Search.

- *Contents.* A table of contents that you can browse through
- *Index.* Similar to the index in the back of a book
- *Search.* Enables you to search the Help system for a particular word or phrase

Help is written for the Classic Style Desktop in which you double-click a filename to open it. If you use the Web Style Desktop and Help prompts you to double-click, you need to single-click.

Using the Contents Feature

Using the Contents feature of Help is similar to using the table of contents in a book: You find the major categories. When you select a topic, it expands to display subtopics from which you can choose (shown in Figure 3.7). The book icons represent topics and subtopics; document icons represent actual Help pages. Selecting a document displays information on that topic in the right pane.

To Do: Using the Contents Feature

Follow these steps in Windows 98 to use the Contents feature:

1. If needed, press F1 or click the Start button and select Help to display the Help dialog box.
2. Click a topic that has a book icon, and it expands to reveal subtopics.
3. If needed, click a subtopic to expand it.
4. Click a topic that has a document icon to display its contents in the right pane of the Help window (see Figure 3.7).
5. After reading the contents of the Help window, you may choose either of the following options:
   - *Click here.* Click this link to launch related applications and wizards.
   - *Related Topics.* Some Help windows display a link at the bottom of the window. If you click this link, a small window appears from which you can select a related topic.
6. To close Help, click the Close button.

FIGURE 3.7.

When you select a topic, it expands.

Major topic —

Subtopics —

Help pages —

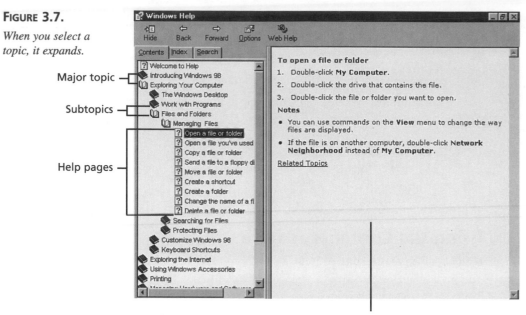

The topic that you
select is displayed here

In Windows 95, just press Start, select Help, click the Contents tab, and double-click a desired category. If you see a book icon next to the topic, the topic expands, enabling you to double-click a narrower category of interest.

Using the Index Feature

Help's Index feature is similar to an index that you might find at the back of a book. To use it, simply type the word for which you're looking, and it appears in a list (shown in Figure 3.8). Select a topic from this list, and it's displayed in the right pane.

To Do: Using the Index Feature

Follow these steps to use the Index feature:

1. Type a word or phrase in the text box. As you type, Help searches the Index for a match, so you might not actually have to type the entire word for which you're looking.

2. Double-click the topic in the list that you'd like to display. The topic appears in the right pane. (A dialog box of selections may appear. If so, select the subtopic that you want and click OK.)

FIGURE 3.8.

*Use the Index to locate
a specific word or
phrase.*

![Windows Help window showing the Index tab with "dialog boxes, shortcut keys in" and a topic pane titled "Using shortcut keys in dialog boxes"]

To	Press
Cancel the current task	ESC
Click a button if the current control is a button	SPACEBAR
-Or-	
Select or clear the check box if the current control is a check box	
-Or-	
Click the option if the current control is an option button	
Click the corresponding command	ALT+underlined letter
Click the selected button	ENTER
Move backward through options	SHIFT+TAB
Move backward through tabs	CTRL+SHIFT+TAB
Move forward through options	TAB
Move forward through tabs	CTRL+TAB
Open a folder one level up if a folder is selected in the **Save As** or **Open** dialog box	BACKSPACE
Open **Save In** or **Look In** in the **Save As** or **Open** dialog box	F4

Using the Search Feature

Index enables you to search for a match to your word or phrase within a topic heading.
Search enables you to search for a match within the contents of the topic itself; this
expands the possibility of locating a match. After using the Contents and Index features
to locate what you want, try using Search.

To Do: Using Search

Follow these steps to use the Search feature:

1. Type the word or phrase in the text box for which you want to search, and press
   Enter or click List Topics.
2. A list of topics is displayed. When you double-click a topic, it appears in the right
   pane (shown in Figure 3.9).

Using the What's This? Feature

Many Windows dialog boxes include a What's This? button (see Figure 3.10). After you
click it, you can click any option within that dialog box and view a description of it. This
enables you to quickly decide which options within a dialog box to use.

Select a match here

FIGURE 3.9.

*Search enables you to
search the text within
Help topics.*

Type your word or
phrase here

Select a topic
from this list

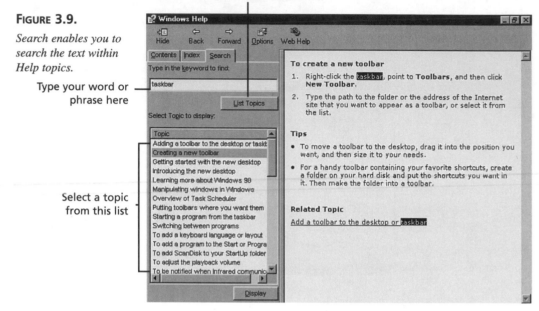

What's This? button

FIGURE 3.10.

*The What's This? fea-
ture helps you identify
which dialog box
options you might want
to use.*

When you click an
option with the
What's This? pointer,
a description appears

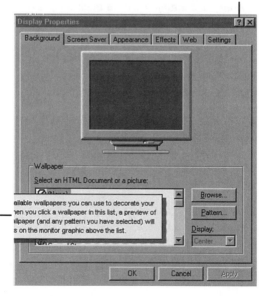

To Do: Using the What's This? feature

To Do

Follow these steps to use the What's This? feature:

1. Click the What's This? button. The mouse pointer changes to a question mark.
2. Click any option within the dialog box. A description of that option appears.
3. After reading the description, click anywhere in the dialog box to remove the dialog box from the screen.

▲

> To display a description of a dialog box more quickly, just right-click it and select What's This? from the shortcut menu that appears.

Using Web Help

For users who have access to the Internet, Windows 98 includes a nice feature that you can use to find answers to common questions about Windows.

To Do: Using Windows 98 Web Help

▼To Do

To locate answers to common Windows questions, follow these steps:

1. If needed, connect to the Internet.
2. Click the Start button and select Windows Update. Internet Explorer starts and connects to Microsoft's Update site.
3. Click Technical Support. You might be asked whether you would like to register. Click Yes and follow the instructions in the Registration Wizard that appears.
4. You may see a security warning. Click Yes to continue.
5. Select a topic that interests you from the My Search Is About list.
6. In the I Want to Search For text box, type the keywords of the item for which you want help.

▲ 7. Click Find.

You might also want to click the How To or the Glossary links displayed in the left frame. They provide additional help: How To describes how to search for information, and Glossary defines Windows' terms.

Obtaining Help in Updating Your System

If you have access to the Internet, Windows Update can help you keep your system current. For example, if you experience an odd problem with your computer, you can use

3

Windows Update to update your Windows software, download the latest drivers for your hardware, and obtain service updates and bug fixes. Updating your system often solves your problem.

Although Windows 95 updates can also be downloaded from Microsoft's Web site free of charge, Windows 98 makes the update process a whole lot easier for the user—no more pawing through oodles of Web links to find the right update to download!

NEW TERM A *driver* is a special program that enables a particular hardware device—such as a CD-ROM or a sound card—to communicate with your computer.

To Do: Using Windows Help to Update your Computer

To update your Windows system, follow these steps:

1. If needed, connect to the Internet.
2. Click the Start button and select Windows Update. Internet Explorer opens and connects to Microsoft's Windows Update site.
3. To update your system, click Update Wizard. You're taken to the Update Wizard site.
4. Click Update.
5. If any of your system programs or drivers needs to be updated, you see them in the Available Updates list. Select an update and click Install to copy it to your system.

Help from Within Microsoft Applications

Many Microsoft applications, such as Word 97, enable you to link to a special Web site that offers help, tips, and other free resources such as new program templates, wizards, and clip art. To access this online help from Word 97 and other supported applications, launch the desired application, and select Help, Microsoft on the Web. You see a large menu of options including links to frequently asked questions about the application, free stuff, product news, and so on.

Installing a Printer

When Windows was first installed on your computer, it checked for any locally attached printers and set them up automatically. If you've purchased a new printer recently, however, you need to install it before you can use it to print your Windows documents.

To Do: Installing a Printer

To install a new printer, follow these steps:

1. Click Start, select Settings, and select Printers. The Printers folder window appears.
2. Click (or double-click) the Add Printer icon. The Add Printer Wizard appears.
3. Click Next >.
4. Select either Local printer or Network printer. (Local is most likely the appropriate choice.) Click Next >.
5. Select the manufacturer of your printer from the Manufacturers list. Then select your printer from the Printers list. If a floppy disk came with your new printer, click Have Disk, select the file, and click OK. Click Next >.
6. Select the port you that want to use and click Next >.
7. Enter a name for your printer, and select whether you want this printer to act as the default printer for your system. Then click Next >.
8. Select Yes to print a test page, and click Finish. You might be asked to insert your Windows disks or CD-ROM; do so if prompted. The icon for your new printer appears in the Printers folder.

Setting a Default Printer

If you use more than one printer—for example, a color printer and a laser printer—you can designate one of them as the default. The default printer is the printer that your applications use to print your documents unless you specifically select a different printer from the Print dialog box.

The first printer set up on your computer is automatically established as the default printer.

To Do: Changing Your Default Printer

You can designate a different default printer by following these steps:

1. Click Start, select Settings, and select Printers. The Printers folder window appears.
2. Right-click the icon of the printer that you want to make the default. (The current default printer appears with a small check mark next to its icon.)
3. Select Set as Default from the shortcut menu that appears.

Printing from an Application

When you initiate a print command from within an application, the document is prepared and then passed to the print queue, where it waits in line behind any other documents you have already set to print. After the document is passed to the print queue, command of the computer is then returned to you so that you can continue working either in that same application or some other program. You don't have to wait as your document is being printed; the Windows print queue handles the entire process.

To Do: Printing a Document

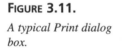

To print a document from within an application, follow these steps:

1. Open the program's File menu and select Print. A Print dialog box appears (similar to the one shown in Figure 3.11). Alternatively, you can click the Print button on the toolbar (if present), but the Print dialog box doesn't appear. This also gives you only one copy of the document printed with the default settings.

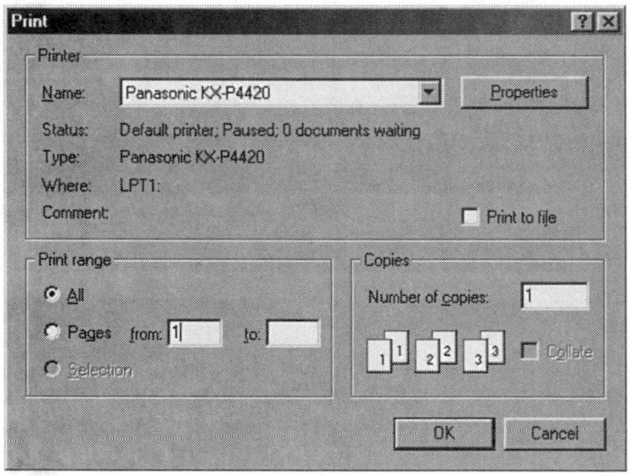

FIGURE 3.11.

A typical Print dialog box.

Print	? X
Printer	
Name: Panasonic KX-P4420 ▼	Properties
Status: Default printer; Paused; 0 documents waiting	
Type: Panasonic KX-P4420	
Where: LPT1:	
Comment:	☐ Print to file

Print range	Copies
● All	Number of copies: 1
○ Pages from: 1 to:	
○ Selection	☐ Collate

| OK | Cancel |

2. The Print dialog box within your application might be slightly different, but it still contains certain elements:

    • From the Printer list, select the printer that you want to use.

    • Select the pages that you want to print.

    • If the option is available, select the number of copies that you want to print.

▲   3. After selecting your options, click OK.

> If you'd like to preview your print job before you actually print it, most applications offer a Print Preview option on the File menu.

Controlling the Print Job

When you send a document to the printer for printing, it's placed behind any other documents that are already waiting to be printed. You can reassign the order of printing, cancel a print job, or simply pause the printer while you reprioritize the print queue.

> Pause a document currently printing so that you have more time to move your document from the end of the line to the beginning of the line. Press Pause on the printer, reshuffle the print queue, and resume printing. The current document finishes printing, and you're next!

When you view the print queue (shown in Figure 3.12), each document is listed, along with its print status, owner, number of pages, and the time and date that printing was initiated.

FIGURE 3.12.

Documents waiting to be printed appear in the print queue.

Panasonic KX-P4420 - Paused				
Printer Document View Help				
Document Name	Status	Owner	Progress	Started At
Microsoft Word - June Sales...		Jennifer Fult...	27 page(s)	9:00:03 PM 3/19/98
garden club members.xls		Jennifer Fult...	2 page(s)	9:00:20 PM 3/19/98
Microsoft Word - PC Buyers ...	Spooling	Jennifer Fult...	287 bytes	9:00:41 PM 3/19/98
3 jobs in queue				

To display the print queue, do either of the following:

- Double-click the Printer icon on the taskbar.
- In the Printers folder, double-click the icon for the printer whose queue you want to check.

Pausing and Resuming the Queue

You can pause the print queue at any time. This might be necessary if the printer is jammed or some other problem has developed. By pausing the print queue, you can easily correct the problem and resume printing when you're ready.

To Do: Pausing the print queue

To pause the printing, follow these steps:

1. Double-click the Printer icon on the taskbar to open the print queue.
2. Open the Printer menu and select Pause Printing. A check mark appears next to this command.

To resume printing, open the Printer menu and select Pause Printing again to remove the check mark.

> If your printer runs out of paper, Windows automatically pauses the printing process and displays a message indicating what's happened. If you don't respond, Windows automatically retries the printer in five seconds.

Deleting a Print Job

If you notice that you've sent the wrong document to the printer or that you need to make some small change, it's not too late. You can delete a print job from the queue to prevent it from being printed.

To Do: Deleting a Document in the Print Queue

To delete a print job, follow these steps:

1. Double-click the Printer icon on the taskbar to open the print queue.
2. Select the document that you want to delete from the queue.
3. Open the Document menu and select Cancel Printing, or press the Delete key.

To remove all documents from the print queue, open the Printer menu and select Purge Print Documents.

Summary

This was one of those let's-see-how-much-we-can-stuff-into-an-hour chapters. Although you may feel a bit overwhelmed about now, you at least have a firm grounding in Windows basics such as how to use the desktop, how to find help, and how to print a document and modify the print queue.

In the next hour, you learn about menus, toolbars, and dialog boxes.

Workshop

The following workshop helps you solidify the skills that you learned in this lesson.

Quiz

Take the following quiz to see how much you've learned.

Questions

1. Which statement about the Active Desktop is false?

    a. You can access the Active Desktop in Windows 98 and Windows 95 provided that you have the right stuff installed.

    b. The Active Desktop enables you to single-click an item rather than double-clicking it.

    c. The Active Desktop and the Web Style option are the same thing.

2. Which of the following are Windows help methods?

    a. Index

    b. Contents

    c. What's This?

3. Which printing capability is not available in Windows?

    a. Reorder the printing queue

    b. Delayed printing

    c. Delete a print job

Answers

1. c. They are two different things. In fact, you can use the Web Style option with the Active or Classic Desktop.

2. a, b, c. All three are valid methods for seeking help in Windows.

3. b. Delayed printing would be a cool feature (bosses could print those pink slips after they've left town); unfortunately, it doesn't exist at this time.

Activity

Using the information that you learned in this chapter, experiment with using Windows in the various modes. Give the Active Desktop a try. See what using Web Style is like. Play with the taskbar until you have it where you want it. By the time you're done, you should have a desktop that works well for you.

HOUR 4

Working with Menus, Toolbars, and Dialog Boxes

In this hour, I introduce you to what could be considered the heart of using Windows: its menus, toolbars, and dialog boxes. Not only are these elements important in using Windows, but they're also an integral part of using Windows software in general. You see a lot of menus, toolbars, and dialog boxes in Hours 16 through 24—the chapters we devote to some popular software that you may already have on your new computer. The following questions are also answered in this hour:

- How can I resize a window?
- How do scrollbars work?
- Can I display more than one window on my screen at a time?
- What kinds of toolbars are available?
- Can I move a toolbar if it gets in my way?

What Is a Window?

A window is a container for data, such as files, folders, programs, icons, and so on.
Depending on your preference, a window can occupy a particular region of the screen
or the entire screen. Figure 4.1 shows the parts of a typical window.

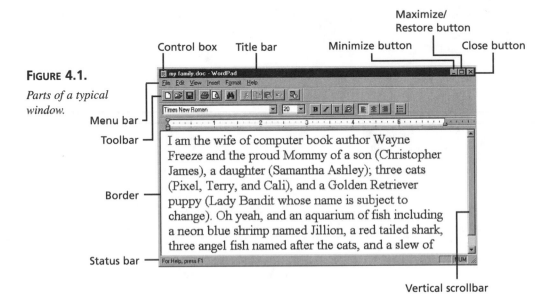

FIGURE 4.1.

Parts of a typical window.

The following is a brief description of each window element:

- *Control box.* Provides a menu with commands for sizing, closing, and moving the
  window. Generally the control box contains the identifying icon for the program
  that uses this window. For example, in Figure 4.1, the icon for WordPad serves as
  the control box. On an Active Desktop Item (a window that contains Web content),
  the control box looks like a down arrow.

- *Border.* The frame that surrounds the window. You can resize a window by stretching its border.

- *Title bar.* Displays the title of the window, which includes the name of the program
  and the name of its active file (if applicable).

- *Minimize button.* Click this button to remove the window temporarily from the
  screen.

"Remove from the screen temporarily" is less ominous than it sounds. When a window is minimized, Windows leaves the button for it on the Windows taskbar. Getting the window back is as easy as clicking its respective button.

- *Maximize/Restore button.* Click the Maximize button, and the window fills the screen; click the Restore button to return the window to its former size.
- *Close button.* Click this button to close (exit) a window and its associated program.
- *Vertical scrollbar.* Use this scrollbar to view data hidden above or below the displayed data.
- *Horizontal scrollbar.* Use this scrollbar to view data hidden to the left or right of the displayed data.
- *Menu bar.* Contains the main categories of commands that you give to an application. When you click one of these main categories, its list of associated commands drops down, and you can select a command or pull up a submenu from that list.
- *Toolbar.* Most applications use toolbars; they contain buttons that you can click to perform common commands such as printing, opening, and saving a document.
- *Status bar.* Like toolbars, most applications include a status bar at the bottom of the window. It alerts you to changes in the program and provides other useful information.

Opening a Window

Generally, windows open themselves when you launch an application or when you open a document within that application.

When you launch an application from the Start menu, an Explorer listing (you learn more about Windows Explorer in Hour 11), or by double-clicking its icon on the Desktop, the application responds by opening its own main window. For an application such as WordPad, which comes with Windows, the window that pops up is empty, ready for you to enter data and to save that data as a document file. For more sophisticated applications, such as Word 97, that empty document window might be contained within the application's main window.

Double-clicking typically means "Open up!," but if you're using the Web Style option, you can set up Windows to open a window with a single-click of a filename, folder, or icon. (See Hour 5, "Customizing Windows," for help.)

Switching Between Windows

Before you work with the contents of a window, that window must be active. For example, to use a particular program, you must activate the window in which it's contained. Regardless of how many windows you have open at the time, you can only have one active window. The active window appears with a brighter title bar than the other open windows (typically blue).

To activate a window (in other words, to switch from one window to another), you can perform any of the following tasks:

- Click any part of the open window that you want to make active.
- Press Alt+Tab to scroll through the list of open windows.
- Click the desired window's button on the taskbar.

Sizing a Window with Maximize, Minimize, and Restore

A window can be maximized (made to fill the screen) or minimized (removed from the screen temporarily). To maximize a window, click its Maximize button (refer to Figure 4.1). When the window is already maximized, this button changes to the Restore button. Click this button to restore the window to its former size, revealing part of the Desktop. You might want a window to be maximized when you're concentrating on its application specifically.

On the other hand, when you're working with more than one application at a time—you can with Windows 98—you might want to see all respective windows simultaneously. In that case, you want to leave them at their restored size. To quickly maximize a window, double-click its title bar. Then, to restore a window to its original size, double-click the title bar again.

The Minimize button removes the window from the Desktop without terminating (closing) its program. To restore the window so that you can start using the program again, click that program's button, which appears on the Windows taskbar.

To Do: Minimizing All Windows

To minimize all your windows at once so that only the Desktop is visible, do the following:

1. Right-click an empty portion of the taskbar (where there are no minimized application buttons).

2. From the pop-up menu that appears, select Minimize All Windows.

To restore your windows, right-click the taskbar again and select Undo Minimize All.

If you're currently displaying the Quick Launch toolbar on your taskbar, you can use it to minimize all your open windows. Simply click the Show Desktop button.

> Using the Minimize All Windows command doesn't affect the Active Desktop Items (the windows that contain Web content) that you might be displaying on your Active Desktop. To remove them temporarily, switch back to the Classic Desktop. Right-click the Desktop, select Active Desktop, and then select View as a Web Page to turn the option off. Repeat these steps to return to the Active Desktop whenever you like.

4

Sizing a Window's Borders

While a window is not maximized, you can change its size by dragging its border. When you stretch or shrink a window, you can move one side or corner at a time.

To Do: Resizing a Window

To change the size of a window, do the following:

1. Move the mouse pointer to one edge or corner of the window. The pointer changes to a black two-headed arrow.

2. While the pointer is a two-headed arrow, click and hold down the left mouse button.

3. Drag the mouse pointer in the direction that you want to stretch or shrink the window.

>
> If you are using Windows 98, the window size changes as you drag its border. This is different from Windows 95, where all you see is an outline of the window as it's resized.

4. When the window is the size that you want, release the mouse button.

Many applications' windows have minimum applicable sizes. So if the window doesn't budge but the pointer continues to move, the window is shrunk as much as it can be.

Using Scrollbars

Scrollbars are used to display a window's offscreen contents. You use a scrollbar to display contents that extend beyond the window's current viewing area. Figure 4.2 shows a window with both horizontal and vertical scrollbars.

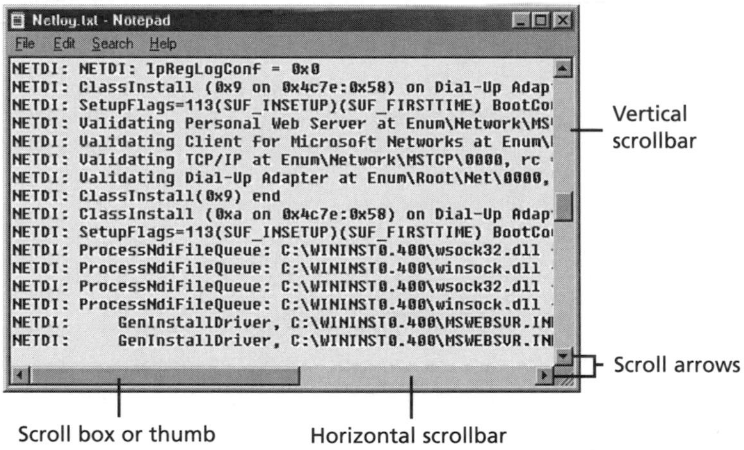

FIGURE 4.2.

A window with both scrollbars active.

Vertical scrollbar

Scroll arrows

Scroll box or thumb   Horizontal scrollbar

Use scrollbars in the following ways:

- To move by a small amount, click the arrow at either end of the scrollbar that points in the direction you want to move.
- To move by a larger amount, click the open space on either side of the scroll box.
- To move quickly through a document, drag the scroll box along the scrollbar to whatever position you choose. Many Windows programs move the contents of the window as you move the scrollbar; others wait until you release the button to execute the move. Some programs, such as Word 97, provide a ScreenTip that displays the relative page number in the document as you drag the scroll box. This enables you to quickly scroll to the exact page that you want.

Moving a Window

The title bar displays the name of the program being used by the window, as well as the name of the current active document. The supplemental function of the title bar is as a handle of sorts. To move a window onscreen, click and drag the window's title bar. When you move a window in Windows 98, the contents of the window follow your movements. If you want to switch back to the Windows 95 method (which displays only the window outline as you move), right-click the desktop, select Properties, click the Effects tab, and deactivate the Show Window Contents While Dragging option.

> You can't move a window that's been maximized.

You can also move Active Desktop items, such as that shown in Figure 4.3.

Title bar   Close button

FIGURE 4.3.

Moving an Active Desktop item is similar to moving any other window.

4

To Do: Moving Active Desktop Items

To move an Active Desktop item, follow these steps:

1. Move the mouse pointer toward the top of the Active Desktop item. A title bar should appear.

2. Click this title bar and drag the window wherever you like.

▲   3. Release the mouse button. The window is repositioned.

Arranging Windows on the Desktop

When you have more than one window open simultaneously and all are pertinent to the job on which you're working, stretching and shrinking them so that they all fit precisely might cease to be convenient. Thankfully, Windows has a few ways for you to automatically arrange several windows without the drag-and-drop maneuver.

Cascading Windows

All the windows in a cascaded set overlap one another so that the upper and left borders are always visible—not unlike the way you'd fan out a hand of Gin Rummy. (Figure 4.4 shows a set of four cascaded windows.)

FIGURE 4.4.

A set of cascaded windows.

To Do: Cascading Open Windows

You can make Windows automatically cascade all open windows on the Desktop by following these steps:

1. Right-click an empty portion of the taskbar.
2. From the shortcut menu that appears, select Cascade Windows.

By the way, the Cascade Windows command doesn't affect Active Desktop items.

Tiling Windows

By comparison, no window in a tiled set overlaps in any way, whether the tiling is horizontal or vertical. (Figure 4.5 shows the same four windows as Figure 4.4, this time tiled horizontally.)

FIGURE 4.5.

A set of horizontally tiled windows.

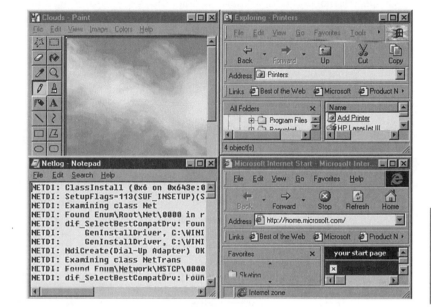

All tiled windows are of equal size. Obviously, if you have a large number of windows open, tiling can result in rather small windows.

To tile your open windows, right-click the taskbar and select either Tile Windows Horizontally or Tile Windows Vertically. The Tile commands don't affect Active Desktop items.

Closing a Window

When you're finished with a window, you should close it. This frees up system resources for other activity. Closing a program's window, by the way, is the same thing as exiting the program.

Some windows immediately close themselves when you click the Close button. Other windows—especially programs with open files—prompt you to save information before closing the window. This gives you an opportunity to save your open files before exiting the program. You can also close a window from the taskbar; just right-click the program's button and select Close.

4

You can close an Active Desktop item by clicking its close button (refer to Figure 4.3). Closing an Active Desktop item temporarily removes it from the Active Desktop.

To Do: Retrieving a Closed Active Desktop Item

To get the window back, follow these steps:

1. Right-click the Desktop and select Active Desktop from the shortcut menu.

2. Select Customize my Desktop.

3. Click the Web tab, and then click the box in front of the Active Desktop item that you want to redisplay. A check mark appears in front of the window that you selected.

▲   4. Click OK.

Using Toolbars

A toolbar is a collection of buttons that represent commands. When you click a button, the associated command is executed. Last hour, you learned how to use the Windows 98 toolbars. Windows programs use toolbars, too. Not every Windows program uses a toolbar, but many do. Because toolbars offer access to the most common commands, many programs have toolbars that contain the same buttons. Figure 4.6 shows Windows Explorer and its toolbars.

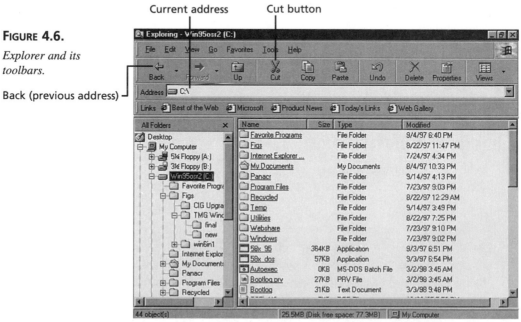

FIGURE 4.6.

Explorer and its toolbars.

The Cut button is indicative of one type of common toolbar button. You select the files that you want to move and then click the Cut button. Notice the order of events here: You always select the object of your command first, and then click the button—not the other way around.

The Back button in Explorer is another type of button. The down arrow to the right of the icon indicates the presence of a drop-down list. If you click the Back button, the Explorer window moves back to the previous directory (or Web page). But if you click the down-arrow portion of the Back button, a menu drops down, showing the most recent directories (or Web pages) in Explorer's history buffer. You then choose the directory to which you want to move back by clicking it in the list.

The Address box is an example of the third type of toolbar button: a drop-down list box. Like the Back button, the Address box drops down when you click the down-arrow button, revealing a menu—in this case, the hierarchy of the current directory. You choose the directory to which you want Explorer to move by clicking it.

Most toolbars you use are composed of some combination of these three types of controls. In the application hours of this book, Hours 16-24, you learn more about common application toolbars.

Working with Toolbars

Both My Computer and Explorer come with several toolbars that enable you to work with your files more easily. Initially, the Standard Buttons toolbar is displayed, along with the Address and Links toolbars (shown in Figure 4.7.)

To Do: Display a Toolbar

To display a toolbar, follow these steps:

1. Open the View menu and select Toolbars.

2. Select the toolbar that you want to display from the cascading menu (currently displayed toolbars have a check mark next to them):

    - *Standard Buttons*. This toolbar provides file management commands such as copying and deleting. (You learn the purpose of each of these buttons later in this hour.)

    - *Address*. This toolbar enables you to type an Internet address for display in the file list area. You can also select local addresses (such as a different drive) from the Address list.

    - *Links*. This toolbar provides quick access to popular locations on the Internet, such as Microsoft's home page.

    - *Status bar*. This presents information such as the number of objects in a folder, the amount of free disk space, and so on.

FIGURE 4.7.

*Toolbars provide quick
access to common
commands.*

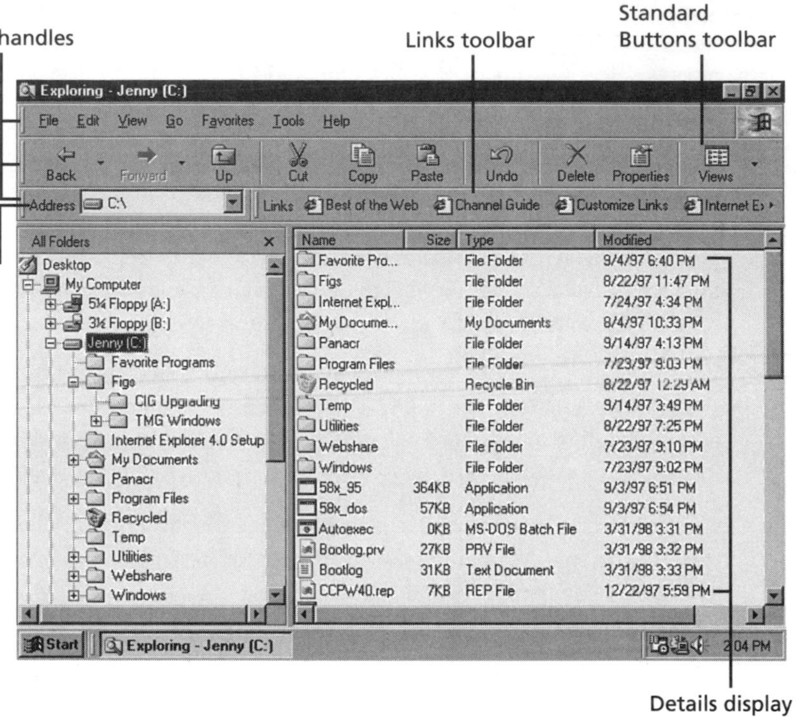

To use a toolbar, simply click the button whose command you want to execute. To use
the Address toolbar, click its text box and type the address of the site that you want to
view, or select an address from the drop-down list.

To avoid crowding the toolbars on one line, you can display one toolbar under another
(refer to Figure 4.5). Simply click the toolbar's grab handle and drag it to its new
location.

The Standard Buttons Toolbar

The Standard Buttons toolbar appears in both Explorer and My Computer. (Table 4.1
lists each button and its purpose.)

TABLE 4.1. THE BUTTONS ON THE STANDARD BUTTONS TOOLBAR.

Button	Name	Purpose
 Back	Back	Redisplays a previously displayed folder.

Button	Name	Purpose
Forward	Forward	After you use Back, this button displays the original folder that you viewed before the current folder.
Up	Up	Moves up one level in the folder hierarchy.
Cut	Cut	Moves the selected file or folder to the Clipboard.
Copy	Copy	Copies the selected file or folder.
Paste	Paste	Copies the file or folder from the Clipboard to the current location.
Undo	Undo	Undoes the last action.
Delete	Delete	Deletes the selected file or folder.
Properties	Properties	Displays the properties of the selected file or folder.
Views	Views	Enables you to change the file list display.

Moving Toolbars

Not all toolbars in Windows can be moved from place to place. A clear signal that a toolbar can be moved is the presence of a single ridge near the left edge (or the top edge in the case of a vertical toolbar). The reason that you might want to move a toolbar to a different location has to do with short-term convenience. For example, you might want to move a toolbar into the work area to make it easier to work with a particular bit of text or a graphic image.

The following are some general methods for moving toolbars:

- To move a toolbar into the work area, click an empty space on the toolbar and drag the toolbar wherever you like. Typically, the toolbar takes on a more rectangular shape, which you can adjust as you might adjust the size of a window.

- To move a toolbar so that it appears beneath another toolbar, drag it over the toolbar under which you want it to appear, and release the mouse button.

- To adjust the boundaries between two toolbars that are horizontally adjacent to each other, position the pointer between the two toolbars so that it changes to a black two-headed arrow. Then drag the border in either direction.

- To swap positions between two toolbars sharing the same line, click the ridge of one of the toolbars. Then drag the ridge past the ridge of the other toolbar.

Using Menus

The menu bar is a Windows program's chief device for presenting you with its available commands. Menu bars are typically placed just under the title bar in a window (see Figure 4.8), although some newer programs enable you to move the menu bar to a different position onscreen (Windows Explorer is one such example).

FIGURE 4.8.

A typical menu.

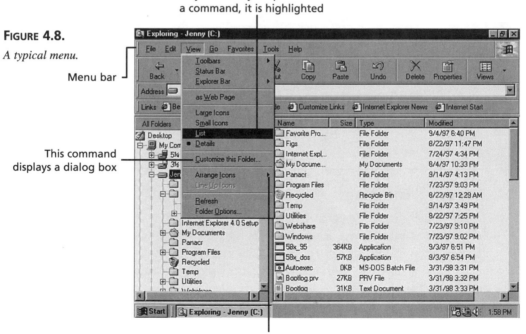

When you open one of the menus on a menu bar, it drops down a list of related commands from which you can choose. A brief listing follows of what typically happens when you choose a command:

- The program executes most operations immediately after you select them. Cut and Paste are classic examples. When you select them, the program carries them out without delay and without asking you anything else.

- If a command has a right-pointing arrow, a submenu (a cascading menu) with additional choices appears. For example, in Explorer, if you open the File menu and select New, a submenu appears. The submenu in this case lists various objects, such as folder, shortcut, bitmap image, and so on, that answer the question "New what?"

- If a command is followed by an ellipsis (…), the command requires more information from you before it can be executed. Thus, when you select such a command, a dialog box appears with several options from which you can choose. For example, the File, Open… command displays a dialog box from which you can select the file that you want to open.

Choosing Menu Commands

To select a menu command with the mouse, you click one of the menus so that it drops down, and then you click one of the menu commands. If a submenu is involved, it pops up to the right of that command (or to its left if there's no room to the right). At that point, just move the mouse pointer onto the submenu and click the command you want.

If you don't see the command you need, or if you just change your mind, you can click anywhere outside the menu area to dismiss the menu altogether. Or you can move the pointer to another menu category, without clicking, to have its menu drop down instead.

To use the keyboard to select a menu command, press and hold down the Alt key as you press the underlined letter of the menu command. For example, to open the File menu, press Alt+F. After the menu is opened, press the underlined letter of the command you want. For example, to select the Open command from the File menu, press the letter O. You can also use the up- and down-arrow keys on the keyboard to move the highlight line to the command you want and then press Enter to select the command.

Using Shortcut Keys

You can select many commands from the keyboard, without having to open the menu first. For example, the common commands Cut, Copy, and Paste have shortcut key combinations that you can press to select them: Ctrl+X for Cut, Ctrl+C for Copy, and Ctrl+V for Paste. To issue the Copy command, for example, select what you want to copy and press and hold down the Ctrl key as you press the letter C. Shortcut keys are listed next to their corresponding command on menus. For a complete listing of the shortcut keys associated with the program you're using, consult that program's Help system, under the term "shortcut keys" or "keyboard shortcuts."

4

Using Shortcut Menus

As an alternative to using the menu bar or toolbars, you can issue commands to many Windows programs using a right-click method, which opens a so-called shortcut menu or context menu. With this method, you point to the item onscreen that serves as the object of your command—for instance, a highlighted sentence or a row of cells in a worksheet. You then right-click. If the program supports shortcut menus, one pops up onscreen near the pointer (see Figure 4.9). From there, you can click a menu command to issue that command to the program or click outside the menu area to dismiss the menu.

FIGURE 4.9.

You can access common commands with a shortcut menu.

The reason that a shortcut menu is also called a context menu is that the displayed commands are related to whatever the mouse was pointing to when you right-clicked.

Shortcut menus are available outside applications as well. For example, if you right-click the Desktop, a shortcut menu appears from which you can select commands that arrange your icons, switch you between the Active and Classic Desktops, and change the Desktop's properties.

Using Dialog Boxes

In this section, you learn how to select options using all types of dialog box elements, such as text boxes, list boxes, option buttons, and check boxes.

When a Dialog Box Appears

A dialog box typically appears after you select a menu command marked with an ellipsis (…). This indicates that the command you selected requires more information from you before the program can execute it. The dialog box provides the means by which you can set the options that the program uses with the command.

Selecting Dialog Box Options

Windows uses a handful of standardized elements that work the same way for any dialog box you encounter. To move through the objects in the dialog box, press the Tab key. To back up to the previous element, press Shift+Tab. The following is a listing of the elements and how to use them:

- *Text box.* A box into which you type text, such as the name of a file, the key number on the back of the Windows 98 CD, or a password to access the Windows 98 Desktop. To replace existing text, drag over the text to highlight it, and type what you want to replace it. (Figure 4.10 shows a dialog box from Paint that contains a text box control.)

FIGURE 4.10.

A text box and a list box.

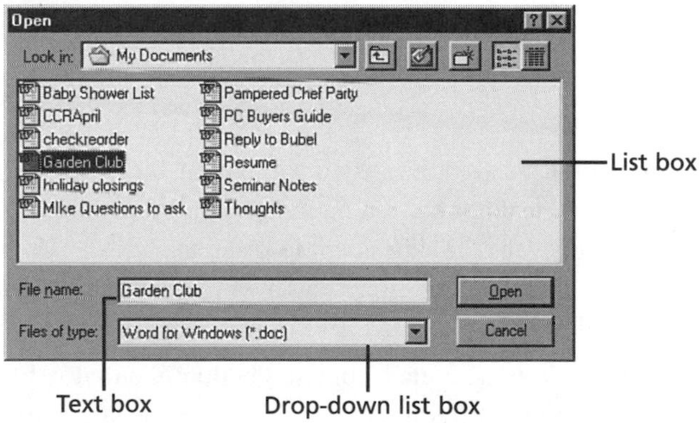

List box

Text box   Drop-down list box

4

- *List box.* A rectangle that lists several choices, the way a menu does. If the list has more entries than can be displayed at once, a scrollbar appears along the right or bottom edges. For a list box that supports multiple choices (such as a file list), and to select more than one item at a time, hold down the Ctrl key and click each item. You can also hold down the Shift key and click the first and last item in a range to select all the items in that range. (A list box is shown in Figure 4.10.)
- *Drop-down list box.* A variation of a standard list box. The list is revealed when you click the down-arrow. To select something from the list, click it. You can't change or add to the items in a list. (Figure 4.10 shows a drop-down list box.)

- *Combo box.* A hybrid of the text box and list box. The top line of a combo box works like a regular text box, featuring a blinking cursor. You may type a choice into this box or choose one from the list below the text line. A combo box supports only one choice at a time.

- *Check box.* Like a voting square, in which you register your x to show your support for the choice labeled beside it. Check boxes may be grouped together. If they are, you can choose more than one option. (Figure 4.11 shows a group of check boxes.)

Tabs create several pages
within a dialog box

FIGURE 4.11.

*A tabbed dialog box
featuring check boxes
and option buttons.*

You can select only
one option button

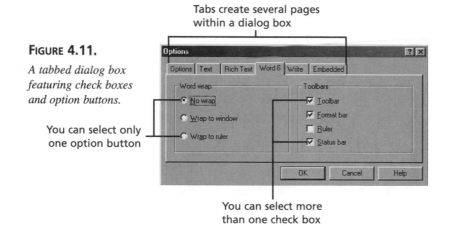

You can select more
than one check box

- *Option button.* Also known as a radio button, an option button is one of a set of such controls that represent a multiple-choice situation. Like the check box, you click the dot or the label beside it to make the choice. Unlike the check box, you can choose only one option in the set. (Figure 4.10 shows a dialog box with a set of option buttons.)

- *Command button.* The most common button in a dialog box. The OK and Cancel buttons on the most frequently seen dialog boxes are command buttons. After making selections in a dialog box, click OK to issue the command with the options you selected, or click Cancel to not issue the command. Most dialog boxes have a default command button, which is generally the OK button. Press Enter any time the dialog box is active to activate the default command button. Press Esc to dismiss the dialog box without issuing the command.

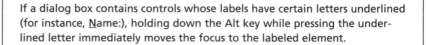

If a dialog box contains controls whose labels have certain letters underlined (for instance, Name:), holding down the Alt key while pressing the underlined letter immediately moves the focus to the labeled element.

Tabbed Dialog Boxes

Many dialog boxes have tabs that compartmentalize the information into multiple pages. A tabbed dialog box looks a little like a file drawer in which you thumb through tabs sticking up in order to find the folder you want. (A tabbed dialog box is shown in Figure 4.11.) To change pages in a dialog box, click one of the tabs. Using the keyboard, press Ctrl+Tab to move to the next tabbed page in the sequence, or press Shift+Ctrl+Tab to move to the previous one.

Summary

This hour taught you everything that you need to know about working with windows, toolbars, menus, and dialog boxes. Not only do you know the way around a windows screen like a champ, but you know how to execute commands the way you prefer—by mouse or by keyboard.

In the next hour, we take a break from all the nuts and bolts and explore ways to customize Windows further.

Workshop

The following workshop helps you solidify the skills you learned in this lesson.

Quiz

Take the following quiz to see how much you've learned.

Questions

1. Which choice is not a window resizing option?

    a. Return

    b. Restore

    c. Minimize

2. How does stretching and shrinking windows in Windows 98 differ in Windows 95?

    a. In Windows 95, you see the window's contents shrink and grow with the window's size.

    b. In Windows 98, you only see the outline of what would be the new window size.

    c. In Windows 98, you see the window's contents shrink and grow with the window's size.

4

3. Can you move a toolbar?

    a. No, they're set permanently in place.

    b. Yes, you can move them in a variety of ways.

    c. Yes, but you can only change its size, not its location.

Answers

1. a. Although Return sounds a lot like Restore, it's not a proper windows resizing command.

2. c. Windows 98 enables you to see the contents change size as you drag the window's size.

3. b. This hour showed you several ways to alter a toolbar's appearance.

Activity

In this hour, you saw how a shortcut menu's selections change based on where the mouse pointer is located. Launch the application that you anticipate using most. Most likely it's Microsoft Word 97.

Place the mouse pointer over the Windows taskbar and right-click. What kinds of selections do you see?

Now put the mouse pointer over the application's workspace. Are the selections the same, or different?

Try right-clicking over the empty toolbar space. Did you expect to see what you see?

HOUR 5

Customizing Windows

The thought of getting into the guts of Windows to make it look and behave differently may be intimidating, but with this hour you learn more than a dozen ways to make your Windows environment unique. You also uncover the answers to the following questions:

- Can I change the color of my Windows desktop?
- How do I create my own screen saver?
- What can I do to fit more on my computer screen?
- Can I adjust the way icons appear on my desktop?
- How do I change the date and time on my computer?

Arranging Icons on the Desktop

The icons on your Windows Desktop provide quick access to the programs you use most often. If the icons are placed on the Desktop haphazardly, however, it becomes difficult to find the icon that you want when you need it.

To Do: Arrranging Desktop Icons

You can, of course, drag each icon into place manually. But to quickly arrange the icons on the Desktop in neat rows, follow these steps:

1. Right-click the Desktop and select Arrange Icons from the shortcut menu.
2. Select a command from the cascading menu that appears:
   - *By Name*. Arranges the icons alphabetically.
   - *By Type*. Arranges the icons by their type (their filename extensions).
   - *By Size*. Arranges the icons by the size of their files.
   - *By Date*. Arranges icons by their file date (the date they were created or changed).
   - *AutoArrange*. Arranges icons automatically. If you add an icon to the Desktop, it's automatically arranged with the other icons in neat rows.

> You can sort your icons by any of the first four methods, and then use AutoArrange to line them up. The first four sort options are mutually exclusive whereas AutoArrange is an on/off switch that can be applied to any of the sorting methods to line the icons up in the specified order.

You can also arrange your icons in neat rows by right-clicking the Desktop and selecting
▲ Line Up Icons. This method merely lines up icons; it does not sort them.

Changing the Background of the Desktop

Initially, the Desktop is a solid teal color. Instead of a plain color, you can use a graphic as wallpaper to cover the background. You can choose a Windows graphic, or use one of your own. (If you want to simply change the color of your Desktop background, and you don't want to use a graphic or a pattern, see the section "Changing the Appearance (Colors) of Windows" later in this hour.) You can also choose a pattern to use as your Windows background, but you can't use both a wallpaper graphic and a pattern. You can even edit these patterns to customize the look of your Desktop if you like.

> In Windows 95, wallpaper and pattern can be used at the same time. If the wallpaper is smaller than the entire size of the screen (and is not tiled), the pattern appears everywhere except where wallpaper is located.

To Do: Put a Graphic on Your Windows Desktop

Follow these steps to select a graphic for your Windows Desktop:

1. Right-click the Desktop and select Properties. The Display Properties dialog box (see Figure 5.1) appears.

FIGURE 5.1.

Wallpaper your Desktop with a nice graphic.

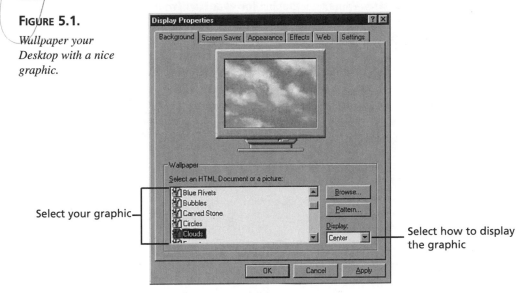

Select your graphic

Select how to display the graphic

2. Select a graphic from the Wallpaper list. A preview of your selection appears at the top of the dialog box.

3. Select either Tile or Center from the Display drop-down list. Tile arranges the graphic across the Desktop in neat rows. Center places the graphic image in the center of the Desktop.

4. To test the graphic on your Desktop, click Apply. If you don't like the result, select another graphic and click Apply again.

▲ 5. When you're satisfied with your selection, click OK.

5

You might notice a small degradation in performance when you use a graphic or a pattern as a background because they both use more of your system resources.

To Do: Put a Pattern on Your Desktop

Follow these steps to select a pattern for your Windows Desktop:

1. Right-click the Desktop and select Properties. The Display Properties dialog box appears (refer to Figure 5.1).

2. If you were previously using a graphic for your background, select None from the Wallpaper list.

3. Click Pattern. The Pattern dialog box appears.

4. Select a pattern from the list. To edit the pattern, click Edit Pattern. Otherwise, skip to step 6.

5. Click within the Pattern box to change the pattern one pixel at a time. You can give your variation a new name by typing that name in the Name text box. When you're through, click Change to save your changes. Then click Done.

6. In the Pattern dialog box, click OK.

7. To test the pattern on your Desktop, click Apply. If you don't like the result, follow steps 3 through 6 to select another pattern, and click Apply again.

8. When you're satisfied with your selection, click OK.

Adding a Screen Saver

It used to be that a screen saver prevented a display from remaining static for a long period of time, which might have caused a permanent imprint (or burn-in) of the screen on your monitor. Few monitors need this level of protection anymore, yet the screen saver has lived on as a source of entertainment.

You can purchase any number of entertaining screen savers, or you can use the screen savers that come with Windows.

To Do: Enable a Windows Screen Saver

To activate the Windows screen saver, follow these steps:

1. Right-click the Desktop and select Properties. The Display Properties dialog box appears (refer to Figure 5.1).

2. Click the Screen Saver tab. The Screen Saver page appears (see Figure 5.2).

3. Select the screen saver that you want to use from the Screen Saver list. A preview appears at the top of the dialog box.

4. In the Wait text box, enter the number of minutes of inactivity that you want Windows to wait before initiating the screen saver.

▼ FIGURE 5.2.

Windows 98 offers several screen savers from which to choose.

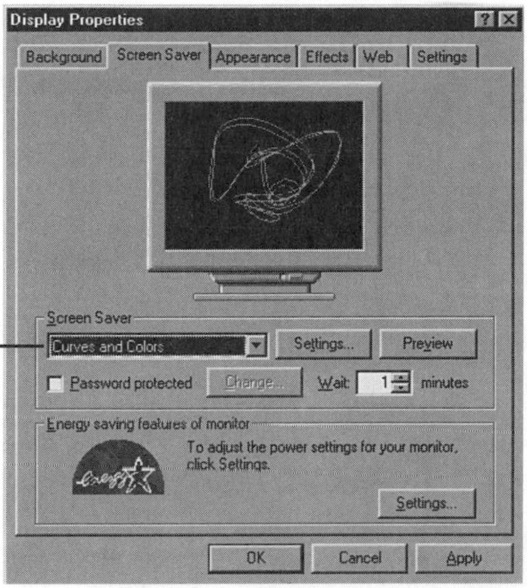

Select the screen saver you want to use from this list

5. Click Settings to access the options available for the particular screen saver you selected. Make your changes and click OK.

6. If you want to protect your PC from unauthorized use when you're away from your desk, select the Password Protected option, click the Change button, enter a password, and click OK. You then have to enter this password to gain access to your system whenever the screen saver is initialized.

▲ 7. Click OK when you're through.

5

Changing the Appearance (Colors) of Windows

Windows uses a particular color scheme by default. This color scheme determines the color of the title bars on active and inactive windows, the color of the Desktop, the style of the window text, the size and spacing of icons, and so on. You can select a different color scheme entirely, or change only the colors of individual elements.

To Do: Bring Your Favorite Color to a Window Near You

To change the appearance of Windows, follow these steps:

1. Right-click the Desktop and select Properties. The Display Properties dialog box appears (refer to Figure 5.1).

2. Click the Appearance tab. The Appearance page appears (see Figure 5.3).

▼ FIGURE 5.3.

*Windows enables
you to customize its
appearance.*

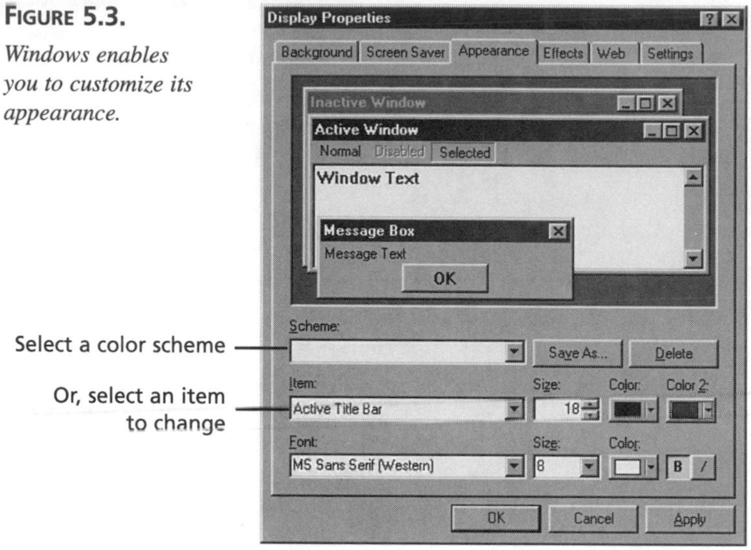

Select a color scheme ──

Or, select an item
to change

3. Select a color scheme from the Scheme drop-down list. A preview of the scheme appears at the top of the dialog box.

4. If you want, you can change the color and style of individual Windows elements. Simply select the element that you want to change from the Item drop-down list and then select the color or style that you desire.

▲ 5. When you're through making selections, click OK.

Changing How Icons Are Displayed

When you first install Windows, your Desktop has several icons for basic Windows items, such as My Computer and the Recycle Bin. You can exchange these icons for something else if you think they aren't meaningful.

In addition to changing the icons on the Desktop, you can also elect to show larger icons, and to display those icons using the entire spectrum of colors available to your monitor.

To Do: Make the Icons Look the Way You Want

To change the icon options, follow these steps:

1. Right-click the Desktop and select Properties. The Display Properties dialog box appears (refer to Figure 5.1).

2. Click the Icons tab. The Effects page appears.

▼ 3. To change one of the Desktop icons, click it and then click Change Icon. Windows opens a file of default icons from which to choose. Select one and click OK. (If you have another icon file that you want to use instead, click Browse to select the file first.)

4. If you want to use large icons, or you want to display your icons using all possible colors, select those options.

▲ 5. When you're done, click OK.

Changing the Screen Resolution

Resolution settings are identified by the number of pixels (or dots) used horizontally and vertically. For example, 640-by-480 resolution uses 640 pixels horizontally and 480 pixels vertically. 640-by-480 resolution is typically the lowest you can use. In addition to the number of pixels, you can control the range of colors that your monitor uses. The more colors, the better the display of certain graphics, but this takes up more video memory.

When you use a higher resolution, the images might become clearer, but your icons and text become smaller because, with more pixels onscreen, the relative size of each pixel is smaller. To compensate for this, you can choose the Large Fonts option; just click the Advanced button in the Settings dialog box. (To increase the size of the icons, use the Effects tab, as explained in the preceding section.)

To Do: Change Your Screen's Resolution to Meet Your Needs

To change your screen resolution, follow these steps:

1. Right-click the Desktop and select Properties. The Display Properties dialog box appears (refer to Figure 5.1).

2. Click the Settings tab (see Figure 5.4). If you're using more than one monitor, select the monitor whose settings you want to change.

3. To change to a higher resolution, drag the Desktop area slider toward More. To switch to a lower resolution, drag the slider toward Less.

4. Select the number of colors you want to use from the Colors drop-down list box.

5. If you're using two monitors and you'd like to use them in sync (to display a single image of your Desktop), select the second monitor in step 2 and then select the Extend my Windows desktop onto this monitor option.

▲ 6. Click OK when you're done.

5

FIGURE 5.4.

*Changing the resolu-
tion affects how items
are displayed
onscreen.*

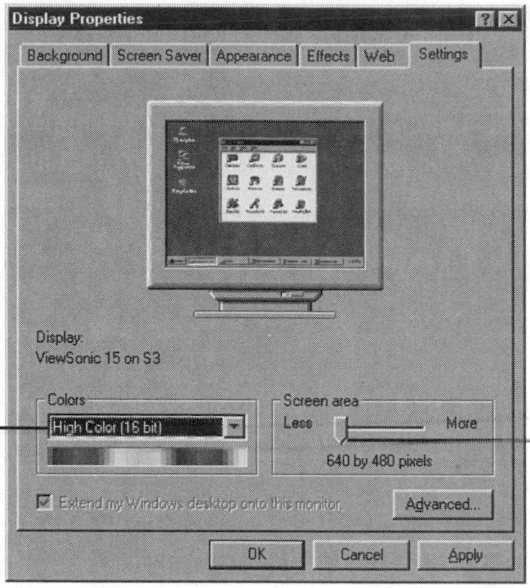

Select a color palette ————

Move slider to change
screen resolution

Changing the Taskbar

The taskbar is your Windows lifeline, providing access to your programs, Windows settings, often-used documents, and Help. This section shows you how to customize the
taskbar to suit your work style.

To Do: Set Your Taskbar Options

Windows provides several options with which you can customize the taskbar and its Start
menu. Follow these steps:

1. Click the Start button and select Settings. Then select Taskbar & Start Menu from
   the cascading menu that appears. The Taskbar Properties dialog box appears.

2. Select the options that you want:

   - *Always on Top*. This option causes the taskbar to appear on top of any win-
     dow, so you can always see it.

   - *Auto Hide*. This option causes the taskbar to disappear. To make it reappear,
     move the mouse pointer toward its former location.

   - *Show Small Icons in Start Menu*. The main Start menu uses large icons,
     which can make it quite wide. (Submenus off the Start menu use small
     icons.) To make the main Start menu less wide, choose this option.

   - *Show Clock*. This option causes the current time to display on the taskbar.

3. When you're done, click OK.

Reorganizing the Start Menu

When you install a new program, that program automatically adds a command to start itself to your Start menu. You might prefer to reorganize the commands for your programs into groups that you find more logical. You may also want to add your DOS programs (because they don't automatically add their commands to your Start menu), or you might prefer quick access to some of your folders.

To Do: Organize Your Start Menu

In any case, it's easy to customize the Start menu, as these steps show:

1. Click the Start button and select Settings. Then select Taskbar & Start Menu from the cascading menu that appears. The Taskbar Properties dialog box appears.

2. Click the Start Menu Programs tab. To add a new command to the menu, click Add.

   To remove a menu command, click Remove. Then select the command that you want to eliminate and click Remove.

3. Type the path to the command that you want to add, or click Browse and select it from the file list. Click Next>.

4. Select the menu (folder) under which you want your command to appear. You can create a new menu by clicking New Folder and typing a name. Click Next>.

5. Type a name for the command as you want it to appear on the menu. Click Finish.

To clear the Documents menu (which normally shows the last 15 files on which you've worked), click the Clear button on the Start Menu Programs page in the Taskbar Properties dialog box.

5

You can reorganize the commands that are already on the Start menu by opening the Start menu, clicking an item, and simply dragging it wherever you would like it to be.

Creating Your Own Toolbars

In previous hours, you learned that Windows 98 comes with several toolbars that provide fast access to the Internet and to some commonly used programs, such as Internet Explorer. These toolbars initially appear on the taskbar, but they can be dragged onto the Desktop if needed.

You can create your own toolbars to add to this collection. The toolbar displays the contents of whichever folder you select.

> If you want to create a toolbar that has icons for your favorite programs, create a folder and then add program shortcuts to it. To create a program shortcut, open Explorer and drag the program's file into the folder you created.

To Do: Build Your Own Toolbar

To create a toolbar, follow these steps:

1. Right-click an open area of the taskbar and select Toolbars from the shortcut menu that appears. Select New Toolbar from the cascading menu.

2. Select a folder, or type an Internet address (if you want to create a toolbar that you can later drag onto the desktop to display that Web page in a window).

3. Click OK. The toolbar appears on the taskbar.

To remove the toolbar from the taskbar, right-click it and select Close from the shortcut menu. This deletes the toolbar permanently; you need to redo the preceding steps to re-create it. You can, however, keep the toolbar on the taskbar as long as you like—even restarting your PC won't remove it. You can also drag the toolbar off the taskbar onto the Desktop just like the other toolbars; doing so does not delete your new toolbar.

Changing the Sounds for System Events

You can replace the sounds that are played for system events (such as displaying a program error and exiting Windows) with ones you create or download from the Internet. You can also replace the default Windows sounds with another sound scheme, such as Jungle.

To Do: Change the Sounds Windows Makes

Follow these steps to modify the sounds that Windows plays for certain system events:

1. Click the Start button and select Settings. Then select Control Panel from the cascading menu that appears.

2. Click or double-click the Sounds icon. The Sounds Properties dialog box appears (see Figure 5.5).

3. From the Events list, select the event whose sound you want to change.

4. Select a sound file from the Name list, or click Browse and select your own sound file. To listen to the sound, click the right-arrow button in the Preview area.

5. Click OK.

FIGURE 5.5.

Change how Windows sounds with the Sounds Properties dialog box.

Select an event

Select a sound for the event

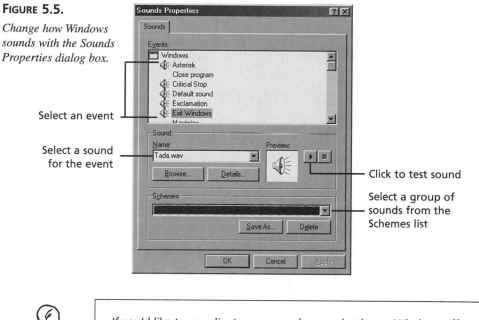

Click to test sound

Select a group of sounds from the Schemes list

If you'd like to coordinate your sounds around a theme, Windows offers several sound Schemes from which you can choose.

Altering the Date and Time

The time that appears on the taskbar is based on the clock setting for your computer. Although Windows automatically adjusts for daylight savings time and other such events, you may still find that you need to adjust the computer clock from time to time.

To Do: Reset Your Computer's Clock

To reset the clock, follow these steps:

1. Click the Start button, select Settings, and then select Control Panel. In the Control Panel window, click or double-click the Date/Time icon. The Date/Time Properties dialog box appears.

To display the Date/Time Properties dialog box quickly, double-click the time icon on the right end of the taskbar.

▼

▼　　2. To change the system date, click a new date.

　　　3. To change the system time, use the spinner that appears under the clock.

▲　　4. Click OK.

Modifying Mouse Settings

If you find that you're having trouble getting the mouse to click or double-click properly, you might try adjusting its sensitivity. You can also increase the size of the mouse pointer if you find that you're having trouble locating the mouse onscreen.

To Do: Make Your Mouse Obey Your Commands

To change these and other mouse settings, follow these steps:

1. Click the Start button, select Settings, and then select Control Panel. In the Control Panel window, click or double-click the Mouse icon. The Mouse Properties dialog box appears.

2. If you're left-handed, you can switch the functions of your mouse buttons by selecting the Left-handed option from the Button configuration panel. To adjust the speed at which your mouse recognizes a double click, drag the slider in the Double-click Speed panel. For example, if you find it hard to click twice fast, move the slider toward Slow. To test the setting, double-click the box in the Test area. If a jack-in-the-box appears when you double-click, the setting is fine. Make adjustments as needed.

3. Click the Pointers tab. Here you can select a different set of mouse pointers from the Scheme list box. For example, you might want to select Animated Hourglasses or 3D Pointers to jazz things up. Or, you might want to select Windows Standard (Large) or Windows Standard (Extra Large) if you're having trouble seeing the mouse pointer.

> Although these animated pointers may be cute, they're among the biggest hogs of system resources. If you use one, be prepared to experience some reduced system performance.

4. Click the Motion tab. To adjust the speed at which the mouse moves across the screen, drag the Pointer Speed slider. If you use a laptop and you find that the mouse pointer is getting lost, activate the Show Pointer Trails option and use the slider to adjust its speed.

▲　　5. Click OK when you're done selecting options.

Summary

I'll bet you never thought that playing with Windows could be so much fun! In this hour, you learned how to gain full control over your Windows desktop. From turning a favorite image into a piece of wallpaper to making Windows play jungle sounds, you've done it all.

In the next hour, we return to some of the more mundane (but vitally important) tasks involved with using a computer—working with drives, files, and folders.

Workshop

The following workshop helps you solidify the skills you learned in this lesson.

Quiz

Take the following quiz to see how much you've learned.

Questions

1. Can I make my Windows desktop any color I want?
    a. As long as it's not chartreuse.
    b. You can use only colors that match the Windows color scheme.
    c. Pretty much.

2. What happens when you increase the resolution of your display?
    a. Icons and print are bigger.
    b. Icons and print are smaller.
    c. Nothing; it just means your monitor promises to perform better.

3. What happens when you have to move the clocks forward or backward an hour?
    a. Windows takes care of it all by itself.
    b. You have to go digging deep into the Windows settings in order to change the clock.
    c. You must perform a Vulcan mind-meld with your computer to achieve the desired results.

5

Answers

1. c. Gee, isn't Windows versatile?

2. b. The increased number of pixels per inch actually makes the display smaller
        and sharper.

3. a. Windows really does take care of it itself, provided you've selected the prop-
        er time zone in the clock's initial setup.

Activity

Changing desktop colors can be a lot of fun, but certain colors can be very hard on the
eyes after an extended period of time. Give yourself ample time to tweak your system's
colors, sounds, and icon configuration until you come up with something you like. But
most of all, make sure that what you choose feels easy on the eyes. The time you invest
in doing this now may very well save you from getting an eyestrain headache by the time
you finish this book.

Hour 6

Working with Drives, Files, and Folders

In this hour, you learn about the elements that help you manipulate and organize all the information that's stored on your computer—the drives, files, and folders.

Although the information about dealing with drives, relocating files, using toolbars, and so on is universal whether you use Windows 98 with the Active Desktop or Windows 95 with the Classic desktop, you notice that My Computer and Windows Explorer are the tools most radically affected by the difference in setups. If you should run across an exercise in this hour that doesn't go the way you expect it to, try turning your desktop into an Active desktop to see whether that fixes things.

In addition to learning gobs of information about disk drives, files, and folders, you find the answers to the following questions:

- What is a file extension?
- What does Windows Explorer do?

- Can I change the way I view my folders and files?
- How do I select more than one file at once?
- What can I do to organize my files?

Understanding Drives, Folders, and Files

As you saw in Hour 1, your computer comes with at least two disk drives—the hard disk drive and the floppy disk drive. The hard disk drive provides large-capacity storage for your programs and the data files that you create. Windows itself is also stored on the hard disk drive. The floppy disk drive enables you to transfer data easily from one computer to another.

The drives are assigned letters so that the computer can tell them apart. Typically, the hard disk is drive C and the floppy disk is drive A. Your PC might have more than one hard disk, or the hard disk might be divided into separate partitions. If so, the additional drives are labeled D:, E:, and so on. If your PC has more than one floppy disk drive, it is labeled B:. If your PC has a CD-ROM drive, it's assigned the first available drive letter, such as D: or E:.

Typically, a new folder is created for each program that you install on the hard disk. You can create additional folders to organize your data into manageable units, just as you might organize your work papers into various folders within your file cabinet. Files are placed into each folder, just as you might place individual pieces of paper into a file folder. Files are of two basic types: program files (files that are used to run an application) and data files (files that contain data created by an application). You can mix both types within a folder if you want.

Filenames under Windows can contain up to 255 characters, with a three-character extension. Although you can't use some characters (/ \ ; * ? > < |), you still have a fair amount of freedom in assigning files names that help you later identify their purpose, such as "Sales for 4th Quarter 1997." Note that filenames can include letters, numbers, and spaces.

NEW TERM A file's *extension* identifies its purpose. For example, a filename that ends with the extension .TXT contains only text. A filename that ends in .EXE is a program file, and a filename that ends in .BMP is a bitmap graphic file. There are many other file types, such as .DOC for a Word 97 document, but you don't need to learn them because Windows specifies the type of file in the Type column in both My Computer and Windows Explorer. To make these file extensions appear, launch Windows Explorer, choose View, Options from the menu bar, and remove the check mark next to the Hide MS-DOS file extensions option.

Using My Computer

Windows offers two programs with which you can view your files, folders, and drives—My Computer and Windows Explorer. Both are remarkably similar, as you will soon see. (My Computer is shown in Figure 6.1.)

Menu bar   Column headers

FIGURE 6.1.

You can view your files, folders, and drives with My Computer.

Standard Buttons toolbar

Address toolbar

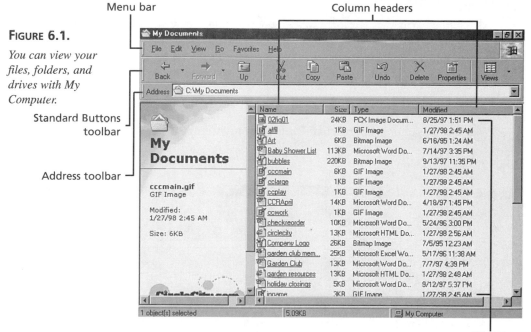

File list

As you learn in upcoming lessons, you use both My Computer and Windows Explorer in the following ways:

- To start My Computer, double-click its icon on the Desktop.
- To display the contents of a drive or folder, double-click it.
- To move back up the folder hierarchy to a previous folder, click the Up button.
- You can also move from folder to folder or to a different drive by selecting it from the Address drop-down list box.
- To return to a recently displayed folder, open the File menu and select the folder from the list near the bottom of the menu.
- To refresh the display (for example, if you switch floppy disks in a drive and you want to display the contents of the new disk), press F5 or open the View menu and select Refresh.

6

My Computer does not include a folder hierarchy list (called the All Folders list) in a separate panel on the left; however, Windows Explorer does. This is the main difference between the two programs. The presence of this list might make it easier for you to quickly jump from folder to folder as you browse (in which case you might prefer to use Windows Explorer), or it might confuse or annoy you (in which case you might prefer to use My Computer).

Also, unlike Windows Explorer, My Computer opens a new window with each folder or drive that you explore. You can change this by simply switching to Web style (explained later in this lesson).

Using Windows Explorer

Windows Explorer is not much different from My Computer (see Figure 6.2).

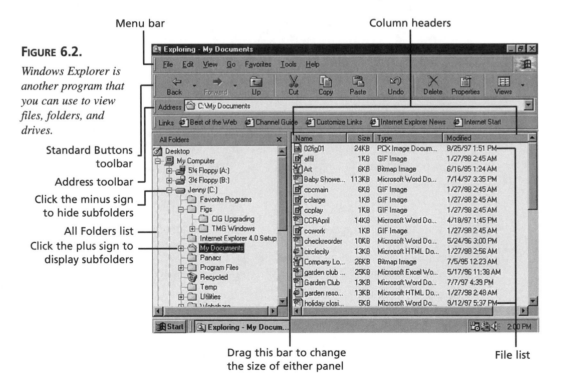

FIGURE 6.2.

Windows Explorer is another program that you can use to view files, folders, and drives.

As just mentioned, Windows Explorer contains a folder hierarchy (the All Folders list) that you can use to jump from one drive or folder to another. Another difference between

My Computer and Windows Explorer is that Explorer enables you to use the Tools, Find command (Find is also available on the Start menu) to search your computer for a particular file or folder. My Computer makes the Find command available only in its main window. (You learn how to search for files and folders later this hour in the section titled, "Searching for a File.")

To use Windows Explorer, follow these steps:

- To start Windows Explorer, open the Start menu, select Programs, and select Windows Explorer.

- Select a folder or file to view from the All Folders list by clicking it.

- If a folder in the All Folders list is preceded by a plus sign, it contains subfolders. To display them, click the plus sign to the left of the folder. To hide them again, click the minus sign that appears.

- In addition to using the Up button, you can move from folder to folder by clicking a folder that you want to view in the All Folders list.

- You can change the size of either panel by dragging the bar that divides them.

Understanding Web Style Versus Classic Style

In Hour 3, we talked a bit about the Active Desktop and Web Style. They can be confusing with their subtle and not-so-subtle differences, so I'll take this opportunity to elaborate on the concepts while discussing their use with My Computer and Windows Explorer.

If you use the Active Desktop, you might be interested in using the Web Style option within My Computer and Windows Explorer. With Web Style, the purpose of clicking and double-clicking is changed. Instead of clicking to select a file, you simply point to it. And instead of double-clicking to open a file, you click it. This change affects not just Windows Explorer, but My Computer and the Desktop as well.

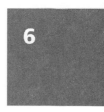

In addition, if you change to Web style and then use My Computer, each folder that you open is displayed in the same window instead of separate windows. If you want to use Web style's single-click method for selecting and opening folders and files but want to retain the use of multiple windows in My Computer, then use the Custom option.

To Do: Changing to the Web Style Option

To change to Web style from within My Computer or Windows Explorer, follow these steps:

1. Open the View menu and select Folder Options.
2. On the General tab, select the Web style option.

Separate from Web style, but often associated with it, is Web view. In Web view, the contents of your folders are displayed as Web pages, with icons representing subfolders and files. To display a folder in Web view, click the Views button and select as Web page.

The following are some tips on using Web Style:

- To open a subfolder, you click it, just as you might click a link within a Web page.
- To select a file, simply point to it. A description of the file appears.
- You can also browse the Web using Windows Explorer or My Computer. Simply type the address of the page you want to view in the Address list box.

If you don't want to use Web Style, you can select Classic Style (shown in Figures 6.1 and 6.2 earlier in this hour).

When you use the Active Desktop, Classic Style is activated by default.

Changing the Display in My Computer and Windows Explorer

As you learned in the preceding section, My Computer and Explorer on the Active Desktop are remarkably similar. All the tasks that you learn in this and subsequent lessons can be performed in either program (unless noted). For simplicity, I show only Windows Explorer in the figures.

The main difference between the My Computer and Explorer displays is the presence of the All Folders list in Explorer (see Figure 6.3). To provide more room for the file listing, you can easily remove this list by opening the View menu, selecting Explorer Bar, and selecting None. You can also click the Close button at the top of the All Folders list.

If you want to display the All Folders list but you'd like it to take up less room, you can resize the All Folders panel by dragging the bar that separates it from the file list.

You can't display the All Folders panel in My Computer; it is strictly an Explorer option.

FIGURE 6.3.

The All Folders list provides quick access to your folders.

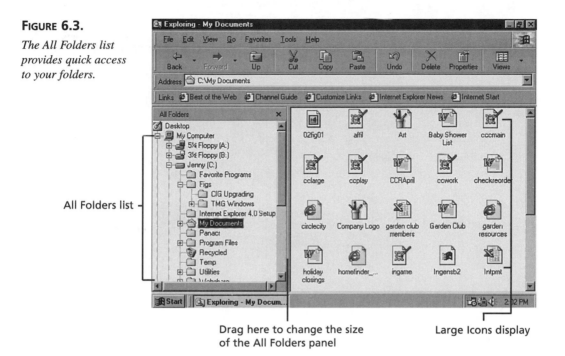

All Folders list →

Drag here to change the size
of the All Folders panel

Large Icons display

Changing the File List Display

In Figure 6.3, files are displayed using large icons. This is just one of many ways in which you can list your files. To change the File List display, open the View menu and select the view option that you want—Large Icons, Small Icons, List, or Details, which provides the file's name, size, type, and date of last modification (shown in Figure 6.4). The current option appears with a dot beside it on the View menu.

> If the Standard Buttons toolbar is displayed, you can use its Views button to change views. Click the Views button's down arrow and select the file list view that you want. (If the Standard Buttons toolbar isn't displayed, see the section "Working with Toolbars" for help.)

6

Normally, file extensions such as .DOC, .TXT, .BAT, and so on do not appear in the file list. If you want to see the extensions, open the View menu, select Folder Options, click the View tab, and select the Hide File Extensions for Known File Types option. To display hidden files (such as the system files WIN.INI, AUTOEXEC.BAT, and so on), select the Show All Files option as well.

FIGURE 6.4.

The Details view.

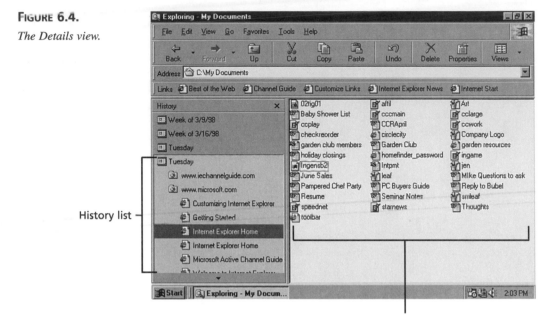

History list ⟶

Small icons display

Controlling the Order of the File List Display

As shown earlier in Figure 6.3, files are displayed in alphabetical order, with folders appearing at the top of the file list.

To Do: Changing the Order of Your File List

To change the order of the list, follow these steps:

1. Open the View menu and select Arrange Icons.

2. From the cascading menu that appears, select the option that you want: by Name, by Type, by Size, or by Date.

3. If you're using the Large Icons or Small Icons view, you can select the Auto-Arrange option to automatically arrange the icons in neat rows. To arrange the icons one time, select the Line Up Icons command on the View menu.

Replacing the All Folders List

The All Folders list can be replaced with other Explorer Bar panels:

- *Search*. Displays a Web page that enables you to search the Internet. (You learn how to perform searches in Hour 15.)

- *Favorites*. Displays a list of your favorite Internet sites. You add to this list just as you would within Internet Explorer (see Hour 11 for help).

- *History*. Displays a list of previous Internet sites you've visited. To visit a site, simply click it, and it's displayed in the file list window. (The History list is displayed in Figure 6.5.)

- *Channels*. Displays a list of channels to which you can subscribe (see Hour 12 for more information on channels).

To display the Explorer Bar panels in either My Computer or Explorer, open the View menu, select Explorer Bar, and select the panel that you want to display. (You cannot display the All Folders list in My Computer, but you can display any of the others listed here.)

Previewing Files

You can preview the contents of a file by right-clicking it and selecting Quick View from the shortcut menu. You can use this technique to view graphics files, Word document files, Excel worksheet files, and many other file types.

If you're viewing the folder as a Web page and you select a file, it is automatically previewed in the left panel. For example, if you select a graphics file, the graphic is displayed in the left panel, along with other file information, such as the file size and date of last modification.

Customizing Folders in Web Style

When you select Web Style, the contents of your folders are displayed as Web pages, with icons representing each file or subfolder. A Web page gives you total freedom to organize and display files within the folder.

If you don't want to go to the trouble of creating a Web page, you can display a graphic as a background for the folder. Although this option doesn't help you organize a folder's contents to suit your needs, it does enable you to add some spice to the display.

To Do: Creating a Web Page for a Folder

To create a Web page for your folder, follow these steps:

1. Open the View menu and select Customize this Folder.

2. Select Create or edit an HTML document. Click Next.

3. Windows prepares to start your HTML (Web page) editor. Click Next.

▼   4. Make your changes to the Web page, save them, and close your HTML editor.

▲   5. Click Finish.

To Do: Adding a Graphic to the Background of Your Folder

To add a graphic to the background of your folder, follow these steps:

1. Open the View menu and select Customize this Folder.

2. Select Choose a background picture. Click Next.

3. Select a bitmap graphic from the Background picture for this folder list, or click Browse and select your own bitmap.

4. If needed, change the Text color for the icons in the folder. (You might need to change the color for the text to show up clearly on top of the graphic that you selected.) If the text still doesn't show up clearly, you can display it on top of a colored Background (instead of directly on top of the graphic). Click Next.

▲   5. Click Finish.

You can remove your customization for this folder by selecting the Remove customization option in the Customize this Folder dialog box.

Selecting Multiple Files and Folders

Before you can copy or move a file or folder, you must select it. When you select a file or folder, it becomes highlighted. You can select more than one file or folder at a time in order to move or copy multiple files or folders in one step.

To select a file or folder, do the following:

- Click the file or folder that you want to select.
- If you have the Web style option activated, point to the file you want to select. After a second or so, the file is highlighted so that you know it's selected.

To select contiguous files or folders (files or folders listed next to each other; see Figure 6.5), do one of the following:

- Click the first file or folder in the list, and then press and hold the Shift key as you click the last file that you want to select.
- If you're using the Web style option, point at the first file or folder that you want to select and then press and hold the Shift key as you point to the last file that you want to select.

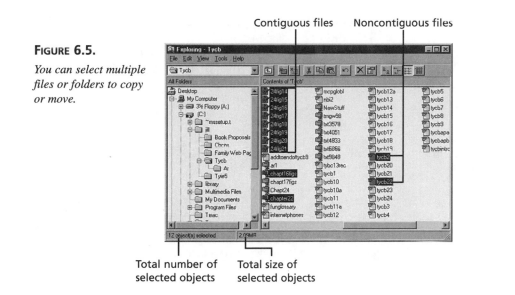

FIGURE 6.5.

You can select multiple files or folders to copy or move.

Contiguous files   Noncontiguous files

Total number of selected objects

Total size of selected objects

To select noncontiguous files or folders (files or folders that are not listed next to each other; see Figure 6.5), do one of the following:

- Click the first file or folder that you want to select, and press and hold the Ctrl key as you click each additional file or folder.
- If you're using the Web style option, point at the first file or folder that you want to select, and press and hold the Ctrl key as you point to each additional file or folder.

Copying and Moving Files and Folders

After the files or folders with which you want to work are selected, you can copy or move them as needed. When you copy a file or a folder, the original file or folder remains as is, and a copy is placed in the location that you choose. Thus, two copies of the file or folder exist.

When you move a file or folder, it is deleted from its original location and placed in the new location you select. In this scenario, only one copy of the file or folder exists.

The simplest way to copy or move a file or folder is to use drag-and-drop. Basically, you drag the objects to their new location and then drop them where you want them. In order to drag and drop successfully, you must be able to see within the My Computer or Explorer window—both the original location of the file or folder and the location to which you want to copy or move it (see Figure 6.6). If you can't see both locations, you can still copy or move your files, but you want to use the copy and paste or cut and paste method (explained later in this section).

6

FIGURE 6.6.

To make drag-and-drop easier, make sure that both the original location and the destination location are visible.

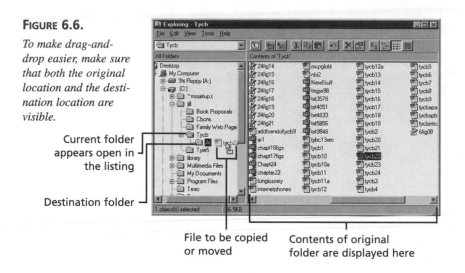

Current folder
appears open in
the listing

Destination folder

File to be copied
or moved

Contents of original
folder are displayed here

> Because you can display the file hierarchy in Explorer's All Folders list, it's easy to arrange things so that you can see both the original and the final location of your files. I recommend using Explorer when attempting to drag and drop files to copy or move them.

To Do: Copying a File or Folder

To copy a file or folder, follow these steps:

1. Select the file or folder that you want to copy.
2. Press and hold down the Ctrl key as you drag the file or folder to its new location.
3. Release the mouse button.

If neither the original nor the destination location is visible, you can follow these steps to copy your files or folders:

1. Select the file or folder that you want to copy.
2. Click the Copy button on the Standard Buttons toolbar, or open the Edit menu and select Copy.
3. Select the folder or drive to which you want to copy.
4. Click the Paste button or open the Edit menu and select Paste.

To Do: Moving a File or Folder

To move a file or a folder, follow these steps:

1. Select the file or folder that you want to move.

2. Press and hold down the Shift key as you drag the file or folder to its new location.

3. Release the mouse button.

> If you're moving files to the same drive—for example, from a folder on drive C to another folder on drive C—you don't have to hold down the Shift key as you drag. In addition, if you're copying files from one drive to another, you don't need to hold down the Ctrl key.

If neither the original nor the destination location is visible, you can follow these steps to move your files or folders:

1. Select the file or folder that you want to move.

2. Click the Cut button on the Standard Buttons toolbar, or open the Edit menu and select Cut.

3. Select the folder or drive to which you want to move.

4. Click the Paste button or open the Edit menu and select Paste.

> If you copy or move the wrong files or folders, you can undo your mistake by clicking the Undo button on the Standard Buttons toolbar or by opening the Edit menu and selecting Undo.

To Do: Right-Drag Your Files to a New Location

Another way to quickly place files where you want them is with the right-drag method. The advantage of this method is that it works the same whether you're copying or moving files:

1. Select the files that you want to move or copy.

2. Point to the files and click and hold down the right mouse button.

3. Drag the files where you want them and release the mouse button. A context menu appears. From there, you can select the Copy or Move command as needed.

6

Creating Shortcuts

Rather than actually copying or moving a file into another folder, you can create a short-cut to it. A shortcut is simply an icon that points to the real file, wherever it might actual-ly be. Shortcuts are used to open files and programs without having to select them from the Start menu or from their permanent location on the hard disk. You find most shortcuts on your Desktop, although they can exist anywhere.

To create a shortcut, follow the steps in the preceding section for right-dragging: select the file to which you want to create a shortcut, click and hold down the right mouse but-ton, and drag the file to its final destination. When you release the mouse button, select Create Shortcut Here from the pop-up menu that appears.

Shortcuts, by the way, appear as normal icons, except that they also have a tiny bent arrow in their bottom-left corner. This arrow indicates that the icon is a shortcut and not an actual file. Thus, you can safely delete a shortcut icon without accidentally deleting any real file.

To use your shortcut, simply double-click (or click) it. The program associated with that file opens automatically.

To Do: Using Send to Copy Your Files

If you often copy files to a floppy disk or to a particular folder, you can use the Send To menu option to perform that task more quickly.

To use the Send To menu option, follow these steps:

1. Select the file or folder that you want to send.
2. Open the File menu and select the Send To command.
3. Select the destination for the file or folder from the Send To menu.

   The Send To menu option contains these destinations:

   - *Floppy Drives*. This command enables you to copy files to available disk drives.
   - *Desktop as Shortcut*. If you send a file to the Desktop, it appears as a short-cut icon. You can then open the file by clicking (or double-clicking) it.
   - *Fax Recipient*. This command enables you to send a file directly to your fax machine.
   - *Mail Recipient*. This command enables you to create a quick email message with the file that you select attached to it.
   - *My Briefcase*. This command places the file in your briefcase, for eventual transfer to your laptop PC.
   - *My Documents*. This command moves the file to the My Documents folder.

To Do: Adding Your Own Destination to a Send To Menu

You can add your own destinations to this menu. Follow these steps:

1. Select the destination you want to add. For example, select the folder that you want to add to the menu.

2. Press and hold down the right mouse button as you drag the folder to the Send To folder, which is located within the Windows folder on your hard drive.

3. Select Create Shortcut Here from the shortcut menu that appears.

> Consider adding WordPad to this list so that you can pull up text files in a snap.

Creating a Folder

Windows provides a My Documents folder for your data files, but you might prefer to organize your files by creating subfolders within the My Documents folder. Alternatively, you might want to create your own folders somewhere else on your hard drive. For example, each member of the family might have his or her own folder with a number of subfolders.

To Do: Creating a New Folder

To create a new folder, follow these steps:

1. Select the drive on which you want to place your new folder. To create a subfolder, select the folder into which you want your new folder placed. For example, select the My Documents folder to create a subfolder for it.

2. Open the File menu and select New.

3. Select New Folder from the cascading menu that appears. A folder is created in the current directory.

4. Type a name for the folder and press Enter. You can give the folder any name, up to 255 characters long, including spaces.

Deleting a File or Folder

When you delete a file or folder, it's placed in the Recycle Bin. This gives you a chance to get back an accidentally deleted file. You learn how to use the Recycle Bin in the next section. When you delete a folder, by the way, you delete all files contained in it, as well as the folder itself.

6

> Even with the Recycle Bin, it's possible to still lose a file, so you might want to back up your files to floppy disks before you delete them.

To Do: Delete a File or Folder

To delete a file or folder, follow these steps:

1. Select the files or folders that you want to delete.
2. Click the Delete button on the Standard Buttons toolbar, or press the Delete key on the keyboard. The Send to Recycle Bin dialog box appears.
3. Click Yes to delete the files or folders.

> If you notice right away that you've made a mistake deleting a file or folder, click the Undo button on the Standard Buttons toolbar or open the Edit menu and select Undo to restore the file. Otherwise, read the next section to learn how to retrieve your file or folder.

Emptying the Recycle Bin

After a file or folder is sent to the Recycle Bin, it stays there until you empty it.

To Do: Retrieving a File from the Windows Recycle Bin

To retrieve a file or folder from the Recycle Bin, follow these steps:

1. Open the Recycle Bin by clicking (or double-clicking) it. You find an icon for the Recycle Bin on the Desktop.
2. Select the items that you want to restore.
3. Open the File menu and select Restore. The items that you selected are restored to their original locations.

> The Recycle Bin can't be used to restore files that were deleted from a floppy disk. These files aren't saved to the Recycle Bin, so be careful when removing files from a disk.

Now, because you might have deleted several files or folders to make more room on your hard disk, and because all those deleted files and folders were actually moved to the Recycle Bin and not really removed from the hard disk, you need to empty the Recycle Bin to regain extra hard disk space.

To Do: Cleaning Out the Recycling Bin

To empty the Recycle Bin, follow these steps:

1. Open the Recycle Bin.

2. Open the File menu and select Empty Recycle Bin, or click the Empty Recycle Bin link if the Recycle Bin is displayed as a Web page.

If you want to remove only one or two items from the Recycle Bin, you can. Just select them and click the Delete button on the Standard Buttons toolbar, or press the Delete key on the keyboard.

> You can actually empty the Recycle Bin without opening it. Right-click the Recycle Bin icon and select Empty Recycle Bin from the shortcut menu that appears.

Bypassing the Recycle Bin

You can delete files or folders without sending them to the Recycle Bin. This saves you the step of emptying the Bin later to actually get rid of the files; however, it also removes your safety net.

To Do: Deleting Files Without Recycling Them

Follow these steps to delete files without recycling them:

1. Select the file or folder that you want to permanently delete.

2. Press and hold down the Shift key.

3. Right-click and select Delete from the shortcut menu.

4. Click Yes to confirm.

You can deactivate the Recycle Bin for all your file deletions if you want, although it might be dangerous to do so because you have no way to restore accidentally deleted files. To deactivate the Recycle Bin, right-click its icon on the desktop and select Properties from the shortcut menu. Select the Do Not Move Files to the Recycle Bin option and click OK.

Renaming Files and Folders

You might want to rename a file or folder if it turns out that the original name that you chose doesn't clearly identify the purpose of the file or folder.

To Do: Renaming a File

To rename a file or folder, follow these steps:

1. Select the file or folder that you want to rename. (You can rename only one object at a time.)

2. Open the File menu and select Rename.

3. Type the new name for the selected file or folder and press Enter. Be sure to type the same file extension as before. For example, if the filename ended in .DOC, be sure to use .DOC at the end of the filename you type. (Keep in mind that you must have the Windows Explorer Hide File Extensions option deactivated in order to see these extensions.)

If you're using the Classic style (single-click) option, you can click a file to select it and then click it again to rename it. The second time that you click the file, a cursor appears in the filename. Make changes as needed, and then press Enter to save the new filename.

Searching for a File

With the large hard drives in use today, it's easy to lose track of a single file. In Windows Explorer (not My Computer) you can search for your lost files by entering a complete or partial name, the date the file was created, the file type, or the file's size. You can even look for some matching text within the file.

If you're unsure of the exact spelling of a filename, you can use wildcards when entering a filename to search for. Two wildcards are available for use: an asterisk represents multiple characters, and a question mark represents a single character in the filename. (Table 6.1 lists some sample uses of wildcards.)

TABLE 6.1. EXAMPLES OF WILDCARD USE.

Wildcard Entered	Search Results
sales*.doc	sales95.doc, sales 96.doc, sales.97.doc
sales.*	sales.doc, sales.xls, sales.ppt
sales?.doc	sales1.doc, sales2.doc, sales3.doc
sales??.doc	sales11.doc, sales12.doc
sa*.xls	sailing.xls, sales97.xls, sam.xls
sa*.*	sailing.xls, sales97.doc, sam.ppt

To Do: Searching for a Misplaced File

To search for a file or folder, follow these steps:

1. In Explorer, open the Tools menu and select Find. Then select Files or Folders from the cascading menu that appears. The Find: All Files dialog box appears (shown in Figure 6.7).

FIGURE 6.7.

Searching for a lost file.

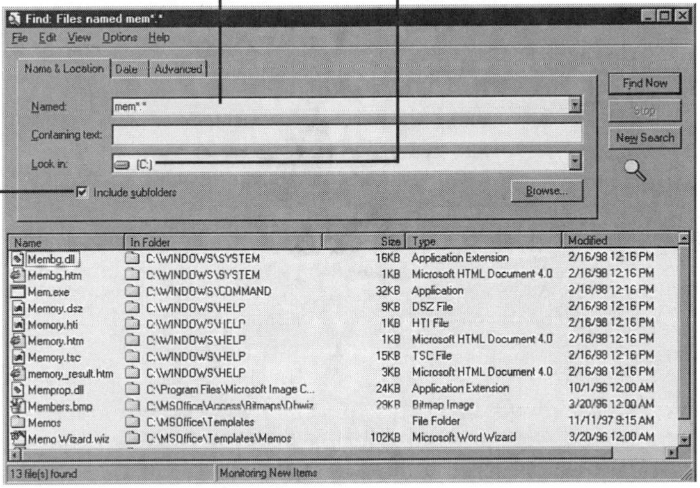

Type a filename for which to search

Select a drive or folder to search

Be sure to check this option to include subfolders in the search

You can initiate a search without starting Explorer: Just click the Start button, select Find, and select Files or Folders.

2. Type the name for which you want to search in the Named text box. You can use wildcards if you like. If you've searched for this file recently, you can select it from the drop-down list box.

3. If you want to search for a file that contains a particular phrase, type that phrase in the Containing text box.

4. Select the folder in which you want to search from the Look in drop-down list box, or click Browse to select it from a list. To search a drive, such as drive C, select it instead. To search an entire drive, make sure that the Include subfolders option is selected.

6

▼   5. To search for a file with a particular creation date or last modification date, click
       the Date tab, and select the date options that you want.

    6. To search for a file of a particular type or size, click the Advanced tab and select
       the options that you need.

    7. When you're through selecting options, click Find Now. The results appear in a
       window under the Find dialog box.

    8. If you didn't get the results that you wanted, you can modify your search criteria
▲   and click Find Now again, or click New Search to erase the criteria and start over.

Summary

This hour probably taught you more than you ever wanted to know about drives, files,
and folders, but at least now you're prepared for just about anything. You're able to
manipulate files with the best of them thanks to all your newfound skills.

Coming up next hour, we look at how to use Windows applications in general and get
a feel for some of the neat applications hidden in Windows.

Workshop

The following workshop helps you solidify the skills you learned in this lesson.

Quiz

Take the following quiz to see how much you've learned.

Questions

1. What's missing in My Computer that you find in Windows Explorer?

    a. Toolbars

    b. File lists

    c. Hierarchical file lists

2. How do you select a group of files that are listed right next to one another?

    a. Just click each file's name.

    b. Click the first file in the list, press and hold Shift, and click the last file that
       you want to select.

    c. You can manipulate only one file at a time.

3. When you delete a file, where does it go?

    a. The Recycle Bin

    b. The circular file

    c. Sorry, Charlie, it's gone for good!

Answers

1. c. Hierarchical is the key term here.

2. b. B is the proper sequence of steps.

3. a. Unless you purposely empty it, Windows holds deleted files in its Recycling Bin, at least until it overflows.

Activity

For this activity, I'd like you to think about who is using your new computer. Are they likely to generate a lot of word processing files? Do you have multiple ventures or activities that would be served well by separate folders? Think about how each user's endeavors could be effectively divided, and take some time to plan out a file structure for your new computer. It makes finding things a heck of a lot easier down the road!

6

HOUR 7

Using Windows 98 Applications

Consider this a friendly warning: This hour is packed with information. You not only get a feel for how Windows applications behave in general, but you discover all kinds of neat applets buried within Windows itself. You find answers to a lot of questions, including the following:

- How do I draw a picture with the Paint program?
- Can I play an audio CD in my computer?
- What can you play with the Media Player?
- Am I able to adjust the volume on my computer?

Starting a Windows Application

Whether you're using a Windows-based word processor or spreadsheet, Windows applications have many of the same basic capabilities. Luckily, these similar capabilities often mean identical keystrokes or menu commands for you.

To use an application, you must start it. When a program is installed, a command to start it is placed on the Start menu. To access the proper command, click the Start button, select Programs, and then select the folder in which the program's Start command is stored (see Figure 7.1).

FIGURE 7.1.

Programs are stored in their own folder.

Folder for the Internet Explorer suite of programs

Programs menu

Command to start Internet Explorer

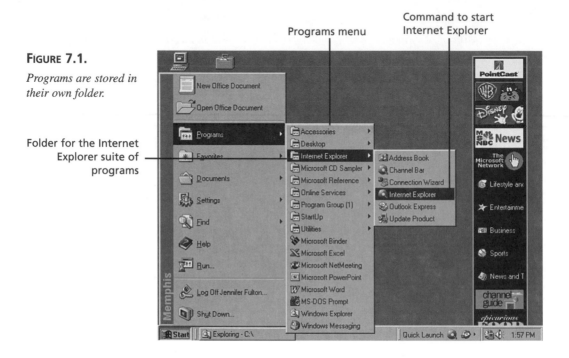

 Some programs, like many of the Microsoft Office suite of applications, place a program icon rather than a folder in the Program menu.

The following are several other ways to start programs:

- *With the Run command.* If the program that you want to start doesn't have a command on the Start menu, click the Start button and select Run. Click Browse, select the path of the executable file (.EXE) for the program, and click OK.

File extensions not visible? Open Windows Explorer (press Start and select Programs, Windows Explorer). From the menu bar, select View, Options. On the View tab, make sure that the Hide MS-DOS File Extensions box is not checked.

- *By file association*. When a program is installed, it registers the types of files that can be created with it. You can then use these file associations to start the program with a particular document. For example, if you select a file with a .DOC extension within My Computer or Explorer, you can open the document and start Microsoft Word at the same time. Simply double-click a file, and the associated program starts.

- *With the Documents or Favorites menu*. The documents you've worked on most recently are displayed on the Documents menu. You can use it to start the associated program with the selected document open and ready for you to work on. In addition, you can save documents to the Favorites or the My Documents folders and access them through the Start menu. Just click the Start button, select Documents or Favorites, and select the document that you want to open. To access documents in the My Documents folder, select it after selecting Favorites.

- *When you start Windows*. You can select certain programs and have Windows start them for you automatically when you start your computer. Just right-click a program's startup file and then drag it into the Startup folder, which you find in the \Windows\Start Menu\Programs folder. From the menu that appears, select Create Shortcuts Here.

- *With a shortcut icon*. You can create an icon for your program and place it on the Desktop. Then, to start the program, all you need to do is double-click the icon. To create a shortcut, right-click the program's start file, and drag the file out onto the Desktop. (You might have to resize Explorer so that you can see the Desktop.) From the menu that appears, select Create Shortcuts Here.

- *With the Quick Launch toolbar*. You can drag an application's start file (EXE file) to the Quick Launch toolbar on the taskbar to create an icon. You can then click this icon to start the program.

Creating and Opening Documents

After starting your Windows application, you might want to begin a new document or open an existing one. This is one of the instances in which nearly all Windows applications behave the same way.

- *Begin a new document*. Open the program's File menu and select New. You might need to make additional selections if your program can create more than one type of new document.

- *Open an existing document*. Open the program's File menu and select Open. The Open dialog box appears. (For most programs, it looks something like Figure 7.2.)

Select the folder in which your document is located from the Look in drop-down
list box. Select your document from those listed and click Open.

- *Open a recent document.* You can find the most recently opened documents listed
  at the bottom of the program's File menu. Simply open the File menu and select
  the document that you want to open from those listed at the bottom of the menu.

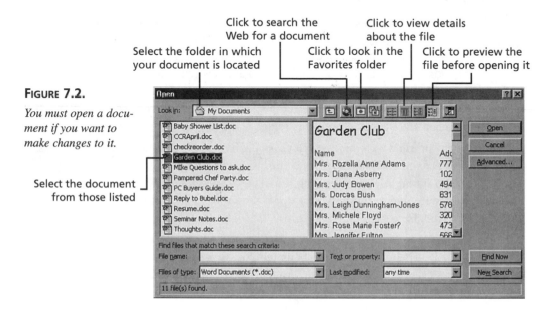

FIGURE 7.2.

You must open a document if you want to make changes to it.

You can open several documents at one time and switch between them as needed. First,
open as many documents as you need. Then open the program's Window menu and select
the document to which you want to switch from those listed.

Copying and Moving Information

When you copy or move data within a Windows application, it's first placed on the
Clipboard. The Clipboard is a kind of holding area for the data while the copy or move
operation is being carried out. The Clipboard is part of Windows, and not the program, so
you can easily use it to copy or move data between applications as well as between documents within an application.

Selecting Text and Graphics

Before beginning a copy or move operation, you must select the item with which you
want to work. The item that you select appears highlighted, so you can easily distinguish

it from unselected objects. To select text, click at the beginning of the text that you want to select and drag over the text.

You have several alternative ways to select text. (See Hour 16, "Microsoft Word 97 Essentials.") Much of what you learn in Word 97 applies to Windows applications in general.

To select a graphic, click it. Small boxes, called handles, appear around the graphic to show that it's highlighted (shown in Figure 7.3).

FIGURE 7.3.

When you select a graphic, handles appear.

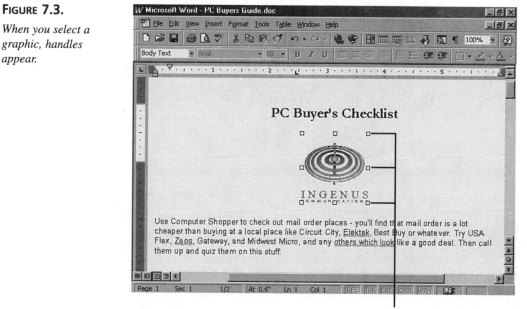

Handles

Consult Hours 16 and 17, "Unleashing the Power of Microsoft Word 97," to learn how to copy, cut, paste, and move elements in a Windows program.

7

Saving and Closing Documents

After you're through working on a document, you should close it to free up system resources for other applications. Before closing a document, you need to save it so that you don't lose any changes that you've made.

To Do: Saving a Windows Document

To save a document, follow these steps:

1. Click the Save button on the toolbar (if you have one), or open the File menu and select Save. If this is the first time you've saved the file, the Save As dialog box appears (similar to the one shown in Figure 7.4). This dialog box does not appear the next time you save this same file.

Choose a folder in
which to save the file

FIGURE 7.4.

The Save As dialog box.

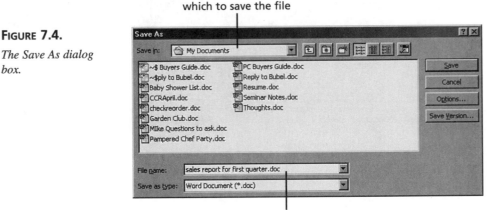

Type a filename here

2. Select the folder in which you want your document saved from the Save in drop-down list box.

3. Type a name for the file in the File Name text box. The name can contain up to 255 characters (including spaces), followed by a period and a three-character extension. You might not have to type the extension; most programs add the appropriate extension to the filename that you type.

4. Click Save.

After you save a document, it remains open so that you can continue working on it. If you make additional changes, save them by clicking the Save button or opening the File menu and selecting Save.

To close a document, open the File menu and select Close. If the document contains changes that haven't yet been saved, you're prompted to save them.

Exiting a Windows Application

Before you exit an application, you should save your open documents. To exit the application, do one of the following:

- *Use the File menu.* Open the program's File menu and select Exit. If you have any open documents that haven't been saved yet, you're asked whether you want to save them.

- *Use the program's Close button.* You can also click the program's Close button (×) to exit a program.

- *Use the keyboard shortcut.* If you prefer to use the keyboard, you can press Alt+F4 to close the program's window and thus exit the program.

Creating and Editing a Document in WordPad

WordPad is a basic word processing program that you can use to create letters, memos, reports, and other documents.

To create a document with WordPad, select Start, Programs, Accessories, WordPad and start typing. To create another new document later, click the New button on the toolbar (see Figure 7.5).

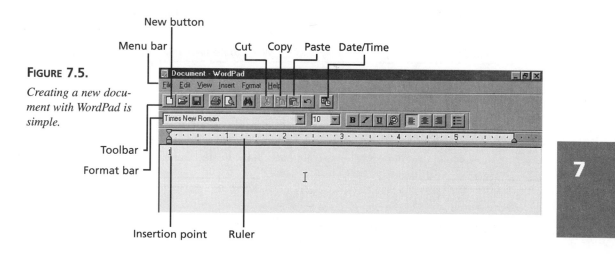

FIGURE 7.5.

Creating a new document with WordPad is simple.

7

Typing Text

When typing text into your document, remember these tips:

- *Text is inserted at the insertion point.* To move the insertion point, simply click the document at some other point. You can also move the insertion point using the keyboard. To type over existing text, switch to Overtype mode. To do so, press the Insert key. What you type replaces existing text, beginning at the insertion point. To switch back to normal (insertion) mode, press the Insert key again.

- *Erase a mistake.* Press the Backspace key; characters to the left of the insertion point are deleted. If you press the Delete key instead, characters to the right of the insertion point are deleted. You can also select text and press the Delete key to remove it.

- *Select text.* Click at the beginning of the text that you want to select and then drag over the text to highlight it. You can select text with the keyboard by pressing and holding down the Shift key as you use the arrow keys to highlight text.

To move the insertion point with the keyboard, use the keys listed in Table 7.1.

TABLE 7.1. KEYS YOU CAN USE TO MOVE THE INSERTION POINT.

Key or Key Combination	Description
Arrow key	Moves up or down one line, or left or right one character
Page Up or Page Down	Moves to the previous screen or the next screen
Ctrl+left arrow or Ctrl+right arrow	Moves left or right one word
Ctrl+Page Up or Ctrl+Page Down	Moves to the top or bottom of the screen
Home or End	Moves to the beginning or end of the line
Ctrl+Home	Moves to the beginning of the document
Ctrl+End	Moves to the end of the document

Drawing in Paint

With the Paint accessory (see Figure 7.6), you can create colorful graphic images for use in your documents or as Windows wallpaper. You can start Paint by selecting Start, Programs, Accessories.

FIGURE 7.6.

Paint is ready for you to create your graphic.

Toolbox

Paintbrush width box

Color palette

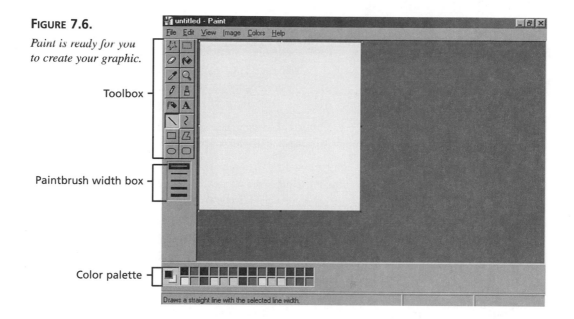

To create your image, you use the tools in the Toolbox. You can change the color of the objects that you draw with the Color palette. (I explain more about the use of color in the next section.) You can also change the size of the lines that you draw (and the size of the outline of drawn objects) with the Line Size box.

Table 7.2 explains how to use each tool.

TABLE 7.2. PAINT TOOLBOX TOOLS.

Tool	Tool Name	How to Use Tool
	Free Form Select	Drag around the area that you want to select.
	Select	Click at the upper-left corner of the area that you want to select, and then drag down and to the right to select the entire area.
	Eraser	Drag over any part of the drawing that you want to erase.
	Fill with Color	Click any part of the drawing and that area is filled with the current foreground color.

continues

7

TABLE 7.2. CONTINUED

Tool	Tool Name	How to Use Tool
	Pick Color	You can change the foreground color to any color in the drawing by simply clicking that color.
	Magnifier	Click to zoom that area of the drawing. Click the area again to zoom back out.
	Pencil	Drag to draw a freehand line. To draw a straight line, press and hold down the Shift key as you drag.
	Brush	Select the size of brush tip that you want to use from the Size box. Drag to brush the drawing with the current foreground color.
	Airbrush	Select the amount of spray you want from the Size box. Drag to spray the drawing with the current foreground color.
	Text	Use this tool to add text to a drawing. (I explain how to do this in the section "To Do: Adding Text to a Graphic.")
	Line	Select the line width that you want to use from the Size box. Then click where you'd like to place one end of the line and drag to draw the line. To create a straight line, press and hold down the Shift key as you drag.
	Curve	Select the line width that you want from the Size box. Click at the point where you want the curve to begin, and drag to create a straight line. Then, click where you want the line to curve, and drag outward to bend the line. Repeat to add another curve to the line if you want. (A line can have no more than two curves.)

Tool	Tool Name	How to Use Tool
▢	Rectangle	Select from the Fill Style box whether you want a filled or unfilled rectangle. Click to establish the upper-left corner of the rectangle, and then drag downward and to the right until the rectangle is the size that you want. To create a square, press and hold down the Shift key as you drag.
▱	Polygon	Select a filled or unfilled polygon from the Fill Style box. Click to establish the first corner of the polygon, and then drag to create the first side. Continue dragging to create each side in turn. Double-click when you're through drawing the polygon.
◯	Ellipse	Select a filled or unfilled ellipse from the Fill Style box. Click to establish the upper-left edge of the ellipse, and then drag downward and to the right until the ellipse is the size that you need. To create a perfect circle, press and hold down the Shift key as you drag.
▢	Rounded Rectangle	Select a filled or unfilled rectangle from the Fill Style box. Click to establish the upper-left corner of the rectangle and drag downward and to the right until the rectangle is the size you want. To create a square, press and hold down the Shift key as you drag.

If you make a mistake while drawing an object, open the Edit menu and select Undo to remove it.

Adding Color and Fill

The left side of the Color palette (shown in Figure 7.7) contains two overlapping squares. The upper square indicates the foreground color, and the lower square determines the background color. In Paint, the foreground color is used for the outline of the object that you draw, and the background color is used for the fill (that is, if you choose to draw a filled object). To change the foreground color, click a color in the Color palette. To change the background color, right-click instead.

7

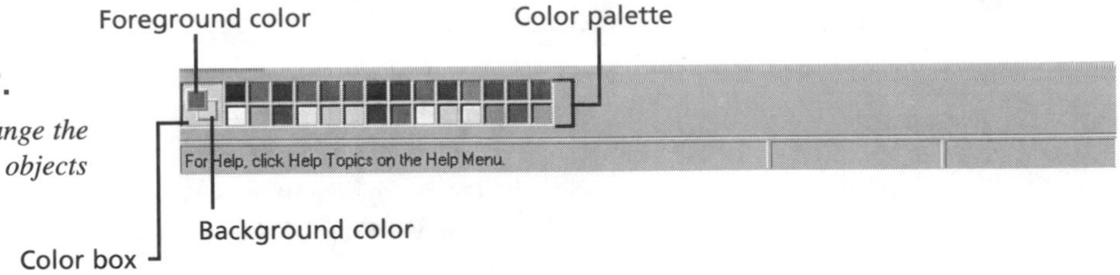

FIGURE 7.7.

You can change the color of the objects you draw.

Foreground color   Color palette

For Help, click Help Topics on the Help Menu.

Background color

Color box

Before drawing an object such as a rounded rectangle, you can choose whether you want it to be filled or unfilled. Simply click the appropriate icon in the Fill Style box—Outline Only, Outline with Fill, or Fill Only.

To Do: Adding Text to a Graphic

To add text to your drawing, you use the Text tool and follow these steps:

1. Click the Text tool.
2. Select whether you want the background of your text box to be filled or unfilled by clicking the appropriate icon in the Fill Style box.
3. Click to establish the upper-left corner, and drag downward to create a text box.
4. Use the Fonts toolbar to select the font, size, and text attributes you want to use.
5. Type your text. When you're through, click outside the text box.

> You can't go back and correct your text after you click outside the text box, so be sure it's correct.

Using CD Player

With CD Player, you can play audio CDs from your CD-ROM drive while you work with other applications.

To Do: Playing an Audio CD Using CD Player

Follow these steps to play a CD:

1. Insert a CD into the CD-ROM drive. The CD Player starts (shown in Figure 7.8).
2. The music begins playing. To pause the playback, click the Pause button. Click it again to resume. You can click other buttons as well (shown in Figure 7.9).
3. Use the Toolbar buttons to control the playback and display. (If the Toolbar is not displayed, open the View menu and select Toolbar.) The following list of buttons explains their functions:

▼

- *Track Time Elapsed.* Displays the track number and play time elapsed.
- *Track Time Remaining.* Displays the track number and time remaining for that track.
- *Disc Time Remaining.* Displays the time remaining on the disc.
- *Random Track Order.* Plays the tracks in random order.
- *Continuous Play.* After the last track has played, play continues with the first track.
- *Intro Play.* Plays only the first few seconds of each track. This helps you find the track you want to play.

4. When you're through listening to your CD, click Stop if needed to stop the playback. (The player may have stopped itself if it played through the entire CD.) Then

▲ click Eject or press the Eject button on the drive itself to eject the CD.

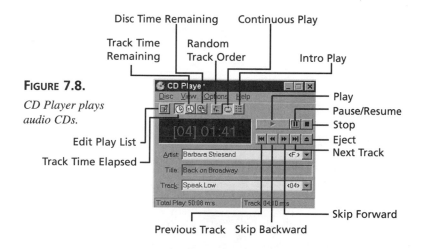

FIGURE 7.8.

CD Player plays audio CDs.

Using Media Player

With Media Player, you can play various types of multimedia (sound and video) files, including these formats: .WAV (sound), .MID (sound), .RMI (sound), .AVI (video), and .MPEG (video).

Media Player should not be confused with the RealPlayer plug-in for Internet Explorer that is used to listen to RealAudio and RealVideo files over the Web. The Windows Media Player enables you to play the above file types locally, so the files must reside on your system, not the Web.

7

To Do: Playing a File Using Media Player

To use Media Player, follow these steps:

1. Click the Start button, select Programs, Accessories, Entertainment, Media Player. The Media Player window opens (shown in Figure 7.9).

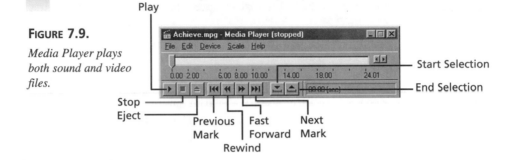

FIGURE 7.9.

Media Player plays both sound and video files.

2. Open the Device menu and select the device that you want to use. The Open dialog box appears.

3. Change to the drive and folder that contain the file you want to play, choose it from those listed, and click OK.

4. Click the Play button. You can click the following buttons as well:

   • *Stop*. Stops the playback.

   • *Eject*. Ejects a CD-ROM from its drive.

   • *Previous Mark and Next Mark*. Rewinds or fast-forwards to the beginning or end of the file, or to the nearest selection mark.

   • *Rewind and Fast Forward*. Rewinds or fast-forwards one increment at a time.

   • *Start Selection and End Selection*. Use these buttons to mark a segment of the file to play. Simply move the slider into position and then click either one of these buttons to mark it.

> To quickly fast-forward or rewind, simply drag the slider forward or backward to the desired position in the file.

5. When you're through listening to or viewing your file, click the × button to exit Media Player.

Using the ActiveMovie Control

The ActiveMovie Control is usually used as a helper application for your Web browser, enabling it to play any ActiveMovie files you encounter on the Web. It is also used in conjunction with Explorer, My Computer, and any other application that supports embedded video objects. The control itself is very simple, so you might prefer to use Media Player to play your ActiveMovie files instead (see the preceding section for help).

Using Sound Recorder

With Sound Recorder, you can play sound files (.WAV). You can also record your own sounds using a simple microphone attached to your sound card. You can even add special effects to sound files!

To Do: Playing a Sound File Using the Sound Recorder

To play a sound file, follow these steps:

1. Click Start and select Programs, Accessories, Entertainment, Sound Recorder. Sound Recorder opens (shown in Figure 7.10).

FIGURE 7.10.

Sound Recorder plays .WAV files.

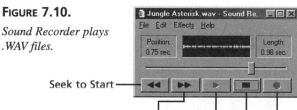

2. Open the File menu and select Open. The Open dialog box appears.

3. Change to the drive and folder that contain the sound file you want to play. Select it from those listed, and click Open.

4. Click Play. To stop the playback, click Stop. You can drag the slider to rewind or fast-forward as needed.

To Do: Recording a Sound Using Sound Recorder

To record a sound file with Sound Recorder, follow these steps:

1. Open the File menu and select New.

2. Click Record and begin speaking into your microphone.

3. When you're through, click Stop.

7

▼ 4. To review what you've recorded, click Play. When you're satisfied, open the File menu and select Save to save the recording to a file. The Save As dialog box appears.

5. Change to the drive and folder in which you want to save your file. Type a name
▲   for the sound file in the File name text box, and click Save.

Using the Volume Control

The Volume Control gives you power over Windows sound. With it, you can control the balance between your left and right speakers, adjust the volume, and even mute particular devices.

To Do: Changing the Volume by Using the Volume Control

To use the Volume Control, follow these steps:

1. Double-click the horn icon on the taskbar. The Volume Control appears (see Figure 7.11).

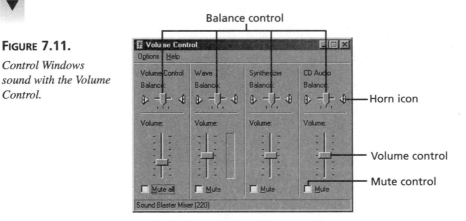

FIGURE 7.11.

Control Windows sound with the Volume Control.

2. Initially, the controls for playback devices are displayed. To display the controls for a recording device, open the File menu and select Properties, Recording. Make sure the device that you want to control is selected, and click OK.

3. To adjust the balance between the left and right speakers, drag the Balance control for that device to the left or right as needed.

4. To adjust the volume for a device, drag the Volume control for that device up or down.

5. To mute a device, click its Mute option.

▲ 6. When you're through, click the × button to exit the Volume Control.

> To quickly adjust the overall volume in Windows, click the horn icon on the taskbar. A volume control appears. Drag the slider up or down to adjust the volume. A beep sounds so that you can judge the volume you selected.

Using Calculator

Windows 98 comes with a handy calculator that you can use to calculate anything you need, from balancing your checkbook to adding up the latest sales figures. You find Calculator on the Accessories menu.

Using Calculator is remarkably similar to using a regular pocket calculator: Use the + button to add, – to subtract, / to divide, and * to multiply. To clear the last entry, click CE or press the Delete key. To clear a calculation completely, click C or press the Esc key. To compute the final value, click = or press the Enter key.

You can store the result of a calculation (or any number) and recall it when needed. To store the displayed value, click MS. To recall it, click MR. To add the displayed value to the value stored in memory, click M+. To clear the memory, click MC.

> You can perform scientific calculations with Calculator. Simply open the View menu and select Scientific.

Using Imaging

With Imaging, you can view your graphic images. You can zoom, rotate, and print the previewed image. You can also view a fax image.

To Do: Previewing an Image Using Imaging

To preview an image, follow these steps:

1. Click Start, and then select Programs, Accessories, Imaging.
2. Click the Open button on the toolbar.
3. Select the image you want to view, and then click Open. The image appears in the Imaging window (shown in Figure 7.12).

▼

7

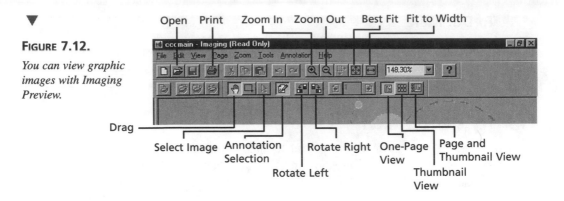

FIGURE 7.12.

You can view graphic images with Imaging Preview.

4. The following are some of the more useful toolbar buttons and their purposes:

- *Open*. Opens an image for previewing
- *Print*. Prints the displayed image
- *Zoom In*. Zooms in on the displayed image
- *Zoom Out*. Zooms the image back out
- *Best Fit*. Zooms the image to fit the window
- *Fit to Width*. Zooms the image to fit the width of the window
- *Drag*. Enables you to move the image within the window by dragging
- *Select Image*. Enables you to select an area of the image
- *Annotation Selection*. Selects an annotation for copying, moving, deleting, and so on
- *Annotation Toolbar*. Displays/hides the Annotation toolbar
- *Rotate Left*. Rotates the image to the left
- *Rotate Right*. Rotates the image to the right
- *One-Page View*. Displays one page of the document
- *Thumbnail View*. Shows multiple pages of the document at once, in small thumbnail-sized windows
- *Page and Thumbnail View*. Combines the One-Page and Thumbnail views

Using Phone Dialer

With Phone Dialer, you can place phone calls using your computer and its modem. This saves you the trouble of having to look up a number and then dial it. When needed, Phone Dialer can even dial your long-distance access code or calling card number. It also tracks your calls in a convenient log that you can review when needed.

To Do: Make a Call Using Phone Dialer

To Do

To use Phone Dialer, follow these steps:

1. Click Start, and then select Programs, Accessories, Communications, Phone Dialer. Phone Dialer appears.

2. Type the number that you want to dial into the Number to dial text box, or click a Speed Dial button.

> To add a phone number to a Speed Dial button, click an available button, type the name and phone number of the person you're entering, and click Save.

▲ 3. Click Dial.

Phone Dialer logs each call, along with the call's duration. To view the log, open the Tools menu and select Show Log.

Summary

I'll bet you didn't realize Windows had so many surprises in store for you, did you? You've seen just how similar Windows applications can be, and you've uncovered a host of useful and, in many cases, fun tools inside Windows. So pop in your favorite audio CD, and get back to work!

Workshop

The following workshop helps you solidify the skills that you learned in this lesson.

Quiz

Take the following quiz to see how much you've learned.

Questions

1. What do you do with the Paint program?

    a. Change the color of your Windows desktop

    b. Draw and color objects

    c. Preview a paint color mixture before you buy it for your house

7

2. What do you use the Media Player for?

   a. To play selected sound and video files residing on your computer

   b. To have Web-published newspapers read to you by a digital voice generator

   c. To play RealAudio files found on the Web

3. True or false? You can only record sounds with the Sound Recorder.

   a. True.

   b. False. You can also view video files with it.

   c. False. You can also play sound files with it.

Answers

1. b. You can draw all kinds of things with this little applet even if you have no artistic talent (like me).

2. a. The Media Player does not do either of the last two things.

3. c. You can also play sound files (.WAV).

Activity

Have you ever bought an entire CD for just one or two songs? Me too. Thanks to the Windows CD Player, you have the flexibility to listen to only the songs you want to.

Now for the big challenge: Insert a CD that you like only one or two songs on. Launch CD Player, and then choose Disc, Edit Play List. Even though I haven't stepped you through the directions, I'm betting that you can use the onscreen prompts to create a play list for that CD that includes only the songs you like. Aw, come on, you can do it! Put all that newly acquired computer knowledge to the test. Stretch yourself a bit; I believe in you!

HOUR **8**

System Maintenance and Troubleshooting Issues

This hour, dedicated to heading system problems off at the pass, is the shortest chapter in the book. It's a good thing, too. I wouldn't want you to be discouraged that countless things will go wrong with your new investment before you even have a chance to use it!

This book has more on troubleshooting and maintenance advice than is found in this hour. I've tried to incorporate additional tips where the given topic is covered more thoroughly. For example, you find advice about installing and configuring your modem in the next hour where I introduce you to the Internet.

We look at all kinds of maintenance and troubleshooting issues, including the answers to the following questions:

- How do I back up my hard disk?
- What if I need to restore the files on my hard disk?
- What does it mean to defragment a hard disk?
- When do I need to scan my hard disk for errors?
- Can I schedule any of these maintenance tasks through Windows?

Backing Up Your Hard Disk

To protect your valuable data, it's best to make an extra copy of it. The easiest way to do so is to back up your files onto disks or tape. Then, if something happens to the original file, you can restore the backup copy onto your hard disk.

When you perform a backup, it's not necessary to back up every file on your hard disk. You should back up your document files and certain system files, but you don't need to back up program files, because they can be reinstalled, if needed, from their original installation disks.

To Do: Performing a Backup of Your Hard Disk

To back up some or all the files on your hard disk, follow these steps:

1. Click Start, select Programs, Accessories, System Tools, Backup.

2. The first time you start Microsoft Backup, it checks to see whether you have any backup devices (such as a tape drive) on your computer. If Backup can't find any such device, it asks you to confirm. If you do have a backup device, click Yes and follow the steps in the Add Hardware Wizard to install it. If not, click No. (If you've used Microsoft Backup before, skip to step 7.)

3. Next, Backup asks you whether you'd like to create a set of emergency disks. You can use these disks to start your PC and restore your most recent full backup when your PC malfunctions. Click OK.

4. To create the emergency disks, files are copied onto your startup disk, which you created when you installed Windows. If you don't have a startup disk, click Startup Disk to create one. Otherwise, insert the startup disk into its drive and click Next.

5. Insert a second disk when prompted and click OK.

6. Click Finish.

7. A welcome screen appears (see Figure 8.1). Select Create a New Backup Job, and click OK.

▲ To Do

▼

▼ FIGURE 8.1.

Welcome to Microsoft Backup.

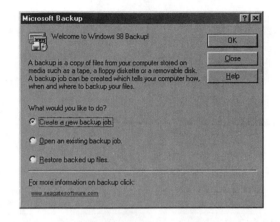

8

> After you create a backup job, you can use it to back up the same files later. When you select Open an Existing Backup Job in step 7, you're taken to the main Backup screen where you can begin the backup. You can also change the parameters of the original job if needed.

8. Select Back Up My Computer or Back Up Selected Files, Folders, and Drives. Click Next>. If you selected Back Up My Computer, skip to step 10.

9. Select the items that you want backed up (selected files appear with a check mark, as shown in Figure 8.2). You have the following selection options:

   • To back up all the files on a drive, click next to a drive letter.

   • To back up all the files in a folder, click next to a folder.

   • To select only some files in a folder, click the folder's plus sign to display its files in the panel on the right, and click the files that you want to select.

   • To deselect a particular file, click it again to remove the check mark.

10. Click Next>.

11. Select All Selected Files or New And Changed Files. Click Next>. If you select New And Changed Files, files are backed up only if they've changed since the last backup you performed. If you select this option, do not use the same backup disks that you used before. Use a new set of disks.

12. By default, backups are stored in the root directory of drive C. To select another drive or folder, click the folder icon and select the drive and folder on which you want your backup stored. Click Next>.

▼

▼ FIGURE 8.2.

Select the files that you want to back up.

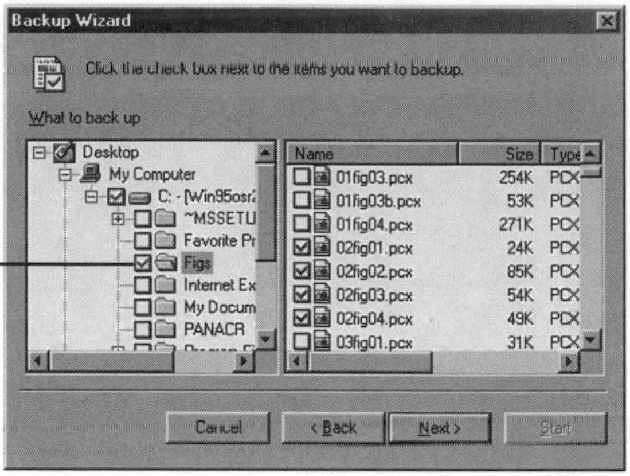

A check mark indi-
cates a selected file

13. Select the options that you want, as described in the following list, and then click Next>:

   - *Compare original and backup files to verify data was successfully backed up.* This option makes the backup process longer, but it does guarantee that all files are backed up successfully.

   - *Compress the backup data to save space.* This option compresses (shrinks) your files so that they take up less space on disk.

14. Type a name for this backup job, such as Full Backup. You can later reuse this job to complete the same type of backup procedure. Click Start.

15. When the backup is complete, you see a message indicating so. Click OK.

16. Click Report to review the backup summary. Click OK when you're through.

▲ 17. The main Microsoft Backup window appears. Click its Close (x) button to exit.

To Do: Restoring Files to Your System

If a file is accidentally deleted or damaged in some way, you can restore it from your most recent backup. Follow these steps:

1. Click Start, and select Programs, Accessories, System Tools, Backup.

2. Select Restore Backed Up Files, and then click Next>.

3. Click the folder icon, and select the drive and folder on which your backup is stored. Click Next>.

4. Select the backup set that contains the files you want to restore. Click OK.

5. Select the files that you want to restore (selected files appear with a check mark) and then click Next>. You have the following selection options:

   - To restore all the backed-up files on a drive, click next to a drive letter.

▼

- To restore all the backed-up files in a folder, click next to a folder.

- To restore only some of the backed-up files in a folder, click the folder's plus sign to display its files in the panel on the right, and click the files that you want to select.

- To deselect a particular file, click it again, and the checkmark is removed.

6. Select whether you want files restored to their Original Location or an Alternate Location (another drive or folder). If you select Alternate Location, click the folder icon and select the drive and folder that you want to use. Click Next>.

7. Select the replacement option that you want to use:

  - *Do not replace the file on my computer.* Use this option if you only want to restore files that no longer exist on your hard disk.

  - *Replace the file on my computer only if the file is older.* This restores all files, provided that they are newer than the files already on the hard disk.

  - *Always replace the file on my computer.* This option restores all the files on the backup, even if some of those files are older than the ones already on your hard disk.

8. Click Start.

9. You see a message asking you to get your backup files ready. Click OK.

10. When the restoration is complete, you see a message indicating so. Click OK.

11. Click Report to review the restoration summary. Click OK when you're through.

▲ 12. The main Microsoft Backup window appears. Click its Close (x) button to exit.

Defragmenting Your Disk

When a file is stored to a disk, it's broken into chunks, and each piece is stored in the first available sector. After the disk starts getting full, and files are deleted (making certain sectors available), file parts are no longer saved in adjacent sectors.

Thus, a file may be scattered (or fragmented) over the disk, which can slow down its retrieval. To improve the speed of your PC, you should defragment your hard disk. Defragmenting reorganizes the parts of each file so that they are once again adjacent to each other on the hard disk, eliminating excess search time.

To Do: Defragmenting Your Hard Disk

To defragment your hard disk, follow these steps:

1. Click Start and select Programs, Accessories, System Tools, Disk Defragmenter. The Disk Defragmenter Optimization Wizard appears.

▼

▼   2. Select Create a Log Now to Optimize My Disk. This causes Disk Defragmenter to analyze how you use your programs so that it can place the programs you use the most in an optimal spot on the hard disk, thereby speeding up your access to them. Click Next>. (If you've already created a log file, or you don't want to create one, select that option and skip to step 7.)

    3. Exit all your other programs, return to the Wizard, and click Next>. Disk Defragmenter conducts its analysis.

    4. Select the programs that you use by clicking them (shown in Figure 8.3). Do not select a program if you've never used it before. Click Next>.

FIGURE 8.3.

Select the programs you actually use.

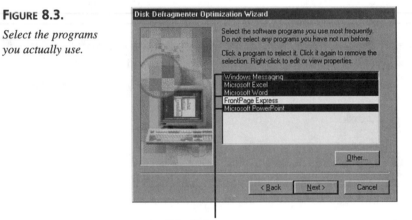

Selected programs

 If you use a program that isn't listed, click Other, then click Browse, and select the program's start file.

    5. Click Next>.

    6. Each of the programs that you selected in step 4 is opened, one at a time. You are asked to close each one in turn. After you close a program, return to the Wizard and click Next> to continue to the next program.

 Do not attempt to run any programs or perform any other computer tasks while this process is going on.

▼

▼ 7. Click Finish.

8. The defragmentation process begins. You can work while this process continues, although you find that your computer is much slower than usual. To stop the defragmentation process temporarily, click Pause. To stop it completely, click Stop.

▲ 9. When the process is complete, you see a message indicating so. Click OK.

Scanning Your Disk

Sometimes a file isn't stored to disk properly, and the computer loses part of it. This sometimes happens when a file is deleted, and the references to all the parts of the file aren't removed from the main file directory (File Allocation Table). In any case, it's a good idea to periodically check your hard disk for this type of error, and to let the computer fix the problems that it finds.

To Do: Scanning Your Hard Disk for Errors

To scan your hard disk for errors, follow these steps:

1. Click Start, and select Programs, Accessories, System Tools, ScanDisk.

2. Select the drive that you want to scan.

3. Select the type of scanning that you want to perform. Standard checks the hard disk for file errors. Thorough checks for errors and examines the surface of the hard disk itself.

4. If you want ScanDisk to fix any errors that it finds (rather than reporting those errors to you and providing various options), select the Automatically fix errors option.

5. When you're ready, click Start.

6. When the scanning is through, you see a message indicating so. Click Close.

▲ 7. You're returned to the ScanDisk dialog box. Click Close.

Scheduling Tasks

With the Windows Maintenance Wizard, you can schedule regular maintenance tasks to be performed on your computer's hard disk. These tasks include the following:

- Scheduling programs to open when you start your PC
- Defragmenting the hard disk
- Checking the disk for errors using ScanDisk
- Deleting unneeded files

To Do: Scheduling Your PC for Maintenance

Like cars, PCs need regularly scheduled maintenance. To schedule tasks, follow these steps:

1. Click Start, and select Programs, Accessories, System Tools, Maintenance Wizard.

2. Select Express or Custom, and click Next>.

3. Select a time period when you might want to have maintenance done, and click Next>. If you selected Express in step 2, skip to step 8. If you selected Custom, continue to step 4.

4. A listing of the programs that are currently scheduled to be run at start-up appears. To prevent a program from running at start-up, click it to remove the check mark. Click Next>.

5. To schedule Disk Defragmenter to run automatically, click Yes, Defragment My Disk Regularly. If you want to change the time at which this occurs, click Reschedule. To change the drive to defragment (and other options), click Settings. When you're ready, click Next>.

6. To schedule ScanDisk to run automatically, click Yes, Scan My Hard Disk for Errors Regularly. If you want to change the time at which this occurs, click Reschedule. To change the drive that you want scanned (among other options), click Settings. When you're done, click Next>.

7. To have Windows delete unneeded files, click Yes, Delete Unnecessary Files Regularly. To change the time at which this occurs, click Reschedule. To change the types of files that are automatically deleted, click Settings. When you're done, click Next>.

8. A summary screen appears. Review the tasks that have been scheduled. If you see a mistake, you can click < Back to return to a previous screen. If everything's okay, click Finish. (If you want the tasks you selected to be performed now, select When I Click Finish, Perform Each Scheduled Task for the First Time.)

Summary

See? Scheduling your PC for regular maintenance isn't so bad. In fact, in many ways it's a lot easier than dealing with a car; you don't have to wait in a long line at the shop, and you don't need to rely on someone's subjective opinion of what's wrong!

This concludes our journey through the Windows operating system. In the next part of the book, we look at how to use the Internet.

Workshop

The following workshop helps you solidify the skills that you learned in this lesson.

Quiz

Take the following quiz to see how much you've learned.

Questions

1. Why back up your hard disk?

   a. You have a second copy of critical files in the event of disaster (or a simple hard disk failure).

   b. There are too many homeless disks in the world; we need to put them to good use.

   c. If you have nothing better to do....

2. What does having a fragmented file mean?

   a. The text files contain only parts of sentences (or fragments) as opposed to having complete sentences.

   b. The file parts are stored in several locations on the hard disk because they are stored where space is available.

   c. There is no such thing as a fragmented file.

3. What activities can you schedule for service with Windows?

   a. Defragmenting your disk

   b. Scanning your disk

   c. Deleting unneeded files

Answers

1. a. If you don't know the answer to this one by now....

2. a. Just kidding, it's actually b!

3. a, b, and c. All three can be scheduled for maintenance with the Windows Maintenance Wizard.

Activity

There's no time like the present—fire up the Windows Maintenance Wizard while you're thinking about it, and schedule your PC for regular checkups. Doing so helps your system perform at its very best.

PART III

The Internet and World Wide Web

Hour

HOUR 9

Introducing the Internet and World Wide Web

An estimated 40 million people in the United States are connected to the Internet, and that's just counting people over 16 years of age. The Internet is growing at astounding rates as parents, senior citizens, and school children turn to the Internet for entertainment and education. What was once an experience for a privileged few has become commonplace.

In this hour, you learn why the Internet has become so popular and how you, too, can join in the fun. You'll also uncover the answers to the following questions:

- What is the Internet?
- Will I be able to send email to friends in other countries?
- What equipment will I need to get online?
- Are there special software requirements?
- What kinds of information will I find on the World Wide Web?

What Is the Internet?

If you've watched the news much in the past year or two, undoubtedly you've noticed all the hoopla over the Internet. Although the Internet, or its forerunner ARPANET, has been around since the late 1960s, you would think that the worldwide network of computers magically became connected during the last two to three years. The Internet has been the hot topic lately, and it doesn't seem likely that the topic will cool down in the near future.

The Internet's popularity has fueled the demand for books, such as this one, designed to help ease you into what, at first, must seem like a technological hodgepodge. The Internet may seem insurmountable. By the time you finish this part of the book, however, you'll think of yourself as an Internet expert. You'll understand Web browsers and email programs, as well as channels and subscriptions, and you will likely be showing other, less-informed users how to access search engines and chat rooms.

Access to the Internet is access to a wealth of information, from online shopping to academic research to stock market quotes (see Figure 9.1) to information on sports, local weather, and national news.

FIGURE 9.1.

The Quote.Com financial service provides current stock quotes.

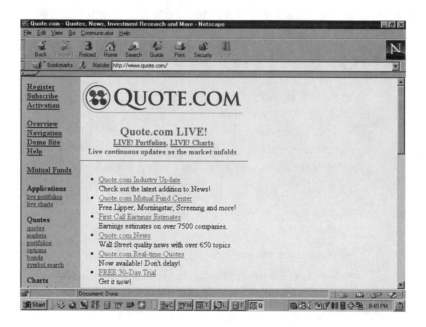

Originally designed as an academic-exchange medium, the Internet has become a favorite target of burgeoning entrepreneurs who sell everything from stocks, bonds, and mutual funds to compact discs, music boxes, and vintage wines.

The Internet's access and appeal have also naturally caught the attention of most major computer hardware and software manufacturers and vendors. They've found that the Internet, or "the Net," is an excellent way to reach and provide information and upgrades to their customer base and potential customer base. Besides Intel (whose home page is shown in Figure 9.2), other well-known computer vendors with a presence on the Net include IBM, Compaq, Novell, Apple, and, of course, Microsoft.

FIGURE 9.2.

Intel's Home Page.

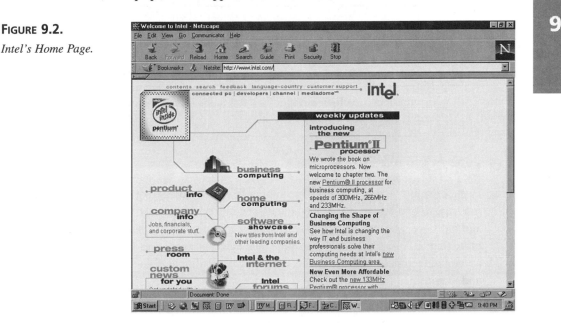

Pieces of the Internet: How They Fit Together

The Internet is a worldwide series of interconnected computer systems and a series of several types of computer services. Although many of you might already have heard a lot about the World Wide Web, you may be less familiar with Gophers, newsgroups, and FTP sites. The following sections outline some of the more popular services available on the Internet.

Email

Email is the oldest Internet service, dating back to the mid 1970s. The basic concept behind email is fairly simple: you log in to a computer system and write and address a text message to a user on another system. The message is then routed through the maze of interconnected computer systems until it is delivered to its intended destination.

Email allows you to send text messages, but you can also attach other types of files, and encrypt messages to prevent anyone but the intended recipient from reading it. There are even free email-only services you can subscribe to if your only interest in the Internet is email. Hour 13, "Using Outlook Express for Email," explains more about sending and receiving email messages using the Outlook Express email program.

Sending email can save you a fortune in long-distance telephone charges. Say you live in Maryland, but your best friend from college lives in Massachusetts. If you're both connected to the Internet, you can correspond as much as you want for free (not counting your Internet service provider's charges of course). Of course you still have to pay your monthly Internet connection fees, but that's still less money spent than if you kept calling that friend long distance.

Usenet

Usenet refers to a service somewhat similar to email, except that instead of sending a message to one person, you post the message in a common area for many users to view and reply to. Usenet is an immensely popular Internet service that has grown to include more than 10,000 topics that users post messages and responses to, ranging from computer and technical topics to social, religious, and political discussions to music, books, and movies.

Newsgroups can also be a good source of information from other users who have used certain products, have seen certain movies or shows, or have had experiences with certain companies.

If you think you might be interested in joining or participating in a newsgroup (or two or three), check out Hour 14, "Reading Newsgroups with Outlook Express." It explains how to find them and how to join in on the discussion.

Before you jump head-first into posting your own news article, be sure to "lurk" in the target group for a while. Monitoring the group gives you valuable insight into what is and isn't appropriate to discuss there, and it could potentially keep you from embarrassing yourself by asking a question that is already answered in the newsgroup's FAQs (frequently asked questions). You'll learn more about newsgroup etiquette in Appendix B.

NEW TERM *FAQ* is an abbreviation for "frequently asked questions." FAQs and their answers exist to keep a newsgroup from getting bogged down with the same questions over and over again. Some groups post their FAQs periodically, although others maintain a Web site of them. If you don't see mention of them after a couple of weeks of steady lurking, just ask.

FTP

FTP (File Transfer Protocol) refers to both an Internet service and a UNIX utility (it's also now a Windows utility). The Internet service FTP is a series of computer file servers that archive and distribute files. Many FTP sites are operated by computer hardware and software manufacturers who use their FTP sites to distribute their software and software updates. Netscape, one of the major Internet Web browser companies, uses its FTP site to distribute its Web browser, Netscape Navigator.

FTP sites are also run by colleges and universities that use them to make shareware and software utilities available to a broad range of users. In Hour 14, you'll learn more about using FTP to download shareware.

The World Wide Web

The World Wide Web, often referred to simply as the Web, is without a doubt the most popular service on the Internet.

Part of the Web's attraction is the fact that it is the only multimedia service on the Internet.

The Web also seems to have no boundaries for the type of information you can find on Web sites. A lot of it may seem to be trivial, but Fortune 500 companies have been attracted to the Web in droves, and part of the Web is gradually becoming the cyber marketplace of the '90s.

You can also find information from or about:

- Government agencies (federal, state, and local)
- Colleges and universities
- Professional and amateur sports teams
- Political organizations
- Social and cultural organizations
- Health and science
- Computer hardware and software manufacturers
- Celebrities from film, music, television, and sports

- Hobbies and collectibles
- Business opportunities on the Web

Chatting

Chatting allows users to congregate in a common area and communicate by typing a conversation. Microsoft Chat, which is covered in Hour 15, "Participating in Other Internet Activities," allows you to choose a character and choose emotions that are graphically portrayed to all the people in the chat room.

Don't expect to find too many highbrow discussions among Rhodes scholars and rocket scientists in a chat room. A considerable percentage of the discussion groups center around popular and adult topics. Occasionally, however, when there is a hot topic in the news, you might find several chat rooms that banter the subject around.

Hardware and Software You Will Need to Access the Web

Now that I've piqued your curiosity about what you'll find on the Internet, it's time to take a look at what you'll need to get connected. If you recently purchased a new PC, odds are most everything you'll need is already installed on the machine. If it hasn't been included, don't worry; you'll know what to do before the hour's over.

The Hardware You'll Need

If you purchased the computer from a retailer or manufacturer in the last couple of years, you'll have no problem accessing the Internet as long as the required hardware and software is in place. If, on the other hand, you "inherited" a computer from a friend or relative who recently upgraded, there potentially could be some snags.

Although it's possible to access the World Wide Web with any computer that will run Windows, you need a fairly powerful system to take full advantage of what the Web has to offer. A practical minimum configuration for using Windows 95 or Windows 98 is a Pentium 133 with 16MB (megabytes) of memory (RAM). Unless you plan to download a tremendous volume of files, your hard disk requirements don't need to be gargantuan; a minimum hard disk of 1GB (gigabyte) is more than sufficient. You will also need VGA graphics. And although you can get by with a video card that supports only 256 colors (if you like viewing what appear to be "washed-out" graphics, or opt to use a text-only Web browser), most of the graphics you will encounter will look a lot better with a video card that supports more than 256 colors.

And last but not least, you need a modem to navigate the Web. The minimum speed for a modem you should even consider is 28,800bps (bits per second). (A 14,400bps modem isn't just sluggish, it is downright torturous.) Get a 56k modem if you can, because that's the maximum speed some phone lines can support.

Now, if you want to get past a "minimum" configuration and start looking at a more realistic Net-surfing configuration, start with at least a Pentium 200 with 32MB of memory, a 2GB hard disk, a video card with 4MB of video RAM (which will support more than 256 colors with no problem), and a 56,000bps modem. In each case, the faster or bigger, the better.

> If you can only afford to upgrade one thing on your PC, go for the RAM. Although 16MB is a good number, I've found 32 to be better. It makes scrolling back and forth among cached Web pages smoother, and it's even made my Web browser less prone to crashing due to lack of memory.

Another item you will want to invest in is a sound card. Much of the Web now boasts multimedia extensions, most notably sound, and you will need a sound card as well as speakers or a headphone to hear Web-based audio. If you also plan to experiment with any of the Web-based telephony products, you will also need a microphone.

Last, you will want to consider adding a CD-ROM drive if you don't already have one. Although a CD-ROM drive is not essential for accessing the Web, you will find that nearly all commercial software is now being distributed on CDs instead of floppy disks.

After you get your hardware assembled, you'll be ready to tackle the Internet and the World Wide Web. This book shows you how to access the Internet directly through an Internet service provider (ISP), not through a local area network (LAN) that has an Internet gateway. For information on configuring an Internet connection through a LAN, talk to your local system administrator. For information about connecting to the Internet through an online service such as CompuServe or America Online, see Hour 10, "Choosing an Internet Service Provider and Getting Connected."

NEW TERM   A means of "passing through" or "connecting to" a system different from the one you are using is called a *gateway*. An Internet gateway for a local area network is merely a means of providing Internet access to users on a LAN.

To get online, you need an Internet account with an ISP. If you don't have an Internet account yet, see Hour 10 to learn how to select an ISP.

You also need a means of communicating with your service provider. This book assumes that your connection is over a standard telephone line using a modem.

High-Speed Paths to the Information Superhighway

It's likely that after battling rush hour on the Information Superhighway, you'll wish you had a bit more speed with which to surf. A communication technology that looks to have a big impact on higher speed Internet usage is ISDN. ISDN (Integrated Services Digital Network) is literally "digital telephones." Rather than convert your computer's digital signals into analog (sound waves) to be transmitted over standard telephone lines as a modem does, ISDN transmits a digital signal over digital telephone lines. The advantage is a communication connection up to 128Kbps (kilobits per second) as opposed to today's 28.8Kbps connections. In many parts of the country, ISDN is available in roughly 70–90% of the local Baby Bells' service areas.

In addition to its lack of availability in some locales, the downsides to using ISDN lie in the difficulty of locating a knowledgeable telephone company sales office, and in its cost. Many regional telephone sales offices still respond "…ISD-what?" And when you do find service in your area, pricing is still geared more towards businesses than consumers. But don't despair. ISDN pricing is going down and availability is still improving.

Even if you do find someone at your local telephone company that is knowledgeable enough about ISDN to be able to place your order, the installation of ISDN can still be a formidable task. Although the phone company might be able to successfully run the line to your computer, getting the special ISDN adapter properly configured and working will still largely be your responsibility (or your problem depending on how you want to look at it). But most ISDN adapter vendors have now made it easier than ever to get ISDN service working in your home.

Another connection option that is getting lots of headlines but that is still moving at a snail's pace is the "cable modem." Instead of getting service through your telephone company, you would connect to the Internet through your cable TV provider. Getting the proper equipment in place by the providers is still the largest roadblock. Most of the current cable TV system is still designed as a one-way system (they provide service to you). To convert to a two-way service, fiber-optic cables need to be installed along with the necessary routing communications equipment. Even if Internet service demand continues at its present rate (meaning that there is still a strong profit motive in providing Internet access), cable modems are still 18 months to two years away for most of us.

The Software You'll Need

Windows 98, 95, and NT provide all the software you need to connect to the Internet. The primary tool you will use to access the information on the Web is a browser. Hours 11, "Using Microsoft Internet Explorer," and 12, "Customizing Microsoft Internet Explorer," explain some of the basics of the two most popular browsers: Netscape Navigator and Microsoft Internet Explorer. Although our primary focus is on Internet Explorer, you'd find many of the same features in Netscape. Hour 13 takes a look at how to use Microsoft Outlook Express as an email client, and in Hour 14 as a newsreader.

> Luckily, both the Microsoft and Netscape products listed previously are available for free download on the Web. Just surf over to www.microsoft.com or www.netscape.com, and follow the directions provided. This is a great and economical way to keep your Internet software up-to-date.

The Internet Setup Wizard makes it easier to connect to the Internet. This utility should already be installed on your machine. Take a peek at Hour 10 to learn how to get set up using the Internet Setup Wizard.

Summary

In this hour, you learned about each part of the Internet. You learned what they do, and how they work together. You also got the lowdown on what hardware configuration you should have to maximize Internet performance. Finally, we took a look at the software you'll need to connect to and participate in the Internet. In a vast majority of cases, the software you need will already be installed in your PC when you buy it.

In the next hour, you learn how to find the Internet service provider that's right for you. Additionally, you see how to set up and test your Internet connection.

Workshop

The following workshop helps you solidify the skills you learned in this lesson.

Quiz

Take the following quiz to see how much you've learned.

Questions

1. Which service is not available on the Internet?

    a. Email

    b. STP

    c. The World Wide Web

2. What is not a valid modem speed?

    a. 56,000 baud

    b. 28.8kbps

    c. 4GB (gigabytes)

Answers

1. b. I'm visually impaired so I can't drive, but even I know STP is a motor oil company!

2. c. Gigabytes is a measure of size not speed.

Activity

Now that you know what the Internet has to offer, come up with a list of five things you want to learn more about using the various Internet services. Maybe you want to learn more about a medication you're taking, or maybe you want to help your son search for the perfect college. Tired of your current job? Why not use the Internet to shop for a new one?

Hour 10

Choosing an Internet Service Provider and Getting Connected

Now that you've decided you want to surf the Net, you've got a bit of work to do. First, you need to select an Internet service provider (ISP) or online service. After you've made that big decision, you need to configure your computer to talk to the provider you've selected. Finally, you should test that connection to verify that it works. In this hour, you learn how to do all this, and you get the answers to these questions and more:

- What kind of Internet service is right for me?
- What questions should I ask when talking to the various providers?
- What information do I need to have on hand to configure my software?
- Where do I begin setting up my software?
- How can I test my connection to the Internet?

What Is Internet Service?

Internet access comes in a variety of connection choices and account types, depending on who provides the service and what hardware and software you use. This hour examines the service options available.

You Can Get Access Through Your Online Service

Many of the commercial online services, such as CompuServe, America Online, and The Microsoft Network, offer Internet access. Internet access through these services is usually quick and easy to set up. It is also "portable." This means that if you have an account on a national service and you move to another state or take your computer with you on an extended vacation, you can still dial in with a local call. The downside to using a commercial online service used to be that the "meter was constantly running" every minute you were connected. Although most of the online services have adopted a flat rate fee structure to compete head-to-head with the legion of Internet service providers who had been luring away their customer base, you should be aware that there are still online services out there that have timed service and time limits—avoid them.

Of course, now there is a new "downside" to using a commercial online service—getting access! The chief complaint many of the online services hear now is that "it is next to impossible to get through," and that users attempting to dial in almost always get a busy signal. This happens because these providers are constantly sending people disks to try their service for free for a limited period of time. People often try the service, then bail out when the trial period is over. Unfortunately, this transient crowd can make daily access for the providers' regular subscribers a challenge at best.

Another factor to consider is many online service providers require you to use certain—sometimes even proprietary—software to use their accounts. Although the software may be good, you're stuck with it whether you like it or not. If it hasn't been upgraded for a while, it may not support the hottest new Internet technologies.

Commercial online service providers counter with the argument that they offer a wide array of additional services (vendor forums, email, file/program downloading, chat rooms, and so on) all neatly organized and easily accessed through a familiar or easy-to-learn interface. When you become familiar with the Internet, however, you will find that most, if not all, of these services are available at a fraction of the cost elsewhere. You only need to know where to look.

The questions to ask yourself are

- What is access like in my location?
- Will I need to access the Internet from multiple area codes?

- How much time do I (or a member of my family) plan to spend on the Internet each month?

- What is it worth to me to have these services laid out in a neat little package?

Selecting an Internet Service Provider

Now that you know something about the types of Internet accounts available, you need to know how to go about selecting an Internet service provider. Don't attempt to make the determination solely on the basis of price. Read through the following questions, consider which of the service options are important to you, and discuss them with potential service providers.

- Is the call to your ISP a local call? The whole idea is to keep your costs to a minimum, which means avoiding long distance or toll telephone charges.

- Do they charge a flat rate, or by the minute/hour? Flat-rate providers are most common, but some providers keep the meter running and charge you by the hour. Some hourly rate providers give you a minimum number of hours before the meter starts. Some give you as few as 3 hours per day, although others give you as many as 100 hours per month.

- How many incoming telephone lines do they make available? The least expensive provider is not a bargain if all you get when you dial in is a busy signal. You may also ask them what their modem-to-user ratio is if the first question gets you a cryptic answer. A good answer is around one modem to five users. It isn't likely that you will get a busy signal with that kind of ratio.

- What communication speeds do they offer? You set your modem to this speed to communicate with your provider's modems. Hardly any service providers offer speeds less than 14,400 bits per second (bps). If you're using a modem with a speed of 28,800bps, make sure your provider has phone lines that talk to your modem at least this speed. If your provider has plenty of modems that are faster than yours, their modems will also be able to communicate with your modem at the slower speed. Note that some providers will also support 56Kbps modems. Because two standards exist for 56Kbps modems, make sure your provider's equipment is compatible with yours. Otherwise, your connect speed will be limited to about 33.6Kbps. If you think you might upgrade to ISDN connections sometime in the future, inquire as to whether your provider can support these connections.

- What are their technical support hours? If you will primarily surf at night, it'd be nice to know that technical support will be available when you'll need them most.

10

- Everyone offers email, but do they let you build your own Web site? Also you may want to consider how many newsgroups they carry. (You'll learn more about email and newsgroups in Hour 13, "Using Outlook Express for Email"). If you are using Windows 95 or Windows NT 4.0, see if they fully support Microsoft Dial-Up Networking to save your username and password. If not, they might require that you type in your username and password each time (which might not be a bad idea in some cases).

If you're wondering how to find an Internet provider, the answer might be right under your nose. Most new computers come with free 30-day trials to one or more providers like MSN or AOL. A leading PC manufacturer, Gateway 2000, has even started to dabble in the ISP business, giving its customers free trial periods with the purchase of a new system.

If you don't find something you like there, look for ads in Internet magazines, check the yellow pages, read the business section of your local paper, or ask someone about his or her provider. You might even receive Internet information with your phone bill because many phone companies and long distance carriers have started getting into the Internet business. If you have a friend who uses the Internet, you could ask them to help you research a particular provider. Internet providers maintain their own Web site with information about their services, including prices and features. This information can be useful when you want to make detailed comparisons of multiple providers.

> What's in a name? You might be tempted to go with a major provider that everyone's heard of, but don't discount the local guys. There are some compelling reasons why you should look at the new guy in town. First, to survive and be competitive, they need to offer something extra. Whether that "something extra" is rock-bottom pricing, extended tech support hours, or the inclusion of popular Web-browsing software at no charge, it may well be something that will sway your decision. Second, because they rely on customer satisfaction to succeed, the local provider will probably be attentive to your concerns. Finally, because providing Internet service is the local guy's first priority, you're more likely to see regular system upgrades and response to new trends.

Also, if you want to "sample the goods," many state-run universities and libraries have started providing Internet-access terminals in student union buildings and libraries where anyone can literally walk in off the street and get on the Internet. Some colleges and universities are providing their students with Internet access in their dorm rooms, having recognized the Internet's potential as a valuable research source.

Getting Started with America Online and The Microsoft Network

Because America Online and The Microsoft Network (which comes packaged with Microsoft Home Essentials 98) are the online service providers you'll encounter most, we'll look at them a little closer in the sections that follow.

America Online

America Online, usually just referred to as AOL, is currently the largest of the major online services with a reported user base of more than 10 million. If you've bought a computer in the last six months, chances are you already have AOL software because many computers now come with AOL software pre-installed. The major online services have also been feverishly distributing their disks and CD-ROMs attached to virtually any and every computer magazine that has anything to say about the Internet. The Internet has been the hot computer topic during the last year, and all the online services are trying to cash in on this groundswell.

10

If you haven't picked up a computer magazine lately or received an AOL mailing, you can call AOL at (800) 827-3338 and order its software.

AOL is only available on the Windows and Macintosh platforms. In the following paragraphs, you will learn how to install AOL on a Windows 95 platform. AOL is not particular about running on either Windows 95, 98, or NT, and none of the flavors of Windows has an advantage when running AOL.

To Do: Installing AOL

To install AOL, follow these steps:

1. Place your AOL disk into your drive (floppy disk or CD) and choose File, Run.

2. At the Run prompt, type x:\setup, where x is the drive you placed the disk in.

▲ 3. Follow the prompts to complete the installation.

Double-click the AOL icon to start the program. When you start AOL the first time, you have to sign up for the service. Follow the prompts to sign up for AOL. The setup takes approximately 3–5 minutes.

You will need a credit card number when trying this service so AOL can charge your account directly without sending you a bill. If you think ending that trial is a simple phone call or email away, I've got bad news—AOL requires you to cancel in writing.

When you complete the setup, follow the prompts to the AOL main menu shown in Figure 10.1.

Note that AOL is continually improving their product, so the screens you see may vary from those shown in these figures.

FIGURE 10.1.

AOL's main menu.

From the main menu, click Internet Connection to proceed to AOL's gateway to the Internet (see Figure 10.2).

In the Internet Connection window, click the World Wide Web icon to start AOL's Web browser.

FIGURE 10.2.

AOL's Internet Connection.

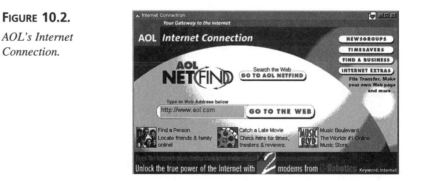

AOL's Web browser works much the same way as Netscape Navigator and Microsoft Internet Explorer. You enter the URL of the Web page or site you want to visit, and in a few seconds the page appears on your screen. (For more information about how Web browsers work, see Hours 11, "Using Microsoft Internet Explorer" and 12, "Customizing Microsoft Internet Explorer.")

The Microsoft Network

The Microsoft Network software is bundled with the popular Microsoft Home Essentials 98 suite of software and as part of Windows 95.

To Do: Installing MSN

To Do

If you are running Windows and you didn't install MSN when you installed Windows, adding MSN is a snap. Follow these steps:

1. Open the Windows 95 Control Panel and click Add/Remove Programs.

2. Select the Windows Setup tab in the Add/Remove Programs Properties dialog box. Select the check box next to The Microsoft Network and click OK.

3. Follow the prompts to install The Microsoft Network. Make sure you have your Windows installation CD or disks handy. You will be prompted to insert them so the installation program can copy the appropriate files to your PC.

4. When the installation is completed, you should see a new icon on your desktop for The Microsoft Network. Double-click the MSN icon to start the program.

5. Follow the initial sign-on prompts until you see the main menu (see Figure 10.3).

10

FIGURE 10.3.

MSN's main menu.

▼

▼   6. Click United States to access the English language section or the language you
         would prefer to use.

      7. In a few seconds, the Internet Explorer browser appears, displaying the MSN
         Home Page located at www.msn.com (see Figure 10.4). For more information about
         Internet Explorer, see Hour 11.

FIGURE 10.4.

The MSN home page.

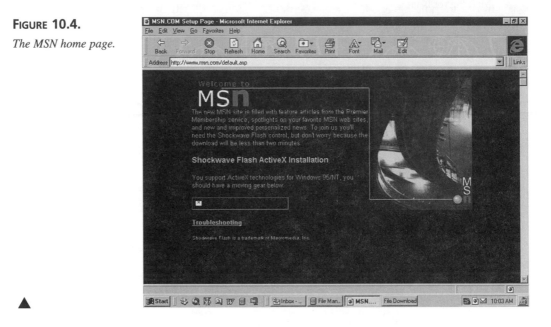

▲

Using Windows to Connect to an ISP

Most people use Windows to connect to a conventional ISP. Before you create a connection to your ISP, you should get a copy of their installation instructions to determine if
they have any special requirements. Generally the ISP's instructions ask you to use the
Internet Setup Wizard discussed in the following section. Before you start, however, you
should gather the information discussed in Table 10.1, so you are ready to answer the
questions from the Internet Setup Wizard.

TABLE 10.1. INFORMATION NEEDED FROM YOUR ISP.

Information	Definition
IP Address	The 12-digit IP address (nnn.nnn.nnn.nnn) that the ISP assigns you.
Subnet Mask	Another 12-digit address formatted nnn.nnn.nnn.nnn.
Gateway Address	Another 12-digit address formatted nnn.nnn.nnn.nnn.

Information	Definition
Host Name and Domain Name	If used (some providers tell you to leave this blank), your provider should supply it. The host name refers to your computer, and the domain name refers to all the computers on the ISP's subnet.
Mail Server Name	Your email server's domain name (often `mail.provider.com`).
Domain Name Server (DNS)	Your provider should give you at least two DNS server IP addresses, again, formatted `nnn.nnn.nnn.nnn`.
News Server Name	Your news server's domain name.
Email Address	Your email address in the form of `username@mail.provider.com`, or `username@provider.com`.
Commands used to log in to the ISP	Commands such as "Enter username and password" and any subsequent commands you need to follow to log in to the provider.
Type of IP Address (dynamic or static)	Your provider assigns you a permanent IP address to use if it's static.
Dial-Up Phone	The phone number you dial to connect to your provider.

Sometimes, ISPs have "express" phone numbers for people who like to pop in and check their mail, and then quickly disconnect in 15 minutes or less. See if your provider will give you this second phone number to use as a backup should the first be consistently busy.

Running the Internet Setup Wizard

The Internet Setup Wizard is found on the Internet Tools menu under Accessories. In the pages that follow, you will see step-by-step how to supply the information the Setup Wizard needs to create your Internet connection. Remember, your use of the Internet Setup Wizard will differ if you use a different provider and connect from a different city.

Check with your ISP before using the Internet Setup Wizard, to see if there are any special steps you must follow to connect to their system.

To Do: Starting the Internet Setup Wizard

To start the Internet Setup Wizard, follow these steps:

1. Select the Start button on the taskbar and choose Programs, Accessories, Internet Tools, and Internet Setup Wizard (see Figure 10.5).

FIGURE 10.5.

The menu path to the Internet Setup Wizard.

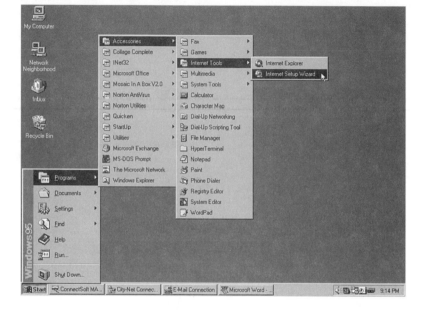

2. At the opening screen, click the Next button to begin. If your modem is not already set up, Windows 95 prompts you to set up your modem.

3. In the How to Connect dialog box, click the I Already Have an Account with a Different Service Provider option button as shown in Figure 10.6. Then click the Next button.

FIGURE 10.6.

Installing Internet support with your own ISP (Internet service provider).

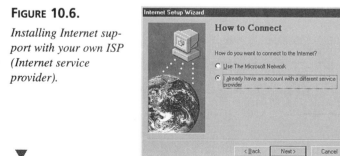

4. In the Service Provider Information dialog box, enter the name of your Internet service provider. This is just a label that identifies the shortcut icon you will use to connect to your provider. It can be anything you like. Click the Next button to continue.

> You may also want to indicate the telephone number you are dialing if your ISP has more than one access number.

5. In the Phone Number dialog box, enter the phone number of your provider. Even if you're dialing a local number, enter the area code and country code (select the correct code from the Country Code drop-down list). Finally, select the Bring Up Terminal Window After Dialing check box. You will use the terminal window to log in to your ISP (see Figure 10.7). Click the Next button to continue.

FIGURE 10.7.

Supply your provider's phone number.

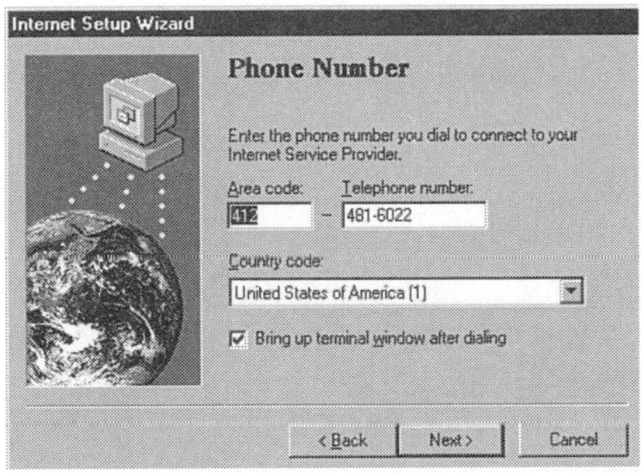

> If your area requires you to dial 10-digit telephone numbers for local calls, enter all 10 digits in the Telephone Number box and leave the Area Code box empty.

6. In the User Name and Password dialog box, enter the login name (username) and password set up for you by your provider. (Even through you enter your username and password here, some login systems by some providers won't accept these unless you also type them in the terminal window.) Click the Next button to continue.

7. In the IP Address dialog box, select how you get your user IP address. Your provider should supply you with this information (see Figure 10.8). Click the Next button to continue.

▼ **FIGURE 10.8.**

Supply your IP address information.

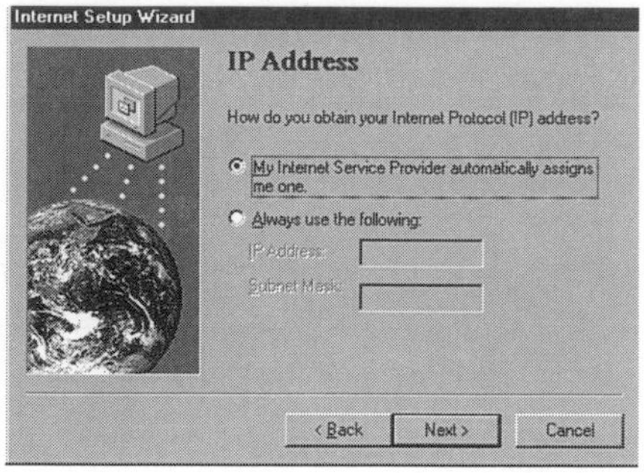

8. In the DNS Server Address dialog box, enter the IP address of your DNS (Domain Name Server) server. Your provider should supply you with this information. If your provider also supplies you with an Alternate DNS server, enter that address in the second field. Select the Next button to continue.

9. In the Internet Mail dialog box, click the Use Internet Mail check box, and then enter your email address and the name of your mail server. (Your provider should supply you with this information.) Click the Next button to continue.

NEW TERM The *DNS (Domain Name Service)* is the means by which a 12-digit IP address (nnn.nnn.nnn.nnn) is converted into a recognizable name.

10. In the Exchange Profile dialog box, enter the Microsoft Exchange profile name to use for Internet mail. Type the name Internet Mail Settings, as you see in Figure 10.9, which is the default profile name. Click the Next button to continue.

FIGURE 10.9.

Set the profile name for Internet mail.

11. Finally, click the Finish button to complete your wizard setup. When the setup is complete, the wizard creates an Internet icon on your desktop. You can select that icon to connect to the Internet through your provider.

Bear in mind that what you enter to connect to your provider might be different than what you see in this hour. The figures in this hour show a sample connection to an Internet provider using a Point-to-Point Protocol (PPP) connection over a 28.8Kbps modem.

> To double-check the information you receive from your Internet provider, compare it to the list shown previously in Table 10.1. It's possible that your ISP provided you with more information than is listed in the table, but you should not have received less.

To Do: Connecting to the Internet

What you see here should be enough additional information to help you connect to the Internet:

1. Click the Internet icon located on your desktop to start the Microsoft Internet Explorer browser. The Connect To dialog box appears (see Figure 10.10).

FIGURE 10.10.

Connecting to your provider with Internet Explorer.

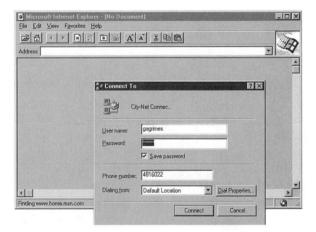

2. In the Connect To dialog box, click the Connect button to dial to your provider. You'll see a dialog box indicating that the provider's phone number is being dialed.

> If your connection setup didn't dial, your modem might not be installed correctly. Check the manual supplied by your modem manufacturer, and check the Modems configuration utility in the Control Panel.

To Do

10

▼ 3. If you connect to your provider, the Post-Dial Terminal Screen window now appears and prompts you to enter the information supplied by your provider (see Figure 10.11). Enter the following information as needed: login name, password, and so on. (In this example, the provider required that PPP be entered to select a Point-to-Point Protocol connection.) When you finish, click the Continue button or press F7.

FIGURE 10.11.

The Post-Dial Terminal Screen window.

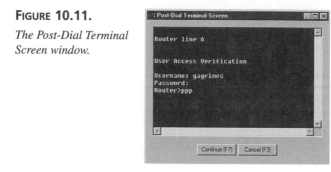

4. If your connection settings are correct and you enter the correct information required by your provider, in a few seconds, a message indicates that you are connected.

You may find it convenient now to minimize the Connect To window, however do not close it. Closing this window will break the connection to your Internet provider.

▲

Testing Your Connection

Before you get started browsing or experimenting with other Internet activities, you can verify the information you entered with WinIPCfg (Windows IP Configuration utility).

To Do: Verifying Your IP Information

1. Click the Start button on the taskbar and choose Run. Enter `winipcfg` in the text box and press Enter to run the WinIPCfg utility program. In a few seconds, the IP information you see in Figure 10.12 appears.

2. Click the More Info button to display the information shown in Figure 10.13.

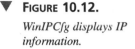
FIGURE 10.12.

WinIPCfg displays IP information.

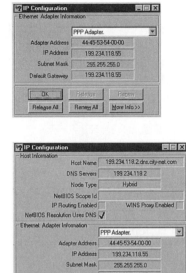

FIGURE 10.13.

More information from WinIPCfg.

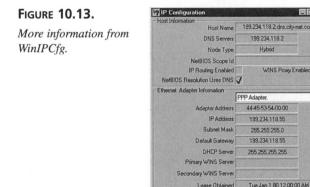

10

Most of the information displayed by WinIPCfg probably won't mean much to you, but the information can be used to verify that any information you entered was entered correctly. Also, you can use this utility while you are connected, to determine information such as your IP address and host name that was determined dynamically during the connection process.

Summary

In this hour, you learned all about your options for Internet access. Whether you choose The Microsoft Network, AOL, or a local ISP, you are now armed with everything you'll need to get up and running. You have a solid set of questions to ask prospective providers, and you know the ups and downs of each type of access.

After you've tested your connection, you're ready to begin your grand adventure. In the next hour, you'll learn how to use Microsoft Internet Explorer 4.01 to browse the Web.

Workshop

The following workshop helps you solidify the skills you learned in this hour.

Quiz

Take the following quiz to see how much you've learned.

Questions

1. What is AOL?

    a. Absent, on Leave

    b. An online service provider

    c. A manufacturer of high-performance modems

2. What is The Microsoft Network?

    a. An online service provider

    b. A television network featuring the nightly news anchored by Bill Gates

    c. A cable system featuring programming for techies only

3. What are the potential downfalls of subscribing to online service providers such as AOL?

    a. You'll be flooded by a sea of disks containing free trial software

    b. Frequent busy signals due to large numbers of people just trying out the service

    c. Both of the above

Answers

1. b.

2. a. The Microsoft Network is one of the newest online service providers to come on the scene.

3. c. Unfortunately, both statements can be true. The disks will still come whether you've subscribed already or not. The good news is you can recycle them. I have AOL to thank for many document backups.

Activity

To help you find the best Internet access given your specific needs, I recommend that you prioritize the following items before interviewing prospective ISPs. These priorities along with the ISP's answers to the questions presented earlier in this hour should give you a clear indication of which providers are best and worst for you.

- Money is tight for me, so I need the least expensive access possible.
- I'm a little afraid of this Internet stuff; I want an ISP who will be there to answer my questions when I need them.
- My friend told me Netscape Navigator is the best Web browser out there. I don't want to be locked into someone's software; I want to make the choice myself.
- I can only surf in the evening like most people, so I want to minimize the likelihood of getting a busy signal.
- I don't want to mess with separate software packages for email, chat, Web, and so on. Just give me one thing to learn.
- My whole family will be surfing the Web, so one day I'd like to get ISDN so multiple people can surf at once.
- Because I live in the country, getting a local dial-up number may be next to impossible. However I can't afford a toll call each time I go online.

10

Hour 11

Using Microsoft Internet Explorer

Internet Explorer 4.0, sometimes called IE4, is a suite of tightly integrated programs that connects you and your computer to the world of information available through the Internet and the World Wide Web. Internet Explorer not only acts as a browser to display the data, but it also helps you find, incorporate, and interact with that data. Internet Explorer includes all the tools needed for you to communicate your message globally (such as Outlook Express, which you'll learn more about in Hour 13, "Using Outlook Express for Email").

Chances are, you received IE4 pre-installed on your computer when you bought it. Why not put it to good use?

In this hour, you learn the basics of using Internet Explorer. You also learn the answers to these questions:

- What do all those buttons do?
- How do I mark a Web page so I can visit it again later?

- I have too many Favorites on my list; how can I organize them?
- Can I place a shortcut to my most frequently visited Web site on my Windows desktop?

Starting Internet Explorer

Before you can start Internet Explorer, you must install the program on your computer. In the majority of cases, IE will already be installed on your machine. If it isn't, however, you can learn how to do it by reading the installation instructions in Appendix A, "Installing Windows Applications."

Depending on the type of Internet connection you have set up, you may need to connect to your ISP directly before starting Internet Explorer. Check with your ISP's technical support department.

Because of Internet Explorer's tight integration into the Windows 95 and 98 operating systems, there are several ways to start the program.

To Do: Starting Internet Explorer

No matter how you have installed the program, you can always start Internet Explorer by following these steps:

1. From the Windows taskbar, click the Start button.
2. From the Start menu, click Programs.
3. From the Programs submenu, click Internet Explorer, found in the Internet Explorer Suite.

On most Windows desktops, you can double-click the Internet icon to start Internet Explorer.

If you are connected to the Internet, Internet Explorer opens your Start Page. (Later in this hour, you learn how to customize your Start Page.)

Touring the Screen Layout

Before you begin exploring the Internet and other capabilities of Internet Explorer, take a moment to familiarize yourself with the components of the screen. Table 11.1 describes the different sections of the screen and their uses, as shown in Figure 11.1.

FIGURE 11.1.

Sections of the Internet Explorer 4.0 screen.

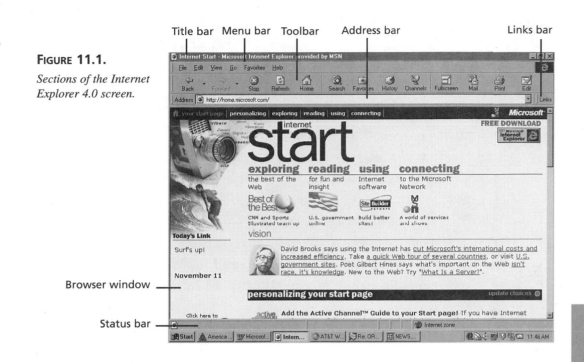

Title bar   Menu bar   Toolbar   Address bar   Links bar

Browser window

Status bar

TABLE 11.1. SECTIONS OF THE INTERNET EXPLORER 4.0 SCREEN.

Screen Element	Function
Address bar	Displays current Internet address
Browser window	Primary display area
Links bar	Provides shortcuts to regularly updated Web pages
Menu bar	Enables access to the Internet Explorer menu commands
Status bar	Displays information on connection status
Title bar	Displays program and current Web page title
Toolbar	Provides shortcuts to basic program commands

All the toolbars can be moved and resized with a simple click and drag on any bar area not covered by a button.

11

Exploring the Toolbar

The shortcuts available in the toolbar across the top of Internet Explorer's screen go a long way toward simplifying your exploration of the World Wide Web. You'll find yourself returning to them time and again for both basic and more advanced operations.

The following is a brief outline of the function of each toolbar button, from left to right:

- Back displays the previous Web page.
- Forward returns to the most recent Web page (if you have clicked the Back button).
- Stop interrupts the transfer of any Web page from the Internet to your computer.
- Refresh reloads the current Web page.
- Home opens the user-definable Start Page.
- Search opens a list of search engines used for finding a particular topic on the Web.
- Favorites opens a list of your favorite Web pages.
- History opens a list of the Web pages you've visited, in reverse chronological order.
- Channels opens a list of currently available subjects you can subscribe to.
- Fullscreen expands the screen to its fullest size by temporarily hiding most of the toolbars and menus.
- Mail opens Internet Explorer's electronic mail and newsgroups menus.
- Print sends the current Web page to your printer.
- Edit opens the current Web page in the Internet Explorer editor, FrontPage Express, used for creating and updating Web pages.

> **NEW TERM** A *Web page* is a document created for the Internet that uses the HTTP protocol to link to one another and to convey not only text, but also multimedia sounds, graphics, and video. A *Web site* is a collection of Web pages.

Quitting Internet Explorer

When you've finished your Internet Explorer session, you can quit the program by any of these standard methods:

- Select File, Exit from the menu bar.
- Click the Close (X) button in the upper-right corner of the Internet Explorer window.
- Use the keyboard shortcut, Alt+F4.

Going to a Web page

When you begin to explore the Internet, you start by visiting specific Web pages. The Web page address, or *URL*, could be given to you by a friend or a colleague, or perhaps it is one you jotted down from an advertisement or announcement.

NEW TERM An *URL* (*Uniform Resource Locator*, pronounced "earl" or "u-r-l") is a unique name used as an address by the Internet. An URL begins with a protocol specification (such as "http://"), followed by the specific Web site name. The last part of the URL designates the type of site; for instance, .com is for commercial, .edu is for educational institutions, and .gov is for governmental agencies.

Internet Explorer, like all browsers, revolves around URLs. Finding, remembering, and managing these Internet addresses are a lot of what Internet Explorer is about. Starting Internet Explorer takes you to your first URL, the Internet Explorer Start Page. After you are up and running, getting to a specific URL is easy.

To Do: Going to a Specific Web Page

Follow these steps to go to a specific Web page:

1. Start Internet Explorer.

   The Internet Explorer Home Page is loaded. The status bar tells you what is happening. When the home page is completely loaded, the status bar displays Done.

2. Move the mouse pointer over the Address box. The pointer changes into an I-beam shape.

3. Click once anywhere in the Address box to select the current URL.

4. Type the URL. The first letter you type replaces the previous highlighted URL.

5. When you have completed typing the Internet address, press Enter.

   ▲ Internet Explorer connects to the requested Web page.

Internet Explorer remembers URLs that you have visited. The next time you type in the address of a previously visited site, Internet Explorer automatically completes the address. Then you just press the Enter key to accept the completion and go to that Web page.

Exploring a Web Site

Few single Web pages exist by themselves in cyberspace. Most are part of a larger structure called a Web site. Because all Web sites are designed independently, there is no common user interface among them. Most Web sites open with a home page that contains links to other pages within their site.

11

Most commercial URLs are variations of the http://www.company.com format. If you type just the main part of the Web site address (the company
part above) and press Ctrl+Enter, Internet Explorer puts an "http://www." at
the beginning and a ".com" at the end, and then connects to your requested site.

NEW TERM *Link* is short for a key concept on the World Wide Web: hypertext links. When a
link is clicked, Internet Explorer opens that link, whether it's another Web page
(in the same or different site) or a downloadable graphic or sound. Figure 11.2 shows a
typical opening page for a Web site.

To Do: Checking Out a Web Site

To explore a Web site such as this one, follow these steps:

1. Go to a specific URL by typing an Internet address in the Address box and pressing Enter.

2. Move the pointer over the various elements of the page to identify the potential
   links:

   - Underlined words that are a different color from the rest of the text.

   - Buttons or icons with clear directional signs.

   - Graphic images, possibly surrounded by a border.

   - Portions of a large graphic image.

   - When your mouse pointer passes over a link, the pointer changes to a hand.

3. Click once on any link to go to that Web page.

4. If you want to return to the previous page, click the Back button in the toolbar.

5. If you see a link on the new page that interests you, click it to go to that page.

Exploring a Web site is a combination of following your nose and retracing your steps.
Clicking links that lead from one page to another takes you down a particular path.
Clicking the Back button on the toolbar brings you back the way you came, one page at
a time.

FIGURE 11.2.

The mouse pointer changes to a hand to identify a link on the Museum of Modern Art's Web site (www.moma.org).

Mouse pointer ——

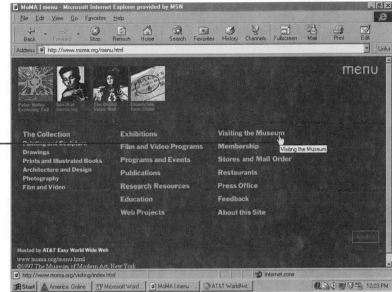

Revisiting Favorite Web Pages

After a short time, you may want to revisit Web sites that have valuable information you need to review or are updated frequently with new information. Internet Explorer enables you to mark any Web page as a "Favorite" so you can easily return there.

To Do: Marking a Favorite Web Page

Follow these steps to mark a Web page as a Favorite:

1. Go to the Web page you want to mark.

2. Click the Favorites button on the toolbar.

3. From the Favorites drop-down list, select Add to Favorites.

4. In the Add Favorite dialog box, Internet Explorer places the title of the Web page in the Name text box. This is the name this page will be under in your Favorites list. If you want, you can modify the page name by typing a new name in the box.

5. By default, Internet Explorer lists a new entry alphabetically in the Favorites folder. To list your selection in a different subfolder, click the Create In button.

6. The Add Favorite dialog box extends to display the available subfolders (see Figure 11.3):

▼

- To list the entry under an available folder, click that folder to open it.
- To create a new folder, click the New Folder button and type in a new name. Press Enter.

7. The Add Favorite dialog box also handles Web page subscriptions, discussed in the next hour. Make sure the No, Just Add the Page to My Favorites option is selected.

8. Click OK.

FIGURE 11.3.

You can easily add and categorize your Favorite Web pages.

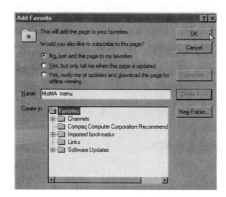

▲

To Do: Accessing a Favorites Web Page

To access a Web page that has been added to your Favorites collection, follow these steps:

1. Start Internet Explorer.

2. Click the Favorites button on the toolbar.

3. Highlight the desired Web page or folder where the Favorite is stored, and click the Favorite name.

> If you installed the Integrated Shell option, you'll find an additional category on the Windows 95 Start menu after installing Internet Explorer: Favorites. Click Start, then Favorites, and then any Web page you want to revisit. If Internet Explorer is not already running, it will open and go directly to the requested Web page.

Organizing Favorite Web Pages

After you get into the habit of adding Web pages to your list of Favorites, it's hard to stop. Soon your list is to the bottom of your screen, and remembering why you selected every entry is next to impossible. It's time to organize your favorite Web pages. Internet Explorer 4.0, like Windows 95 and 98, uses folders as a primary organizational aid. Folders take up almost no physical hard drive space and they can help you find your files more quickly while avoiding clutter. Internet Explorer provides the Organize Favorites dialog box for arranging your favorite Web pages.

To Do: Arranging Your Favorite Web Pages

Follow these steps to organize your favorite Web pages:

1. From the Favorites menu, select Organize Favorites.

2. The Organize Favorites dialog box opens, as shown in Figure 11.4, and displays the folders and Web sites selected in Internet Explorer. If you installed the Integrated Shell, Favorites selected in other Office 97 programs such as Word 97 are displayed as well.

3. When the Organize Favorites dialog box opens, all the command buttons, with the exception of the Close button, are inactive. Click any file or folder to activate the buttons.

4. From the Organize Favorites dialog box, select any of the following options:

   Move. Opens the Browse for Folder dialog box to display all folders in your Favorites collection. Click any folder to move the selected file there. Click OK.

   Rename. Highlights the name of the selected file or folder. Type in a new name and press the Enter key.

   Delete. Places the selected file or folder in the Recycle Bin. Before proceeding, Internet Explorer asks for confirmation. From the Confirm File Delete dialog box, choose Yes to delete, No to cancel.

   Open. Opens the selected file or folder. This is useful if you don't remember what the Favorite is.

5. To create a new folder, click the New Folder button in the dialog box toolbar. Enter the new folder name and press Enter.

6. When you've finished organizing your Favorites, click OK to close the dialog box.

To Do

11

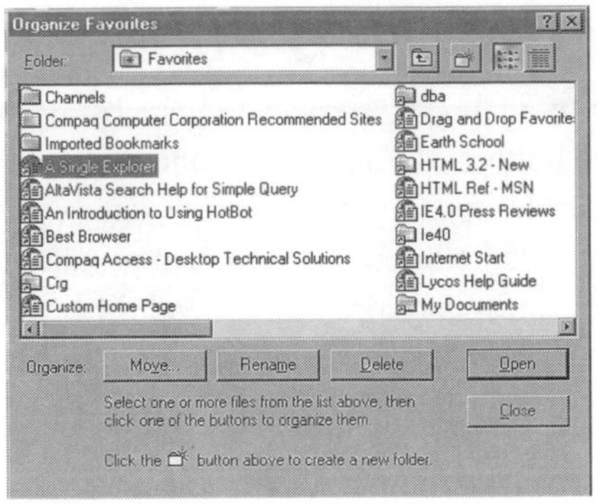

FIGURE 11.4.

The Organize Favorites dialog box arranges all your selected Web sites.

Viewing Thumbnail Favorites
===========================

After you have organized your Favorites, you still might have trouble remembering what each of the filenames means. If you installed the Integrated Desktop, Internet Explorer provides a visual alternative to often cryptic filenames: thumbnails. Thumbnails are basically small pictures used as reminders. This feature is not available if you have not installed the Integrated Desktop.

To Do: Viewing Your Favorites As Thumbnails

To view your Favorites as thumbnails, follow these steps:

1. Click in the Address bar and type `c:\windows\favorites`.
2. Press Enter. Your Favorites are displayed in the browser window.
3. From the View menu, select Thumbnails.

   The view switches to Thumbnail view (with a Windows Explorer toolbar).
4. To go to any Favorite shown, double-click the thumbnail.
5. To return to your previous Internet Explorer page, click the Back button in the toolbar.

> You can display what's inside other folders besides the Favorites folder. Select a folder you want to display and right-click to reveal the Quick Menu. From the Quick Menu, select Properties. From the Properties dialog box, on the General tab, check Enable Thumbnail View.

Using the Favorites Explorer

In addition to accessing your Web site Favorites through the menu, you can also use the split-window Explorer feature. Just as with the Search, History, and Channel buttons, clicking the Favorites button on the toolbar opens a frame on the left side of the screen to display a list while keeping Web pages visible in the frame on the right. Using the Favorites Explorer enables you to quickly review your current selections so you can print, rename, or delete them.

To Do: Accessing Your Web Sites with Favorites Explorer

To use the Favorites Explorer, follow these steps:

1. Click the Favorites button on the toolbar.

   The screen splits into two frames, as shown in Figure 11.5. The frame on the left contains a listing of your Favorites. The currently selected Web site is in the frame on the right.

FIGURE 11.5.

Explore your collection of favorite Web pages through the split-screen Favorites feature.

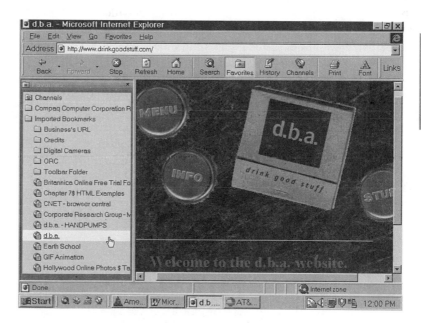

2. To go to a Web page Favorite, click the page name.

   The Web page opens in the right frame.

3. To look inside a folder, highlight the folder and click it.

   The Web pages in the folder are displayed in an indented list.

▼   4. Right-click the Favorite when you want to print, rename, or delete it. Choose your action from the Quick menu that appears.

5. To close the Favorites frame and expand the right frame to full-screen, click the
▲   Favorites button.

Saving Link Shortcuts and Using Quick Links

Those Web sites you access the most frequently can be set up for one-click access from the desktop or from the Links toolbar. Although the Favorites menu is convenient for most revisits to Web pages, there are times when you want to go to a site again and again; you might need to look up a zip code often or keep in touch with a competitor's Web site. Internet Explorer has two features for these circumstances: Link Shortcuts and Quick Links. A shortcut is an icon that acts as a pointer to a program or, in this case, a link to a Web page. Shortcuts are usually found on the Windows desktop, although they can exist in any folder.

To Do: Creating a Link Shortcut

To Do

To create a shortcut to a link, follow these steps:

1. Go to the Web page containing the link to which you want to create a shortcut.

2. If your Internet Explorer screen is maximized, click the Restore button in the title bar.

3. Click the link you want, drag it to the desktop, and release the mouse button.
▲   A Link Shortcut is created on the desktop.

To access your Web page via the Link Shortcut, double-click the desktop shortcut. If Internet Explorer is open, the Web page loads; if not, Internet Explorer opens and then loads the Web page.

> If you have the Desktop Integration mode turned on, you can bring the desktop to the front just as you would any open window. Click the Surface/Restore Desktop icon on the right side of the taskbar. Check out Hour 3, "Windows Desktop Basics," to learn more about the Integrated Desktop.

A Quick Link is a user-specified button on the Links toolbar. Internet Explorer has room for up to five Quick Links.

To Do: Connecting a Web Site to a Quick Link Button

To connect a Web site to a Quick Link button, follow these steps:

1. Go to the Web site containing the link you want to make into a Quick Link.

2. If the Links toolbar is not fully visible, click the word Links.

3. Click your desired link, drag it up to any of the other buttons on the Links toolbar, and release the mouse button.

   The Quick Link dialog box opens, as shown in Figure 11.6.

4. From the Quick Link dialog box, click Yes to set the Quick Link to the selected Web address or click No to cancel.

5. If you clicked Yes, the name of the Quick Link button changes to your selected site.

6. Click the Quick Link button to load the chosen Web page.

7. Click the word Links to shrink the Links toolbar.

FIGURE 11.6.

Quick Links can give you a custom toolbar.

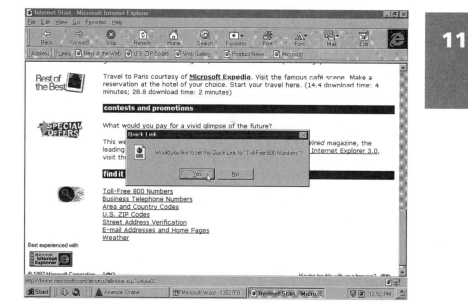

Summary

In this hour, you learned everything you'll need to know to begin surfing the Web with Internet Explorer 4.0. You got acquainted with the various buttons and menus, and even discovered how to define and manage your list of favorite sites.

In the next hour, you'll uncover several ways to personalize your Internet Explorer 4.0 browsing environment.

Workshop

The following workshop helps you solidify the skills you learned in this lesson.

Quiz

Take the following quiz to see how much you've learned.

Questions

1. What does the History button do?

   a. Plays a sound file of Bill Gates telling the evolution of Microsoft

   b. Lets you study U.S. history with a series of links

   c. Displays a list of recently visited Web sites

2. What happens when you view thumbnail favorites?

   a. You see a small picture of a few of your favorite Web pages to help you remember which site is which.

   b. You get a close-up view of what's been lurking under your fingernails.

   c. A group of images, literally the size of your thumbnail, appears.

3. What is a Favorite?

   a. IE4 keeps count of how many times you visit a page, then logs that page as a Favorite. Naturally, the Favorites are rank-ordered according to the number of times you've visited them.

   b. When you come across a Web site you'd like to revisit with some degree of regularity, you can save it as a Favorite. Then you can revisit it by clicking its page title.

   c. A set of must-see sites selected by Microsoft.

Answers

1. c. History lists can be a great way to retrace your steps by leaps and bounds.

2. a. Mercifully, the pictures are a bit larger than your thumbnail; otherwise, they'd be virtually useless. These images can be particularly helpful if a Web page carries an "Untitled" title.

3. b. Favorites are a great way for you to quickly revisit Web sites.

Activity

Consider this activity a license to surf. Type the following URL into the IE4 address box: www.yahoo.com. You'll see a broad list of topics from which you can drill down to more focused topics. For instance, you can start with Sports, go to Auto Racing, focus on NASCAR, then hone in on a specific driver. Your mission for this activity is to spend some time clicking your way through the Yahoo! subject index until you find at least three Web sites you want to save to your Favorites list. When you find them, save them as Favorites for future reference.

11

HOUR 12

Customizing Microsoft Internet Explorer

You may be new to the online world, but that doesn't mean you have to miss out on some of Internet Explorer's coolest features. By the time the hour's over, you'll have IE4 doing everything you want it to. Well, almost....

In this hour, you learn how to customize the IE4 display and Start Page. You also learn the answers to these questions:

- Is it true I can "subscribe" to a Web page?
- Can I use subscriptions if I don't have a full-time connection to the Internet?
- Can I change the size of the text on my IE display?
- How can channels work for me?
- What will I need to make IE play sounds on the Web?

Customizing IE4

There are tons of neat ways to customize your Web-browsing environment with IE4. From setting a new default Start Page to adjusting the way pages are displayed, you'll learn them all in the next few sections.

The IE4 Start Page

Every time Internet Explorer opens, it goes to its Start Page. The default Start Page is maintained by Microsoft and offers an excellent entry into the Internet. One advantage that this page has over others is that you can get daily headlines (and their links) in a variety of categories. You also get to choose the categories and the content providers used. For example, you could pick the Sports and Stock Ticker categories or you could opt for Technology, Money, and Entertainment categories.

To Do: Personalizing Your Start Page

Follow these steps to personalize the Internet Explorer Start Page:

1. Start Internet Explorer.

2. From the Microsoft Start Page, click the Personalizing button located at the top of the Web page.

3. From the Personalizing page shown in Figure 12.1, click the category under step 1 that you want to alter.

4. For each category, different options appear under step 2. Select any desired option by clicking its logo.

5. To step through the categories one at a time, click the Next button under step 3.

6. When you have made all your choices, click the Finish button under step 3.

▲   Your Start Page is reloaded with your new options enabled.

> The Stock Ticker option needs a small program called an ActiveX control to run on your Start Page. After you click the Finish button, the ActiveX control downloads and installs on your system. This may take several minutes.

Selecting a New Start Page

In some circumstances, you might want to choose an entirely different Start Page. If your business has its own Web site, you might prefer using that home page as your starting point. Or, you might have a news source specific to your industry that is not available through Microsoft. Internet Explorer enables you to choose your own Start Page as well as your own Search and Quick Link pages that were covered previously in Hour 11, "Using Microsoft Internet Explorer."

FIGURE 12.1.

Personalize your Start Page to give you the headlines you want.

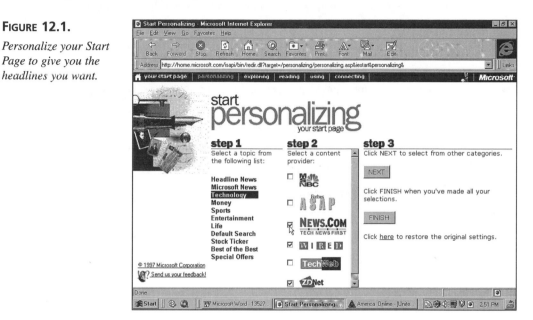

To Do: Selecting a Web Site As Your Start Page

To select a Web site as your new Start Page, follow these steps:

1. Go to the Web page that you want to set up as your Start Page.
2. From the View menu, select Internet Options.
3. Click the General tab.
4. In the Home page section, click the Use Current button. The current URL appears in the Address box.
5. Click OK.

12

Tailoring Your Web Page Display

If you enter a Web site with intensive graphics and multimedia elements, the World Wide Web can become the World Wide Wait. Internet Explorer enables you to turn off certain elements to speed up the downloading of Web pages. You can independently control pictures, sounds, and videos with Internet Explorer. IE4 also enables you to customize the colors of your Web browser. Many Web pages, particularly the text-intensive ones, use the browser defaults when displaying background, text, and link colors. Use this feature to reduce eyestrain or increase the contrast between text and background.

To Do: Modifying Your Web Browser's Display

To alter your Web browser's display, follow these steps:

1. From the View menu, select Internet Options. The Options dialog box appears.
2. From the Advanced tab, remove the check mark next to the multimedia elements to stop the pictures, sounds, or videos from automatically displaying (see Figure 12.2). Click again to enable them.
3. To change the colors, click the Colors button on the General tab.
4. From the Colors dialog box, click Use Windows Colors to deselect it.
5. Click the box next to Background to open the Color Picker dialog box.
6. Click a desired color, and then click OK.
7. Repeat steps 4 and 5 to choose the text color.
8. You can follow the same procedure to alter either of the Visited or Unvisited Link colors. If you click the Use Hover Color box, text links change to the specified color when your mouse passes over them.
9. Click OK.

FIGURE 12.2.

Customize your Web browser with the Options dialog box.

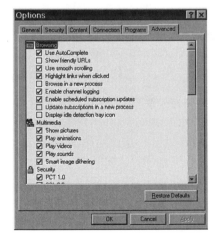

Altering the Browser Fonts

With Internet Explorer, you can alter the size of the font normally used to display Web page text. This is useful when you need to make the text larger for presentation purposes or smaller to see more on a page. These changes are also reflected in any printouts of the page. You can either alter the font size temporarily or specify your new size as the default.

To Do: Changing the Size of the Font

To temporarily alter the size of the default font, follow these steps:

1. From the View menu, select Internet Options. The Options dialog box appears.

2. From the General tab, click the Fonts button.

3. Select one of the five available sizes ranging from Largest to Smallest. Medium is the default.

4. Open a Web page to see the resulting changes.

5. To make your new font size the default, click the Set as Default button.

Unless you've made it the default, the new font size stays in effect until you change it using the preceding method or until you close Internet Explorer.

What Are Subscriptions?

Subscriptions are a way to save time getting the Internet information you want. A subscription doesn't replace surfing or searching the Web to locate information, but it automates the process of downloading from Web sites current information that you read frequently, such as an online magazine or newspaper. You can use a subscription to download newspaper stories, financial information, or sports scores while you're away from your computer (perhaps at lunch or overnight) and have the information waiting for you to read, offline and at your leisure, when you return. In the following sections, you'll learn how to program IE to perform these updates.

Internet Explorer 4.0 uses a Web crawling agent to go online at scheduled intervals, visit specific sites, check for changed information at each site, and then either download the new Web pages or notify you that pages have changed so you can choose which ones to download.

NEW TERM   A Web crawling agent, or *Web crawler*, is a software program that goes online to search out and download Web sites and follows links to more Web sites—all without your guidance or attention. It's like a robot Internet surfer.

12

To Do: Subscribing to a Site

You must add a Web site to your Favorites list, and then subscribe to it and set a schedule for the Web crawler to check it for changed information. To subscribe to a site, follow these steps:

1. In your browser, open the Web page you want to subscribe to.

2. In the browser window, click Favorites, and then click Add To Favorites.

3. In the Add Favorites dialog box (see Figure 12.3), click one of the following options:

    • Select Yes, but Only Tell Me When This Page Is Updated if you want to be notified of changes but don't want the pages downloaded automatically.

    • Select Yes, Notify Me of Updates and Download the Pages for Offline Viewing if you want to have changed pages automatically downloaded.

    If you check the latter option, your first wizard step asks whether you want to download this page only or all linked pages. Be careful about downloading all linked pages because you may end up downloading many megabytes of information.

FIGURE 12.3.

Subscribing to a new favorite.

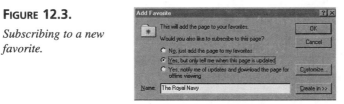

4. Click Customize. The Subscription Wizard starts.

5. In the first wizard step, you can choose to be notified of changes via email. This is helpful if you're on the road with your laptop and checking in with your home-base computer. If you select the No option, a small red asterisk appears on the page icon in the Subscriptions dialog box to notify you of changes.

Make certain your modem is connected to the phone line during scheduled downloads, or IE can't perform the update. Although desktop system users may never unplug their modems, laptop users may because the modem jacks are fragile and prone to breaking.

6. In the second wizard step, fill in any username and password required by your sub-scribed site (if it's a site you normally have to log into with a password, the Web crawler needs your password to check the site for you). Most Web sites don't need passwords, however. Click Finish to complete your subscription.

7. Click OK to close the Add Favorites dialog box. The Web page is added to your Favorites list and will be checked on the schedule you set. (See the following sec-tion, "Customizing Subscription Settings," for details on setting up a schedule.)

If the site is already on your Favorites list, follow these steps to subscribe:

1. In your browser window, click Favorites.

2. Right-click the site you want to subscribe to, and then click Subscribe.

3. Follow steps 5 through 7 of the preceding task to complete the subscription.

Customizing Subscription Settings

When a subscribed site has changed, your notification appears as a red asterisk on the page icon in your Subscriptions dialog box, like the ones shown in Figure 12.4. You can switch your subscription settings from mere notification to actually downloading the changed information, and you can change the site-checking schedule.

FIGURE 12.4.

Two of the subscriptions have changed contents, as indicated by the aster-isks on their icons.

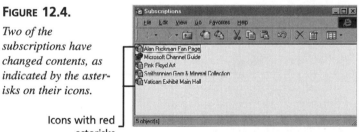

Icons with red asterisks

To subscribe to a site, you must add it to your Favorites list, and then subscribe to it and set a schedule for the Web crawler to check it for changed information.

To Do: Switching Notification Settings

To switch your notification settings, follow these steps:

1. In your browser window, click Favorites, and then click Manage Subscriptions.

2. In the Subscriptions dialog box, right-click the Web site you want to change, and then click Properties. The Subscription tab (see Figure 12.5) shows your current subscription settings.

12

FIGURE 12.5.

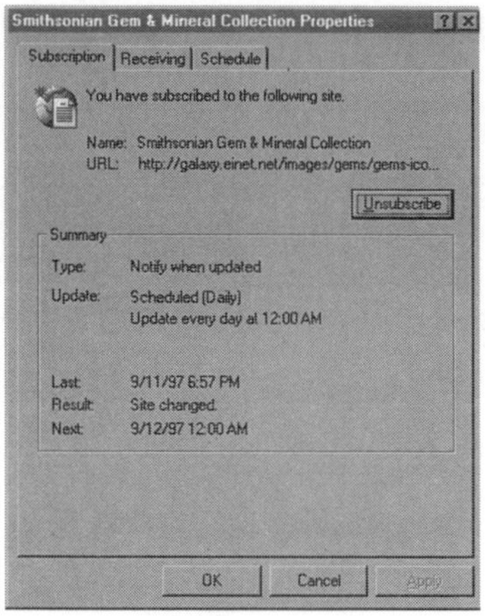

The Subscription tab, where you'll find your current settings.

▲

Changing Notification Settings

On the Receiving tab (see Figure 12.6), you can change the settings for notification of site changes.

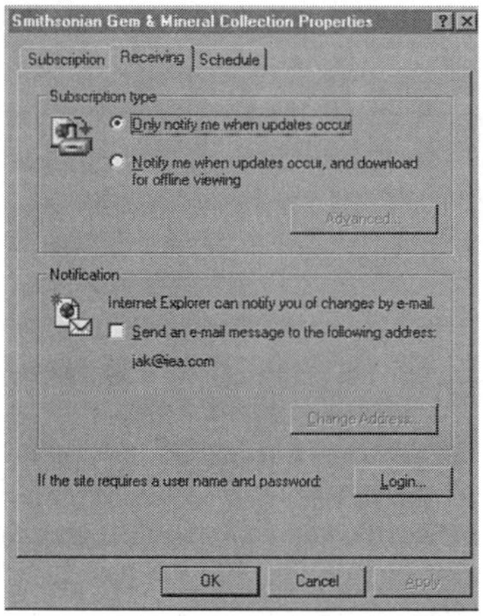

FIGURE 12.6.

Set notification preferences on the Receiving tab.

These are the settings you can select on the Receiving tab:

- Be notified by email of changes in the Web site.
- To select notification only, click the Only Notify Me When Updates Occur option. This option is much faster than actual automatic downloading and enables you to download the changed site separately from other subscribed sites.

- To direct the Web crawler to download the site automatically whenever it changes, click the Notify Me When Updates Occur and Download for Offline Viewing option. Then click the Advanced button to select download options from the Advanced Download Options dialog box.

- In the Advanced Download Options dialog box (see Figure 12.7), you can set a maximum size for downloads, and choose which types of page content to download (images, sounds, video, and so on). You can direct the Web crawler to download only the subscribed page, or follow links on that page and download other pages within that Web site (up to five levels deep).

Note that the more types of content you download, the more time your browser has to stay connected to the Internet. Although this may not be a problem for late-night checks, it could become one during the day when the Internet is sluggish and slow. In extreme cases, if you subscribe to a large number of pages and request all multimedia content from these pages each hour, you may find Internet Explorer ties up your phone line nonstop.

FIGURE 12.7.

The Advanced Download Options for a specific site.

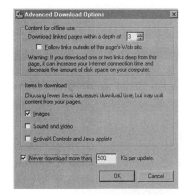

12

After the Web crawler downloads a changed page, it disconnects itself from the Internet. So if you point to a link on a page you've downloaded, you'll see a *not* symbol (a circle with a diagonal slash). To follow the link, click the link, and then click the Connect button in the dialog box that appears. Your browser connects and opens the link.

Changing Schedule Settings

On the Schedule tab (see Figure 12.8), you can change the Web crawler's update
schedule.

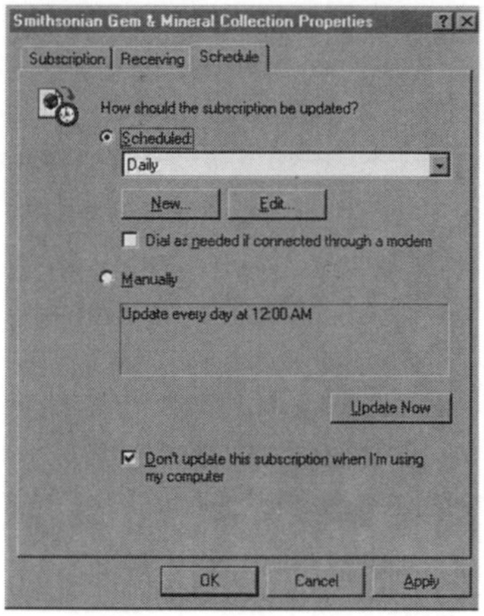

FIGURE 12.8.

*Set an update schedule
on the Schedule tab.*

The following are the settings you can select on the Schedule tab:

- Scheduled enables you to set a schedule for the Web crawler to go online and
  check your subscribed sites for changed information. You can set a daily, weekly,
  or monthly schedule, and set a time for downloads (overnight is a good choice if
  your Web crawler will be downloading lots of information). You also can have the
  Web crawler repeat the check at hourly intervals if you need to catch late-breaking
  news.

- Manually directs the Web crawler to check for changes in a Web site only when
  you tell it to do so, rather than automatically.

Downloading Subscriptions Now

If you've set your Web crawler to the Manually schedule, you can send it online to
download changed information whenever you choose. If you think it will be a long
download, send the Web crawler out before you go to lunch, and your new pages will be
waiting for you when you return.

Even if you have your subscriptions set to download automatically, you can update them
off-schedule whenever you want. This comes in handy if you're on your way out of town
and want to check a subscribed site once more before you leave.

To Do: Downloading All Your Subscriptions

To download changed pages from all your subscribed sites at your command, follow these steps:

1. In the browser window, click Favorites.

2. Click Update All. The Web crawler goes online and checks each of your subscribed pages for changes. A Download Progress message box appears while the Web crawler is at work and disappears when the Web crawler is finished.

   Click the Details button to watch the progress of the downloads. To stop the download at any point, click the Stop button in the Download Progress message box.

   To skip downloading a specific site, click that site, and then click the Skip button.

To Do: Downloading a Single Site

To download changed pages from a single subscribed site, follow these steps:

1. In your browser window, click Favorites, and then click Manage Subscriptions.

2. Right-click the site you want to check for updated information.

3. Click Update Now. The Web crawler goes only to that site to check for changed pages. If there are changes in that site, a red asterisk appears on the icon, and you can open the page by double-clicking it.

To Do: Viewing a Changed Site

When changed information has been downloaded, follow these steps to view the downloaded page:

1. In the browser window, click Favorites.

2. Point to Subscriptions, and then click Manage Subscriptions.

3. In the Subscriptions dialog box, double-click the page you want to read.

To Do: Deleting a Subscription

To unsubscribe to a site, follow these steps:

1. In your browser window, click Favorites.

2. Right-click the site you want to unsubscribe, and click Unsubscribe.

3. In the Confirm Item Delete message box, click Yes. Your subscription is canceled, but the site remains on your Favorites list so you can visit it when you want.

12

What Are Channels?

Channels are Web sites that come to your computer the way television channels come to your television set. They are a specialized form of subscription to Web sites. You cannot navigate to a channel by typing a URL in your browser; but after you subscribe to a channel, you can view it in your browser window by clicking a channel button on the Channel bar found on the Windows desktop.

If your computer is on a network that has constant Internet access (a constant open line to the Internet so channels can *push* information into the network), any channel you subscribe to is automatically updated by the channel's provider. You just open the channel on your computer to see the latest information. If your computer isn't connected full-time to the Internet, channels work like subscriptions—you update them manually or on a Web crawler schedule to get the latest information.

Internet Explorer 4.0 comes with built-in access to many channels, but as time goes by, more channels may become available on the Internet, and you will be able to add them to your Channel Guide.

Because few of us can afford full-time connections to the Internet, we are best served by subscriptions, as described earlier. Should you find yourself with a sudden windfall of money (and a full-time connection to the Internet), rest assured that channels work similarly to subscriptions. You'll get the hang of them in no time.

Enhancing Your Web Browser's Capabilities with Plug-Ins and Add-Ons

Internet Explorer provides you with a robust, full-featured Web browser. It's great for surfing the World Wide Web, searching for your favorite Web sites, and downloading great files and software. Believe it or not, you can extend and enhance the capabilities of Explorer with browser add-ons and plug-ins.

Add-ons and plug-ins can function as Explorer enhancers, increasing the capabilities of the browser. They can also function as helper applications to provide support for things that Explorer cannot do, such as view certain file types or play certain types of Web files—for example, sound, video and multimedia files—within the browser window.

NEW TERM A *browser add-on* is a mini-program that runs in conjunction with the browser and supplies you with additional Internet tools, such as a special communication interface like Microsoft NetMeeting.

Add-ons and plug-ins can do a variety of things. For instance, add-ons such as NetMeeting and Microsoft Chat enhance Explorer's communication capabilities. Both add-ons provide you with the ability to communicate in real time with other users on the World Wide Web. Other add-ons and plug-ins, such as DirectShow, ShockWave, and RealPlayer, help Internet Explorer play video, audio, and multimedia files you can find on the Web.

You will also come across add-ons and plug-ins that function outside of Internet Explorer as self-contained mini-programs. Microsoft DirectShow (shown in Figure 12.9) and NetShow play special Web files in special players outside of the Explorer Window.

FIGURE 12.9.

Some add-ons and plug-ins such as DirectShow play special Web files outside the browser window.

Microsoft FrontPage Express is an Explorer add-on that provides you with an HTML editor you can use to design your own Web pages. Web Server add-ons such as the Microsoft Publishing Wizard and the Personal Web Server help you publish your FrontPage Express content and get it onto the Web.

Popular Explorer Add-Ons

Microsoft offers several excellent add-ons for Internet Explorer 4. These add-ons range from the highly visual and fun Microsoft Chat to Microsoft Wallet, an add-on you can use with your Explorer Web browser to make secure purchases over the Internet.

Don't know which add-ons you already have? No problem; Microsoft offers a special Active Setup page for the various Internet Explorer add-ons that actually can tell you which components you have installed.

To Do: Determining the Add-ons You Have Installed

1. Connect to your Internet service provider or online service and open Internet Explorer.

▼ To Do

12

▼ 2. In Internet Explorer's Address Box, type the following and press Enter:
      `http://www.microsoft.com/ie/ie40/download/addon.htm`.

   3. The Explorer components download page opens. The page asks you to wait while
      initialization takes place. The Active Setup dialog box appears and asks you
      whether you want it to determine which Explorer components are installed on your
      computer, as shown in Figure 12.10.

   4. Click Yes to continue. Active Setup determines the status of each Explorer add-on
      listed on the page. Add-ons already installed on your computer are marked
▲   "Already Installed" in the status area to the right of the component's name.

After you determine which add-ons aren't installed on your computer, you can use this
Web page to select and install the ones you want.

FIGURE 12.10.

*The Internet Explorer
components download
page will help you
determine which
Explorer add-ons you
currently have
installed.*

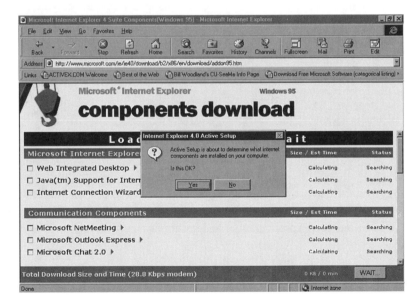

Finding Add-Ons and Plug-Ins

A number of Web sites provide you with a library of Internet Explorer add-ons and plug-
ins. Because new add-ons and plug-ins are created constantly (sometimes there seems to
be a total flood of new add-ons and plug-ins for a Web browser), it pays to check these
sites periodically to see what new items have become available.

The first place to check for new add-ons and news about IE4 is its page at the Microsoft
Web site. The address is `http://www.microsoft.com/ie4/`. This page will lead you to
the plug-ins and add-ons that work best with IE4.

Summary

See? You can now have IE4 load the page you want when the application is launched; you know how to make IE's fonts larger; and you have everything you need to put Web site subscriptions to work for you!

In the next hour, we'll explore Outlook Express's email capabilities.

Workshop

The following workshop helps you solidify the skills you learned in this hour.

Quiz

Take the following quiz to see how much you've learned.

Questions

1. You can suppress graphics and other multimedia files from loading to speed up the browsing of text.

    a. False

    b. True

2. Can you set your own Start Page that loads automatically when IE is launched?

    a. Of course!

    b. That capability will be available in the next version of IE.

    c. What's a Start Page again?

3. What's the difference between subscriptions and channels?

    a. Subscriptions are for magazines and newspapers, and channels are for televisions and radios.

    b. The two are similar, except channels allow one with a full-time Internet connection to get constant updates to channels they subscribe to. Subscriptions, on the other hand, must have scheduled updates or be downloaded manually.

    c. Channel is a perfume; a subscription is something you get for a newspaper.

12

Answers

1. b. If you've forgotten how, you can go back and skim through the necessary steps in this hour.

2. a. And you don't even have to wait for the next version of IE!

3. b. Although I guess an argument could be made for A as well....

Activity

Play around with some of the IE configuration options to find a background color, type font, and so on that makes Web browsing most comfortable for your eyes.

HOUR 13

Using Outlook Express for Email

Email in the '90s is becoming what faxes were in the '80s—indispensable. For worldwide business, interoffice, and even personal communication, electronic mail is fast, inexpensive, and convenient. Internet Explorer 4.0 includes a powerful email component called Outlook Express that makes sending all forms of electronic communication—notes, documents, graphics, and even multimedia files—a breeze.

In this hour, you find the answers to the following questions:

- How do I retrieve my email messages with Outlook Express?
- Can I make my message look nicer by adding special formatting, colors, and so on?
- Are you able to attach Word files and other documents to your messages?
- How do I store an email address in my address book?
- What can I do to keep my mail organized?

Defining Email

Email stands for electronic message, and you can send and receive messages to anyone with an email address. Email has no real cost. You do pay a price to your Internet service provider for Internet access, but most ISPs do not charge for messages sent and received. If it does charge for these, I suggest you find another ISP right away!

What's My Email Address?

To receive mail, you must have an email address. Your Internet service provider assigns this address to you. Usually, you can select your user name, which often is the first part of your email address. An example of an address is

ChrisandSam@Chrissam.com

The first part is a user name, and the second part defines the server or Internet provider where the mail is sent. The two parts are separated by an at (@) sign; an email address always has this sign. Again, check the information sent to you by your ISP to find out your email address.

 People often use their first initial followed by their surname as a user name. Note that email addresses are not case sensitive, so you may capitalize letters as needed to clarify your chosen name.

How Does Email Work?

When someone sends you a message, that message is sent to the server that you use for your Internet connection and stored there. When you log on and check your mail, the message is then sent from that server to your PC. Likewise, when you send mail, you send a message to the recipient's server (where they get the Internet connection). The message is stored there until the recipient checks his or her mail; the mail is then sent to that person's PC.

Introducing Outlook Express

To check your mail, you first log on to your Internet service provider and then start the mail program by pressing Start, selecting Programs, Internet Explorer, Outlook Express. (Alternatively, if you already have Internet Explorer open, it has a toolbar button and menu command for accessing your mailbox.) As soon as Outlook Express is up and running, it scans your mail server for email.

Outlook Express gives you the following choices when you receive a message:

- *Read and close the message.* To close the message and keep it in your inbox, click the Close (x) button for the message window.
- *Print the message.* To print the message, click the Print button in the toolbar or a Choose File, Print command from the menu bar.
- *Delete the message.* To delete the message, use the Delete button in the toolbar.
- *Reply to the message.* If you want to send a reply to the sender, click the Reply button in the toolbar. You see a message reply window (see Figure 13.1). When you reply, the address information is complete. The reply may also contain the text of the original message. You can type your response and click the Send button to send the reply.

FIGURE 13.1.

You can reply to messages you have received.

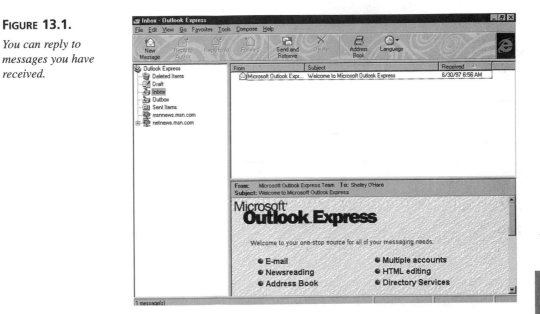

- *Forward the message.* To forward the message to another person, click the Forward button. In the To text box, type the address of that person and click the Send button.

Understanding the Outlook Express Email Window

After you start Outlook Express, you see the program window shown in Figure 13.2. You find the Outlook Express menu bar at the top of the window, with commands for accessing all the mail features. You also see a toolbar with buttons that you can use as shortcuts to common tasks such as checking mail or creating a new message.

FIGURE 13.2.

You can send and receive messages by email or to newsgroups with Outlook Express.

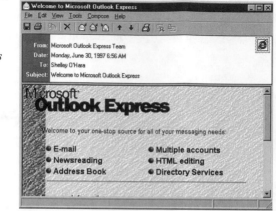

Outlook Express initially lists the message headers in a window referred to as the inbox. This line indicates the sender, subject, and date that the message was received. You can easily tell which messages have been read and which have not. Messages with headers in bold have not been read, and messages with an envelope icon that appears to be open have been read.

Outlook Express divides its workspace into several window panes. The left pane lists the folders for handling and storing mail (and also newsgroups as discussed in Hour 14). The top-right pane—the inbox—contains message headers. The bottom-right pane displays the contents of the selected message.

Reading Mail

After you get your email address, you can tell your friends, family, and coworkers so that they can send you messages.

To give you a little practice at reading messages, Microsoft usually includes a message or two in your inbox. Although you need not connect to your mail server to retrieve them, they do provide practice in reading and navigating the various window panes.

To Do: Reading Your Email

To check your mail, start Outlook Express, and review any messages in your inbox. Follow these basic steps:

1. Make sure that you have an active connection to the Internet, and start Outlook Express as described earlier.

2. Outlook Express checks for messages automatically when you start the program.

3. Your mail program collects all the messages on your mail server and displays them in your inbox.

4. To read a message, double-click it. You see the contents of the message in a separate message window (see Figure 13.3).

FIGURE 13.3.

When you double-click a message header, you see the entire message.

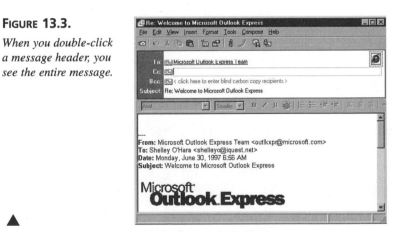

13

Composing and Sending a Message

Because you most likely need to send mail to receive it, follow these steps to send a message to friends and family on the Internet:

To Do: Creating an Email Message and Sending It

1. If it is not already running, start Outlook Express.

2. Click the Compose Message icon on the toolbar.

3. The New Message form opens as shown in Figure 13.4.

FIGURE 13.4.

The New Mail form, filled out and ready to send.

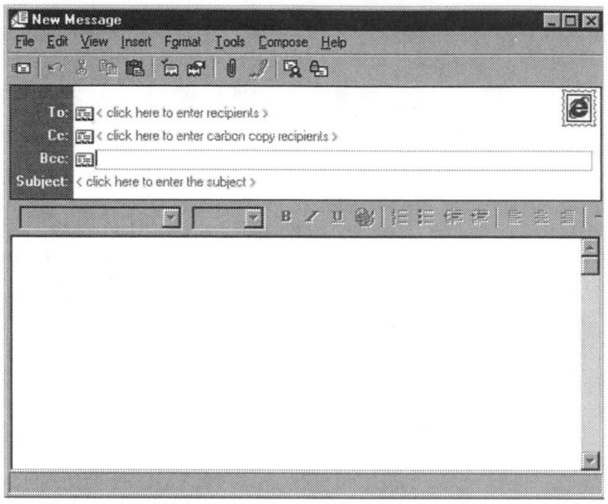

4. Type the recipient's email address in the To box—for example, ChrisandSam@Chrissam.com.

5. Press Tab to move to the next box.

6. Enter any additional recipients in the Cc and Bcc boxes and press Tab.

7. In the Subject box, type your email message title and press Tab.

8. Type your text in the message area. You can use any of the formatting options available in the toolbar above the message area, including bold, italic, underline, font (name, color, and size), alignment, and bulleted or numbered lists.

> Keep in mind that not everyone has an email program capable of displaying all the fancy font colors and styles, so you may not want to spend extra time making your notes look nice until you know that the recipient's mail program can read it.

9. To send your message, click the Send button (the envelope) on the Outlook Express toolbar.

Suppose your teenage daughter is tying up the phone line again. With Outlook Express, you can compose messages offline and save them to the Outbox to be mailed at a later time. Just follow the preceeding steps to compose your message, but instead of executing step 9, go to the File menu and select Send Later. The message is placed safely in the Outbox so that you can send it off when the phone line is finally free.

Replying to Messages

When everyone has been informed of your new email address, you're bound to start getting a fair amount of mail, some to which you'll undoubtedly want to reply. (And yes, this includes junk mail much like the stuff that clutters your snail-mail box.)

To Do: Replying to Your Email Messages

Follow these steps to reply to a message in your Inbox:

1. Open Outlook Express, if it isn't already running.
2. From the Message List, click the message to which you want to respond.
3. Click the Reply to Author button on the toolbar.

   The Reply form opens with the To and Subject boxes filled in. The insertion pointer is in the message area.
4. Type your reply.
5. Click the Send button on the Reply form toolbar.

By default, Outlook Express includes the original message after your reply. To disable this feature, select Mail Options from the Tools menu. On the Send tab, uncheck Include Message in Reply. Click OK.

13

Attaching a File

One of email's most powerful features is its capability to attach any document to your message. This feature has greatly enhanced productivity between working groups by enabling them to share files across the office or the country. Word processing documents, spreadsheets, or graphics all can be sent with equal ease. You have to be certain only that whoever is receiving the files has the capability (or software) to view them. For the home, this may mean sending a scanned image of your kids or new puppy to relatives across the country, exchanging recipe databases with your best friend, and so on.

To Do: Attaching Files to Email Messages

To attach a file to your email, follow these steps:

1. Compose a new message or respond to a previous message.

2. From the Message toolbar, click the Insert File button (it looks like a paperclip). The Insert Attachment dialog box appears.

3. From the Insert Attachment dialog box, select a file and click OK.

4. An icon for the file appears in a box below the message area, as shown in Figure 13.5. To send additional attachments, repeat steps 2–4.

▲   5. Click the Send button to send the email message with the attachments.

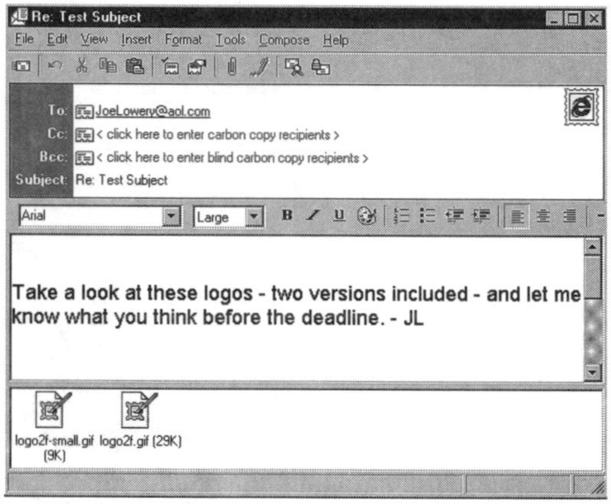

FIGURE 13.5.

An email reply with attachments.

When the email is sent, your message is sent first and then the attached file or files are uploaded. The time it takes to send the entire email message and attachments depends on the size of the files and the speed of the Internet connection.

> Need to let someone know that this email is urgent? Click the stamp with the Internet Explorer logo in the upper-right corner. A drop-down list gives you High, Normal, and Low priority options.

Using Your Address Book

The Address Book is a key component of any email system. Internet Explorer and Outlook Express use the central Windows Address Book found in Outlook and all Office 97 applications. This address book enables you to organize information on a variety of personal and business contacts, ranging from email address to home phone number. You can use the information in your address book to quickly address messages to one or more persons. In the following sections, I show you how to enter contact information, how to use that information to address correspondence sent from Outlook Express, and how to modify contact entries.

Adding Contacts to the Address Book

To put this time-saving tool to work for you, you need to enter the information on important contacts whether it's your boss, your daughter's gymnastics coach, or your grandmother's new Web TV email address.

To Do: Adding an Address

To create a new address book entry, follow these steps:

1. With Outlook Express running, click the Address Book button.

2. Click the New Contact button.

3. Enter the individual's first, middle, and last name in the appropriate fields (shown in Figure 13.6). These names are combined to create an automatic display name. You also can choose to fill in a nickname for the individual whom you're adding.

FIGURE 13.6.

The Properties dialog box, from which you can add a New Contact.

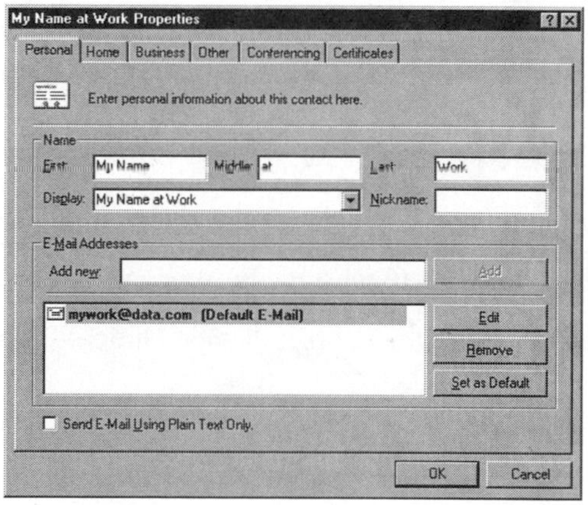

My Name at Work Properties	? ×

Personal | Home | Business | Other | Conferencing | Certificates

Enter personal information about this contact here.

Name
First: My Name   Middle: at   Last: Work
Display: My Name at Work   Nickname:

E-Mail Addresses
Add new: Add

✉ mywork@data.com [Default E-Mail]   Edit
   Remove
   Set as Default

☐ Send E-Mail Using Plain Text Only.

OK   Cancel

13

4. In the E-mail Addresses section, click the Add New field and type the full address you want to use, such as jack@whitehouse.gov.

5. Click the Add button.

6. If you want to send only plain text messages to these individuals, check the Send Email Using Plain Text Only check box at the bottom of the screen.

▼   7. Click the Home tab. On this tab, you can store the personal mailing information
        about your contact. Included on this page is space for the individual's Personal
        Web Page address. Be sure to leave `http://` attached to the front of the page
        address.

     8. Click the Business tab. This screen enables you to store all the business informa-
        tion for your contact, including an address for his or her business Web site.

     9. Click the Other tab, and you can store notes about this particular individual such as
        a birthday, names of kids, or whatever.

    10. From the Select or Add New drop-down field, select an email address to use to find
        the contact.

▲   11. When you finish entering the contact information that you want to track, click the
        OK button.

Why Use the Address Book to Address Messages?

As I mentioned earlier, using the Address Book can speed up the time it takes to address
a message, especially if you don't know the address by memory. No more poring through
old messages to track down the desired address! It can also make addressing messages
more accurate, because once the information is entered correctly in the Address Book,
your messages always carry the correct email address. No more worrying about typos
during those late night email sessions! It's also a great way to define groups of people to
whom you like to write as a whole. For instance, you might like sending the same family
update to all your relatives, or you may have a group of friends with whom you trade
funny jokes found on the Net.

To Do: Addressing Email with Your Address Book

Follow these steps to send an email message to someone in your Address Book:

     1. After you're connected to the Internet, launch Outlook Express and press the
        Compose Message button.

     2. From the Compose Message form, click the Address Book icon (the Rolodex card)
        next to the To box. The Select Recipients dialog box opens (shown in Figure 13.7).

     3. From the Name List on the left, double-click the name of the intended recipient.
        The name appears in the To box.

     4. To add additional recipients, repeat steps 3 and 4.

▲   5. Click OK.

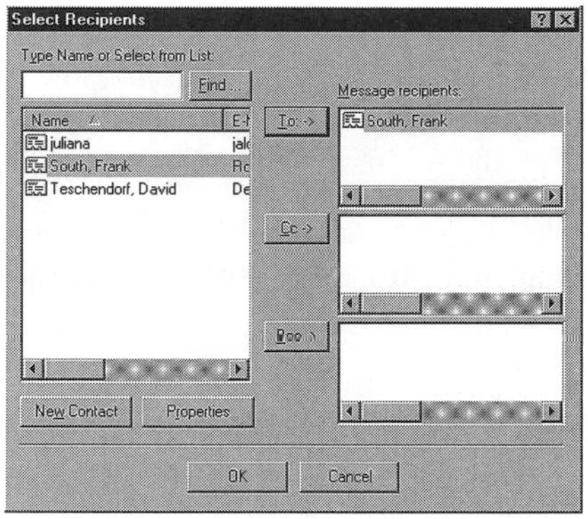

FIGURE 13.7.

The Address Box maintains a list of all your contacts through the Select Recipients dialog box.

Editing a Contact

People's personal information is constantly changing, and when it does change, you want to make a note of it in your address book.

To Do: Changing Information in the Address Book

The following steps walk you through editing an entry in your Contact list.

1. With the Address Book open, select the entry that you want to edit.

2. Click the Preferences button, or open the File menu and select Properties (Alt+Enter).

3. Click the tab storing the information that you need to edit. Most likely this is the Personal tab because you probably want to edit the email address.

4. To edit the email address, click the Edit button.

5. Place your cursor in the highlighted email field, and edit the entry to reflect the necessary changes to the email address.

6. When you finish making your changes, click the OK button.

Adding a Group

Groups are used to organize mass delivery of email messages. As you develop groups of friends on the Internet, you may find yourself sending those individuals the same email messages. Maybe your family is scattered across the country, and you want to send them all the same newsy letters whenever something exciting happens. To make this process easier, simply collect those names under a single nickname, and send your messages.

13

To Do: Creating a Group Mailing List in the Address Book

The following steps help you create a group mailing list:

1. In Outlook Express, click the Address Book button.

2. Click the New Group button.

3. Type an easily identifiable name such as family or college friends in the Group Name field (shown in Figure 13.8).

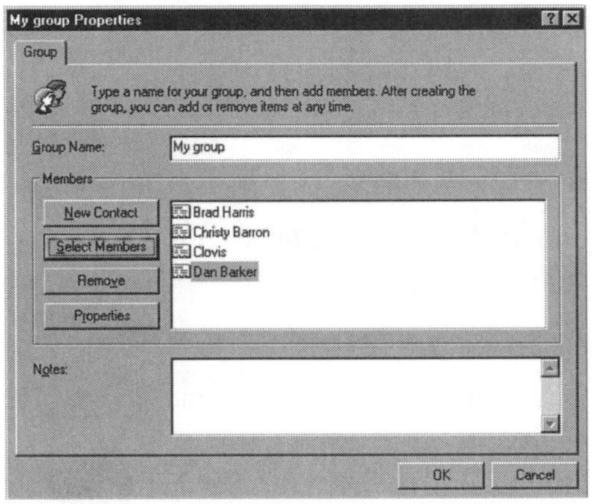

FIGURE 13.8.

The Group Properties dialog box enables you to create personal groups for distributing mass mail messages.

4. Click the Select Members button. If you want to create a New Contact, you can do so by clicking the New Contact button.

5. From the Select Group members dialog box, click the names of the individuals whom you want to include in your group from the left window. Hold down the Control key to select multiple names.

6. Click the Select button (see Figure 13.9).

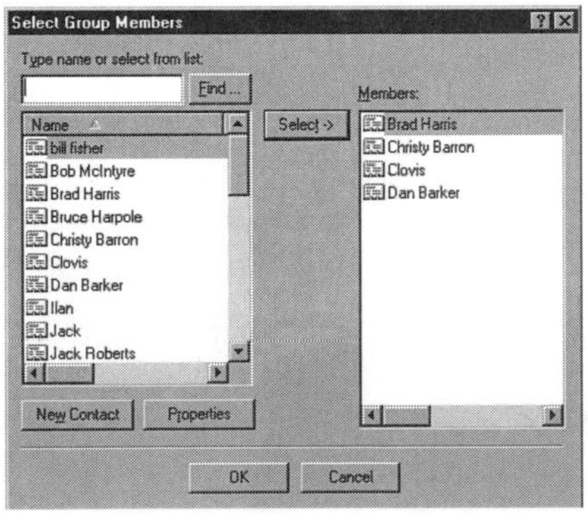

FIGURE 13.9.

The Select Group Members dialog box enables you to add members to your groups.

▼

7. When all your names have been added to the Members list, click OK.

8. Click OK on the Group Properties dialog box. You see your new group listed below the main Address Book icon on the left side of your Windows Address Book

▲   screen.

Deleting an Entry

Addresses change often, or you may no longer want to correspond with someone. In this case, you may want to delete a Contact.

To Do: Deleting Contacts from the Address Book

Follow these steps to delete addresses:

1. With the Windows Address Book open, select the entry that you want to delete.

2. Click the Delete button on the toolbar, or open the File menu and select Delete. The entry immediately disappears from your Contact list and from all your groups.

Internet Address Directories

You'd be amazed at how many old friends and acquaintances you can track down on the Net! A wide variety of internationally accessible email address books are located on the Internet. By using these LDAP (Lightweight Directory Access Protocol) email address books, you can quickly and effortlessly add the addresses that you find to your Windows Address Book.

Outlook Express provides you with immediate access to the most popular LDAP directories. These directories include: Four11 (http://www.four11.com), Switchboard (http://www.switchboard.com), InfoSpace (http://www.infospace.com), BigFoot (http://www.bigfoot.com), and Who/Where (http://www.whowhere.com).

To Do: Using LDAP Directories to Find People

When you need to look up an individual on these systems, you can use the following steps:

1. From the Windows taskbar, open the Start menu, select Programs, and then Windows Address Book. If you already have Outlook Express open, you can click the Address Book button, or you can open the Tools menu and select Address Book (Ctrl+Shift+B).

2. Click the Find button, or open the Edit menu and select Find (Ctrl+F).

3. Select the directory service that you want to use from the Search list (see ▼   Figure 13.10).

13

The Find People dialog box enables you to search both your local Address Book and a variety of Internet directories.

4. Enter the information for which you want to search, whether it is a user's name, email address, postal mail address, or phone number in your local Address Book. If you have selected one of the Directory services, enter either a name or email address.

5. Click the Find Now button.

6. If the individual for whom you're looking is listed with that service, that person's name appears in the search results window.

7. Select the name that you want to add to your Address Book, and click Add to Address Book.

▲ 8. Click Close.

Organizing Your Email

One of the most frustrating things about email is the lack of organization. All your messages automatically come into one folder and stay there until you have the time to do something about it. In Outlook Express, this problem is compounded if you have multiple email addresses from which messages are collected. Fortunately, you can easily have this information sorted and stored for you.

Outlook Express includes some useful tools for separating this information. You can easily retrieve mail for all your personal and business accounts and keep it separate. Outlook Express enables you to create subfolders within the Inbox or any other folder that you want. This means that you can easily filter all your incoming mail into specific areas, so personal messages can go into one folder, business-related messages can automatically be placed in another folder, and each of your mailing list messages can be sorted into a folder of its own. This can save you time, and it enables you to tackle the important messages, leaving the rest for later.

Creating Folders

Folders can quickly bring order to the chaos of dozens of saved email messages. Finding a certain message amidst a sea of hundreds of email messages can be like looking for the proverbial needle in the haystack. If, on the other hand, those messages were grouped into folders such as Humor, Work Stuff, and the like, finding it would be much easier.

To Do: Creating Folders for Email

The following steps walk you through creating a folder:

1. Open the File menu, select Folder, and then select New Folder. The Create Folder dialog box appears.

2. Type the name for your folder in the Folder Name field. For example, you might type Personal Inbox as the name of a subfolder in which you want to store your personal messages.

3. You can place your new folder wherever you want in your Outlook Express folder hierarchy. Simply highlight the name of the folder in which you want to create the subfolder. For example, click Inbox.

4. Click the OK button.

Moving Messages into Folders

After you have created a series of folders, you need to organize your existing messages into them.

To Do: Moving Messages into Folders

Follow these steps to move your messages into the folders that you have created:

1. Select the first message that you want to move to your new folder.

2. Right-click the entry and select Move To from the shortcut menu that appears. (Alternatively, you can open the Edit menu and select Move to Folder.)

3. Select the folder in which you want to place your message, such as the Personal Inbox folder that you created under the Inbox.

4. Click OK.

Deleting Old Email Messages

Part of maintaining a well-organized email system is deleting the messages that you no longer need (the ones that are simply taking up important space). To delete a message, select its message header from the list in your folder, and click the Delete button on your toolbar or press the Delete key on your keyboard.

When you delete a message, it automatically goes to your Deleted Items folder. It remains there until you empty that folder or your scheduled backup runs, whichever comes first.

13

Deleted messages DO NOT go to the recycle bin. When you remove them from the deleted items folder by executing the Edit, Purge deleted messages command, they are gone for good.

Compacting Mail Folders

After moving and deleting messages, you want to compact your mail folders. This might sound odd, but it's a necessary form of maintenance for keeping Outlook Express functioning well.

NEW TERM   When you *compact* a message folder, you simply reorganize the files it contains so that they take up less space on your hard drive. This process also removes any messages that you have marked for deletion.

To compact all your mail folders, open the File menu, select Folders, and then select Compact All Folders.

If you want to compact a single folder, switch to the folder that you want to compact, click the folder name heading, and select it from the list of available folders. Then open the File menu, select Folder, and select Compact.

Summary

With everything you learned this hour, you're ready to begin using email like a pro! In addition to the basics of sending and receiving messages, you learned how to compose messages offline to be sent later, how to attach files to your notes, and how to make the most of your address book.

In the next hour, we build on everything that you learned here by exploring Outlook Express as a newsreader.

Workshop

The following workshop helps you solidify the skills that you learned in this lesson.

Quiz

Take the following quiz to see how much you've learned.

Questions

1. Which of the following represents a properly formatted email address?

    a. Cali*kittycat.net

    b. Terry#Labonte.com

    c. Pixel@computer.net

2. If you want to pass on to your mother a recipe that your friend sent you, you would _____ it.

    a. forward

    b. reply to

    c. compact

3. What does compacting folders in Outlook Express do?

    a. Cuts down on bulky trash in landfills

    b. Frees up space on your hard drive by reorganizing files so that they take up less room

    c. Magically shrinks outgoing messages so that they take less time to send

Answers

1. c. Email addresses must always carry the at sign.

2. a.

3. b.

Activity

Begin collecting email addresses from all your friends and family, and enter them in your address book. Don't forget to create a group entry if you have a list of people to whom you'd commonly like to send the same mailing.

13

Hour **14**

Reading Newsgroups with Outlook Express

If you think the Web is filled with exotic content, wait until you see the newsgroups. Currently more than 10,000 highly focused discussion groups cover virtually every and any interest, lifestyle, or belief. Newsgroups can be a tremendous source of entertainment, enlightenment, advice, and news. They can also be a highly emotional forum, so before you jump into the thick of things, I suggest that you browse Appendix A of this book for some invaluable rules of the road.

In the meantime, this hour presents ways to use outlook Express as your newsgroup reader. In addition, the following questions are answered:

- How are newsgroups structured?
- How do I find a newsgroup of interest to me?
- Can you tell which articles have been read?
- What are threads?
- How do I reply to the author of an article?

What Are Newsgroups?

Newsgroups are electronic discussion groups. The name is a bit of a misnomer; news-groups don't involve late-breaking news, sports, or weather, unless that happens to be the topic of discussion. Newsgroups are more like an electronic version of a bulletin board or online club, where users exchange messages. In these groups, users discuss various top-ics ranging from aviation and alien visitors to Zen and zoology. Each of the 10,000 or more newsgroups usually limits discussion to just one topic.

The discussions take the form of posted messages. For example, one person posts a mes-sage asking for tips on training a new puppy. After posting the message in the Dog Training newsgroup, other users can read the message and respond with their thoughts, suggestions, or opinions.

Although newsgroups are single-topic by definition, as you browse through a few, you see that a topic can have many sidetracks or threads. For example, a newsgroup about dog training may also lead to a discussion of pet care products or veterinary medicine.

In the early days of the Internet, a special program, called a newsreader, was needed to read and post newsgroups' messages. Now you can use Internet Explorer 4.0's Outlook Express to access newsgroups. Most newsgroups are part of a larger network called Usenet (user's network). Usenet sets the standard for how newsgroups exchange and post messages.

NEW TERM The term *Usenet* predates the Internet. It refers to an early system of connecting mainframe computers using standard telephone lines and crude versions of desk-top modems to transfer discussion articles.

Looking at Newsgroups' Names

Newsgroups' names are unique. Like other Internet locations, newsgroups have an address, usually made up of two or three parts, as in rec.sports.nascar. The first part in the address, rec, reflects the general topic, which in this case is recreation. The second part, sports, specifies the specific topic itself. The third part, nascar, narrows the topic by category, as in the sport of NASCAR racing.

The abbreviated newsgroups' names are sometimes difficult to decipher. The following is a list of common newsgroup abbreviations to help you:

- *alt.* Alternative topics that may not fit elsewhere in the newsgroup hierarchy. Because creating an alt newsgroup is far easier than creating a rec newsgroup, topics may also venture into the unusual and possibly offensive, although obviously this is not a general assumption.

- *comp.* Computer topics
- *misc.* Miscellaneous topics
- *news.* Newsgroup-related topics
- *rec.* Recreational topics
- *sci.* Science topics
- *soc.* Social issues
- *talk.* Controversial topics (talk show format)

You may find many newsgroups on the Internet offensive. Keep this in mind when you're first learning how to view and subscribe to newsgroups. You can always unsubscribe to any questionable newsgroups that you encounter.

Configuring Your Server

When you run Outlook Express, you need to make sure that you're connecting to the proper news server.

To Do: Connecting to a News Server

To connect to a news server, follow these steps:

1. From the Windows taskbar, open the Start menu, select Programs, Internet Explorer, and then select Outlook Express.

The first time you run Outlook Express, the configuration process starts automatically.

2. Open the Tools menu and select Accounts.
3. Click the Add button and select News. This opens a screen similar to the one shown in Figure 14.1.
4. Type your name in the Display Name field, and click Next.
5. Enter your full email address in the E-Mail Address field, and click Next.
6. Type the full address of your news server in the News (NNTP) Server field, and click Next.

14

▼ **FIGURE 14.1.**

The first screen of the
Internet Connection
Wizard for configuring
your news server.

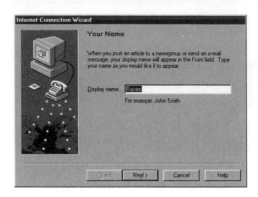

Although most Internet service providers don't require you to log in to the news server you use, you should check with your service provider to see whether logging in is required. If you need to log in, check the My News Server Requires Me to Log In check box, and enter your login name and password on the next screen.

7. Type a name for your news connection in the Internet News Account Name field, and click Next.

8. You now need to indicate how you connect through your provider to your news server. You have three ways to connect to your service provider. Outlook Express Mail enables you to select the method most appropriate for you. Choose from the phone line, local area network, and manual options, and then click Next.

9. If you choose to use a phone connection, you need to select a Dial-Up Networking connection. If you have never connected to the Internet before, you need to create a new dial-up connection. If you have used the Internet previously, you probably already have a connection to use. In that case, select Use an Existing Dial-Up Connection, and select a connection to use. Click Next.

   If you selected either the Local Area Network or the Manual connection, you're done configuring your account. When the Congratulations screen appears, click the Finish button, and you can start using Outlook Express.

10. When you complete the configuration, click the Finish button. If you want to make changes to your settings, click the Back button until you find the option that you want to adjust, make the adjustment, and use the Next button to return to the final screen.

Configuring Your Message Windows

The simplest way to read your news articles is in an easy-to-read font. I recommend a proportional font such as Times New Roman or Arial—they somehow feel more natural to the eye. Doing so, however, may mean either that you miss out on some of the neat ASCII art (letters, numbers, and symbols used to make a larger image or design) that people use in their signatures or that any charts you receive via email may be misaligned. Font selection is very much one of those personal decisions. You have compelling reasons to go either way, but it's a matter of preference in the end.

To Do: Configuring Message Windows

To configure your message window font, follow these steps:

1. Open the Tools menu and select Options.
2. Click the General tab.
3. Check the Make Outlook Express My Default News Reader check box.
4. Click the Send tab to see the options shown in Figure 14.2.

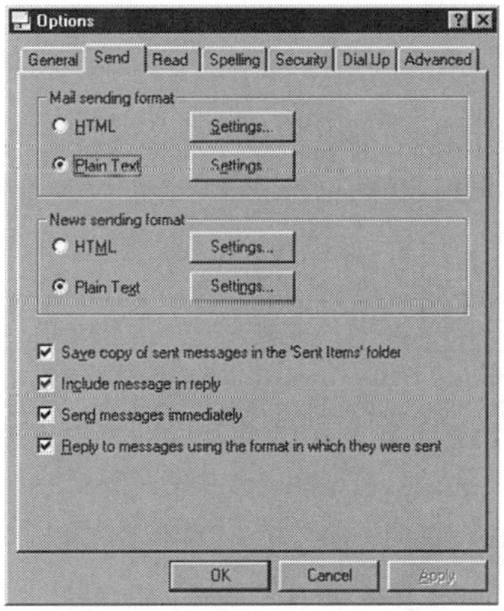

FIGURE 14.2.

The Send tab of the Options dialog box enables you to control the format in which your messages are sent.

5. In the News Sending Format section of the dialog box, select either HTML or Plain Text for your news articles.
6. In the Read tab, press the Fonts button. Use the drop-down arrows to choose the fonts that you want to use.
7. Press the Set as Default button when you're finished.
8. Click the OK button.
9. Click the OK button at the Options dialog box.

14

Finding and Subscribing to Newsgroups

After you configure Outlook Express, the next step is to retrieve a list of available news-groups. Outlook Express has no default newsgroups, so you have to find those that you want and select them yourself. You can also read articles in newsgroups to which you haven't subscribed.

When you subscribe to a newsgroup, the subject information for each article in that newsgroup is automatically downloaded every time you connect to your news server. You don't need to subscribe to a newsgroup in order to review its messages; however, subscribing does make it easier to find the newsgroup again later.

To Do: Finding Newsgroups That Interest You

Follow these steps to find newsgroups and subscribe to them:

1. With Outlook Express running, scroll through the list of folders and select the name of your news server, as shown in Figure 14.3. (Alternatively, you can open the Go menu and select News.) This enables you to automatically connect to your Internet service provider.

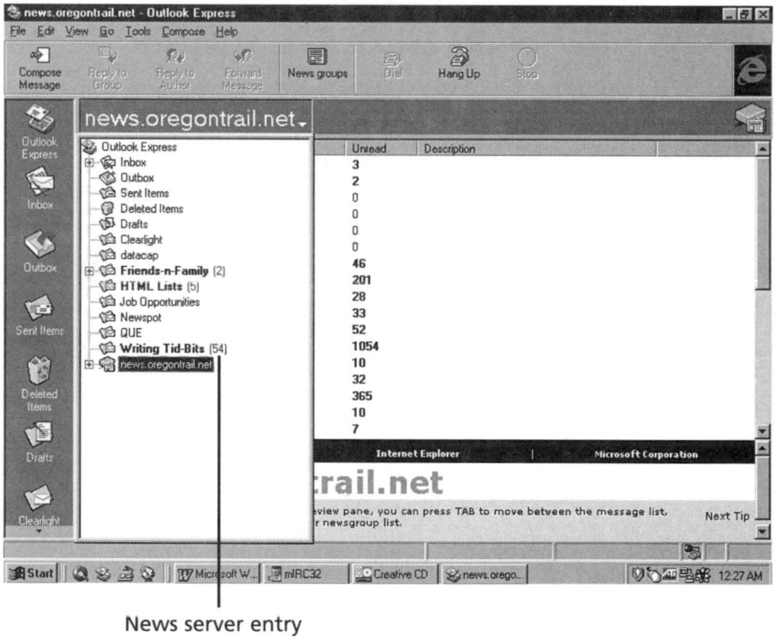

FIGURE 14.3.

The folder list showing your news server entries.

News server entry

▼   2. After you're connected, Outlook Express asks you whether you want to download
       the list of available newsgroups. Click OK, and a list of the newsgroups appears
       onscreen as your news server downloads it to your computer.

    3. When all the newsgroups have been downloaded and sorted, Outlook Express dis-
       plays the Newsgroups dialog box (see Figure 14.4). It lists all the newsgroups to
       which you have access.

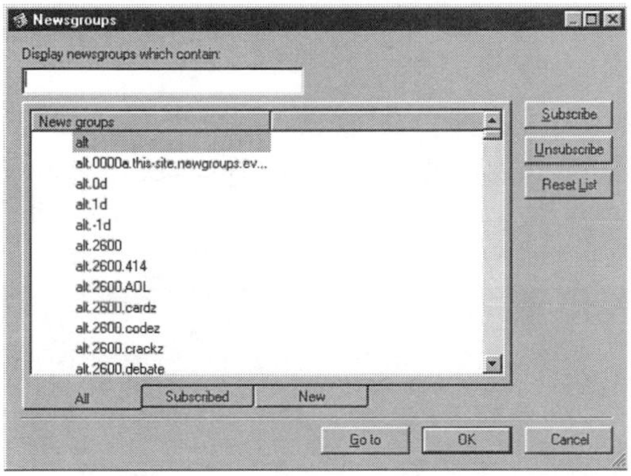

FIGURE 14.4.

*The list of newsgroups
available from your
service provider's news
server.*

> **NEW TERM** *Subscribing* is the process used to mark a list of favorite newsgroups that you
> read frequently. This enables you to access your favorite newsgroups in a manner
> similar to that in which you access your favorite Web sites.

    4. Read through the list of newsgroup names in the Newsgroup list until you find one
       that interests you. Click to select the one that you want.

> To read the messages in a newsgroup that you have not subscribed to, click
> the Go To button at the bottom of your Newsgroups dialog box.

    5. With a group name selected, click Subscribe. You can repeat this process for as
       many newsgroups as you're interested in. In the newsgroup list, a newspaper icon
       appears to the left of each newsgroup to which you've subscribed.

▲   6. To see the list of newsgroups you've subscribed to, click the Subscribed tab.

Downloading Article Headers

Outlook Express enables you to control how much of your time and hard drive space is
going to be taken up by the articles that you download from newsgroups. The first time

you connect to a newsgroup, you have to download the message headers. The headers are the only part of the messages that are downloaded automatically.

NEW TERM The *message header* is the portion of the message containing information about the original author of the message, what group the article was sent to, and the subject of the message.

To Do: Downloading New Message Headers

▼ To Do The following steps show you how to download the new message headers for your subscribed newsgroups:

1. With Outlook Express open, scroll through the folders list and select the newsgroup that you want to read. (Alternatively, you can open the Go menu, select News, and choose a newsgroup from the screen shown in Figure 14.5.)

FIGURE 14.5.

The main Outlook Express window, showing your available newsgroups.

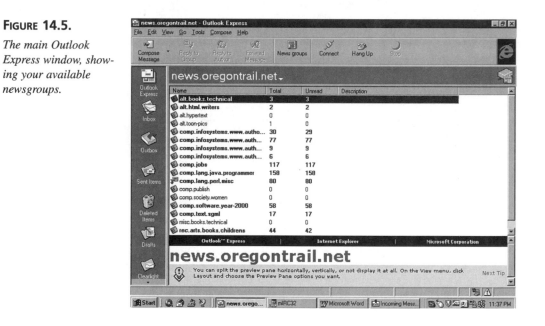

2. Double-click the newsgroup in which you're interested. Outlook Express automatically connects to your service provider, connects to your news server, and downloads the headers for the newsgroup.

▲

  You can print a message only from the message window (see the section "Printing Articles" later in this lesson). You can, however, reply to the original author, reply to the newsgroup, or forward to another individual or group from the preview window.

Outlook Express does not have to automatically download each message when you select it. Instead, you want it to download all selected messages at one time to reduce your connect time (which leaves your phone line open for incoming calls and also keeps your Internet connection charges to a minimum). You can select all the messages that you want to read while you're offline, connect for a few minutes to download them from the server, and then disconnect before reading them.

Tagging Articles

As you read through the message headers, you can find out what type of conversations are taking place and decide whether you want to participate in them. The bodies of messages take up large amounts of space on your hard drive. And if files are attached to the messages, they take up even more space. By taking advantage of the option of reading the message headers before downloading the entire message, you can conserve your online time and your hard drive space—two major considerations when using a computer on the Internet. When you find particular articles that you would like to read in their entirety, you tag them.

To Do: Tagging Articles

To tag an article, perform the following steps:

1. Open Outlook Express but don't connect to the Internet.

2. Open your newsgroups list and select a newsgroup to read—one for which you have already downloaded the headers.

3. Select a message that you didn't view while online. The preview window indicates that the message is not cached and needs to be downloaded.

4. To tag this article, right-click the article's header and select Mark Message for Download from the shortcut menu. Outlook Express displays a green arrow icon to the left of the article. This icon identifies articles that are downloaded the next time you connect to your service provider.

▲

If you tag a message that has multiple replies, Outlook Express automatically downloads all its replies, too.

14

Downloading Selected Messages

In the previous sections, you tagged some messages that you wanted to read. Now you need to get those messages from the news server to your computer.

To Do: Downloading Tagged Messages

To download all tagged messages, follow these steps:

1. Click the Connect button to connect to your service provider.

2. Open the Tools menu and select Download All. This starts the automatic retrieval process for all the articles that you have marked. The Post and Download window shows you the progress of your download.

3. After the articles are completely downloaded, double-click one to see the entire message.

Opening Articles

Generally, you download messages so that you can read them. Outlook Express provides you with a preview window so that you can skim a message quickly, without waiting for a message to open all the way. You can use the preview window to read your messages and to perform any other message-specific action.

When you need to open an article in a true article window, double-click the message header. This opens the message in its own window (see Figure 14.6). If a message is a reply, greater than marks (>>) appear in front of the original message's text. As you can see, this message is a reply to a previously posted message that was also a reply.

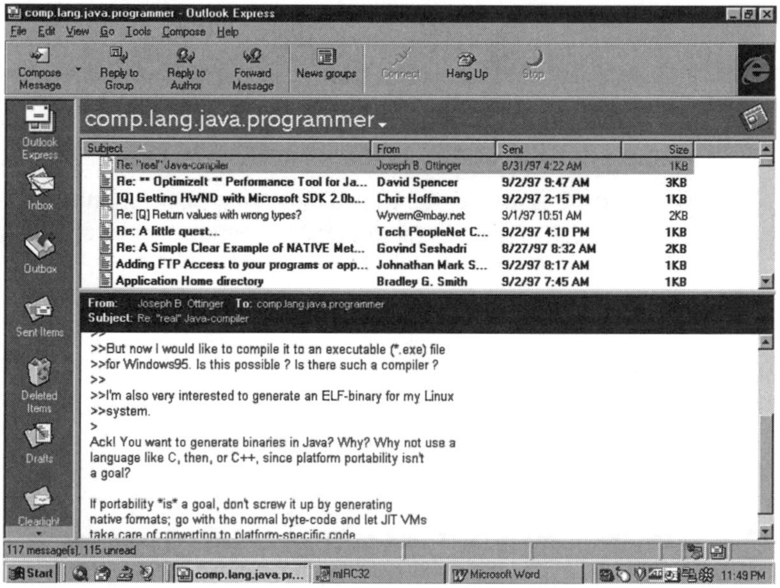

FIGURE 14.6.

The article window showing a message sent to the newsgroup.

Printing Articles

You might read a message and decide that you want to print it to keep on file, for example, or to pass along to a friend. Printing an article is quite easy; just follow these steps:

1. Double-click a message's header to open the message in the message window.

2. Open the File menu and select Print (Ctrl+P).

3. In the Print dialog box, select the printer, number of copies, and print range. Click OK.

> With a message open, you can simply click the Print toolbar button to have the article sent to the currently selected printer.

Threading Articles

A thread is made up of the original message and all responses to that message, chained together to create a flowing conversation. By following a message thread, you can read the original message and everyone's responses to it. Then you can read the responses to the responses until you have read the entire conversation.

In the Outlook Express window, a plus sign next to a message indicates that the message has a thread of responses. You click the plus sign to see the headers of all messages sent as responses to that original message. If any of those responses has generated responses, a plus sign appears next to the first response to show that the thread continues. Again, you click the plus sign to see the next level of responses. A minus sign appears next to a message when you have displayed all of its responses.

To Do: Following a Message Thread

To follow a thread of articles, take these steps:

1. With Outlook Express open, scroll through the messages that you downloaded. Search for one that has a plus sign in front of it. Click that symbol.

2. Scroll through the thread list to see all the responses to the original message (see Figure 14.7). If you see more plus signs, you can click them to expand the thread further.

14

The plus sign (+) notes that the
message is part of an expandable thread

FIGURE 14.7.

*Plus and minus signs
identify a thread—
original messages and
their responses.*

The minus sign (-)
shows that a
message's thread has
been completely
expanded

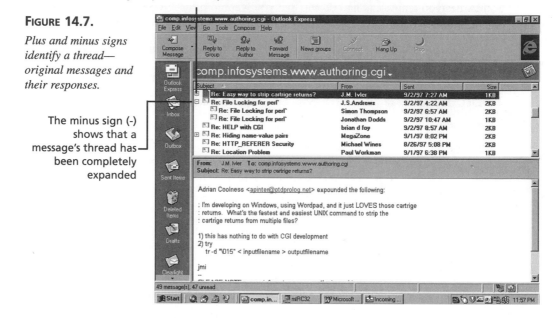

Replying to a Newsgroup

When you want to respond to a news article with a public statement, you respond to the
entire group. This enables everyone, including the casual observer, to read your message.
Posting messages to an entire newsgroup is often the best way to get an answer to your
question.

To Do: Responding to a Newsgroup Article

To respond to an entire newsgroup, perform the following steps:

1. With Outlook Express open, select a message that you have read and on which you
   would like to comment. Click the Reply to Group button. The original message
   opens in the message window.

2. The Newsgroups field automatically displays the original newsgroup's name. The
   Subject field contains the subject of the original message with the reply tag (Re:)
   added, and the cursor appears in the body of the message where you enter your
   comments. Add all the comments that you want.

3. When you finish your message, click the Send button. Outlook Express places a
   copy of your message in the Outbox to be posted to the newsgroup the next time
   you connect to your service provider.

Replying to the Original Author

Sometimes you read something about which you want to talk to the author—and only the author. Maybe you want to clarify a point, or maybe you simply want to get to know that person better because you seem to have a shared interest. No matter the reason, replying to an individual is essentially the same as replying to a group, except that you use the Internet Mail client to send the information.

To Do: Replying Only to the Original Author

Follow these steps to reply to the author:

1. With Outlook Express open, select a message on which you would like to comment. Click the Reply to Author button. The original message opens in a mail window.

2. The To field automatically displays the original newsgroup name. The Subject field contains the subject of the original message with the reply tag (Re:) added, and your cursor appears in the body of the message where you enter your comments. Add any comments that you want.

Because you're legally responsible for email messages in the same way you're responsible for written messages, you need to make sure that your response isn't libelous and that it contains no copyrighted information.

---

3. When you finish your reply, click the Send button. Outlook Express places a copy of your message in the Outbox of the Internet Mail client. The next time you connect to your service provider, the message is mailed to the selected recipients.

▲

Summary

As you made your way through this hour, you've undoubtedly noticed how similar using Outlook Express for newsgroups is to using Outlook Express for email. Having common ground cuts down your learning curve considerably. Now not only do you know how to read and respond to newsgroup articles, but you know exactly how to find groups of interest.

Next hour, we look at a sampling of other Internet activities including searching on the Internet, online chatting, and Internet telephones.

Workshop

The following workshop helps you solidify the skills that you learned in this lesson.

14

Quiz

Take the following quiz to see how much you've learned.

Questions

1. How many newsgroups are there?

    a. 10,000+

    b. 100

    c. 1,000

2. What is a thread?

    a. The cable that hooks your PC to the news server

    b. The ability to place a link to a Web site in a newsgroup post

    c. A news article along with its related responses

3. How do you find newsgroups of interest?

    a. By performing a search using Outlook Express

    b. By clicking your way down through the various newsgroup hierarchies

    c. Both of the above work

Answers

1. a. And the number gets larger by the day!

2. c.

3. c. You can also find useful pointers to newsgroups of interest in specialty magazines and on Web sites dedicated to the topic of interest.

Activity

The challenge of the day: Think about a question you might have or an issue on which you might like input. Now go in search of a newsgroup that might address that issue. When you've found the perfect newsgroup, sit back and lurk awhile—just observe what goes on so that you can determine whether or not your post would be well received. When you're certain you've found the perfect home for your post, get ready to jump in and post it for the world to see.

PART IV

Home Essentials—What You Can Do With It

Hour

Hour 15

Participating in Other Internet Activities

You've learned about Web browsing, email, and newsgroups. What else can you do online? Believe it or not, there are powerful search tools to help you find information on any topic imaginable; there are ways to type back and forth to a friend in "real-time"; there are ways to set up your Web browser to keep you safe online; there are even ways to make free long-distance phone calls over the Internet!

This hour is filled with information about performing searches on the Internet; chatting online; staying secure on the Internet; and an introduction to Internet telephones. In addition, the following questions will be answered:

- Where can I begin my search for information?
- What are these "security zones" I see in Internet Explorer?
- Do I need special software to chat online?
- What's so unusual about Microsoft Chat?
- Is it true you can make free long-distance calls using the Internet?

Starting the Search for Information

After you get comfortable with your new PC, you'll begin to rely on it for all kinds of things. Maybe your daughter just came down with strep throat, and you want to learn more about its treatment and incubation period. Maybe you want to buy a new camcorder, but the salespeople can't give you enough details about each model. Or, how about tracking down that old college friend who swore he was going to take the world by storm?

The World Wide Web is made up of hundreds of thousands of constantly changing Web sites filled with vast amounts of data. How can you find the information you need? Internet Explorer 4.0 gives you quick and easy access to a number of different *search engines* for this very purpose.

NEW TERM *Search engines* are Web sites devoted to cataloging and indexing the World Wide Web. When you submit a search for keywords or a phrase, the search engine returns a list of links to Web pages that are relevant to your search.

Internet Explorer's innovative Search Explorer enables you to see both the list of links returned by your search request and the Web pages connected to those links, as shown in Figure 15.1. With this feature, you can quickly hone in on your information without having to constantly use the Back button to get back to the results list. With Search Explorer, the next site is a simple click away.

FIGURE 15.1.

The Search Explorer lists available search engines.

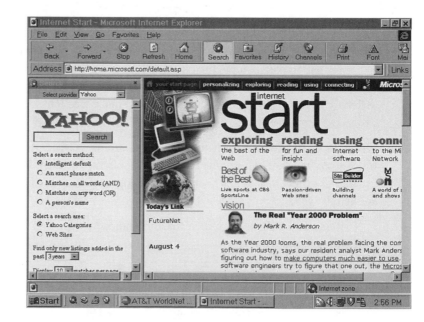

To Do: Using Search Explorer to Find Information

To start a search using Search Explorer, follow these steps:

▼ To Do

1. With Internet Explorer running and an active connection to the Internet, click the Search button on the toolbar. The Search toolbar opens in a frame on the left side of the screen.

2. In the Search box, type the keywords for your search.

3. If you would like to use a particular search engine, open the Select Provider drop-down list and choose a search engine. Currently supported search engines are

   AltaVista (www.altavista.digital.com). Indexes more Web pages than most other services, but does not categorize them.

   Excite (www.excite.com). Searches by concept rather than keyword; Excite includes a directory of reviewed sites.

   HotBot (www.hotbot.com). Has fill-in-the-blank–type boxes for selecting key search criteria such as keywords, dates, and places. You can also search for images and sounds on the Internet.

   Infoseek (www.infoseek.com). Categorizes and includes check marks next to sites that have been reviewed by the staff.

   Lycos (www.lycos.com). Uses WebGuides to highlight specific areas and continuously updates their Top 5% of the Web list.

   Yahoo! (www.yahoo.com). Uses categories more extensively than the other services and includes special local search engines for metropolitan areas.

4. Click the Search button. A list of responses to your search query is returned in the left frame.

5. Move your mouse pointer over the resulting links. If available, a synopsis of the Web page appears.

6. Select a link and click it.

   The selected Web page appears in the right frame as shown in Figure 15.2.

7. To clear the search results and submit a new search, highlight the current keywords and type in your new keywords in the Search box.

▼ 8. To expand the right frame to full-screen, click the Search button.

▼ **FIGURE 15.2.**

The search results on the left frame link to the Web pages on the right.

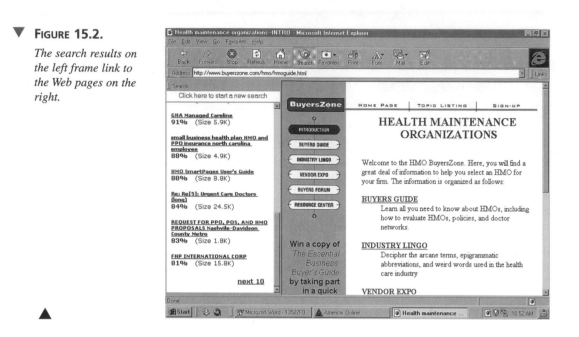

▲

Each search engine has its own style. Try them all to see which one suits you best.

Using Search Engines

Submitting a single keyword for a search will likely result in thousands of responses. It's best to use multiple keywords to narrow your search. For example, "cat" will yield over a million responses; however, "Scottish Fold cat" returns only a handful of responses. The opposite situation—restricting the search too much—can also be a problem. The phrase "travel magazines" returns far fewer responses than "travel magazine" because the former searches only for those sites that indicate they work with multiple publications.

To Do: Setting Up an Effective Search

Follow these steps for better results in searching the Web:

1. Click the Search button in the toolbar.
2. Use the following techniques in any combination to make your search more appropriate:

   Multiple keywords. Search engines look for documents with any of the words specified. Web pages that contain all the keywords are listed first. Example: Maryland gymnastics camp.

▼   *Double quotes.* Use double quotes around a phrase to look for the phrase and not the individual words. Example: "white house." Note that some search engines have drop-down boxes that allow you to search for "any of the words," "exact phrase," "the person," and so on.

Plus sign (+). A plus sign in front of words indicates that the words must be in the Web page, but not necessarily together. Example: +OSHA requirements +CA.

Minus sign (-). A minus sign in front of a word indicates that the word must not be in the Web page. Example: python antidote venom -monty.

Capitalization. Enter all queries in lowercase unless a proper name is desired. Example: "White House."

3. Click Search.

All the search engines have advice for using their particular system better. Go to the search engine's home page and click pages labeled Tips or FAQ (Frequently Asked Questions). You may also see links to advanced queries which guide you through nar-

▲   rowing your search.

> If you want to gain access to some lesser known or more focused search tools, type in the following URL: www.search.com. It has a categorized list for hundreds of search engines that enable you to search recipe databases, medical conditions, and other topics.

Searching by Category

Sometimes, the best way to search for information is to start in a particular category and then enter your keywords. Most of the search engines are organized this way: Yahoo!, Lycos, Infoseek, and Excite are among them.

To Do: Search for a Topic by Category

Follow these steps to search by category:

To Do

1. In the Address bar, type the URL of any of the previously listed search engines.

2. Press Enter.

3. Click any highlighted category. Additional subcategories are listed at the top of the page before the pertinent Web sites.

▲   4. Follow the links through any additional subcategories to your desired topic.

If you find a category page with a number of links that you want to reference, make it a Favorite for quick access. Hour 11, "Using Microsoft Internet
Explorer," explains how to mark any page as a Favorite.

Reexamining Web Sites with the History Explorer

When you're frantically searching for a piece of information, it's easy to forget to save it as a Favorite for future reference. If you were at the Web site earlier in the same session, you can right-click the Back button to choose from a drop-down list of recently visited sites. But what if you were there yesterday or even two weeks ago? Internet Explorer has a new feature that enables you to keep track of—and link to—sites you visited up to three months ago.

The History button is part of the Explorer section on the toolbar, along with Search, Favorites, and Channels. Like those selections, clicking the History button opens a frame on the left side of the screen while keeping your current Web page in a frame on the right.

To Do: Using the History Button

To find a site you previously visited, follow these steps:

1. Click the History button on the toolbar.
2. Choose from one of the days listed in the History frame that opens on the right side of the screen.

    The day chosen expands to show a list of Web sites visited on that day (see Figure 15.3).

3. Click the individual Web site to see a list of Web pages you visited there.
4. Click any individual page to revisit it.

    Internet Explorer displays the selected Web page in the right frame.

5. To close the History frame and expand the right frame to full-screen, click the History button.

You can adjust how many days you want Internet Explorer to track your Web-viewing History. Choose View, Internet Options. On the General tab, change the value in the box next to Days to Keep Pages in History.

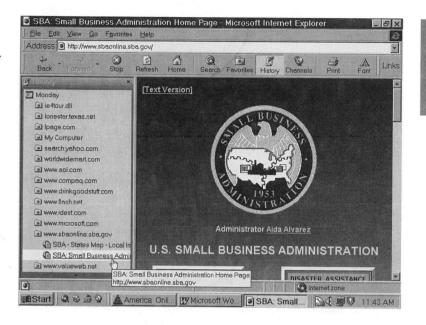

FIGURE 15.3.

You can search your previous Web site visits with the History feature.

Setting Your Security Level

Because the Internet is an interconnected series of networked computers, any information you send can pass through many computers before it reaches your intended destination. This fact gives rise to a number of security concerns—not because there have been a rash of "Information Superhighway robberies," but because the possibility exists that your data (business records, proprietary trade information, or credit-card numbers) might be accessed by unauthorized individuals.

Internet Explorer 4.0 has a wide range of industry-standard security measures in place. For example, most Web sites involving credit-card transactions are run on computers known as secure servers. When Internet Explorer encounters a secure server, a small lock appears in the status bar.

Additionally, before you send information across the Net, Internet Explorer displays an information box telling you that you are about to send information across the Internet, and it may be seen by unauthorized persons. You can opt to go on, or abort your transaction at that point. Likewise, Internet Explorer will alert you that you are about to enter or exit a secure server. You can disable these warnings by clicking the appropriate box located within this warning dialog box.

To keep you even safer, Microsoft has devised a system of security zones because you don't do all your computing with one type of Web site. Some types of network connections can be trusted more than others. Your company intranet, for example, is far more of a known entity than unsolicited email advertisements offering a download too good to be true. You can set different security levels (High, Medium, Low, and Custom) for each zone.

Internet Explorer has four different security zones:

- *Local Intranet*. Defined by your system administrator, this zone incorporates your in-house network connections. The default security level for this zone is Medium.

- *Trusted Sites*. This zone includes sites that you believe to be trustworthy and you are confident enough to download or run files from. You assign the sites to this security zone where the default security level is Low.

- *Restricted Site*. Sites that you deem to be untrustworthy and that you want to prevent from downloading files to your system are grouped in this zone. You assign sites to this security zone where the default security level is High.

- *Internet Zone*. This zone encompasses every site not included in the other security zones. The default security level for this zone is Medium.

To Do: Changing Your Security Settings

To alter the security level settings for any of the zones, follow these steps:

1. Choose View, Internet Options.
2. From the Options dialog box, click the Security tab.
3. From the Security tab as shown in Figure 15.4, select the security zone you want to change from the Zone drop-down list.
4. From the security level area, select one of the following:

   High. Doesn't download certain programs and alerts you to any attempt to do so.

   Medium. Warns of any file attempting to load onto your system.

   Low. Neither warns about, nor avoids, any file download.

   Custom. Enables advanced users and developers to select specific settings for active content and other potential security risks.
5. After you have clicked the option button next to your selection, click OK.
6. Click OK again to close the Options dialog box.

▼ **Figure 15.4.**

The Security tab man-ages Web security.

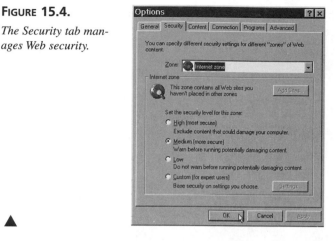

15

▲

Assigning Web Sites to a Security Zone

Two of the security zones depend on you to add Web sites to their lists. Both Trusted Sites and Restricted Sites are completely user-defined.

To Do: Assigning a Web Site to a Security Zone

To assign a Web site to a security zone, follow these steps:

1. From the View menu, select Options.

2. From the Options dialog box, click the Security tab.

3. Select either Trusted Sites or Restricted Sites in the Zone box by clicking the option arrow. The Add Sites button becomes active.

4. Click the Add Sites button.

5. From the Trusted Sites Zone (or Restricted Sites Zone) dialog box, as shown in Figure 15.5, type the URL for the Web site you would like to assign in the Add this Web Site to the Zone box. You must use the complete URL—for instance, http://www.microsoft.com.

6. After you have typed in the complete URL, click the Add button. The URL appears in the Web Sites box.

7. To clear an URL from the list, select it and click the Remove button.

8. Click the OK button when you have finished assigning your Web sites.

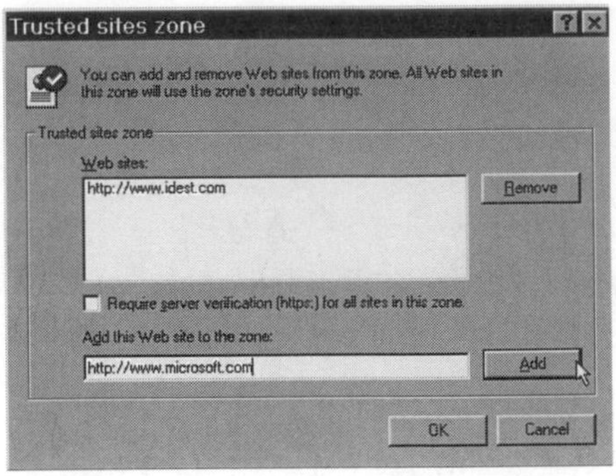

▼ **FIGURE 15.5.**

You can assign Web sites to either the Trusted or Restricted Sites Security Zones.

▲

Web-Based Chat

Whether you frequent a soap-opera Web site or one dedicated to NASCAR racing, you're bound to run across sites hosting real-time chats.

NEW TERM Unlike email where you see a period of time elapse between communication, *real-time chat* allows people to chat with others live about a given topic. It's like talking on the phone, only you type messages to others instead of speak.

So how do you participate in these Web chats? Luckily, you don't even need special software (except for your Web browser of course). Typically, you'll follow a link on the Web site's home page to its chat area. After you get there, you may be presented with a code of conduct for the site. This code basically tells chatters to be considerate of others, stay on-topic, and so on. It'll vary with each site. Then, you may be asked to provide your email address (usually for the host site's information only). Finally, you'll be asked to choose a screen name—a name that other chatters will know you by, thus protecting your privacy.

Each site operates a bit differently, but no need to worry: You'll find plenty of onscreen prompts to guide you through the process.

Introducing Microsoft Chat

Microsoft Chat is the only Internet chat program that gives you the ability to converse inside a comic strip. That's right, you can become your own comic-strip star complete with an "emotion wheel" to modify your facial expressions and gestures. What's more, your conversation appears as word balloons or thought bubbles inside a comic strip. You even get to choose your character's background scene. But if you happen to be chatting with others using different software, you can easily turn off comic-strip mode so your messages will be understood by all.

Microsoft Chat has some other unique features: You can "whisper" (send a private message) to other chat participants, play a sound file, and even save your comic strip for offline viewing and printing. You also have the opportunity to define a self profile which provides other chatters who request it information about you, such as hobbies, email address, Web page address, and so on.

To launch Microsoft Chat, press Start, select Programs, Internet Explorer, Microsoft Chat. You'll see a dialog box like the one shown in Figure 15.6.

FIGURE 15.6.

Microsoft Chat's Connect dialog box asks you to select the chat server you'd like to visit.

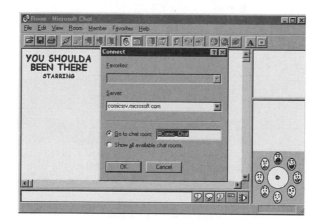

After you've logged on to a Microsoft Chat server, you'll see a viewing area with the following parts:

- A toolbar across the top of the screen with buttons for entering/exiting a chat room, creating your own chat room, and so on.

- A viewing pane where the conversation is displayed.

- A member list pane that lists all the people in a chat room.

- A compose pane (a text box at the bottom of the window) where you type your messages.

- A row of buttons to the right of the compose pane that lets you specify the way your communication should be passed on—for instance, Say, Think, Whisper, Action, or Play a Sound.

- A "starring" pane that displays the title of the chat and lists the participants (this particular pane is only visible when you're working in comic-strip mode).

- A self-view pane that shows what your character looks like (comic-strip mode only).

- An emotion wheel that enables you to control all your character's emotions (comic-strip mode only).

Figure 15.7 shows you what this workspace will look like.

FIGURE 15.7.

The Microsoft Chat workspace is where the chat happens.

Microsoft Chat toolbar

Conversations are displayed here

Chat member list is printed here

See what you look like here

Define your character's emotion here

Enter your text here

Specify whether the text is said, thought, or acted here

Here are some additional things to keep in mind when using Microsoft Chat:

- *Create Your Personal Profile.* Select View, Options, Personal Info from the pull-down menus to begin creating your personal profile for other chatters. Remember that anyone in the chat room who wants to see it can, so be judicious about what you put in there.

- *Get a New Body.* Select View, Options, Character to search for a new identity. You can even use the emotion wheel to test what that character would look like with each expression. (Just click the dot and drag it to the desired emotion.)

- *Adjust the Size of the Comic Strip Displayed.* Select View, Options, Comics View to specify the number of frames you want displayed on each line. You can also change the font type for comic text in this tab.

- *Getting Around the Easy Way.* Use the toolbar at the top of the viewing pane to jump to another chatter's Web site, send a whispered message, or request a personal profile.

What You Can Expect From Internet Phones

15

If real-time chat doesn't quite do it for you, you might be interested in learning a little more about Internet telephones.

Let's begin by separating fact from fiction. It is true you can use these products to talk to virtually anyone, anywhere in the world, provided that person also has a computer using the same or a compatible Internet phone product. And you can make "free" phone calls, provided you have purchased a computer, a sound card, a microphone, speakers, and an Internet connection. Those "free" phone calls can have a startup cost of around a thousand dollars or more.

But if you already happen to have a computer connected to the Internet, and you also happen to have a sound card along with the usual accompanying accouterments (microphone and speakers), then all you need is the right software and you can begin talking to friends and acquaintances who have similar setups.

In fact, the most common video Internet telephones today are packaged with the necessary software and a small camera used to capture your picture. The packages usually cost around $300, but that cost can be made up in no time by the money you save by not having to pay for your long-distance phone calls.

NEW TERM Computers use *standards* to define common ways of communicating with one another. It's always best to use a computer product based on a standard whenever possible because venders will adopt the standard down the road.

How Good Is the Sound Quality?

How good your sound quality will be depends on a lot of factors: how good your sound card and speakers are, the speed of your Internet connection, and most importantly, the software you use to make your Internet phone calls. Some products do a reasonably good job of transmitting the human voice over the Internet. You won't get CD-quality sound, but you can get decent phone-quality sound.

Check it Out!

Want to learn more about the various products available? Fire up your Web browser, surf over to www.zdnet.com, and search for Internet phones. At the time this book went to press, the following products were highly acclaimed by computer professionals:

- Supra Video Phone Kit 3000
- AVer TV-Phone
- US Robotics Bigpicture Video Camera and Capture Card

Summary

In this hour, you rounded out your Internet education by learning about search engines, online chatting, Internet security, and Internet telephones. The Internet gives you a wide variety of ways to stay in touch with friends and family, whether it's the relative simplicity of email or the complexity of a comic-strip chat hosted by Microsoft.

This chapter concludes the Internet section of the book. In the next section, you will begin learning about the various software programs commonly included with new PCs.

Workshop

The following workshop helps you solidify the skills you learned in this lesson.

Quiz

Take the following quiz to see how much you've learned.

Questions

1. Which group of words would focus a search most narrowly?

    a. Auto Racing

    b. NASCAR Terry Labonte

    c. NASCAR

2. Which item is not an Internet Explorer security zone?

    a. Web Zone

    b. Internet Zone

    c. Local Intranet Zone

3. Which of the following products can be used to make Internet telephone calls?

    a. Supra Video Phone Kit 3000

    b. AltaVista

    c. Microsoft Chat

Answers

1. b. Auto racing is the broadest, followed by NASCAR, then the correct answer, b.

2. a. This choice may sound like an authentic security zone, but it's not.

3. a. AltaVista is a search engine, and Microsoft Chat is, of course, a chat program.

Activity

For this activity, I'd like you to think of a focused search that you'd like to perform. After you've settled on a search topic, try searching on it using the following search engines:

- HotBot at www.hotbot.com
- Excite at www.Excite.com
- Lycos at www.lycos.com

The first time around, perform the search using each search engine's default settings. In other words, don't change a thing. Also be sure that the words are in the same order for each search.

Review the results to see if the best sites really do come to the top, and if you like the way results are presented. After you've made note of the search engines' differences and similarities, feel free to play around with some advanced searches. By the time you're finished, you'll surely start to prefer one search engine over another.

15

Hour **16**

Microsoft Word 97 Essentials

Technically, Word is considered a word processor. Although it does a superior job at that, it's really so much more than a word processor. Word can create Web pages loaded with hyperlinks, and it can even produce newsletters that would push the capabilities of many small desktop publishing programs. As a home user, Word 97 can be the application of choice for doing any of the following:

- Producing a professional-looking resume
- Creating a brochure for your son's nursery school fundraiser
- Drafting a college admissions letter

No matter what the written task, Word can come through with professional-quality results in an amazingly short period of time.

Because the majority of PCs sold today come with Word 97 pre-installed, I'm dedicating two hours of this book to showing you the ins and outs of this powerful application.

In this hour, you learn the basic functions of Word 97 from the anatomy of its workspace to the various ways of printing a Word 97 document. In addition, you'll learn the answers to the following questions:

- What are the various parts of Word's workspace called, and what do they do?
- How do I insert and delete text?
- Help! How can I undo a change I've made to my document?
- Is there an easy way to select large blocks of text?
- Do I have to launch Word 97 in order to print a document?

Before You Get Started...

When working with Word 97, you should know a few things from the start. First, virtually anything created in Word 97 is referred to as a "document." As such, Word 97 files are saved with the .doc file extension unless you deliberately specify otherwise.

Secondly, keep in mind that Word 97 behaves just like any other Windows application. Throughout the second part of this book, "Working with Windows," you've learned how to launch an application, how to reposition and customize toolbars, and so on. Much of this applies to Word 97 as well as the other applications covered in the Home Essentials part of the book.

> In case you need a reminder, all you have to do to launch Word 97 is click Start on the Windows taskbar, then select Programs, Microsoft Word 97.

Finally, because Word uses many toolbars and commands found in other Microsoft applications (including FrontPage Express and Microsoft Works 4.5, which you'll read about later), you'd be wise to soak in everything in this hour even if you don't plan to work extensively with Word.

Anatomy of the Word 97 Workspace

Knowing Word 97's screen elements will go a long way toward helping you unleash its power. Figure 16.1 points out all of the critical elements.

Title bar | Menu bar | Standard toolbar | Formatting toolbar | Ruler

FIGURE 16.1.

This figure points out each of the critical Word 97 screen elements.

Insertion point —

End of File marker —

Mouse pointer —

View buttons —

Status bar —

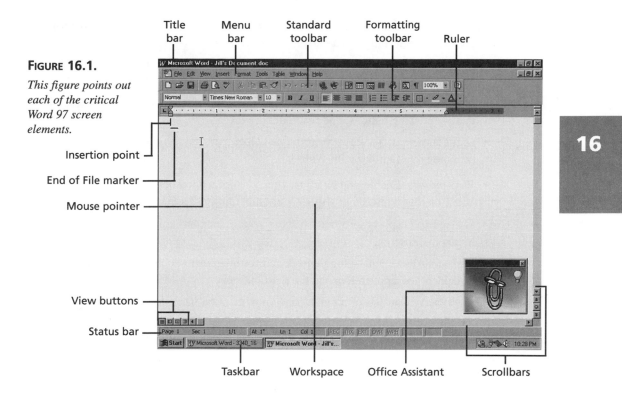

16

Taskbar | Workspace | Office Assistant | Scrollbars

So what do each of these elements do? The quick answer follows, but many of these functions will be explored in greater detail later in the hour.

- *Title bar.* Contains the name of the program and the name of the document, as well as the Maximize, Minimize, Restore, and Close (X) buttons.

- *Menu bar.* Allows you to select from a variety of pull-down menus needed to execute commands in Word 97.

- *Standard toolbar.* Holds shortcut buttons to quickly execute common tasks such as printing, opening a new document, and so on. This toolbar may be modified to meet your specific needs. (For more on customizing toolbars, see Hour 4, "Working with Menus, Toolbars, and Dialog Boxes.")

- *Formatting toolbar.* Presents buttons to quickly format text as you work. Selections include font (Courier, Times-New Roman), font size (expressed in point size 12, 24), text alignment (center, align left, justify), and font style (bold, underline).

- *Ruler.* Provides a quick and easy way to guide the setting of tabs and indents in your documents.

- *Insertion point*. Shows you where the text or graphics will be placed. In other programs, it is referred to as a cursor.
- *End of File marker*. Indicates the end of a document with a short, horizontal line. You cannot move past this point.
- *Mouse pointer*. Moves onscreen as you move the mouse to assist you in accessing menus, clicking buttons, and manipulating text.
- *Office Assistant*. Serves as your online helper. Ask it questions or turn it off as you become more familiar with Word 97.
- *View buttons*. Enable you to adjust your view of a document. Choose from Normal View, Outline View, Page Layout View, and Outline Layout View.
- *Status bar*. Displays information about your document including page count, line number, and so on.
- *Taskbar*. Allows you to toggle back and forth between documents already open, or to launch new applications via the Start button.
- *Workspace*. Consists of a blank page on which you insert text and graphics.
- *Scrollbars*. Move you quickly around a document. Either slide them with your mouse (point to the scroll box, hold down the left button, and drag), or click either side of the box for larger jumps.

If you ever forget what one of these elements is, just rest your mouse pointer over it. A yellow ScreenTip box appears, naming the element in question.

Word 97 Document Defaults

What is a document default? Basically, unless you tell it otherwise, Word 97 automatically assigns certain attributes to a new document. These attributes are referred to as default settings. In the case of Word 97, the application sets page margins, tab stops, and page orientation. Luckily, these settings are pretty standard, so even if you don't define them yourself, you'll be okay.

Every application has default settings that tell the program how to do things even if you happen to forget. For example, Internet Explorer uses a Microsoft home page as its start page unless you select another one.

Word 97's default document settings are listed in Table 16.1.

TABLE 16.1. WORD 97 DOCUMENT DEFAULTS.

Setting	Value
Left/Right Margins	1.25 inches
Top/Bottom Margins	1 inch
Tab Stops	Every 1/2 inch
Page Orientation	Portrait
Font	Times-New Roman
Text Alignment	Align Left

16

Creating a New Document

You can create a new Word document in a number of ways. The way you select will vary depending on your specific document requirements and situation. See Table 16.2 for a quick overview of these methods.

TABLE 16.2. HOW TO CREATE A WORD DOCUMENT.

Use This Method	To Get This Result
Launch Word 97	To get a blank document page using the default settings.
Click the New icon at the far left of the Standard toolbar	To get a blank document page using the default settings. This can be used to create a new document while you're working with an existing document.
Select File, New	To select from a variety of Word 97 templates and wizards. (More about templates and wizards in the next hour.)

Opening an Existing Document

If you need to go back and edit an existing document, how do you do it? You can launch Word 97 and select File, Open, then browse through the various directories on your system until you find the document you're looking for.

If you've recently worked on the document, you have two other options. From within Word, select File and look toward the bottom of the pull-down menu. You'll see the file-names of four of the most recently accessed Word documents. With the left mouse button held down, move the mouse until the desired file is highlighted. Release the button and Word will load the specified document.

You can also find a recently accessed Word document even before you launch Word 97. On the Windows taskbar, click Start, and then click Documents. A list of 15 of the most recently accessed documents appears. Select the desired file by holding the mouse button, highlighting the file's name, then releasing the mouse button. Word will now launch with the requested document rather than a blank document page.

Inserting Text into Word 97

When you launch Word 97 or create a new document, the cursor (or insertion point, as it's often called) blinks in the first position on the page. Simply begin typing to enter the desired text. If you've ever used a typewriter, you won't find working with a word processor much different except that it's far more forgiving of potential errors. You won't need gobs of White-Out to cover your typos—a simple backspace will do.

To insert text in an existing Word document, point your mouse to the desired location, click once to set the insertion point in place, and then begin typing.

Deleting Text

You may delete Word 97 text in one of three ways:

- Use the Delete key to delete characters to the right of the insertion point.
- Use the Backspace key to delete characters to the left of the insertion point.
- Select a block of text (see the section on selecting text in Word later in the hour), then press Delete.

If you delete the wrong block of text or a few more words than you had intended to, don't panic. Word 97 has a great Undo feature that can come to the rescue. Just click the Undo Typing icon (the left-pointing arrow) on the Standard toolbar, or press Ctrl+Z (the Control key and the Z key simultaneously). For those who love working with menus, select Edit, Undo.

Selecting Blocks of Text

Another neat thing about using a word processor is that you can change large blocks of text at one time. Want to make the title of your paper a larger type size, make a certain sentence bold, or center a line of text? To do it quickly, select the desired amount of text, and then perform the chosen operation (that is, clicking the Bold button, changing the font, and so on).

In the sections that follow, you'll learn all the text-selecting tricks Word has to offer.

Selecting Text with the Mouse

Table 16.3 shows multiple ways to select a block of text with a mouse.

16

TABLE 16.3. SELECTING TEXT BLOCKS WITH THE MOUSE.

To Select This	Do This
Word	Double-click inside the word.
Sentence	Ctrl+click inside the sentence.
Paragraph	Triple-click inside the paragraph.
Graphic/image	Click the graphic/image.
Entire document	Move mouse pointer to the left of the text until it turns into an arrow as pictured in Figure 16.2, and then triple-click.
Vertical text block	Hold down the Alt key and drag the mouse over the text.
Large text blocks	Move the mouse pointer to the left of the text until it becomes an arrow, then click the left mouse button and drag the mouse until the desired block of text is highlighted.

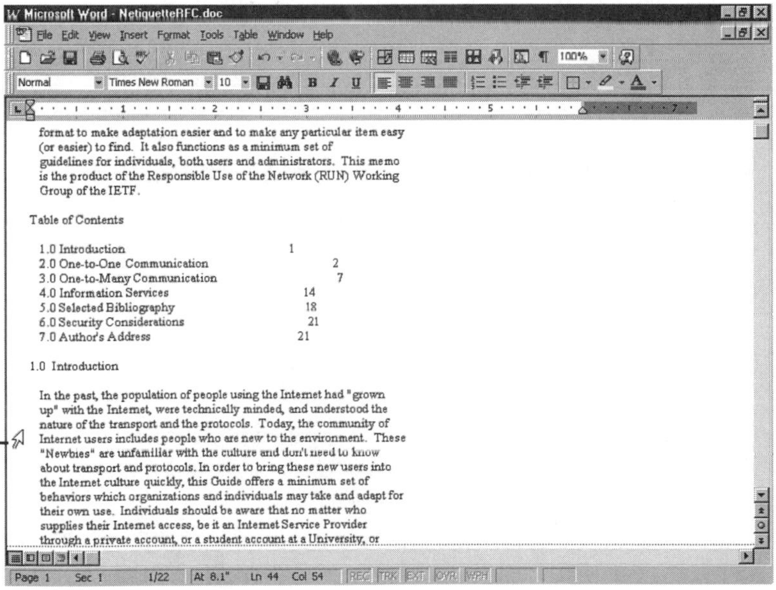

FIGURE 16.2.

Point the mouse to the left margin of the document to turn the mouse pointer into an arrow, and then select text as directed in Table 16.3.

Mouse arrow ———

Selecting Text Blocks with the Keyboard

Some people prefer to work with the keyboard instead of the mouse whenever possible. If you're one of those people, you'll be interested in Table 16.4, the listing of shortcut keys for selecting blocks of text.

TABLE 16.4. KEYBOARD SHORTCUTS FOR SELECTING TEXT.

To Select This	Do This
One character at a time to the left of the insertion point—repeat until the desired number of characters is highlighted.	Shift+left arrow
One character at a time to the right of the insertion point—repeat until the desired number of characters is highlighted.	Shift+right arrow
The insertion point to the beginning of the current word—keep pressing the arrow key to select additional words to the left.	Shift+Ctrl+left arrow
The insertion point to the end of the current word—keep pressing the arrow key to select additional words to the right.	Shift+Ctrl+right arrow
The insertion point to the same position in the previous line.	Shift+up arrow
The insertion point to the same position in the following line.	Shift+down arrow
The insertion point to the beginning of the current paragraph.	Shift+Ctrl+up arrow
The insertion point to the beginning arrow of the next paragraph.	Shift+Ctrl+down
The insertion point to the beginning of the document.	Shift+Ctrl+Home
The insertion point to the end of the document.	Shift+Ctrl+End

Manipulating Selected Text

As mentioned earlier, it's easy to perform a number of major operations on a block of text after it has been selected. In the sections that follow, you'll see how you can dramatically alter the appearance of a document with just a few clicks of the mouse.

Changing Character Fonts

It's amazing how much a well-suited font can enhance a message you're trying to convey. Whether it's the crisp, easy-to-read appearance of Times New Roman for a term paper, or the flowing elegance of Palace Script for the text of a formal invitation, fonts can enhance the appearance of your text.

To choose a new font in Word 97, select the text you want to modify, and then click the arrow next to the Font text box (the second text box from the left on the Formatting toolbar). You'll see a sizable list of fonts from which to choose. With your left mouse button depressed, slide down the list until you spot the font you want to use. After that font is highlighted, release the mouse button. The selected text appears in the chosen font.

> One or two carefully chosen fonts can make quite an impression, but a hodgepodge of random fonts thrown into one document screams amateur. Not only that, it's plain tacky. Impressions aside, you should be aware that some of those nifty-looking fonts can be hard to read in the smaller font sizes.

Change the size of the selected text via the font size text box (located immediately to the right of the font box). Just click the arrow to choose from a type size listed, or click inside the text box to enter a type size manually.

Because making text bold, italic, or even underlined is so common, Word 97 comes with those buttons easily accessible on its Formatting toolbar. Just select the text, click one of the three buttons, and your text is transformed!

Aligning Text

Word 97 text can be aligned four ways—flush left (as this book is), centered, flush right, and justified (stretched out or pushed together to make both margins even). To align your text any of these ways, select the block of text and click the appropriate icon on the toolbar as shown in Figure 16.3. See Figure 16.4 for a sample of how text would look formatted each of the four ways.

Relocating Text

There are things about using a word processor that will spoil you so badly, you'll never want to touch a typewriter again as long as you live. In addition to being able to do all the neat things you've seen earlier in the hour, Word 97 gives you ways to take chunks of text and move it wherever you want it with minimal hassle. Try doing that with a typewriter!

There are two primary methods for moving text: cut and paste, and drag and drop.

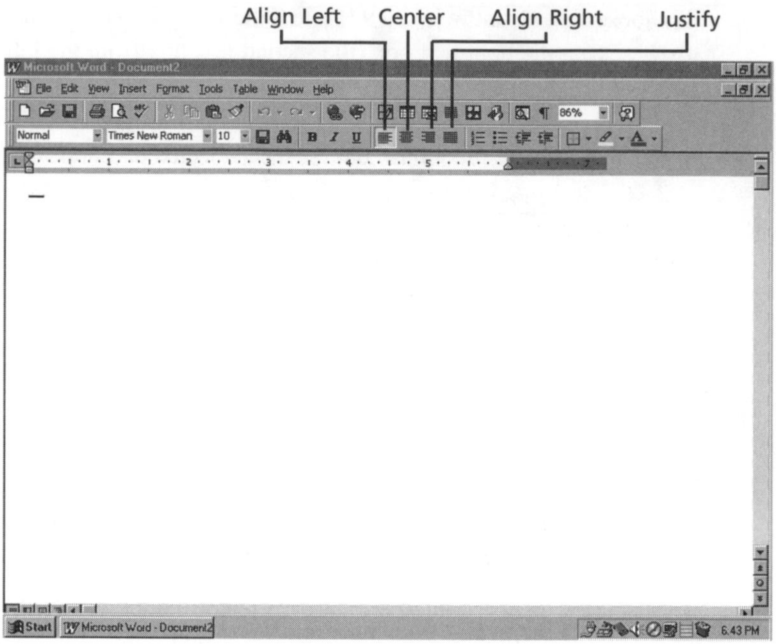

Align Left   Center   Align Right   Justify

FIGURE 16.3.

*Click any of these but-
tons to instantly
realign your selected
block of text after the
text has been selected.*

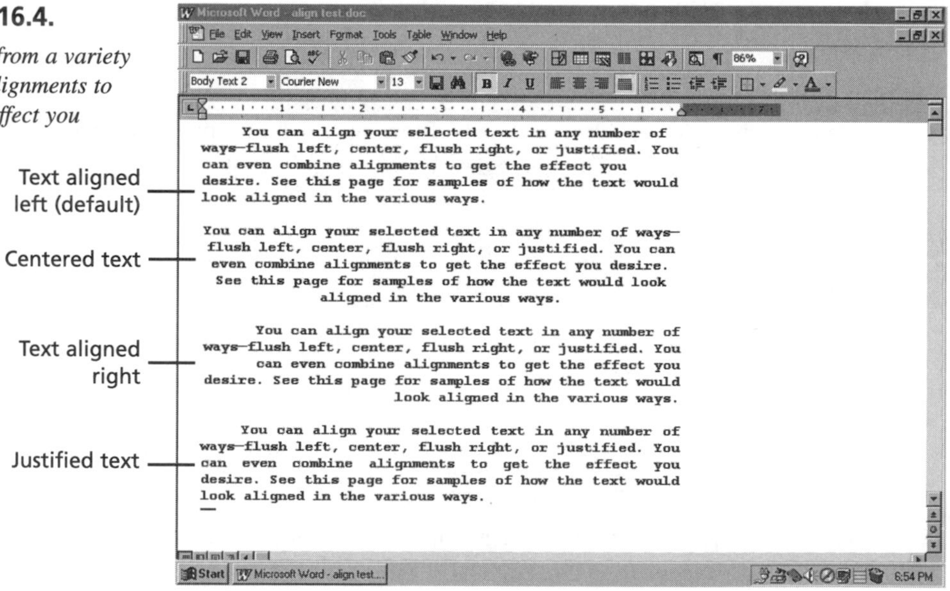

FIGURE 16.4.

*Choose from a variety
of text alignments to
get the effect you
desire.*

Text aligned
left (default)

Centered text

Text aligned
right

Justified text

To Do: Cutting and Pasting Text

One of the most popular ways to move text in Word is to cut and paste it. Just follow these easy steps:

1. Select the text you want to move.

2. Click the Cut button (the scissors) on the Formatting toolbar. The text will disappear from your screen, but don't panic; Word 97 has it safely stored on a virtual clipboard until you're ready to place it.

3. Click the mouse button on the location you'd like to place the text to set the insertion point.

4. Click the Paste button on the Formatting toolbar. The selected text will appear in its new position.

> Say you took this incredible vacation and wrote a lengthy letter to Aunt Bonnie telling her all about it. Now your grandmother wants to hear all about it. With Word 97, you don't have to worry about writing the letter all over again. You can open the letter to Aunt Bonnie, select the text you want to include in your grandmother's letter, click the Copy (instead of Cut) button on your Formatting toolbar, and then Paste it into the letter you started to your grandmother.

To Do: Dragging and Dropping Text

If you have to move a small chunk of text only a short distance, you may want to use drag and drop. This method works best when all the text and its destination appear onscreen.

1. Select the block of text as illustrated earlier.

2. Place the mouse pointer in the middle of the highlighted text and then hold down the left mouse button.

3. While holding the left mouse button down, drag the text to its new location and release the button.

Saving Word 97 Documents

In Hour 7, "Using Windows 98 Applications," you learned about saving documents. There are a few pointers you should keep in mind when working with Word, or any other application for that matter:

- SAVE, SAVE, SAVE!!! You never know when a summer thunderstorm will knock out your power, or a prowling cat will loosen the power cord from its socket. Either of these things will give your system the hiccups, so it's always wise to save your work often.

- Give your documents descriptive filenames. This will save you oodles of time when trying to track down that one document you just gotta have. Instead of saving a document as "letter.doc", try something more specific such as "UMass app letter.doc". That way, you'll be able to find that all-important college application cover letter in a snap.

- When trying to locate an older Word file on your system, be sure you're looking for files with the .doc extension. Some file-browsing windows open with only a certain type of system file specified. For example if you try to search for a Word document while working on your Web page in FrontPage Express, you might be out of luck at first because the program will automatically look for .htm or .html files. You can easily rectify this by modifying the Files of type box. Just click the arrow next to the box and make sure All files is specified.

What if you have WordPerfect at work, but Word at home? Word 97 makes it easy to exchange files with minimal (if any) loss of formatting. Word reads files from various versions of Microsoft Works, WordPerfect, and earlier versions of Word. You can work at home in Word, save your edited document as a WordPerfect file (by clicking the Save as Type drop-down arrow in the Save As dialog box), and then take the file back to work.

Preview Before You Print

To make sure you'll get the output you expect when printing your documents, consider using Print Preview. To do this, click File, Print Preview, or select the Print Preview icon on the Standard toolbar. To close the preview, click the Close button on the Print Preview toolbar. See an example of Print Preview in Figure 16.5.

Printing a Word Document from Within Word 97

Perhaps the most common way to print a document involves using the File, Print command.

FIGURE 16.5.

With Print Preview, you can see what you'll get before you print it.

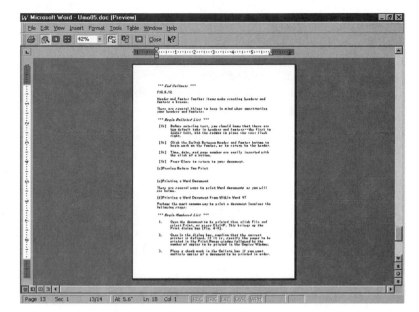

16

To Do: Printing a Document from Word

To print a document from within the Word Print dialog box, complete the following steps:

1. Open the document to be printed, then click File and select Print; or press Ctrl+P. This brings up the Print dialog box (see Figure 16.6).

FIGURE 16.6.

The Print dialog box gives users full control of their output.

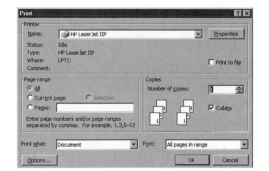

2. In the dialog box, confirm that the correct printer is defined. If it is, specify the pages to be printed in the Print Range window followed by the number of copies to be printed in the Copies window.

▼

3. Place a check mark in the Collate box if you want multiple copies of a document to be printed in order.

4. In a majority of cases, the Print What and Print boxes will be left on their default settings. It should be noted, however, that Word 97 gives its users the flexibility to print just about any part of a document, including

- *All Pages*. This is the default.

- *Current Page*. Be sure you know where the insertion point is set, because Word will print that current page, not the one you may have scrolled to.

- *Pages*. Specify a group of pages separated by a comma (for example, 1,3,5 to print those odd-numbered pages), or select a range such as 5–10 to print that group of pages.

▲

- *Odd or Even*. Click the Print drop-down box to have Word print only the even or odd pages.

> Need just one copy of the document as it appears? Sidestep the Print dialog box by clicking the Print icon on the toolbar. A single copy of the document will be ready in no time.

Printing a Word 97 Document Without Launching Word 97

If you're in a hurry to print a copy of a Word file and don't have Word 97 up and running, you now have an alternative.

To Do: Printing a Document Without Running Word

▼ To Do

1. From the Windows taskbar, click Start and select Open Office Document. The Open Office Document dialog box appears.

2. Locate the Word document you want to print, then click the Commands and Settings icon at the top-right side of the box.

3. Select Print from the pop-up menu, and you're all set without even having to run Word 97.

▲

Closing and Exiting the Document

Now that you're finished with all that hard work, you'll want to know how to close the document and exit Word 97.

First, if you plan to exit the program altogether, there's no need to close the document beforehand. Just save your work, then exit Word by selecting File, Exit, or by double-clicking the program icon in the upper-left corner of the Word 97 screen.

Should you decide to close the current document and go on to another Word document, select File, Close.

Summary

In this hour, you became acquainted with the Word 97 workspace and basic functions. You essentially learned everything you needed to do create a document, modify its text, save it, and print it.

In the next hour, you'll have the opportunity to play with some of the more advanced Word features.

Workshop

The following workshop helps you solidify the skills you learned in this lesson.

Quiz

Take the following quiz to see how much you've learned.

Questions

1. Which two methods can be used to select text in Word?

    a. Mouse

    b. Keystrokes

    c. Text Selection Icon (TSI)

2. How many fonts should you use in a single Word document?

    a. As many as humanly possible. It demonstrates your superior creativity.

    b. Never more than one.

    c. No more than four per page.

3. Word 97 documents can be printed only if Word 97 is up and running:

    a. True

    b. False

16

Answers

1. a. and b. The Text Selection Icon sounds good, but, unfortunately, it doesn't exist.

2. c. One font can make a document boring, but too many can be downright tacky.

3. b. It is possible to print a single copy of the document from the Windows desktop without ever launching Word 97.

Activity

Launch Word 97 and type your name on the blank page. Select the entire name using whichever method comes most natural to you.

Click the drop-down arrow next to the Font text box to see which fonts are currently available on your machine. Pick a few that look interesting, and apply them to your name. How do they look? Are they legible? What does that particular font say about you? Is it playful or formal? Try this with several different fonts.

Now play with the type size. Verify that your name is still selected, click the drop-down arrow and test a few of the sizes. Is 8-point type too hard to read? Can your entire name fit on one line if you use a 48-point font? Is 72-point type really as big as it sounds?

Hour **17**

Unleashing the Power of Microsoft Word 97

Now that you have the basics under your belt, it's time to take a look at some of the more advanced features of Word 97—the very features that enable you to produce documents with pizzazz and professionalism. In this hour, you find the answers to these questions among others:

- How do I set tabs and margins in Word 97?
- Can I create a fancy bulleted list from an unformatted list already residing in a Word document?
- Is Word 97 capable of producing nice-looking tables?
- What do I do to include clip art in my documents?
- Why are headers and footers so useful?

Setting Up Your Page Layout

As you discovered in the last hour, Word 97 automatically sets margins for you when you create a new document. Sometimes, however, the default margins may not be optimal. Perhaps you want to have your term paper bound, but doing so makes a paper printed using the default settings look off-center. Maybe your letter has only one stray line flowing over onto a second page, prompting you to tweak the settings a hair. Maybe you're even trying to do something creative with paper of an unusual size. Whatever the case, you want to be familiar with Word 97's Page Setup tabs.

To Do: Setting New Margins

To change your margins, do the following:

1. From within a Word document, select File, Page Setup.

2. If the Margins tab doesn't appear, click its title to activate it.

3. After you're in the Margins tab, you see four text boxes in which to define each of the margins—top, bottom, left, and right. To modify one that you want, click inside the box to activate it. Repeat this for each margin that you want to set.

> You can either enter the numbers manually or click the up or down arrows to alter the size. If you're like me and can't picture precise measurements in your head, Word 97 gives you a nice big preview window to see what you're getting before you do anything radical.

4. Specify whether you want the newly set margins to apply from this point on in the document, or for the whole document. To do this, click the drop-down arrow next to the box beneath the Preview window and highlight your choice.

5. When you've made the desired changes, click OK to apply them.

Defining the Paper Size and Orientation

If you find the need to work with anything other than an 8 1/2-by-11-inch piece of paper in portrait mode, you'll want to check out the Paper Size tab.

To Do: Defining a Page's Orientation

To define the orientation of a page or a nontraditional size of paper, follow these steps:

1. Open the document that you want to modify, or create a new document if necessary.

2. Select File, Page Setup, and choose the Paper Size tab.

3. Click the drop-down arrow next to the Paper Size text box to choose from some of the more standard-sized paper and envelopes. If you don't see the size of paper

▼ with which you want to work, select Custom size from the list, and enter the
   dimensions in the height and width boxes.

4. Click Portrait or Landscape to define the page's orientation. Note that Word
   assumes portrait.

5. Click the Apply To drop-down arrow to define whether the page orientation should
   apply to the entire document (the default) or be carried out from this point forward.

6. Approve your selections by looking in the Preview window. If everything looks
▲ okay, click OK to apply the new settings.

Setting Tabs in Word

As a default, Word sets a left tab every half inch, which meets your needs a majority of
the time. You can, however, set four different types of tabs in Word—left, right, center, or
decimal. The center and right tabs are useful for advanced formatting, such as centering
column headers for a table, and so on. Decimal tabs (see Figure 17.1) are best used to
line up columns of numbers.

17

FIGURE 17.1.

*The decimal tab can
bring order to the
chaos of numbers.*

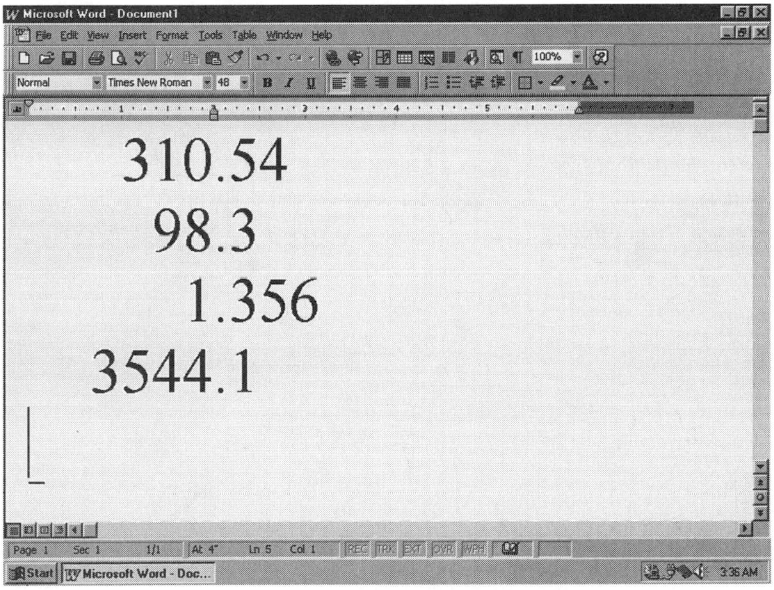

To Do: Setting Tabs

To set tabs, do the following:

1. Make sure the ruler is displayed at the top of your Word workspace. If it isn't, you may retrieve it by selecting View, Ruler.

2. Select the text that you want to format using the tabs. To have them apply to the whole document, just triple-click the left margin.

> Be sure you select the text to which you want to apply the tab before setting it, or the setting applies only to the paragraph containing the insertion point.

3. Click the Tab button (see Figure 17.2) until you see the icon of the tab that you want to create.

4. Click the ruler to set the location of the chosen tab.

5. If the tab already exists, you can move it by dragging it to the new location.

6. To delete a tab, drag it on to the workspace.

FIGURE 17.2.

Use the Tab button to select the desired type of tab.

Tab Button ─

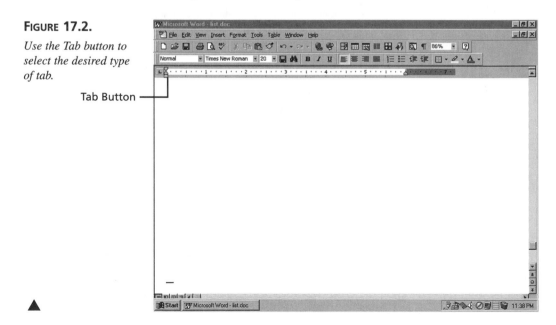

Using Lists to Add Style to Your Documents

You can use bullets or numbers to draw attention to your lists.

To Do: Creating a List from the Beginning

To create either kind of list from the beginning (where no text exists), follow these steps:

1. Type the text leading up to the list as desired.

2. When you're ready to create the list, place the insertion point at the location you'd like the list to appear.

3. Click the Numbered or Bullets button on the Formatting toolbar.

4. Type each section of text and then press the Enter key to set up subsequent bulleted or numbered sections.

▲ When the list is complete, press Enter, and click the Numbering or Bullets button again to turn off the formatting.

> To set your lists off even further, insert tabs before the list.

Generating a List from Existing Text

Maybe you've previously typed a list into Word, but would like to use your newfound knowledge to actually make it look good. To do so, select the text to be turned into a list, and click the desired list button on the Standard toolbar. Keep in mind that each list entry must be followed by a hard return (pressing the Enter key); otherwise, the items are all placed on a single list entry. This requires you to insert returns after you have formatted the list. So, if you were hoping to turn that long list of names separated by commas into a fancy list, you need to go back in and add the returns. Sorry. Word's smart, but not quite that smart.

> Looking for something a little flashier than the typical bullets or numbered lists? Try selecting Format, Bullets and Numbering. You are presented with three tabs from which you can select a variety of bulleted and numbered list formats. If you're really adventurous, you can even create your own!

17

Building a Simple Word Table

Tables can be an excellent way to emphasize important information within a document. Although Word 97 offers some pretty glitzy table generation features, you can create simple tables using the Insert Table button on the toolbar.

Simple tables are defined as tables having a maximum of five columns. The number of rows can easily be expanded.

To Do: Building a Table

To build a simple table in Word, follow these steps:

1. Place the insertion point in the location that you want to begin the table.

2. Click the Insert Table button on the Standard toolbar to open the screen shown in Figure 17.3.

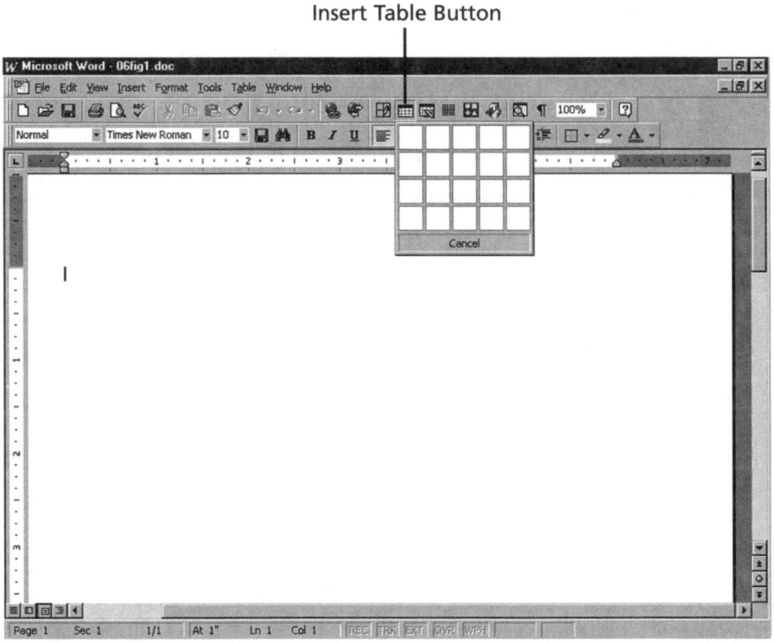

FIGURE 17.3.

Click the Insert Table button to begin creating your table in Word.

Insert Table Button

3. Select the range of cells that equals the number of rows and columns that you want to include in your table. To do this, simply move your mouse pointer down to the drop-down box and highlight the desired number of cells.

> Need more than four rows in your table? It's easy to add more. While in the
> last cell of a table, press Tab to add another row.

4. Enter data in the desired cell by clicking it and typing text as usual. If the text that
   you enter is wider than the cell allows, a second line is created within the cell to
   accommodate the excess.

5. To move to the next cell, press Tab. To return to the previous cell, use Shift+Tab.

> For more complex needs, try selecting Table, Insert Table to define a larger
> number of columns; or if you're really brave, you can draw the table free-
> hand by choosing Table, Draw Table.

17

Using AutoFormat to Improve Your Table's Appearance

Your table might not look like much at this point, but you're about to see the magic of
Word 97.

To Do: Improving Your Table's Appearance

Word 97's AutoFormat tool makes it easy to polish your table's appearance. To do so,
follow these steps:

1. Place the insertion point inside the table.

2. Choose Table, Table AutoFormat to open the Table AutoFormat dialog box (shown
   in Figure 17.4).

3. Choose the format that you want to use in the Formats list. You can preview it in
   the Preview box before applying it.

4. Click OK to confirm your choice and return to the main document.

Emphasizing Content with Borders and Shading

When used judiciously, borders and shading can be extremely effective at drawing attention to selected text.

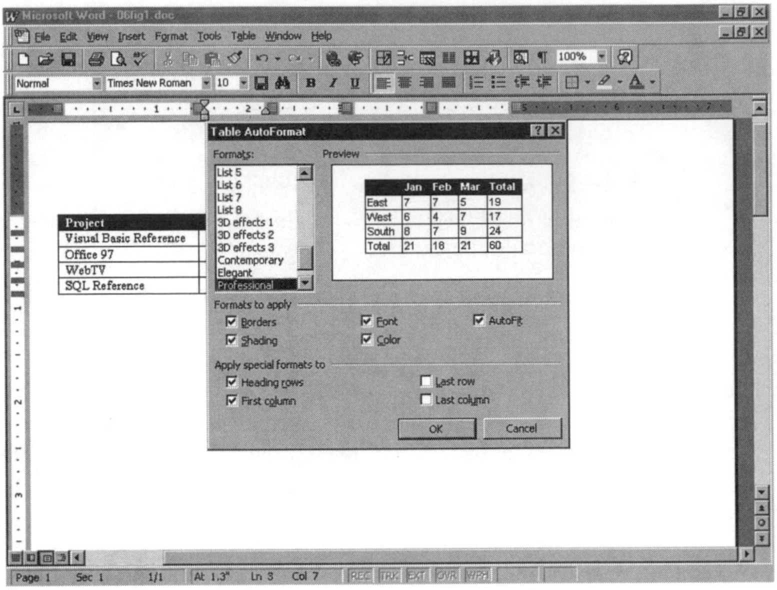

FIGURE 17.4.

From the Table AutoFormat dialog box, you can select from dozens of table formats, including multicolor tables, which are perfect for publishing on the Web.

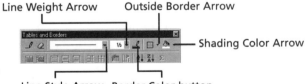

To Do: Adding Borders and Shading

To take advantage of the borders and shading options, follow these steps:

1. Right-click any visible toolbar to open a shortcut menu. Select the Tables and Borders toolbar (shown in Figure 17.5) from the list.

Line Weight Arrow   Outside Border Arrow

FIGURE 17.5.

Use the Tables and Borders toolbar to create dynamic borders and shading effects.

Shading Color Arrow

Line Style Arrow   Border Color button

2. Select the text around which you'd like to place a border (or the section of text that you want to shade) by using the text selection techniques described in the preceding hour.

> If no text has been selected, Word finds the insertion point and applies the formatting to that paragraph.

▼

3. Click the arrow next to the Line Style box to choose a line style for the border.

4. Use the Line Weight arrow to choose the thickness of your border.

5. The Border Color button may be used to add color to online documents or color printer output.

6. Click the arrow next to the Border icon to open a palette of available border styles. Although the desired option is most frequently Outside Border, you have a number of options from which to choose.

7. Click the Shading Color arrow to see a pop-up shading palette from which to make your selection.

8. To close the toolbar and maximize your workspace, click the X at the top-right corner of the box.

▲

Want more border and shading options than the toolbar gives you? Select the text that you want to change and select Format, Borders and Shading to open the Borders and Shading dialog box.

Adding Headers and Footers to Your Documents

Headers and footers may not seem that exciting at first, but they are when you consider the fact that they are what Word uses to apply page numbers to your documents. Headers and footers can also house the date, the document's filename, and other key information.

Adding headers and footers to your documents is less complicated than it may seem. Start by selecting View, Header and Footer to open the Header and Footer toolbar (shown in Figure 17.6).

Keep the following things in mind when constructing your headers and footers:

- Before entering text, you should know that there are two default tabs in headers and footers—the first to center text, and the second to place the text flush right.

- Click the Switch Between Header and Footer button to begin work on the footer or to return to the header.

- Time, date, and page number are easily inserted with the click of a button.

- Click Close to return to your document.

Show/Hide
Document Text

Switch Between
Header and Footer   Show Previous   Show Next   Close

FIGURE 17.6.

*Header and Footer
toolbar items make
creating headers and
footers a breeze.*

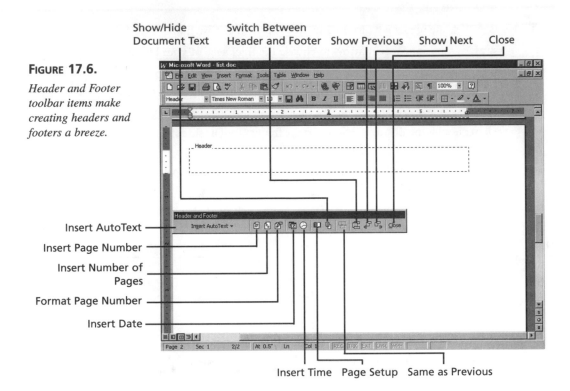

Insert AutoText

Insert Page Number

Insert Number of
Pages

Format Page Number

Insert Date

Insert Time   Page Setup   Same as Previous

Using the Shrink to Fit Feature

And while we're on the topic of useful features, take a look at this cool Shrink to Fit feature! When typing a letter, nothing's more frustrating than to find that two lines of it spill over on to a second page. Word has a feature to save paper (and your sanity) called Shrink to Fit.

To Do: Using Shrink to Fit

To access this feature, follow these steps:

1. Click the Print Preview button on the Standard toolbar. You see your document displayed as it would appear on paper (see Figure 17.7).

2. Click the Multiple Page button so that you can see just how much text hangs over onto the second or final page.

3. To squeeze stray lines onto a single page, press the Shrink to Fit button. The results are shown on the same Print Preview screen.

Multiple Pages Button　　　　Shrink to Fit Button

FIGURE 17.7.

Click the Print Preview button on the Standard toolbar to see just how much of your text falls over to the next page.

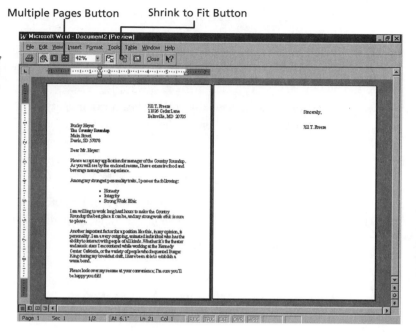

17

Using Word's Auto Features

If you've spent any time wandering through Word 97's menus, you've undoubtedly noticed the overabundance of AutoWhatever options. Although these features are designed to make our time at the computer easier and more productive, some of them can drive you, well, AutoInsane!

Even more upsetting than that is Word 97 fixing and changing things that you're not sure you even want fixed and changed. One day you're innocently working on an outline for a school paper, and it happens: You get to your c sections—notated (c)—and Word's AutoCorrect feature spits out these perfect little copyright symbols. But you don't want copyright symbols! It does it every single time, making you crazier and crazier with each occurrence. Just take my advice and disable the blasted thing until you're absolutely sure that you're ready to deal with it. To do so, select Tools, AutoCorrect. In the AutoCorrect tab, make sure that you remove the check mark in the Replace Text as You Type box.

Having said that, I must say that there are some extremely helpful auto features, too. The following list defines some of these features, what they do, and when to use them. Pay extra attention to AutoComplete, AutoCorrect, and AutoText because their similarities and interrelationships can be particularly confusing.

- *AutoFormat (with the As You Type option activated).* Automatically formats headings, bulleted and numbered lists, borders, numbers, symbols, and so on, as you type a document. To automatically format selected text or an entire document all at once, choose Format, AutoFormat and select your options in the AutoFormat dialog box.

- *AutoCorrect.* Automatically corrects many common typing, spelling, and grammatical errors as you type, and it can automatically insert text, graphics, and symbols. To enable AutoCorrect, choose Tools, AutoCorrect, and choose the AutoCorrect tab. Check the Replace Text as You Type box. This option corrects or replaces programmed text as you type, without prompting you.

Because AutoCorrect does have some powerful spelling error detection, you may decide to delete any troublesome AutoCorrect entries rather than disable the whole tool.

To Do: Deleting an AutoCorrect Entry

To delete an AutoCorrect entry, follow these steps:

1. From within Word, select Tools, AutoCorrect.

2. In the AutoCorrect entry window, find the entry that you want to delete, and click it.

3. After you're certain that you want to delete the highlighted entry, press the Delete key.

4. Repeat steps 2–3 as desired.

5. When you've finished editing your AutoCorrect entries, press OK to close the dialog box.

- *AutoComplete.* Enables you to insert entire items such as dates and AutoText entries when you type a few identifying characters. Unlike AutoCorrect, AutoComplete prompts you with a little yellow ScreenTip box to accept or reject the programmed text. Accepting it is as simple as pressing Enter. To enable AutoComplete, choose Tools, AutoCorrect, and select the AutoText tab. Place a check mark next to Show AutoComplete tip for AutoText or date, and then choose OK to confirm your request.

- *AutoText.* A storage location for text or graphics that you want to reuse. Good candidates for an AutoText entry include a company logo, an organization's mission statement, your business's return address, and so on. AutoComplete uses the programmed AutoText entries to generate its ScreenTips. You can also retrieve AutoText entries from the AutoText toolbar. To display this toolbar, right-click an open toolbar and check AutoText. (AutoText is covered in detail later in this hour.)

- *AutoSummarize*. Automatically generates a summary of your long documents to be saved in a specified location. You can also choose summary attributes to make sure that the summary contains needed data. To use AutoSummarize, choose Tools, AutoSummarize. Word searches the document to generate a summary and offers you various options for placing the summary.

- *AutoSave*. A feature that enables you to automatically save your work at specified intervals. (AutoSave was presented in Hour 16.)

- *AutoRecover*. Nearly synonymous with AutoSave because it offers multiple ways to protect your work.

Adding Graphics to Your Documents

17

We've all heard the cliché a million times—a picture's worth a thousand words. You'll be happy to know that Word 97 makes adding clip art and image files to your document a breeze.

To Do: Inserting Clip Art or an Image

To Do

To insert clip art or an image file, follow these simple steps:

1. Set the insertion point in the location that you'd like to place the graphic.

2. Select Insert, Picture, Clip Art or From File.

3. If you chose Clip Art, Microsoft Clip Gallery 3.0 loads, giving you the opportunity to preview its gallery of art.

4. If you selected From File, the Insert Picture dialog box comes up, enabling you to browse your directories for the desired image. A preview appears in the right window when available.

5. After you've chosen the image or clip art to be included, press the Insert button. The image appears in the document.

▲

If you look closely at the new image, you see that eight white boxes frame it (see Figure 17.8). These boxes, called handles, can be used to resize and reshape the image. As you run the mouse pointer over the handles, you see arrows indicating which direction you can drag the image to resize it. Just click the box and pull the image's border in the desired direction.

FIGURE 17.8.

In this graphic, you can see the resizing arrows on the bottom center handle.

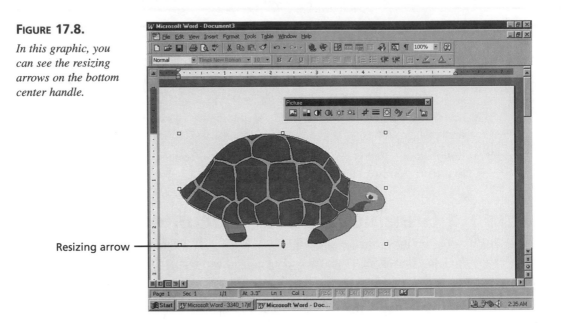

Resizing arrow

After you see the size of the image in relation to your document, you may decide that it's not placed where you want it after all. No need to worry. Just place the mouse pointer inside the image until you see a four-way arrow. This symbol means that you can press your left mouse button and drag the image anywhere you want.

Correcting Spelling and Grammar

Whether you're bleary-eyed from burning the midnight oil, or just plain lousy at spelling like my husband, Word 97's spelling and grammar checker may be just the ticket.

To Do: Setting Spelling and Grammar Options

To set spelling and grammar checking options, follow these steps:

1. From within Word 97, select Tools, Spelling and Grammar. The Spelling and Grammar dialog box (shown in Figure 17.9) appears.

2. If you want Word to check your grammar as well as spelling, check the Check Grammar box.

3. Next, click the Options button. You see the Grammar & Spelling tab (shown in Figure 17.10).

4. Check each of your preferences. Here you specify whether you want problems marked with green (grammar) or red (spelling) squiggly lines as you type, or

▼ whether you want them hidden until you perform a spell check. You can even tell Word what kinds of things to ignore (such as Web and email addresses), and whether or not you want the program to offer suggestions for fixing the problems.

FIGURE 17.9.

Check the Check Grammar box if you'd like Word to review your document for errors in grammar as well.

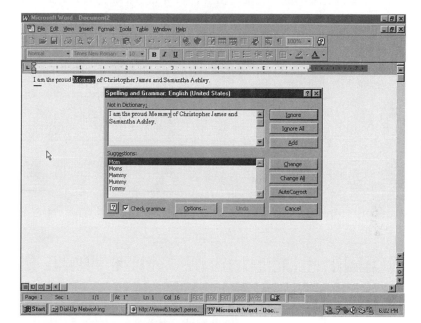

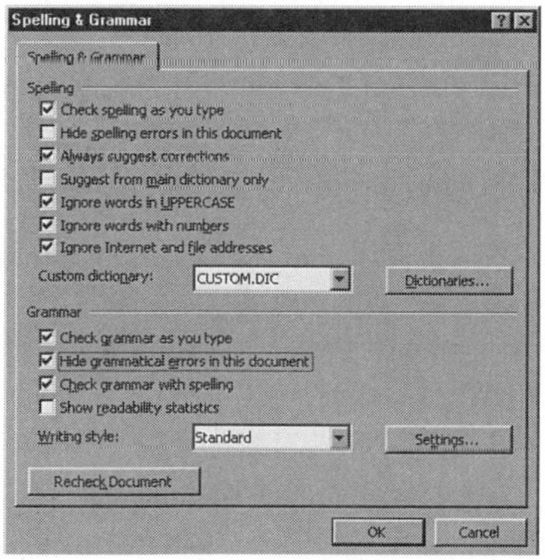

17

FIGURE 17.10.

Use this tab to tell Word what to check for and what to ignore.

5. Press the Settings button to define grammar checking options such as the use of passive voice, the improper number of spaces after a punctuation mark, and so on.

▲ 6. After your options are set, click OK.

To Do: Running the Spelling and Grammar Check

When you're ready to do a spelling and grammar check, do the following:

1. Press F7 to get started. You see a screen like the one in Figure 17.9 where Word 97 provides its suggestions for improvement.

2. In each case, you have the option to accept or reject the suggestion, and in the case of spelling, you have the option to ignore the word in question once or always, or you can add it to your personal dictionary.

3. Word prompts you when the spelling and grammar check is complete. Click OK to continue.

> If you want to address random problems as you work, just right-click any text underlined in red or green. You see a brief description of the problem, a suggestion for improving it where appropriate, and you have the opportunity to accept the suggestion or ignore the problem sentence.

Building Documents with Word 97 Wizards and Templates

One of the great things about using wizards and templates is that they are all very easy to use and self-explanatory. Wizards consist of a series of questions for which you provide answers. These answers are then turned into a customized document. Take, for example, Word 97's Newsletter wizard (see Figure 17.11). It may ask you how many columns you want the newsletter to have, how many stories you want on the front page, and so on. Then, based on your answers, it builds a template-like document to your specifications.

That brings us to templates. Templates are essentially preformatted, professional-looking documents. All you have to do to make them yours is insert custom text. All the hard formatting and font selection is done for you. The Word 97 résumé templates can be particularly useful when you have to put a high quality product together quickly.

To find wizards and templates in Word 97, select File, New, and browse through the tabs until you find something that strikes your fancy. The wizards are clearly marked, so you won't have to worry about missing them.

FIGURE 17.11.

The Word 97 Newsletter wizard helps you generate professional-looking results in no time.

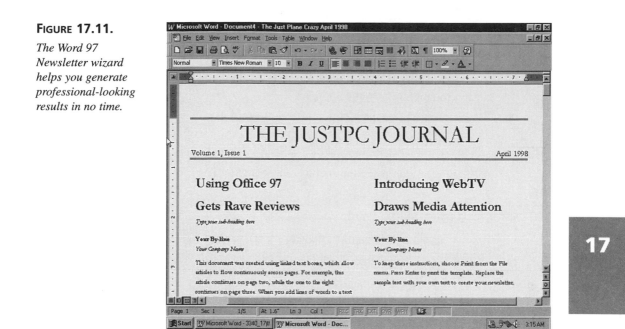

17

Summary

This whirlwind hour covered everything from setting margins to creating great-looking tables to adding text to your documents. In other words, you now have at least a back-grounder on some of Word's more advanced features. If you want to learn more, I strongly urge you to read one of Macmillan's Word 97 titles.

Next up, the Microsoft Works word processing tool.

Workshop

The following workshop helps you solidify the skills you learned in this lesson.

Quiz

Take the following quiz to see how much you've learned.

Questions

1. Why would you use shading and borders?

   a. To keep text from spilling over into other columns

   b. To emphasize important text

   c. Neither of the above

2. What does the Shrink to Fit feature do?

   a. Compresses text when only one or two stray lines are on the last page of a document

   b. A new grammar-checking feature that takes complex words and tries to make them simpler

   c. Takes a table heading and makes it the perfect size to fit the space allotted

3. What's the difference between a template and a wizard?

   a. Wizards make documents magically disappear

   b. Templates ask you a series of questions in order to build a customized document

   c. Neither of the above

Answers

1. b. Borders and shading are very effective ways to draw attention to certain text.

2. a. This feature can truly save your money and your sanity.

3. c. If you're confused at all, go back and read the last section in this hour.

Activity

Just to get a feel for how wizards work, launch Word 97 and select File, New. Look in the Publications tab; you see a newsletter wizard. Pretend that you're doing some kind of newsletter, whether it's one for a favorite cause or a holiday newsletter for all the relatives. Work your way through all the questions to see how Word 97 generates a customized template-like document for you to fill in.

HOUR **18**

Designing Your Own Web Page with FrontPage Express

If you recently purchased a computer and got connected to the Internet, odds are you'll eventually catch the "I want to design my own Web page" bug. Millions of people have done it, and thanks to easy-to-use Web design applications like FrontPage Express, so can you.

This hour gets you started with designing your own Web page, and provides the answers to the following questions:

- How do I define my Web page's title?
- FrontPage Express looks an awful lot like Word 97; are they similar?
- Can I specify the color of my page's hyperlinks?
- How do I preview my Web page to make sure it looks right before I publish it?
- What information do I need from my Internet service provider before I can publish my Web page?

Starting FrontPage Express

One of the reasons the Web has grown so rapidly is that Web pages are easy to make.
The language used to construct Web pages, HTML, is easy enough to learn, but Internet
Explorer 4.0 comes with its own editor that makes building Web pages even easier. The
program, FrontPage Express, is referred to as a WYSIWYG (What You See Is What You
Get) editor, which means that you lay out your page, and all the coding is handled
behind the scenes.

To Do: Starting FrontPage Express

FrontPage Express is a separate program and can be started by following these steps:

1. Click the Start button on the Windows taskbar.

2. Select Programs, and then from the submenu, select Internet Explorer Suite.

▲   3. From the Internet Explorer menu, select FrontPage Express.

Figure 18.1 shows a FrontPage Express screen with a new, blank page, and highlights
some of the key features.

FIGURE 18.1.

*FrontPage Express is
Internet Explorer 4.0's
editor.*

> You can also access FrontPage Express through the Internet Explorer toolbar
> by clicking Edit. This opens FrontPage Express and loads whatever Web page
> is currently open in Internet Explorer 4.0. Click the New icon in the
> FrontPage Express toolbar to start with a blank page.

Setting Up the Basics

When people think of Web pages, they often think of flashy graphics, an occasional sound
clip, and captivating text. But before you even reach that point, you need to define some
basic page properties. You'll want to enter a title for your page, specify its background
color, and indicate which colors you want your text and various links to display in.

Entering the Page's Title

Giving your page a title has even more significance than it might first appear. Remember,
the Web page's title is what shows up on the list when people mark it as a Favorite, so
you want its title to be descriptive and appropriate.

To Do: Creating a Title for Your Web Page

To enter your page's title, follow these simple steps:

1. Launch FrontPage Express, then select File, New, to create a new blank page.

2. Select File, Page Properties, and choose the General tab.

3. Press the Tab key until your cursor appears in the Title field.

4. Type in your Web page's title, and then click OK to return to the FrontPage
   Express editor.

Adding Some Color to Your Page

FrontPage Express makes it a snap to generate flashy background and text color combinations. Just follow these easy steps to add tons of color to your page:

To Do: Changing Text and Background Colors on Your Web Page

1. From within your newly created Web page, select File, Page Properties, and activate the Background tab.

2. Click and hold down the left mouse button on the arrow next to the Background
   setting.

3. Pull the cursor down until you find the desired color, then release the mouse button
   to select that color.

18

▼   4. Repeat the first three steps to define colors for the following: Text, Hyperlink, Visited Hyperlink, and Active Hyperlink.

▲   5. Click OK when you're satisfied with your selections.

Formatting Text

One main feature of a Web page is its computer platform independence. A Web page built on a Windows 95 or Windows 98 machine can be viewed by Windows 3.1, Macintosh, UNIX, and any other system with a basic browser. To reach this degree of universal accessibility, text in Web pages use formatting styles rather than specific font sizes as in a word processing program. Headings, used for titles and subtitles, can be any one of six different relative sizes—Heading 1, the largest, through Heading 6, the smallest.

To Do: Creating Headings and Formatting Text

Follow these steps to enter and format some text on your Web page:

1. Start FrontPage Express.

2. Type in your first heading.

3. Select the text you just entered by clicking in front of it and dragging the mouse across the rest.

4. From the Change Styles box in the toolbar, click the arrow to reveal the drop-down options list.

5. From the options list, click a text style choice. Heading 1 or Heading 2 is suitable for a Web page title. The text changes to the selected size (see Figure 18.2).

6. Keeping the text highlighted, click one of the Alignment buttons to make the text align to the Left, Center, or Right.

7. If desired, click the standard Bold, Italic, or Underline style buttons.

▲   8. Click anywhere on the blank page to clear the highlight.

Repeat these steps to continue to add text to your Web page, varying the text styles between Headings and Normal.

A quick glance at FrontPage Express's toolbars reveals several similarities between it and Word 97. Text alignment, numbered and bulleted list generation, and font styles like bold and italic are accomplished the same way in both applications. You may want to refer to Hours 16, "Microsoft Word 97 Essentials," and 17, "Unleashing the Power of Microsoft Word 97," for techniques that may be useful in FrontPage Express, as well.

FIGURE 18.2.

This sample FrontPage Express screen shows what each heading size of text might look like.

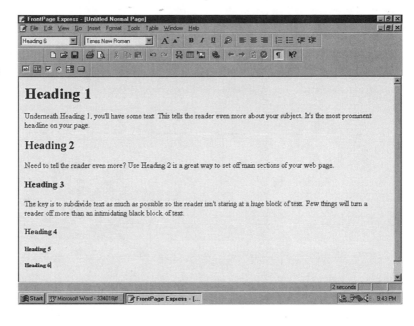

Adding Graphics

18

A major World Wide Web innovation was the inclusion of graphics with text. Most browsers currently support only two types of graphics. The first, GIF format, can have up to 256 colors and is used for drawings, logos, and illustrations. The second, JPEG, can display millions of colors but takes longer to load because it is compressed; JPEG is used primarily for photographs.

Web graphics are inline graphics, which means they can be placed right next to text. Graphics can also be aligned left, center, or right, just like text.

To Do: Adding Graphics to Your Web Page

To place a graphic on your Web page, follow these steps:

1. Move the insertion point where you would like to have the graphic appear. If necessary, press Enter to move down the page.

2. From the Insert menu, select Image.

3. From the Insert Image dialog box, choose the Other Locations tab to select a graphic file from your hard drive or from a Web address. Click OK when finished.

4. To select from one of the available clip art images, click the Clip Art tab and select a category. Click an image to select it, and then click OK.

5. The image is inserted on the page. To re-align the image, select it and click one of the Alignment buttons on the toolbar.

Figure 18.3 shows a Web page with two lines of text and two images.

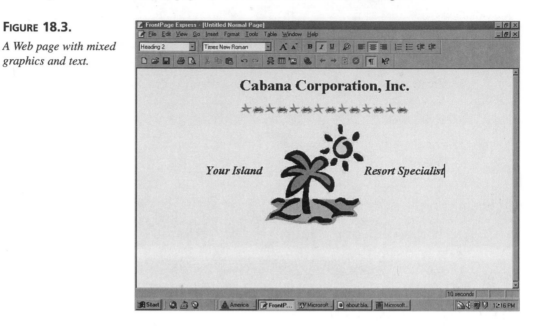

It's a good idea to reuse the same graphic image on the Web site in several places. This gives continuity to a site with no additional download time. This is especially useful for businesses that have developed a fancy, colorful logo. After a graphic has been downloaded, it is temporarily cached on the viewer's system and can be reused without redownloading.

Saving Your Web Page

After you have spent some time creating your Web page, you have to save it before you see it in Internet Explorer. Because Web pages and Web sites (which are usually comprised of more than one Web page) can be made of many separate files (each graphic is an individual file, for example), you'll probably want to create a folder for each Web site you work on. This also makes it easy to find all the files when it comes time to publish your creation to the Web.

FrontPage Express allows you to either publish directly to the Internet (or an internal intranet) or to a file.

To Do: Saving Your Web Page in FrontPage Express

Follow these steps to save your Web page as a file in FrontPage Express:

1. Click the Save button on the toolbar.

2. From the Save As Web dialog box, click the As File button.

3. Create a new folder, if necessary, from the Save As File dialog box by clicking the New Folder icon.

4. Type a new name for your Web page in the Name box and click OK.

5. FrontPage Express asks whether you would like to copy your graphics to the new directory. Click the Yes To All button.

Browsing Your Web Page

You'll want to check your Web page frequently in Internet Explorer as you work. When you are browsing your creation, you can get an idea of how quickly (or how slowly) your page will load. You can also double-check your links and your graphics to make sure everything is in place. If you are eventually posting your page to the Internet (as opposed to an internal network), look at your Web page with different screen resolutions; you can't be sure what your potential readers are using, so it's best to see how your Web page looks under a variety of circumstances.

18

To Do: Reviewing Your Web Page

Follow these steps to browse a Web page previously saved in FrontPage Express:

1. From the Internet Explorer File menu, select Open.

2. From the Open dialog box, click the Browse button.

3. Open the folder in which your Web page is saved.

4. Double-click the filename of the Web page you want to browse. The page loads and the dialog box closes.

The speed with which your page gets loaded using the method in the previous set of steps in no way indicates how fast it will load over the Internet. Putting your Web page on the Internet and retrieving it under the same circumstances as your prospective readers is the only true test of speed (or lack thereof).

Quitting FrontPage Express

When you have finished your FrontPage Express session, you quit the program by any of the standard methods:

- Choose File, Exit from the menu bar.
- Click the Close (X) button in the upper-right corner of the FrontPage Express window.
- Use the keyboard shortcut, Alt+F4.

After you have completed your Web page, you must place it on a Web server, where other people can open and view it with their Web browsers. In the past, the only way to place a page on a Web server was to use a separate FTP (File Transfer Protocol) program. However, FrontPage Express comes with its own file transfer program, called WebPost, that you can access by using the File, Save As command.

Dealing with the Preliminaries

Unless you've been working directly on a *Web server* (a computer that stores Web sites where people browsing the Web can see them), you have to take the additional step of *publishing* your Web pages.

Before you start, you need to make sure you have somewhere to store your Web page. The best place to start is with your Internet service provider. Most providers make some space available on their Web servers for subscribers to store personal Web pages at no extra cost. Call your service provider and find out the following information:

- Does your service provider make Web space available to subscribers? If not, maybe you should change providers.
- How much disk space do you get, and how much does it cost (if anything)? Most providers give you a limited amount of disk space, which is usually plenty for one or two Web pages, assuming you don't include large audio or video clips.
- Can you save your files directly to the Web server or do you have to upload files to an FTP server?
- What is the URL of the server you must connect to for uploading your files? Write it down.

- What username and password do you need to enter to gain access to the server? (This is typically the same username and password you use to connect to the service.)

- In which directory must you place your files? Write it down.

- What name must you give your Web page? In many cases, the service lets you post a single default Web page, and you must call it index.html or default.html. You can name pages that branch off from this default page anything you want.

- Are there any other specific instructions you must follow to post your Web page?

- After posting your page, what will its address (URL) be? You'll want to open it in Internet Explorer as soon as you post it.

If you're using a commercial online service, such as America Online or CompuServe, you may have to use its commands to upload your Web page and associated files. For example, CompuServe has its own Web Page Publishing Wizard. In similar cases, you should use the tools the online service provides instead of trying to wrestle with FrontPage Express.

If your service provider doesn't offer Web page service, fire up Internet Explorer, connect to your favorite search page, and search for places that enable you to post your Web page for free. These services vary greatly. Some services require you to fill out a form, and then the service creates a generic Web page for you (you can't use the page you created in FrontPage Express). At others, you can copy the HTML coded document (in Notepad or WordPad) and paste it in a text box at the site. A couple of other places let you send them your HTML file and associated files. Find out what's involved. Because these types of sites come and go, not to mention change their requirements fairly regularly, it's best to perform the search when you're almost ready to publish your page.

18

You can save yourself some time and trouble by placing your Web page, all its graphic files, and any other associated files in a single folder separate from other files. The Web Publishing Wizard can then transfer all the required files as a batch to your Web server. Make sure you use the correct filename for your Web page file, as specified by your service provider.

Saving Your Page to a Web Server

If you work on an intranet or use a service provider that enables you to save your Web page directly to its Web server, take the steps in the following section to publish your Web page.

To Do: Publishing Your Web Page

1. Open the page you want to place on the Web.

2. Open the File menu and select Save As. The Save As dialog box appears, displaying the name and location of your Web page file.

3. Click OK. If you used any images or other files in your Web page, a dialog box appears asking if you want to save these files to the Web server.

4. Click Yes to All. The Enter Network Password dialog box appears, prompting you to enter your username and password.

5. Type your username in the Username text box, tab to the Password text box, and type your password. Click OK. (FrontPage Express is set up to save your password, so you won't need to enter it the next time you publish a Web page.)

6. The Web Publishing Wizard appears, displaying an explanation of what you are about to do. Click Next. The wizard prompts you to type a name for your Web server.

7. Type a brief, descriptive name (you don't need to type the server's domain name at this point). Click Next. The wizard prompts you to type the URL of your Web page.

8. Type the address of your Web page, as specified by your service provider (for example, `http://www.internet.com/~bfink`). You may be prompted to enter your username and password again.

9. Click Next. The wizard prompts you to select your service provider. If you're unsure, select HTTP Post to place your files directly on a Web server, or select Automatically Select Service Provider. Click Next. You are now prompted to enter information about the server.

10. Enter the server's name and any special command you need to upload your page to the Web server. Your service provider should have supplied this information.

11. Click Next. The final dialog box appears, indicating that the wizard is ready to publish your Web page.

▼
▲

12. Click Finish. The wizard dials into your service provider if you aren't yet connected and uploads your Web page and all associated files to the Web server. Dialog boxes appear, showing the progress.

> If you receive an error message indicating that the wizard was unable to publish the files, you may have entered the wrong username or password, typed the wrong Web server address, or selected the wrong service provider. Check with your service provider to ensure that you have the correct information, and then repeat the preceding steps.

Uploading Files to an FTP Server

Many service providers require that you upload your Web page and associated files to an FTP server. When you open your account, the service provider creates a separate directory on the FTP server that only you can access using your username and password. You rarely deal with this directory, so you may not know its path. Ask your service provider to specify the path to your directory.

To Do: Uploading Files to an FTP Server

After you have the information you need, take the following steps to use the Web Publishing Wizard to upload files to your directory on the FTP server:

1. Open the page you want to place on the Web.

2. Choose File, Save As. The Save As dialog box appears, displaying the name and location of your Web page file.

3. Click OK. If you used any images or other files in your Web page, a dialog box appears asking if you want to save these files to the Web server.

4. Click Yes to All. The Enter Network Password dialog box appears, prompting you to enter your username and password.

5. Type your username in the Username text box, tab to the Password text box, and type your password. Click OK. (FrontPage Express is set up to save your password, so you won't need to enter it the next time you publish a Web page.)

6. The Web Publishing Wizard appears, displaying an explanation of what

18

▼

> Just because FrontPage remembers your password doesn't mean you should forget it altogether. If you forget it and should need to rebuild your system after, say, a hard disk failure, you'll be out of luck.

▼   you're about to do. Click Next. The wizard prompts you to type a name
           for your Web server.

     7.   Type a brief, descriptive name (you don't need to type the server's domain
           name at this point). Click Next. You may be prompted to enter your user-
           name and password again.

     8.   Type the address of your Web page, as specified by your service provider (for
           example, `http://www.internet.com/~bfink`). You may be prompted to enter
           your username and password again.

     9.   Click Next. The wizard prompts you to select your service provider.

     10.   Open the Service Provider drop-down list and select FTP, as shown in
           Figure 18.4. Click Next. You are then prompted to enter information about
           the server.

     11.   Enter the server's domain name (for example, `ftp.internet.com`) in the FTP

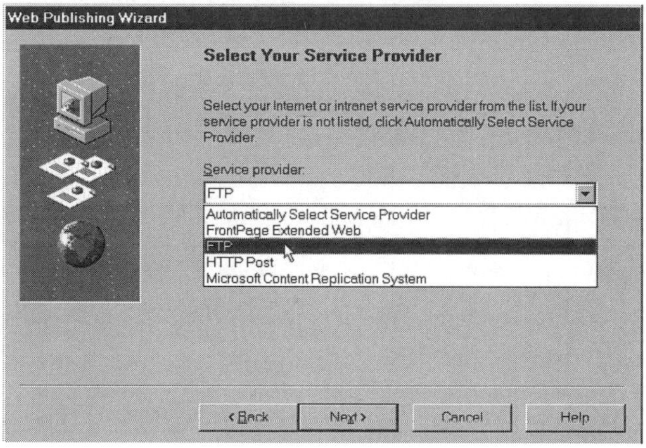

FIGURE 18.4.

*Select FTP as your
service provider.*

           Server Name text box.

     12.   Tab to the Subfolder Containing Your Web Pages text box, and type the path to the
           directory in which you must store your Web pages (for example, /users/bf/bfink)
           (see Figure 18.5). Your service provider should have supplied this information.

     13.   Click Next. The final dialog box appears, indicating that the wizard is
           ready to publish your Web page.

     14.   Click Finish. The wizard dials into your service provider if you aren't yet connect-
           ed and uploads your Web page and all associated files to the Web server. Dialog
           boxes appear showing the progress.

▲

FIGURE 18.5.

The wizard needs to know where to store your files.

Specify the domain name of your FTP server.

Type the path to the directory where your Web page files are stored.

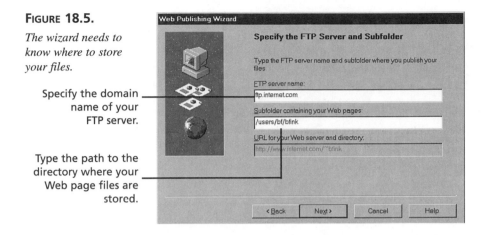

The good news is that you won't have to go through this 14-step process the next time you need to upload your Web page. Choose the File, Save command, and FrontPage Express automatically uploads your Web page and associated files to the FTP server.

18

Summary

In less than an hour, you learned more than enough to create a simple Web page on your own. Not bad! You learned how to give your page a title, add splashes of color to it, and even incorporate graphics.

Next hour, I will introduce you to the word processing functions of Microsoft Works 4.5.

Workshop

The following workshop helps you solidify the skills you learned in this hour.

Quiz

Take the following quiz to see how much you've learned.

Questions

1. FrontPage Express is an application nested inside

   a. Microsoft Works 4.5

   b. Microsoft Word 97

   c. Microsoft Internet Explorer

2. Can you have more than one color of text on your Web page?

   a. No

   b. Yes

   c. It depends

3. What kind of server wouldn't you publish a Web page to?

   a. A mail server

   b. A Web server

   c. An FTP server

Answers

1. c. FrontPage Express is Internet Explorer's editor, so they have a tight relationship.

2. b. You can define any number of text colors for your Web page as long as you go through the necessary steps.

3. a. Both Web and FTP servers are commonly used for publishing Web pages.

Activity

Launch FrontPage Express, and then type in your name. Now give your name some personality—change its color, center it, make it bold, change its type font...anything you want. When you're done, select View, HTML. All that stuff you see onscreen is referred to as HTML source code. Just seeing how much code FrontPage Express produces for your little bit of work gives you a good idea of just how powerful the application is.

HOUR 19

Introducing Microsoft Works and Its Word Processing Tool

As retailers tighten their belts to offer consumers more PC for the money, Microsoft Works 4.5 has emerged as the application of choice to be pre-installed on new systems at costs under $1,000. Less expensive to include than the robust Office 97 suite, Microsoft Works is an integrated software program that combines the features of several tools to help you perform the functions of four different kinds of programs. Works has the added benefit of enabling you to perform a wide variety of functions while working in only one program. This means fewer commands to memorize, and a speedier learning curve.

In this hour, I introduce you to Microsoft Works 4.5 and touch on its Word Processing Tool. The following questions are answered as well:

- What tools are included in Microsoft Works 4.5?
- What's the difference between Word 97 and the Works Word Processing Tool?

- How does a Task Wizard work?
- Does Works contain a Thesaurus?
- What kinds of projects can I do with Microsoft Works Task Wizards?

The Parts of Works and What They Do

Microsoft Works contains a Word Processor, a Spreadsheet, a Database, and a
Communications Program. These programs, or Works Tools as they're called, can be
used separately or together to help you perform tasks.

Each of the following tools is designed to perform a specific function:

- Use the Word Processor to write letters or other documents.
- Use the Spreadsheet tool to create documents that contain numbers in rows and
  columns and perform calculations on those numbers.
- Use the Database tool to keep track of lists of names and addresses, or inventoried
  objects.
- Use the Communications tool to communicate with another computer, sending and
  receiving files (if you have a modem connected to your computer and if you have
  the rights to access the other computer).

Although Microsoft Works calls them tools, the Word Processing,
Spreadsheet, and Database functions of Works are actually scaled-down
computer applications that fall into the software program categories of
word processing, spreadsheet, and database. Their function and design follow the basic function and design of other much larger and more costly programs in the same category.

Table 19.1 lists tasks and projects that you might want to perform on your computer and
the tool you use in Works to perform that task or create that project. The first column in
the table is designed to help you quickly identify your project.

TABLE 19.1. TASKS YOU CAN PERFORM IN WORKS, AND THE TOOLS YOU USE TO PERFORM THEM.

Category	Project	Use
Letters/correspondence	Write a letter Create a report for school	Word Processor tool
Address/mailing lists	Maintain a list of vendors, friends, or newsletter recipients	Database tool

Category	Project	Use
Mass mailing	Create a letter and/ or envelopes Create labels for envelopes	Word Processor and Database tools
Newsletters/letterhead	Create your own letterhead Design a newsletter using columns and inserting graphics	Word Processor tool
Mortgage/loan analysis	See the payment schedule for a loan	Spreadsheet tool
Calendar	Create a calendar for work or home Keep a to-do list	Spreadsheet tool

In the remaining part of this hour, we take a closer look at the Works Word Processing Tool and the Works Task Wizard. In Hour 20, "Using the Works Spreadsheet Tool," we delve into spreadsheets, and databases are the subject of Hour 21, "Using the Works Database Tool."

Starting Works

To start Microsoft Works, you must be running under the Windows operating system, and Works must be installed on your computer. Follow these simple steps to start Microsoft Works:

1. Click the Windows Start button.
2. Select Programs, Microsoft Works, Microsoft Works.
3. The Microsoft Works Task Launcher dialog box appears (see Figure 19.1).

19

FIGURE 19.1.

The Works Task Launcher.

During installation, Microsoft Works 4.5 normally places a shortcut icon on your Windows desktop. You can start Works quickly by double-clicking that icon.

The Task Launcher is the master control for Works. It provides an easy-to-use menu, displaying all of Works features in one window.

The Works Task Launcher

The Task Launcher has the following three tabs:

- *TaskWizards*. Mini programs that assist you in performing your task. For example, you can use the Letter TaskWizard to help you write a professional looking letter. (We examine this particular task in depth later in the hour.)

- *Existing Documents*. Displays a list of the documents that you have created and saved. If you are using Works for the first time, this window is empty. When you create Works documents, you can reopen them by double-clicking the document in the list.

- *Works Tools*. Enables you to access the Word Processor, Spreadsheet, or Database tools without the help of Wizards. This access enables you to create your own documents without assistance, but requires some knowledge in using these types of programs.

To view the selections on each tabbed page, click the tab. The tabbed page on which you clicked appears in front of the other tabbed pages.

Exiting Works

Throughout this book, you've learned to exit an application by selecting File, Exit, or by double-clicking the program control icon. This same method may not work inside Works if the Task Launcher is visible. As a precaution, you should exit Works by clicking the Exit Works button found in the Task Launcher.

What TaskWizards Are

TaskWizards are the heart of the Works program. The purpose of Wizards is to help you become even more productive in a short time period, and to produce professional-looking documents with limited or no experience.

The TaskWizards page in the Works Task Launcher lists categories for types of tasks that you can do with Works. Each task that you select runs a Wizard, a Microsoft term for a miniprogram that assists you in performing your task. For example, when you select Letterhead from the list of tasks, Works starts a program comprised of a series of questions that you answer. The answers that you provide instruct the program, and the program then designs the letterhead for you.

Viewing the TaskWizards Tab

When you first launch Works and click the TaskWizards tab, you'll see the wizards listed by category. (You'll learn how to change the order of these categories later in this hour.) To view a category's contents, click the icon on the left of the category as shown in Figure 19.2. This expands the category. To collapse the category, click its icon again.

FIGURE 19.2.

Expand and collapse categories by clicking their icons.

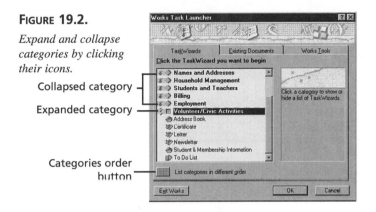

Collapsed category

Expanded category

Categories order button

Icons found to the left of the document names indicate which Works tool is used to create that document (shown in Table 19.2).

TABLE 19.2. DOCUMENT ICONS.

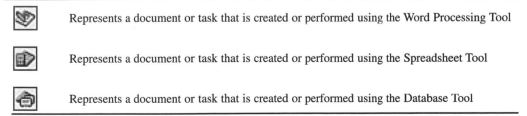

	Represents a document or task that is created or performed using the Word Processing Tool
	Represents a document or task that is created or performed using the Spreadsheet Tool
	Represents a document or task that is created or performed using the Database Tool

19

When you click one of the icons, a brief explanation of what you can do with that wizard is displayed in the right pane of the TaskWizard tab.

As mentioned earlier, when you first see the TaskWizard tab, the wizards are listed by categories. If you'd prefer to organize the wizards another way, however, you have a few options. You can list wizards alphabetically, by the wizards most recently used, or by document type.

To Do: Changing the Order of Categories

To change the order of the tasks in the TaskWizard window, follow these steps:

1. Click the List Categories In Different Order button or use the shortcut key, Alt+O.

2. Indicate a new order for the tasks in the Works Task Launcher dialog box.

3. Click OK to close the dialog box and return to the Task Launcher main window.

Launching the Word Processor

Perhaps your system didn't come with Word 97 in addition to Works 4.5. If that's the case, you surely want to become familiar with the Works Word Processing tool.

To Do: Opening the Works Word Processor Tool

To begin using the Works word processor, follow these steps:

1. Click the Start button on the taskbar.

2. From the Start menu, choose Programs, Microsoft Works, Microsoft Works.

3. The main Works window, called the Task Launcher, opens. The Task Launcher is your starting point. You see three tabs across the top of the window. Click the Works Tools tab.

4. Click the Word Processor button. This opens a blank page, ready for you to begin typing.

The blank page that you see onscreen (see Figure 19.3) isn't really blank. The page is based on a template, a predesigned group of settings that enable you to just begin typing without making any adjustments. These settings, which follow, are based on the requirements of a standard business letter.

Default font settings

FIGURE 19.3.

A blank word processing document.

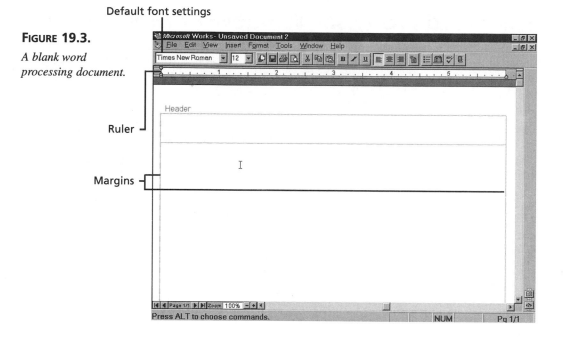

Ruler

Margins

- The margins (edges of the page where you don't type) are set to 1" all around the page
- There are tabs (for indenting text or typing lists in columns) set to every half-inch.
- Line spacing is set to single spacing.
- The font (typeface) is set to Times New Roman, 12 points.

Exiting the Word Processing Tool

When you want to exit the Microsoft Works Word Processing Tool, choose File, Exit Works from the menu. If you have made changes to the document since you last saved it, Works prompts you to save it. Click Yes if you want to save it, No if you want to exit without saving the document, or Cancel if you decide not to exit Works.

Don't exit Works if you only want to go back to the Task Launcher. Click the Task Launcher button on the Toolbar, or choose File, New from the menu instead. That way, you don't need to close your document file. If you just need to open a file created in another Works Tool, choose File, Open, select the file from the Open dialog box, and click OK.

19

The Word Processor Window Contents

The Works word processor window contains tools and features that assist you in creating a document (see Figure 19.4). It also has a Control icon and sizing icons for maximizing, minimizing, and closing the window (explained in Hour 4, "Working with Menus, Toolbars, and Dialog Boxes").

FIGURE 19.4.

The Word Processor window.

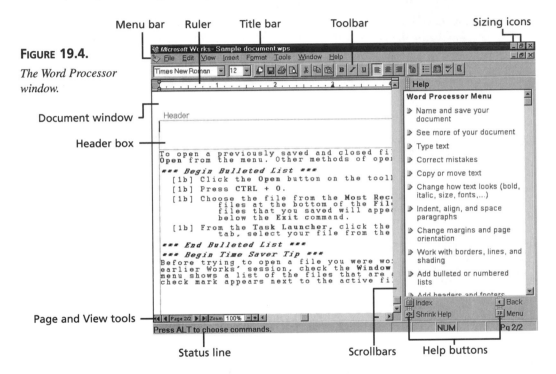

To open a new document and view a blank document window, choose File, New from the menu. In the Task Launcher dialog box, click the Works Tools tab and choose Word Processor.

The main components of the word processor window are

- *Title bar*. This strip across the top of any Windows application displays the name of the software you're using and the document name. (If the document hasn't been saved, Works assigns a title such as "Unsaved Document 1").

- *Menu bar*. The menu bar contains a series of menus that contain commands for doing everything from saving your document to changing fonts.

- *Toolbar*. The toolbar is a row of graphic buttons that represent the most commonly used commands, which are also found in the menus.

- *Document window.* This is the "paper" on which you create your document.

- *Scrollbars.* Found on the right side and across the bottom of your document window, these tools enable you to see the parts of your document that don't fit in the window.

- *Ruler.* The ruler enables you to visually measure your document horizontally and is used for setting tabs, indents, and adjusting the margins.

- *Page and View controls.* These tools appear on the lower-left corner of your document window. You can move forward and backward through a multi-page document, or choose to zoom in on the active page.

- *Status line.* This strip across the bottom of your screen indicates which page you're on, displays additional toolbar button information (when you're pointing to a button), and indicates whether your Num Lock, Insert, or Caps Lock key is on.

- *Help window.* The Help window is a separate window that can appear next to your document. You can shrink it out of view and open it as needed.

Do these elements look familiar? Don't worry; you're not having flashbacks to Word 97. The applications are intentionally similar.

The Word Processor Toolbar

The word processor toolbar contains buttons for the most commonly used commands in the menus. Toolbar buttons represent commands such as Save, Print, and Spell Check. Many of the tools work like toggle switches—one click turns a feature on, a second click turns it off. When a toggle button is in use, it appears depressed on the toolbar. Other toolbar buttons open a dialog box.

19

If you're not sure what a particular toolbar button does, just hover your mouse pointer over it and watch for the yellow screen tip box, which identifies the button.

The first two tools on the toolbar are drop-down list tools. To see the list of alternatives, click the drop-down arrow and select an item from the list. The item that you select appears in the box to the left of the drop-down arrow, which indicates that your selection is now the current setting. (Figure 19.5 shows the Works word processor toolbar.)

Drop lists　　　　　Toggle buttons

FIGURE 19.5.

The Word Processor toolbar.

Buttons in use

Because the way you work with text and formatting in the Works Word Processing Tool is identical to the way that you do things in Word 97, we are moving on to more Works-specific topics. Refer to Hour 16, "Microsoft Work 97 Essentials," should you have any text manipulation or formatting questions.

Moving Around in a Document

As you type your document, you may want to move quickly to the beginning of a previous paragraph, go to the next page, or move to the end of a line. To navigate and reposition your cursor within your document, you can use the scrollbars and click the document to place your cursor. You can also use the following shortcuts, which also work with Word 97:

- Ctrl+Home takes you to the top of the document.
- Ctrl+End takes you to the end of the document.
- The arrow keys on your keyboard move you up or down one line, and left or right one character.
- Add the Ctrl key while pressing the arrows to move up or down one full paragraph, or left or right one full word.
- The Home key takes you to the beginning of the line you're on.
- The End key takes you to the end of the line you're on.
- Press Page Up or Page Down to move up or down one full screen (a full screen doesn't always correspond to one printed page).
- Press Ctrl+G to open the Go To dialog box, and enter the page number to which you want to go. (This feature works only on documents of more than one page.)

Although you can move around the document using the mouse and the vertical and horizontal scrollbars, Works provides an additional aid in the Page and View controls in the bottom-left corner of your screen. The Page controls indicate which page you're on and how many total pages there are, and enable you to move one page up, one page down, or to the beginning or end of the document. The Zoom control enables you to magnify your view of the page, either by clicking the percentage and choosing a magnification from the list or by using the minus (-) and plus (+) buttons to zoom in or out.

Finding and Replacing Text

You can search for a particular word or phrase in your Works (or Word 97) document to assist you with proofreading, and you can replace the text that you find with another word or phrase. This feature is especially useful in longer documents.

To Do: Finding Words in Your Document

To find a word or phrase in an open document:

1. Choose Edit, Find from the menu.

2. In the Find dialog box (see Figure 19.6), enter the text for which you're looking in the Find What box and click Find Next.

FIGURE 19.6.

The Find dialog box.

3. If the text for which you're looking appears more than once in the document, click Find Next again to go to the next occurrence.

4. When you've come to the last occurrence of the text, you are prompted, "Works did not find a match." Click OK, and then click Cancel in the Find dialog box.

> If you start the Find program in the middle of your document, Works stops at the end and asks whether you want to start looking again at the beginning of the document. To avoid this extra step, make sure that your cursor is at the top of the document before you begin the Find process. You can get to the top of the document quickly by pressing Crtl+Home.

To Do: Replacing Words in Your Document

To replace the text that you find, follow these steps:

1. Choose Edit, Replace from the menu.

2. In the Replace dialog box, enter the text that you want to find in the Find What box.

3. Press Tab or click your mouse in the Replace With box. Enter the replacement text exactly as you want it to appear in the document.

19

▼   4. If you want to replace every occurrence of the text without seeing each one, click
         Replace All. Clicking Replace instead enables you to skip some of the found items
▲   if you don't want to replace them all. To skip an item, click Find Next.

The Find and Replace dialog boxes offer some extra features for customizing your
search. You can specify that your search match the case of the text that you enter in the
Find What box, and you can Find Whole Words Only. For example, a search that uses
both of these options would keep you from finding "candy" when you're looking for
"Andy."

Using a TaskWizard to Create a Basic Letter

Because Task Wizards are such a vital part of Works, we conclude this hour with a brief
TaskWizard walk-through to assist you in creating a letter.

To Do: Using a TaskWizard to Create a Letter

To create a basic word processing document with the Letter TaskWizard, follow these
steps:

1. If Works isn't currently open, open it by clicking the Start button, selecting
   Programs, Microsoft Works, Microsoft Works. Works opens and displays the Task
   Launcher.
2. From the Task Launcher's TaskWizards tab, click Common Tasks to see a list of
   tasks. Choose Letter from the list. Click OK to select the Wizard and close the
   Task Launcher.

> When you run any TaskWizard, a dialog box opens and asks whether you
> want to create a new document using a TaskWizard or work with an exist-
> ing document. Choose Yes, Run the TaskWizard to continue with your task.
> If you don't want to see this dialog box every time you run a TaskWizard,
> deselect the Always Show This Message option.

3. The TaskWizard begins by offering you three different types of letters:
   Professional, Simple, and Formal. As you click each one, you see a brief description of that particular type of letter and a sample appears.
4. Choose the Professional letter, and click Next.
5. In the next dialog box, a series of five buttons offers you the chance to customize
   the letter (see Figure 19.7). To accept the Wizard's default and create a simple
▼   blank document that you can fill in with your own content, click Create it!.

▼ **FIGURE 19.7.**

Letter options.

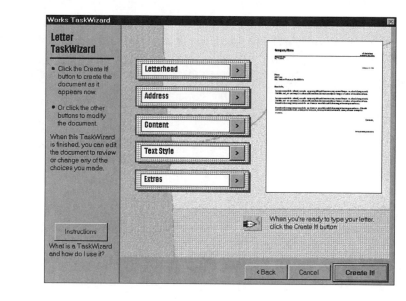

FIGURE 19.7.

Letter options.

> Whenever possible, let the Wizard do the work for you! The TaskWizard creates your letterhead with the fonts, styles, and layout already designed for you. This is the purpose of a Wizard—to take the formatting and design decisions out of your hands.

6. The Wizard's Checklist appears, showing the default settings for your letter:

   • Professional style (based on your choice in the first dialog box)

   • Wizard-designed letterhead

   • Single address

   • Prestige text style

   • No extras

7. To accept these settings, click Create Document. The Wizard begins building the letter, and the resulting document opens in a new window.

Inserting Text into a TextWizard Document

The Wizard creates a letter with sample text built in, such as "Company Name" and a sample phone number to assist you in creating your letterhead. To replace the sample text, highlight it and type your own text to replace it. The text that you type appears in

19

the same font and style as the sample text. (Figure 19.8 shows the letter's sample text replaced with a company name and other letterhead information filled in.)

FIGURE 19.8.

Inserting text.

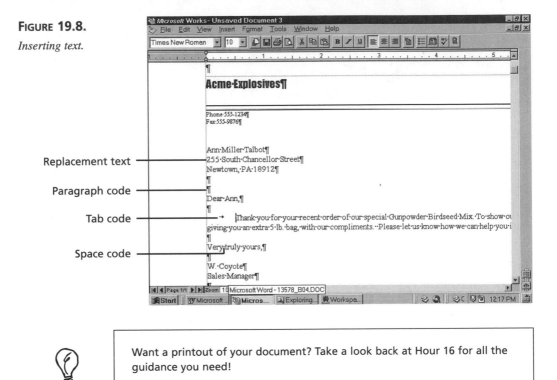

Want a printout of your document? Take a look back at Hour 16 for all the guidance you need!

Using the Thesaurus

Have you ever been writing a paper only to find that you seem to be using the same words time and time again? In Works, you can use the Thesaurus to look up alternative words (synonyms) for words you're using too often, or to get a word's definition by looking at other words that mean the same thing. To use the Thesaurus, select the word that you want to look up, and choose Tools, Thesaurus. The Thesaurus dialog box displays your word and the following two lists:

- A list of potential Meanings for your word appears on the left.
- A list of Synonyms (alternate words) appears on the right in the Replace with Synonym box. Depending on which meaning you choose, the list of synonyms changes.

If you only want to know what the word means, click Cancel to close the dialog box. If you want to replace your word with a synonym, select one from the list, and click Replace.

You can also use the Thesaurus to look up words that aren't in a document. In an open document with no text selected, choose Tools, Thesaurus. In the dialog box, type the word that you want to look up in the Replace with Synonym box, and click Look Up. The word that you inserted moves to the Looked Up box. A list of meanings appears on the left, accompanied by synonyms on the right.

Summary

Whew, what a frantic hour! The good news is that much of this information should be familiar to you because of what you learned about Windows and Word 97. The most important things to take with you from this hour are the way the Task Launcher works and what you can do with the Letter TaskWizard. The rest is primarily a variation of what you've learned earlier in the book.

The next hour should be a bit more subdued as we focus on the Works Spreadsheet Tool.

Workshop

The following workshop helps you solidify the skills you learned in this lesson.

Quiz

19

Take the following quiz to see how much you've learned.

Questions

1. If you want to track the amount of a mail order that you plan to place, which application tool do you use?

    a. Spreadsheet

    b. Database

    c. Word Processor

2. Why didn't we look at manipulating text in the Word Processor Tool?

    a. There wasn't enough room in the chapter.

    b. The author was too lazy to write that section.

    c. Because the Works word processor and Word 97 are so similar, it wasn't worth repeating all the information.

3. When you need to find an alternative to a word that you use too frequently, which tool do you consult?

    a. Grammar Checker

    b. Thesaurus

    c. Spell Checker

Answers

1. a. A spreadsheet is the way to go because you surely need to manipulate numbers.

2. c. The Works version is like buying a car without any options; it works just fine, but it may lack some of the fancy frills.

3. b. The Thesaurus, of course. The other tools don't help you much in this instance.

Activity

Launch Works and locate a project that interests you from the TaskWizard tab. When you've decided on one, make your way through the wizard to see just how the TaskWizard works.

Hour 20

Using the Works Spreadsheet Tool

A *spreadsheet program* is a software application that organizes data into rows and columns. Each entry is placed into a box called a *cell*. With groups of cells, numeric values can be calculated, and text can be sorted. The pages or documents these programs create are called *spreadsheets* or *worksheets*. As you'll see, these spreadsheets look similar to those green ledger sheets used before computers became so popular.

In this hour, you learn all the basics of using the Works spreadsheet tool. You also find the answers to the following questions:

- What is a spreadsheet?
- How do I move from cell to cell?
- After I've entered all the numbers, can I insert another column or row in the middle if I need it later?
- Is there a way to quickly add numbers in a spreadsheet without messing with nasty formulas?
- How can I make my spreadsheet look nice before I print it?

Launching a Spreadsheet

Maybe you don't use spreadsheets on a daily basis at work, so you may be wondering why on earth you'd want to use one at home. Spreadsheets are kind of like cordless phones. You can perform the task just fine the old way (corded phone), but after you've sampled the new way, you won't want to go back.

With spreadsheet programs, not only do you have the functionality of a calculator, but you can also manipulate numbers with ease; turn them into professional-looking tables; and even create charts and graphs based on them.

How many times have you asked yourself "what if" when it comes to finances? Questions like: "What if I got a $10,000 raise?" can be fun to ponder, and thanks to the spreadsheet tool, they're easy to ponder as well.

To Do: Opening the Spreadsheet Tool

To launch the Microsoft Works spreadsheet tool, follow these steps:

1. Open the Microsoft Works program by double-clicking the Shortcut to Microsoft Works icon on your desktop or by clicking Start on the taskbar and then choosing Programs, Microsoft Works, Microsoft Works.

2. From the Works Task Launcher dialog box (see Figure 20.1), click the Works Tools tab.

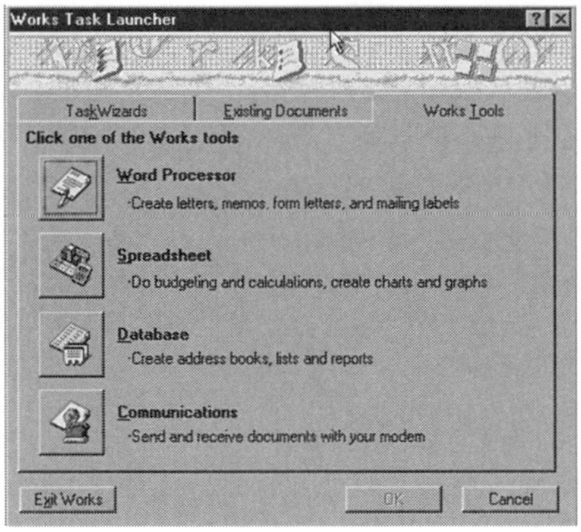

FIGURE 20.1.

The Works Task Launcher dialog box with the Works Tools tab selected.

▲   3. Click the Spreadsheet button.

Understanding the Spreadsheet Window

When you open the spreadsheet tool of Microsoft Works, you see two windows (see Figure 20.2). The main window is the program window for the spreadsheet tool. This window has several parts. Some of them are common to all programs designed to work in Windows: the title bar, Minimize button, Maximize/Restore button, Close (x) button, and the menu bar.

FIGURE 20.2.

The Microsoft Works spreadsheet tool window.

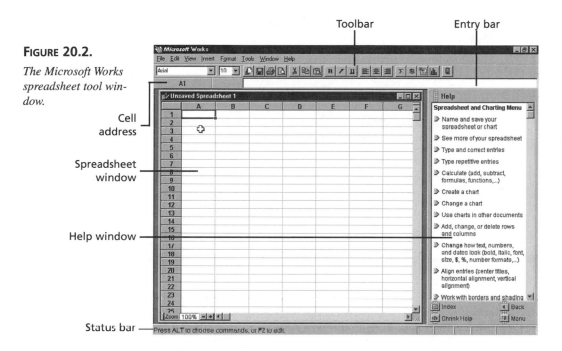

Some parts of this window are unique to the spreadsheet tool; these parts are explained in the following list:

- *Toolbar*. The toolbar allows you to quickly access some of the most frequently used menu commands by clicking the appropriate button. To find out what each button does, point to it. A small ToolTip label will pop up beneath the button to identify it. The status bar (see next list item) also displays a brief explanation of what the tool does. If your toolbar is not showing, choose View, Toolbar from the menu bar.

- *Status bar*. The status bar is the horizontal bar that appears at the bottom of your screen. It displays important information such as your location in the spreadsheet, descriptions of menu commands and toolbar buttons, and keys that are locked

20

(such as the Caps Lock key). If the status bar is not showing, choose Tools, Options from the menu bar, click the View tab, and place a check mark in the Show Status Bar box.

- *Cell address.* The name of the currently active cell in your spreadsheet is displayed below the toolbar, to the left of the Entry bar. The active cell is the cell in which your cursor is placed. Cells are referenced by the column name and row number, so cell A1 is in the first row of the first column.

New Term *Cell addressing* applies to all spreadsheet programs. All columns are named A, B, and so forth, with A starting at the leftmost column. All Rows are numbered 1,2, and so forth, beginning with row 1 at the top of the spreadsheet. The intersection of a column and row is a cell address, named with the column name followed by the row name (A1). This also applies to many tables in word processing programs.

- *Entry bar.* The area below the toolbar where you type or edit information to be entered in a cell on the spreadsheet.

- *Spreadsheet window.* Each spreadsheet you start or open has its own window. The name of the spreadsheet file appears on the title bar of that window (unless you've maximized the spreadsheet window, in which case the filename appears alongside "Microsoft Works" on the title bar of the program window). If you haven't saved the spreadsheet file, "Unsaved Spreadsheet #" appears on the title bar, where # represents the number of this spreadsheet. The number changes depending on how many spreadsheet files you've opened in this particular session; each one is numbered in order as it's opened.

- *Help window.* The Help Window appears to the right of the spreadsheet window. If you don't need the Help window, choose Help, Hide Help from the menu to make it disappear. Choose Help, Show Help to make it reappear. To make the Help Window smaller without having it totally disappear, click the Shrink Help button on the Help window. Click it again to make the Help Window expand.

In the spreadsheet window, you see a grid of small rectangles (see Figure 20.3). Each of these rectangles is called a *cell.* Data is entered in a cell. An *active* cell has a thick border around it and is the cell in which your cursor currently resides. A cell must be active before you can enter data in it.

A cell occurs at the intersection of a column and a row. Columns are identified by letters of the alphabet (A through IV). There is a gray border above the first row of cells that contains the *column headers* that identify the name of each column.

FIGURE 20.3.

The spreadsheet window.

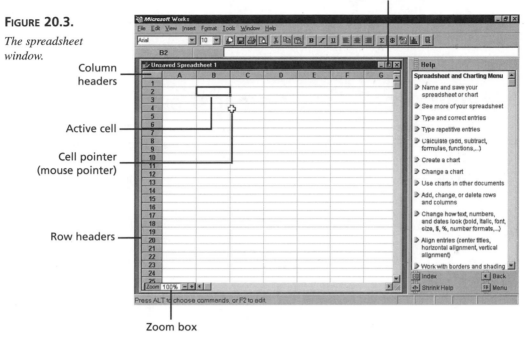

Maximize button

Column headers

Active cell

Cell pointer (mouse pointer)

Row headers

Zoom box

A through IV? What's that? When you reach Z in your column headers, you have to find a new way to label subsequent columns. You might think the sequence of columns would be AA, BB and so on, but they're not. It goes AA, AB, and so on through AZ, then the next set of columns begins with BA, BB, on through BZ. The pattern continues until you reach IV.

To the left of the first column is a gray border that contains the *row headers* that identify the name of each row (1 through 16,384).

Each cell is referenced by its *cell address*. The cell address consists of the column name plus the row name. Therefore, the cell address of the top cell in the first column is A1; the cell address of the last cell on the spreadsheet is IV16384.

To see more of the spreadsheet, you can do one or all of the following:

- Maximize the spreadsheet window by clicking the Maximize button to the right of the title bar on that window.

- Shrink the Help window by clicking the Shrink Help button at the bottom of that window or hide the window by choosing Help, Hide Help from the menu.

20

- Click the Zoom box at the bottom-left of the Spreadsheet window and select the magnification level you want, or click the + button to zoom in or the – button to zoom out.

Moving Around the Spreadsheet

One way to move around the spreadsheet is to use the mouse. All you have to do is click the cell you want. If you can't see the cell you want, use the vertical scrollbar to move up and down the spreadsheet or the horizontal scrollbar to move left or right on the spreadsheet. Using scrollbars is explained in Hour 4, "Working with Menus, Toolbars, and Dialog Boxes."

Another way, which is sometimes the easiest and quickest method of moving around the spreadsheet, is to use the keyboard shortcuts detailed in Table 20.1.

TABLE 20.1. KEYBOARD SHORTCUTS FOR MOVING AROUND THE SPREADSHEET.

Press	To
←	Move one cell to the left
→	Move one cell to the right
↑	Move one row up
↓	Move one row down
Tab	Move one cell to the right
Shift+Tab	Move one cell to the left
Home	Move to beginning of row
End	Move to end of row (last cell containing data)
Page Down	Move one screen down the spreadsheet
Page Up	Move one screen up the spreadsheet
Ctrl+Home	Go to A1 (the first cell on the spreadsheet)
Ctrl+End	Go to the last cell in the spreadsheet that contains data

To go to a specific cell address, choose Edit, Go To. In the Go To dialog box, enter the specific cell address or range you want to go to, or select a range name from the ones listed. Click OK.

Exiting the Spreadsheet

When you want to exit Microsoft Works, choose File, Exit. If you have made changes to the spreadsheet that you haven't already saved, Works will ask if you want to save it. Click Yes if you want to save it, No if you want to exit without saving the spreadsheet, or Cancel if you decide not to exit Works at this time.

If you only want to go back to the Task Launcher, don't exit Works, just click the Task Launcher button on the toolbar instead. That way you don't need to close your spreadsheet file. If you just need to open a file created in another Works tool, choose File, Open, select the file from the Open dialog box, and then click OK.

Entering Text

Entering text into these cells may seem a bit intimidating at first because we're not used to thinking of text in such a way, but it's really not much more complicated than using a word processing program.

To Do: Enter Text into Your Spreadsheet

To enter text in your spreadsheet, do the following:

1. Click the cell (or use the keyboard shortcuts to go to the cell) where you want the text to appear. That cell then becomes the *active* cell.

2. Type the text. As you type, the text will appear in both the cell and in the Entry bar at the top of the spreadsheet.

3. Press Enter or click the check mark next to the Entry bar to accept your text entry.

If you're entering data (text, numbers, dates, or times) and you want to enter information in a series of cells, you don't need to press Enter after each entry. Instead, press the arrow key pointing in the direction you want to go. Works accepts the entry and moves to the next cell all in one motion. If you're entering data by columns, use Tab the same way, pressing Tab after each entry to accept the data, and then move one cell to the right.

20

> Moving through a spreadsheet or a table with the use of the arrow and tab keys can be done in most spreadsheet programs and in most tables in word processing programs.

Entering Numbers

Because this is the spreadsheet tool, you'll undoubtedly want to know how entering numbers differs from entering text. The fact is, there isn't as much of a difference as you may think.

To Do: Entering Numbers into Your Spreadsheet

To enter numbers into the spreadsheet, follow these steps:

1. Click the cell (or use the keyboard shortcuts to go to the cell) where you want the number to appear. That cell then becomes the active cell.

2. Type the number. As you type, the number will appear in both the cell and in the Entry bar at the top of the spreadsheet.

3. Press Enter or click the check mark next to the Entry bar to accept your number entry.

When entering numbers, you may use dollar signs ($), percentage signs (%), and decimal points (.).

Entering Dates and Times

The best way to enter dates is with slashes (1/12/98), especially if you want to use them for calculations such as figuring ages or length of employment. You can always format it later to appear as text (January 12, 1998). If you do enter the date as text (January 12, 1998), however, Works can reformat it later to appear with slashes (1/12/98). Avoid is entering the date with dashes (1-12-98) because Works treats that as text and won't change the date format or recognize it as a date for calculations.

When entering times, add AM or PM for morning or afternoon (10:00 PM) or use the 24-hour, or military, clock (22:00). You can specify time to the second (10:00:03 PM).

To Do: Entering Dates and Times in Your Spreadsheet

To enter dates or times in your spreadsheet, follow these steps:

1. Click the cell (or use the keyboard shortcuts to go to the cell) where you want the date or time to appear. That cell then becomes the active cell.

▼

2. Type the date or time. As you type, the date or time will appear in both the cell and in the Entry bar at the top of the spreadsheet.

3. Press Enter or click the check mark next to the Entry bar to accept your date or time entry.

▲

Using Undo

If you make a mistake in an entry while you are typing it, just backspace and enter the correct text. Don't use the arrow keys to move back and forth, because you'll end up in one of the cells next to the one where you wanted to enter the data, and your mistake will remain in the original cell.

After you accept the entry, the fastest way to fix it is to undo the mistake. Choose Edit, Undo Entry from the menu (Ctrl+Z is the keyboard shortcut for Undo). However, you must use undo immediately after making the error because you can only undo the very last thing you did.

Saving and Closing the Spreadsheet

To avoid losing the data you entered in your spreadsheet, you must save your file. When you save your file for the first time, you must name it and locate it in a folder where you can find it later. A filename can be up to 256 characters, including spaces. To make it easier to find the file later, you should keep the filename as short and simple as you can. Also, put the important part of the name first as files are listed alphabetically. For example, a file called "Report of Monthly Income" will fall under R, although one called "Monthly Income Report" would be found under M.

To Do: Saving and Naming Your Spreadsheet

To save your file the first time and give it a name, follow these steps:

1. Choose File, Save. The Save As dialog box appears (see Figure 20.4).

2. From the Save In drop-down list, select the drive and/or folder where you want to save the file. Click the down arrow next to the list to see the choices and then click the one you want. Refer to Hour 6, "Working with Drives, Files, and Folders," to learn more about how drives, files, and folders are organized in Windows.

3. In the File name box, enter the name you want to give the file.

4. If you want to save the original version of the spreadsheet as is while also saving the version with your changes each time you modify the file, check Create Backup Copy. Just remember that by enabling this option you'll always end up with two files when you save the spreadsheet, and that can take up room on your disk.

▼

▼ To Do

20

▼   Furthermore, your second backup copy will overwrite the first, so bear that in
            mind.

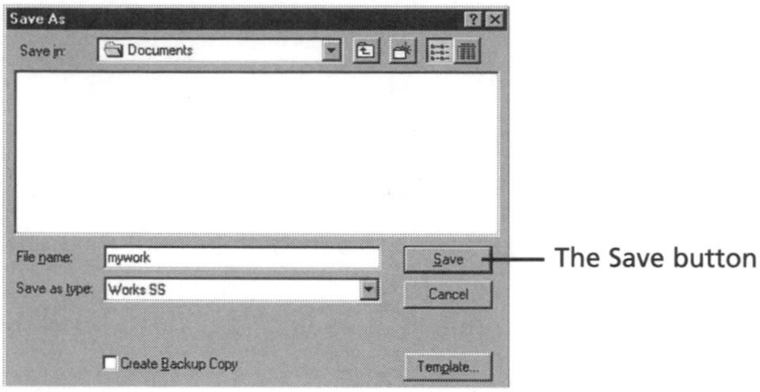

FIGURE 20.4.

*The Save As dialog
box.*

The Save button

▲   5. Click Save.

After you've modified a file, you'll need to save it again. You can use one of the following three methods and Works will save the file to the name you gave it originally without
opening a dialog box:

- Choose File, Save.

 • Click the Save button on the toolbar.

- Press Ctrl+S.

You should save your file frequently so you don't lose any valuable information you've
entered or waste time entering data over again. If you haven't saved your file and the
power goes out or your system crashes, you'll have to re-create it.

On some occasions you'll want to save a spreadsheet as a new file with a different name
so you can make modifications without destroying your current file. For example, if
you've prepared an accounts receivable spreadsheet for the first quarter, you may want to
use the same form for the second quarter. You don't want to lose your first quarter
spreadsheet, so you can save it again but give it a different name. This leaves your old
file intact with its original name and creates a duplicate of the first. You can then change
the duplicate to meet your needs for the second quarter.

To Do: Saving a File to a Different Name

To save a file and give it a different name:

1. Choose File, Save as. The Save As dialog box appears.

2. From the Save in drop-down list, select the drive and/or folder where you want to
   save the new file. Click the down arrow next to the list to see the choices, and then
   click the one you want.

▼   3. In the File name box, enter the name you want to give the file.

▲   4. Click Save.

To Do: Closing a Spreadsheet

After you've finished using a spreadsheet, you will want to close it before you go on to other work.

1. Choose File, Close from the menu bar.

2. If you have made modifications to the file since you last saved it, Works will ask you if you want to save the file. Click Yes if you want to save it, No if you don't want to save it, or Cancel to stop the closing of the file. You are returned to the Works Task Launcher dialog box.

Opening a Spreadsheet

To work on an existing spreadsheet file, you must first open that file (these instructions assume that you've already launched the spreadsheet tool of Microsoft Works).

To Do: Opening an Existing Spreadsheet

1. Choose File, Open from the menu bar. The Open dialog box appears as shown in Figure 20.5.

2. From the Look In drop-down list, select the drive and/or folder where you stored the file.

FIGURE 20.5.

The Open dialog box.

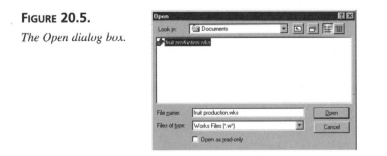

20

3. Select the filename from the list of files.

▲   4. Click Open.

Selecting Cells and Ranges

Before you can delete, move, copy, or format data, you must select the cells to be involved in the operation. The active cell is automatically selected, but if you want to involve additional cells, you must highlight them.

The entries of a highlighted cell have a black background, except for the cell where the selection originated. The first cell in the group (or range) keeps its white background and dark text. The entire highlighted area has a thick border around it, which appears to be a block.

Table 20.2 lists the methods (both keyboard and mouse) for highlighting cells in your spreadsheet.

TABLE 20.2. How to highlight (select) cells.

To Highlight	Mouse Method	Keyboard Method
A cell	Click the cell	Press an arrow key
A group of cells	Starting with the mouse pointer in the first cell, hold down the mouse button, and drag to the last cell in the group	Starting with the first cell in the upper-left corner of the group, press F8, and then use the arrow keys to highlight the rest of the cells
A row	Click the row header	Highlight one cell in the row and then press Ctrl+F8
A column	Click the column header	Highlight one cell in the column and press Shift+F8
The entire spreadsheet	Click the corner header cell where the column headers and row headers meet (upper-left corner of spreadsheet)	Press Ctrl+Shift+F8

When you have to enter data in a large block of cells, highlight the cells first. Then starting in the first cell in the upper-left corner of the block, enter the data and press Enter. Works automatically moves you to the next cell, first going down one column, then moving to the top of the next column to the right, down that column, then to the next column on the right, and so on.

Editing Data

If you have entered data incorrectly and it's too late to undo the entry, you can correct it by replacing the entry or by editing the entry.

To replace information in a cell, click the cell containing the information you want to replace, type the new information, and press Enter. The new entry will wipe out the old one.

To Do: Editing Your Information

To edit the data that is already in the cell, follow these steps:

1. Click the cell that contains the data you want to change.
2. Click the Entry bar to place an insertion point (cursor) there (see Figure 20.6).

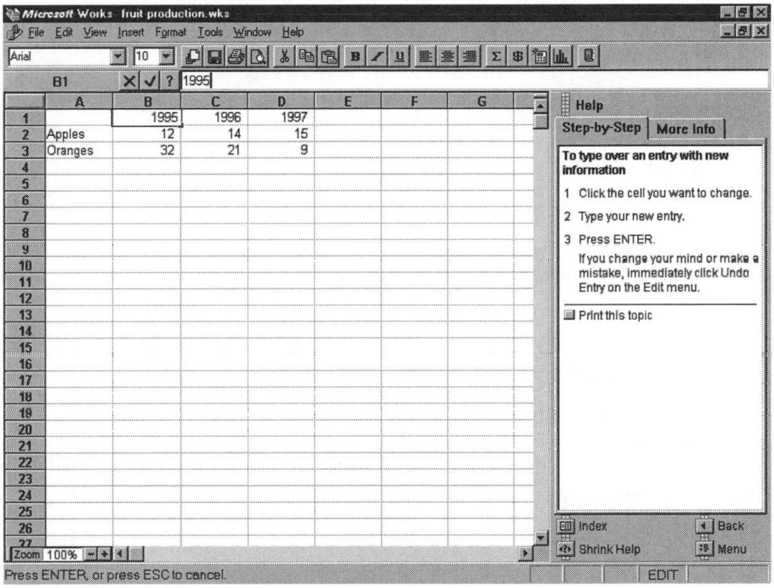

FIGURE 20.6.

The Entry bar while editing an entry.

3. If you want to add characters, click where you want to insert them or use the arrow keys to move the cursor and then type in the new information.

   If you want to remove characters, click immediately after the characters and press Backspace until they disappear. To remove a larger number of characters, highlight them and press Backspace or Delete.

▲ 4. Press Enter or click the check mark by the Entry bar.

Double-click the cell to be edited and make your changes in the cell using the arrow keys to move the cursor and use Backspace and Delete to remove unwanted characters.

Deleting Data

You can easily delete data from either a single cell or a group of selected cells. Keep in mind that if you delete the wrong information, you can retrieve it by quickly choosing Edit, Undo Clear.

To Do: Deleting Data from Your Spreadsheet

To delete data from a cell or group of cells:

1. Highlight the cell or cells that contain the data you want to remove.

2. Press the Delete key or choose Edit, Clear from the menu.

Moving Data

You can move data from one part of a spreadsheet to another, or from one spreadsheet to another spreadsheet.

There are two methods of moving data. This first method works well for moving data within a spreadsheet from one area to another.

To Do: Moving Information from One Area to Another in a Spreadsheet

1. Highlight the cell(s) you want to move.

2. Point to the edge of the highlighted cell or group of cells.

3. When the mouse pointer changes to an arrow with the word "Drag" under it (see Figure 20.7), hold down the mouse button and drag the highlighted cell(s) to a new location. An outline of the cells appears as you drag, and the word "Move" replaces "Drag" under the mouse pointer. Release the mouse button and the data is relocated.

The second method works well within a spreadsheet but also well when moving data from one spreadsheet to another.

FIGURE 20.7.

The mouse pointer when it's ready to move data.

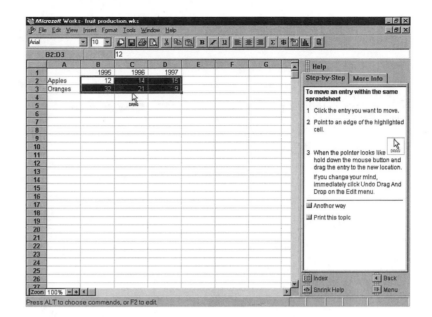

To Do: Moving Data from One Spreadsheet to Another

1. Highlight the cell(s) you want to move.

2. Choose Edit, Cut or click the Cut button on the toolbar.

3. Click the cell (or the top-left corner of a group of cells) where you want the data to appear.

   If you want to insert the data in another spreadsheet, you must open that spreadsheet first, and then click the cell where you want the data to appear.

4. Choose Edit, Paste or click the Paste button on the toolbar (if you need to switch back to the original spreadsheet file, choose Window from the menu and then select the name of the spreadsheet from the bottom of that drop-down menu).

Copying Data

There are two methods of copying data. This first method works well for copying data within a spreadsheet from one area to another.

20

To Do: Copying Information from One Area to Another in a Spreadsheet

1. Highlight the cell(s) you want to copy.

2. Hold down the Ctrl key.

3. Point to the edge of the highlighted cell or group of cells.

4. When the mouse pointer changes to an arrow with the word "Drag" under it, hold down the mouse button and drag the highlighted cell(s) to the location where you want the copy placed. An outline of the cells appears as you drag, and the word "Copy" replaces "Drag" under the mouse pointer. Release the mouse button, and the data is copied.

To Do: Copying Data from One Spreadsheet to Another

The second method works well within a spreadsheet but also very well when copying data from one spreadsheet to another.

1. Highlight the cell(s) you want to copy.

2. Choose Edit, Copy or click the Copy button on the toolbar.

3. Click the cell where you want the data (or the top-left corner of a group of cells) to appear.

   If you want to insert the data in another spreadsheet, open that spreadsheet first and then click the cell where you want the data to appear.

4. Choose Edit, Paste or click the Paste button on the toolbar (if you need to switch back to the original spreadsheet file, choose Window and then select the name of the spreadsheet from the bottom of that drop-down menu).

Using AutoSum

Need to add a bunch of numbers quickly? You can use a calculator to figure out what those totals are and enter the numbers, you could create a formula to calculate the numbers, or you can have Works automatically calculate the total for you using its AutoSum feature.

NEW TERM A *formula* is an algebraic expression using cell addresses that tells Works what operations to perform on the contents of the designated cells. For more information about programming spreadsheet formulas, use the Works EasyCalc feature introduced in the next section, or read Que's *Microsoft Works 4.5 6 in 1*.

To Do: Using AutoSum to Automatically Total Rows and Columns

To automatically total columns or rows, follow these steps:

1. Enter the numbers in your spreadsheet.

2. Click inside the next blank cell (at the end of the column or row), then click the AutoSum button on the toolbar.

3. If totaling the numbers in a column, all the cells in the column are highlighted and a formula appears at the bottom of the column and in the Entry bar.

    If totaling the numbers in a row, all the cells in the row are highlighted and a formula appears at the end of the row and in the Entry bar.

4. Press Enter if these are the cells you want to total.

    If you don't want to total all the highlighted cells, highlight just those cells you want to include in the total and then press Enter. These cells must be contiguous (joined together).

Working with EasyCalc

EasyCalc is a feature of Works spreadsheet that will assist you in writing formulas. EasyCalc is a good tool to use if you are new to spreadsheets.

To Do: Writing Formulas with EasyCalc

To use EasyCalc, do the following:

1. Click in the cell where you want the results of the formula to appear.

2. Choose Tools, EasyCalc from the menu bar or click the EasyCalc button on the toolbar. The EasyCalc dialog box appears (see Figure 20.8).

3. Under Common Calculations, click the button for the type of calculation you want to perform (click Other to see a full list of functions).

4. Follow the instructions in the dialog box to build your formula. If you need to click a cell in the spreadsheet and the dialog box is in the way, point to the title bar of the dialog box and drag it out of the way.

5. Enter whatever values or cell addresses you need to complete your formula (or click the appropriate cells to enter the addresses).

6. Click Next.

7. EasyCalc asks you to confirm the cell address where the formula will go. Enter the correct cell address if it isn't already showing in the Result At box.

20

▼ **FIGURE 20.8.**

The EasyCalc dialog box.

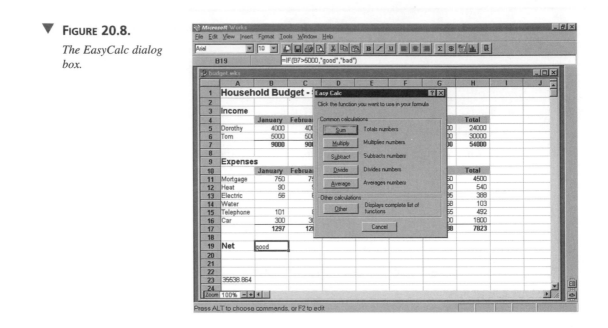

8. Click Finish. The results of the formula now appear in the designated cell and the
▲ Entry bar shows the formula.

Sorting Data

If the thought of creating a database (see Hour 21, "Using the Works Database Tool")
intimidates you, consider using the Works spreadsheet tool as a lightweight database
because it can, after all, sort text and numbers too. There may also be times you need to
enter data as it comes to you, and that data is in no specific order. That can happen if you
hope to catalog your collection of music CDs, or even as you make new friends and
acquaintances and want to add them to your database.

Face it, trying to find information out of order can be a royal pain in the neck. Luckily,
Works provides you with the tools you need to sort the data in a spreadsheet *after* you
have entered it.

To Do: Sorting Your Data

To sort data, do the following:

1. Select the data you want to sort.

2. Choose Tools, Sort from the menu bar. The Sort dialog box appears (see Figure
20.9).

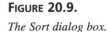

FIGURE 20.9.

The Sort dialog box.

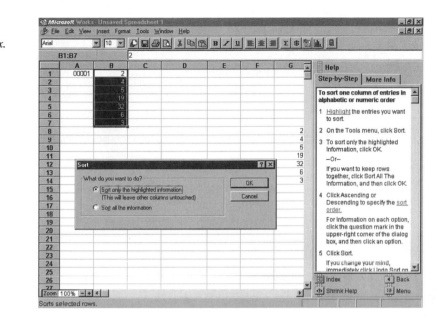

3. To sort one column of entries you've highlighted, click OK. If you want to sort a range of information based on one of the columns in the highlighted range, select Sort All the Information and then click OK.

4. When the dialog box changes, choose the column you want to use for sorting from the Sort By drop-down list.

5. Choose your sort order: Select Ascending to sort the column A-Z, 1-100, Descending to sort Z-A, 100-1.

6. If the first row of your highlighted sort range has column headings, select the Header Row option under the My List Has section so Works will ignore that row when it sorts. Otherwise, select No Header Row.

7. Click Sort.

If you want to sort by more than one column, click the Advanced button in the Sort dialog box. You can then specify a second and third column to sort by. (This is useful if the first column contains last names and the second column holds first names. You might want to sort first by last names and then by first names in case you have more than one person with the same last name). To start the sort from the Advanced options box, click Sort.

20

Inserting Columns and Rows

Suppose that you have this beautiful spreadsheet all laid out but suddenly you discover something's missing. What do you do?

Luckily you won't have to cut, paste, and move things around. You can easily add a column or row as needed.

To Do: Adding Columns to Your Spreadsheet

To add a column to your spreadsheet, follow these steps:

1. Click the column header to the right of where you want to add the column. This will highlight that column.
2. Choose Insert, Insert Column.
3. The columns will move over to make room for the new column.

To Do: Adding Rows to Your Spreadsheet

To add a row to your spreadsheet, follow these steps:

1. Click the row heading below where you want to add the row. That row will be highlighted.
2. Choose Insert, Insert Row.
3. The rows will move down to make room for the new row.

> You can also right-click the mouse to bring up context-sensitive menus while working in the spreadsheet. When you right-click while in the spreadsheet, you will see a menu that includes an option to insert a column or row.

Delete Columns and Rows

When you delete a column or row, be sure that no information remains in that column or row that you want to keep.

To Do: Deleting Columns and Rows from Your Spreadsheet

1. Click the column header or row header of the column or row you want to delete to highlight it.
2. Choose Insert, Delete Column or Insert, Delete Row.

Moving Columns and Rows

If it's rearranging you need to do, that's easy with the spreadsheet tool as well. You'll be surprised how easy it is to move columns and rows after you've done it a few times.

To Do: Moving Rows and Columns in Your Spreadsheet

To move a column or row, you will use the cut-and-paste methods:

1. Click the gray column header to highlight the column you want to move, or click the gray row header to highlight the row you want to move.

2. Choose Edit, Cut from the menu bar or click the Cut button on the toolbar.

3. Click the column header to the right of where you want the column to appear or click the row header below where you want the row to appear.

4. Choose Edit, Paste from the menu bar or click the Paste button on the toolbar. The moved column is inserted into its new location.

Using AutoFormat

Can't make up your mind which colors to use? Don't want to spend time formatting the spreadsheet? Then AutoFormat is for you. AutoFormat offers you a set of predesigned formats that you can apply to your spreadsheet.

To Do: Formatting Your Spreadsheet

To use AutoFormat, complete these steps:

1. Choose Format, AutoFormat from the menu bar. The AutoFormat dialog box appears (see Figure 20.10).

FIGURE 20.10.

The AutoFormat dialog box.

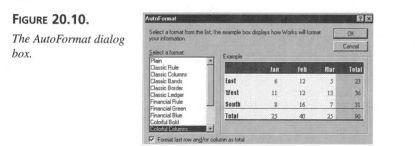

2. Choose a format from the Select a Format list. A sample of that format displays in the Example window.

▼　　3. Select Format last row and/or column as total only if you have totals in the last row or column.

▲　　4. Click OK to close the dialog box and apply the formatting.

Printing a Range

As you learned how to print documents in Hour 3, "Windows Desktop Basics," if you don't want to print the entire spreadsheet, you can specify which pages you want to print. If the portion of the spreadsheet you want to print is not an entire page, however, you can print only a range of cells. To do this, you must set a print area before you open the Print dialog box.

To Do: Printing Ranges in Your Spreadsheet

To set a print range, do the following:

1. Open the spreadsheet.

2. Highlight the portion of the spreadsheet you want to print.

3. Choose Format, Set Print Area from the menu bar.

4. A Works alert box appears asking whether it's okay to set the print area to the high-lighted cells and warning that it will print only the highlighted cells. Click OK.

▲　　5. Print as you learned in Hour 3.

When you no longer want to use the specified area as a print range and would like to go back to printing the entire spreadsheet, you need to remove the print area setting:

To Do: Removing a Print Range

1. Choose Insert, Range Name from the menu bar. The Range Name dialog box appears.

2. In the Select a name box, click Print Area.

3. Click Delete.

▲　　4. Click Close.

After removing the Print Area range name, you can now print the entire spreadsheet.

Summary

Do you feel like a spreadsheet expert now? In one short hour, you learned about the elements of spreadsheets and how to take advantage of some of Works' powerful features designed to make computing easier. You were introduced to AutoSum, EasyCalc, and

AutoFormat, all of which can go a long way toward giving you the results you desire with minimal hassle.

In the next hour, we'll explore the world of databases.

Workshop

The following workshop helps you solidify the skills you learned in this lesson.

Quiz

Take the following quiz to see how much you've learned.

Questions

1. What do you call the boxes that each number or text string is placed in?

   a. Data boxes

   b. Worksheets

   c. Cells

2. What does AutoSum do?

   a. Automatically adds the sum of a group of cells

   b. Generates a summary of your worksheet

   c. Automatically figures out your monthly payments for a new car

3. Why would you use AutoFormat?

   a. When you want lengthy, but perfect worksheet output

   b. When you want a worksheet formatted quickly and without hassle

   c. When you want a detailed tour of the formatting options available to you

Answers

1. c. Individual cells make up the parts of a worksheet.

2. a. AutoSum is the fastest, simplest way to add numbers using the Works spreadsheet tool.

3. b. This feature definitely saves time.

20

Activity

Pick a group of numbers, say your list of monthly expenses, or the products (and their prices) you want to order from a catalog that you have lying around the house. Enter them into a Works spreadsheet. After they're entered, use AutoSum to add up all the numbers. Finally, use AutoFormat to make the worksheet look professionally done (even if the subject matter isn't so professional).

Hour 21

Using the Works Database Tool

The term *database* has a dual meaning: It is used both to describe a type of program as well as the type of file that you create in the program. This is similar to the way we use the term *spreadsheets*.

A database program automates the process of creating, collecting, sharing, and managing almost any kind of information. That information might be a list of names and addresses used for club membership and for tracking dues, or it might be an inventory of your miniature die-cast car collection.

In this hour, I introduce you to the basics of working with databases. In addition, the following questions are answered:

- Why would you use a database?
- What do fields do?
- How do I move around within a database?
- Do I have to design a database myself to maintain an address book, or can I use a Works TaskWizard?
- How can I print a database report?

When Do You Need a Database?

In the last hour, you learned that you can use the Spreadsheet Tool for small database-like jobs. When, however, do you need to turn to the Database Tool? You need a database when you need to keep large lists of data, track status, sort, or extract information from that data. Typical database applications include:

- *Address book*. This is a list of names and addresses that can be sorted by name, address, zip code, or phone number. You can also extract a list of people in a particular area code or zip code.

- *Inventory*. This is a list of personal or business items that can be sorted by status (on hand, on order) location (dining room, warehouse), ordering information, vendor, value, or price of an item.

- *Customer list*. This is a list of customers that can be sorted by location, status (active or inactive), salesperson, or contact name.

The Parts of a Database

As you build a database, you are building a table of information, and like a spreadsheet, a table has rows and columns. The primary components of any database are fields and records.

NEW TERM   A *field* is the smallest piece of data in the database. Fields represent such information as First Name, Last Name, Address, City, and so forth.

NEW TERM   A *record* is a set of fields. In a customer database, each customer is a record.

NEW TERM   A *database* consists of records—one record for each item in the database. Each record is made up of fields. Fields are the pieces of data that you enter about each item, such as First Name, Last Name, Address, and Phone Number in a personal address book.

Fields are displayed in columns in the database table, and the field name appears at the top of the column. Records are displayed in rows in the database table. In the example of a club membership database, each person in the club is a record. (Figure 21.1 shows a database table with records and fields.)

You can add information to the database by typing directly into the table, or you can create forms for entering data. Input forms are easier to read than tables. (Figure 21.2 represents an input form in an employee database.)

FIGURE 21.1.

The database table displays information in columns and rows.

Fields —

Record —

Table —

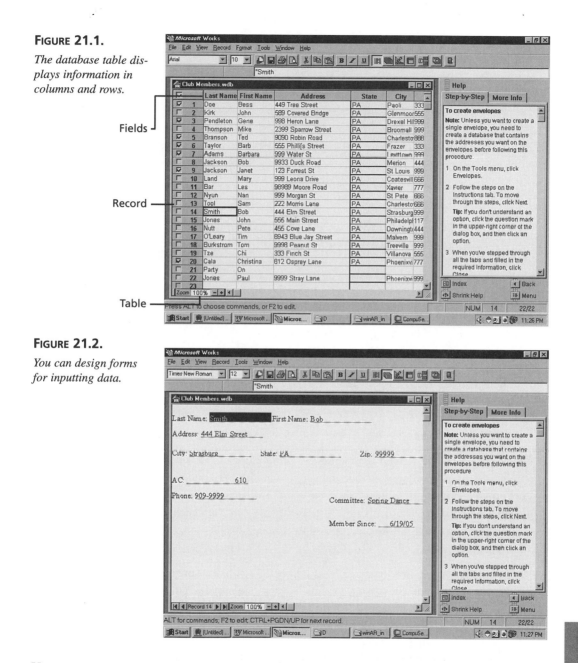

FIGURE 21.2.

You can design forms for inputting data.

21

You create reports when you want to print information from your database. With a report, you can print all or some of your data, and you can sort, extract, and format the appearance of that data. For example, Figure 21.3 is a report created in an employee database, listing all employees whose retirement year is 1997, and sorted by employee number.

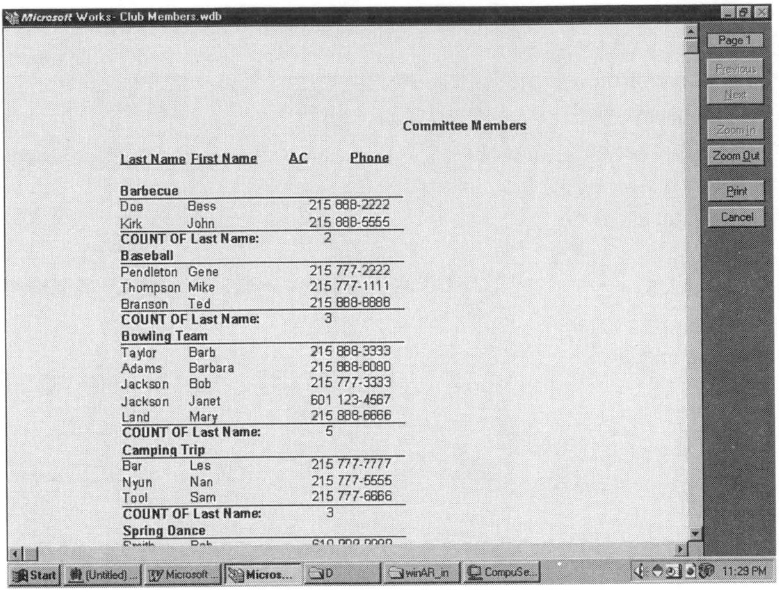

FIGURE 21.3.

Create reports and print your data. Data can be sorted, manipulated, or extracted using Reports.

Database Window Contents

The Database window opens after you have finished creating and entering new fields into a new database or when you open an existing database. If you have left Works and want to reopen a database file, start Microsoft Works. In the Works Task Launcher, click the Existing Documents tab. Locate your database in the document list and click OK.

Databases can be viewed in List mode, Form mode, and Report mode. Figure 21.4 shows the Database Window, which contains two windows—the main window on the left in List view and the Help window on the right. The default mode is List view. (You learn more about views later.) Like all Microsoft windows, the Database window has a title bar, Minimize button, Maximize/Restore button, Close button, a menu bar, a toolbar, and a status bar.

The Database window in List view is laid out much like a spreadsheet or table. Rows in the database window represent records in your database and columns represent fields. The intersection of a row and a column is called a *cell*, the same as it is called in a spreadsheet. (As you can see in Figure 21.4, no data has been entered into the database; therefore, the cells are blank.)

The Database Menu Bar

The Database menu bar contains the features and functions of the program—commands such as File, Open, Edit, and Cut can be accessed by clicking the menu item once.

A drop-down menu appears showing options within that category. You can also access the menu by holding down the Alt key while pressing the underlined letter in the menu. Most of the functions of the program are found in the menu, and the menu is context sensitive—that is, it changes depending upon the view and function you are performing while in the Database tool. If you take a moment to read the menu options by clicking each item in the menu bar, it helps you to become familiar with the features of the Database tool.

FIGURE 21.4.

The Microsoft Works Database tool window.

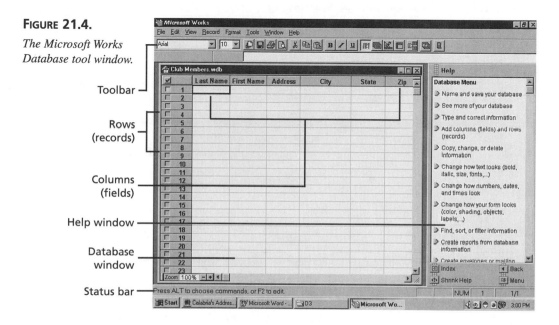

Toolbar

Rows (records)

Columns (fields)

Help window

Database window

Status bar

The Database Toolbar

Like all Windows products and programs, the Database toolbar represents shortcuts for menu commands. You can click an icon in the toolbar instead of selecting a menu item. Not every menu item, however, is represented on the toolbar.

Displaying the toolbar is optional. If your toolbar is not displayed (shown in Figure 21.4), choose View, Toolbar from the menu. Use the same commands when you want to hide the toolbar.

As you point with your mouse to each button on the toolbar, a small yellow box appears below the tool indicating what the tool is. The yellow box is called the *tool tip*. (If your tool tips don't appear, choose Tools, Customize Toolbar, check Enable Tool Tips on the dialog box, and then click OK.) When you point at a toolbar button, a brief explanation

21

of what that tool does is displayed on the status bar at the bottom of the screen. (Table 21.1 lists each icon found on the Database toolbar. Figure 21.5 displays the toolbar.)

FIGURE 21.5.

The Database toolbar.

TABLE 21.1. THE DATABASE TOOLBAR BUTTONS.

Tool	Name	Description
 Arial	Font Name	Applies font to selected text or cells.
 10	Font Size	Changes point size of selected text.
	Task Launcher	Opens the Task Launcher dialog box and gives you access to TaskWizards, existing documents, and Works tools.
	Save	Saves the active document.
	Print	Prints the active document using the current print defaults.
	Print Preview	Displays the active document as it will look when it's printed.
	Cut	Removes the current selection from the document and stores it in the Clipboard.
	Copy	Stores a duplicate of the current selection in the Clipboard.
	Paste	Inserts the contents of the Clipboard at the insertion point (where the cursor is positioned.)
 B	Bold	Makes the current text selection bold (or bold off if the selection is already bold).
 I	Italic	Makes the current text selection italic (or turns italic off if the selection is already italicized).
 U	Underline	Underlines the current text selection (or turns off underline if the selection is already underlined).
	List View	Displays the current selection in List, or table View. This is the default view.

Tool	Name	Description
	Form View	Displays the database records, one at a time, in a form instead of a table. Uses the default form created by Works if you have not designed a form.
	Form Design	Displays the forms design view, enabling you to change the order and appearance of fields, and to add fields, objects or labels.
	Report View	Runs the Report Wizard to create a new report, or displays the last active report.
	Insert Record	Creates a new, blank row in the table at the insertion point so that you can create a new record between existing records.
	Filters	Runs a Wizard to create a filter, applies existing filters, or enables modification of existing filters.
	Address Book	Opens the default Address Book.

Moving Around the Database

Although you may not yet have added data to your database, you can still move around the database window. Move to a field by clicking the cell. Use the vertical scroll bar to move up and down the database, or use the horizontal scroll bar to move left or right on the database table. (For more information on using scroll bars, see Hour 4, "Working with Menus, Toolbars, and Dialog Boxes.") Another way to move around the database is to use the keyboard shortcuts detailed in Table 21.2.

TABLE 21.2. KEYBOARD SHORTCUTS FOR MOVING AROUND THE DATABASE WINDOW.

Press	To
←	Move one cell to the left.
→	Move one cell to the right.
↑	Move one row up.
↓	Move one row down.
Tab	Move one cell to the right.
Shift+Tab	Move one cell to the left.
Home	Move to beginning of row.

21

continues

TABLE 21.2. CONTINUED

Press	To
End	Move to end of row (last cell containing data).
Page Down	Move one screen down the database.
Page Up	Move one screen up the database.
Ctrl+Home	Go to A1 (the first cell on the database).
Ctrl+End	Go to the last cell in the database that contains data.

To move to a particular field, choose Edit, Go To from the menu. In the Go To dialog box, select the field that you want. Click OK.

Creating a Database the Easy Way

Creating a database from the ground up can be a daunting task for even the most experienced computer user, but I show you one of the easiest ways to produce a real database.

In the sections that follow, I walk you through the Works TaskWizard, which can be used to produce one of the most popular types of databases—an address book. This walkthrough not only shows you how to make your own address book, but it also serves as a great example of how to work with databases in general.

Starting Your Address Book

A major benefit of maintaining an electronic Address Book is that, unlike the manual version, you can keep many different books for all the different types of contacts that you have, both personal and business. Each Address Book is a separate file, but all the files can be in one location—your computer. In addition, you can customize the Address Book that you create with Works to include the extra information that you want to keep about your contacts.

To Do: Using the Address Book TaskWizard

You can access the Address Book TaskWizard from the Task Launcher:

1. Choose Address Book from the Common Tasks or Household wizards and click OK. A dialog box appears asking whether you want to run the TaskWizard or see a list of existing documents. Click Yes, and Run the TaskWizard. If you deselect Always Show This Message, you won't see this dialog box in the future.

2. The Wizard begins. Choose the type of Address Book you want to create. Your options are

▼
- Personal
- Business
- Customers or Clients
- Suppliers and Vendors
- Sales Contacts
- Employees

3. For the purposes of this lesson, choose Personal and click Next. (You access the other types of Address Books in the same way.)

4. The next window shows what fields you see in your Address Book. Click Next to move to the next step.

5. The TaskWizard enables you to customize your Address Book in three areas (see Figure 21.6):

- *Additional Fields*. You can add extended phone numbers, personal information about the contact, and a notes area.

- *Your Own Fields*. This dialog box enables you to create up to four new fields. Simply click the field check box and type a name that is no more than 14 characters long.

- *Reports*. Choose either an alphabetized book or a categorized one. You can also choose both options, to enable either type of printout later.

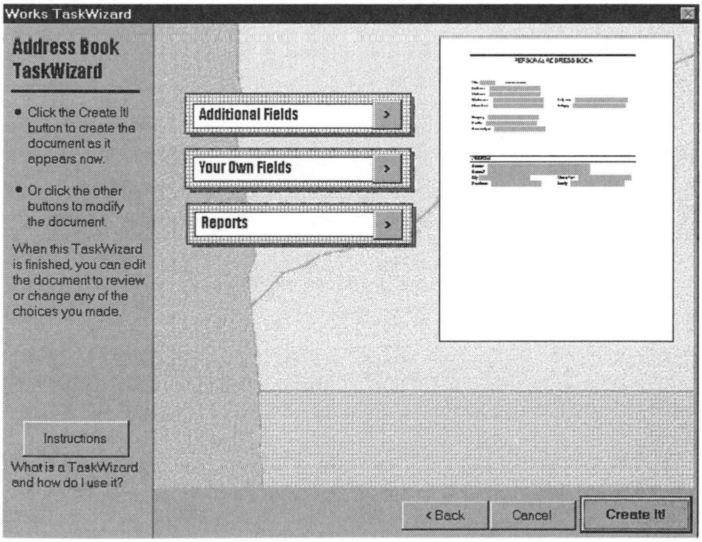

FIGURE 21.6.

Customization options.

▼

▼ 6. To customize your address book, click the desired button. Another box opens with options for customizing the database. Select the options that you want to apply and click OK.

7. Click Create It! to begin the TaskWizard's creation process.

8. Next, you see a checklist of the options you chose in the previous steps. To con-
▲ firm them and create the Address Book, click Create Document.

Entering Your Data

The TaskWizard creates a database entry form (see Figure 21.7) containing the basic Address Book fields for the type of book that you chose to create, as well as the optional fields you added.

To Do: Entering Information into Your Address Book

To begin entering your Address Book records, follow these steps:

1. The shaded box to the right of the Title label is already highlighted, ready for you to enter data. (If it isn't, click the shaded box).

2. Type the contact's title.

FIGURE 21.7.

The Address Book Entry form.

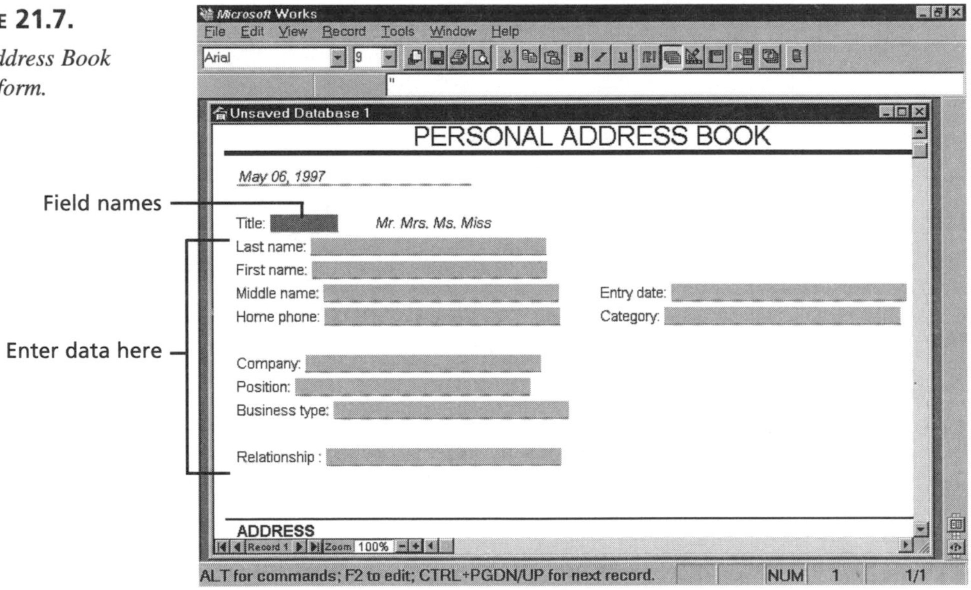

▼   3. To move to the next field, press the Tab key. To move backward, press Shift+Tab.

     4. Enter information into all the fields for which you have data.

> As you enter text into the fields, the text also appears in the Entry bar—a box above the database window. If you make a mistake, you can edit the text that has been typed into a field.

> To make changes, place your cursor in the Entry bar and add or delete existing characters. Press the Enter key to commit to your changes, or click the Enter button (the check mark) and return to the database.

> When entering dates, be sure to type the slashes between the month, day, and year—for example: 5/17/97. This helps the tool recognize it as a date.

     5. When you reach the last field in your record, press Tab to move to the first field in a new, blank record. You can also jump out of the current record and go to a new, blank record by choosing Record, Insert Record. Continue following steps 1–5
▲   to enter data for each record that you want to include in the address database.

Copying and Deleting Records

If you have contacts in one Address Book that you want to duplicate and use in another, you can copy the records from their current location and paste them into the new location. This saves you from typing redundant information.

To Do: Editing Your Database

To copy and paste a record, follow these steps:

To Do

     1. Make sure the record that you want to copy is the currently displayed record. Use the record navigation buttons at the bottom-left corner of the screen to move from record to record.

     2. Choose Edit, Copy Record.

     3. Go to a blank record and choose Edit, Paste Record. An identical record appears.

▼   4. In the pasted record, make any changes to the data that are unique to that record.

21

▼ To delete a record, follow these steps:

   1. Display the record that you want to delete.

▲ 2. From the Records menu, choose Delete Record.

> If you delete the wrong record and you catch your mistake immediately,
> choose Edit, Undo Delete Record. If you didn't notice your error right away,
> you have to reenter the record from scratch.

Address Book Views

You can work in one of two views as you enter records into your Address Book. The
default view is the Form view. You can also work in List view, which shows each record
horizontally. List view looks like a spreadsheet with each field in a column and each
record in a row. To switch between these two views, use the View menu, and choose
either List or Form.

> As you enter data for each record in List view, the field names in the first
> column disappear. To keep your field names visible in the List view, select
> the second column and choose Window, Split from the menu. Now as you
> scroll to the right, your field names remain in view..

Sorting Your Address Book

After you've completed your Address Book, you can sort the records. Sorting refers to
the order in which the database records are presented. The order in which you choose to
display or print your Address Book depends on your perspective—which aspect (field) of
your data contains the information that's most important to you.

To Do: Sorting Records in Your Address Book

To sort your Address Book, do the following:

   1. In either Form or List view, choose Records, Sort Records from the menu.

   2. A dialog box opens with three levels for sorting. In each level, the field names
      appear in a drop-down list.

   3. Choose a field on which to sort, and select Ascending or Descending order.

   4. Use the Then By drop-down list to choose fields for second- or third-level sorts,
      and click OK. The records appear in the order that you specified.

Filtering Your Address Book

You may want to see a listing of only specific people—perhaps those who work for a specific company or live in a particular state. To do this, you must filter out the people who don't meet these criteria.

To Do: Filtering Records in Your Address Book

To see only certain records from within your Address Book database, follow these steps:

1. Choose Tools, Filters from the menu. The Filter Name box appears.

2. Name your filter and click OK. Naming filters enables you to keep track of the filters that you've used before so that you can run them again without setting them up from scratch.

3. From the Field Name drop-down list, choose the field that contains the information that you want to use as a filter (see Figure 21.8).

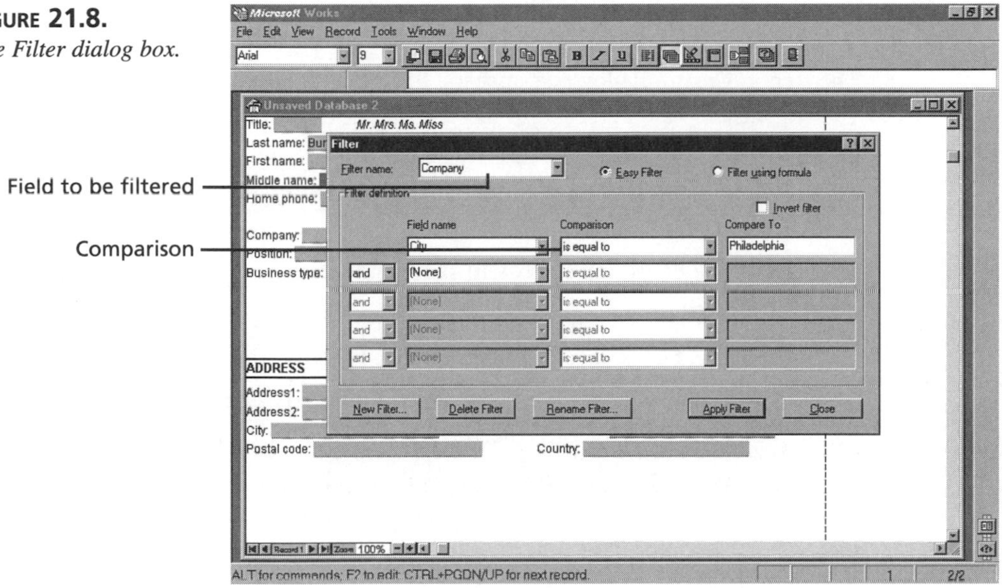

FIGURE 21.8.
The Filter dialog box.

Field to be filtered

Comparison

4. Choose a method of filtering by selecting a phrase from the Comparison drop-down list—such as is equal to, begins with, or greater than.

5. In the Compare To text box, enter the value (field content) that you want as your filter. For example, if you want to find all the residents of Philadelphia in your address book, the field name you want to select is City, the comparison phrase is is equal to, and Philadelphia is the text that you enter in the Compare To box.

21

▼
▲   6. Click Apply Filter. The records that meet your criteria appear one at a time in
         Form view, or as a numbered list in List view.

Creating Address Book Reports

In addition to printing a simple one-page-per-record report, you can design a customized
report that shows only the fields that you need.

To Do: Printing Reports

To create and print a customized report, follow these steps:

1. Choose Tools, ReportCreator.

2. In the Report Name dialog box, give your report a name, and click OK.

> You can change a report's name later by choosing Tools, Rename Report.

3. The Report Creator dialog box appears. Each tab represents a part of the report
    you can customize (click Next to move to the next tab, and Previous to return to
    the last tab).

    • *Title.* Contains options for the name of the report, the paper orientation, and
      the font of the title text.

    • *Fields.* Select which fields will show on the report.

    • *Sorting.* Choose the order in which the records print.

    • *Grouping.* Gives you the option to have records grouped by common data.

    • *Filter.* Choose from filters you named previously or create a new
      filter. Only those records meeting your filter criteria show on the report.

    • *Summary.* Set up your report to display such things as a count of items, sum
      totals, or average values under each group of records.

4. When your report customization is complete, click Done.

5. A dialog box appears offering the option to preview the report or modify it. Choose
    to Preview your report. The report appears in a Print Preview window. You can
    move from page to page by clicking the Next and Previous buttons in the Preview
    window. To enlarge your preview, click Zoom In.

6. To print the report as it appears in the preview, click Print. Click Cancel to exit the
▲   Preview window without printing.

Summary

As you saw during the course of this hour, creating a database can be more than a little complex, with so many concepts unique to databases. At least now you have a general feel for what they are and do, and thanks to the Microsoft Works TaskWizards, you can do so much with databases in minutes that would otherwise take hours.

This hour concludes our discussion of Microsoft Works 4.5. In the next hour, we turn our attention to Microsoft Money 98—an application that can help you organize and manage your finances.

Workshop

The following workshop helps you solidify the skills that you learned in this lesson.

Quiz

Take the following quiz to see how much you've learned.

Questions

1. What is a database field?

    a. Something in which you plow and plant corn

    b. The smallest piece of data in a database

    c. A place where they play databaseball

2. Immediately after making a mistake, what keystrokes do you press to correct it?

    a. Ctrl+Z

    b. Ctrl+U

    c. Alt+Z

3. What is the difference between sorting and filtering?

    a. There is no real difference.

    b. Sorting puts all your records into order or groups, whereas filtering can single out records based on your chosen criteria.

    c. Sorting puts your records in order, while filtering removes all the lint on your disk drive.

21

Answers

1. b. Sorry, there won't be any databaseball world series in the near future.

2. a.

3. b. Try as you might, filtering does not remove the lint from your disk drive!

Activity

Okay, so maybe it's the wrong time of year for New Year's resolutions, but that doesn't mean you shouldn't seize the opportunity to get organized. I challenge you to go rummaging through your desk drawers, wallet, and pockets in search of those business cards and scribbled phone numbers that you vowed to one day put in a safe place. Oh, and don't forget to check those piles of papers stashed in various places throughout your home!

Hour **22**

Getting Started with Microsoft Money 98

Whether you simply want to keep tighter control over your checking account or you want to create a monthly budget to help put some money away for a new house, Microsoft Money 98 may be just what you're looking for.

In this hour, we cover some of Money's basic setup and housekeeping issues. In addition, the following questions are answered:

- How do I create a shortcut icon for Money on my Windows desktop?
- Can I monitor credit card accounts with Money?
- How do I back up my files?
- Help, my computer died; now what?
- Am I able to print checks with Money?

In this hour, it is assumed that you have Money 98 preinstalled on your system as part of Microsoft Home Essentials or some other special offer. If you do not have the program, you can always choose to purchase it and install it yourself. See Appendix A, "Installing Windows Applications," or the installation instructions that come with the software.

Launching Money 98

To launch Microsoft Money 98, click Start on the Windows taskbar, choose Programs, Microsoft Money. The Money home screen (shown in Figure 22.1) is the first thing you see.

FIGURE 22.1.

The Money home screen before any data is entered.

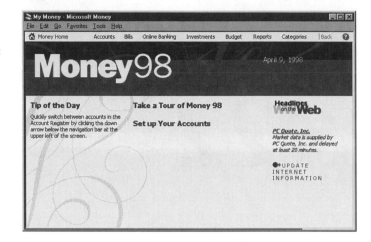

If you've had the opportunity to browse the Web in the past, you notice this home screen's similarity to a Web page. It includes a tip of the day for using Money 98, a link to stock quotes, a chart of the day reflecting your finances (after you've entered data into Money 98), and perhaps a list of bills due in the near future. (You learn how to schedule bills to appear on the home screen in Hour 23, "Using Money 98.")

Launching Money for the First Time?

The first time you start Money 98, you see a File Required dialog box. This asks you to create a file in which to store your Money files. Money 98 stores everything that you enter in this neat little package.

To Do: Creating a File to Store Money 98 Information

To create this file from the File Required dialog box, do the following:

1. Click the Open File button. You see the Open File dialog box with which you've grown so familiar.

2. In the File Name text box, enter a name for your file, preferably something descriptive such as my money, money stuff, or something such as that.

3. Click the New button. The New dialog box appears, holding the filename that you entered in the previous step.

4. Click OK to create the file. After a few seconds, the home screen appears (refer to Figure 22.1).

Create a Shortcut Icon to Launch Money 98

One of the keys to making a program such as Money 98 work well for you is to enter every piece of data regularly. What better way to remember than to place a Money 98 icon on your desktop? Each time you boot your computer to play a game, surf the Net or whatever, you have a gentle reminder staring you in the face.

22

> Money helps you most if you use it faithfully. To help you do this, you may want to create a shortcut icon to Money on your Windows desktop to help remind you. (Refer to Hour 6 to learn how to do this.)

Anatomy of the Money 98 Home Screen

Because this is where all your work with Money begins, it's important that you know all the parts of the screen as well as Money's menus—what they do and where they take you.

The following is a brief description of each element (see Figure 22.1):

- *Menu Bar.* The Money 98 menu bar includes some familiar elements as well as a couple of new ones.
    - *File.* Use this menu item to create a password, back up your files, import files from another program, or print out checks.
    - *Edit.* This menu gives you access to the ever-popular cut, paste, and copy commands.
    - *Go.* This menu mirrors the Navigation bar; it takes you to various sections of Money 98 such as Accounts, Bills, and Categories.
    - *Favorites.* You can even save certain accounts as Favorites using this menu.
    - *Tools.* Use this menu to update the Internet information on the Money 98 home screen, edit your Categories list, or set Money 98 options.
    - *Help.* The Help menu leads you to general program assistance organized similarly to the general Windows help (see Hour 3, "Windows Desktop Basics"). You can also access special help for ordering checks that you can run through your printer.
- *Navigation Bar.* This white bar, located directly underneath the menu bar, is the fastest way to make your way.
- *Back Button.* Pressing this button returns you to the screen that you were viewing previously.

Keeping Your Financial Data Safe

When it comes to your finances, you can never be too cautious. You may want to assign a password to your money files to protect them from unauthorized access.

To Do: Setting a Password for Your Money Accounts

Follow these steps to assign a password to your money files:

1. Launch Money 98.

2. Select File, Password from the menu bar. The New Password dialog box appears (see Figure 22.2).

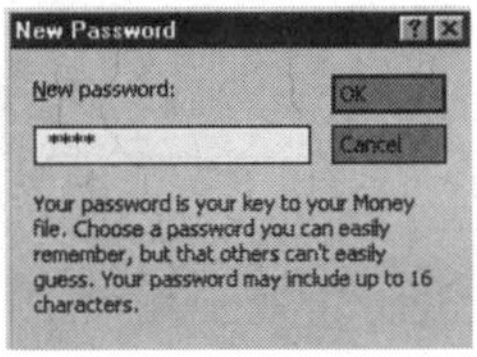

FIGURE 22.2.

The letters in your password appear as asterisks, in case someone is peeking over your shoulder.

3. Enter your chosen password in the text box, and click OK.

> Your password can be up to 16 characters long. When choosing one, be careful not to select something obvious such as a child or spouse's name, the name of a pet, or even the kind of car you drive. Instead, opt for something such as a character from a favorite book or movie, or perhaps a favorite song followed by your favorite NASCAR driver's car number—anything that isn't easily found in a dictionary.

4. You are asked to verify the chosen password by re-keying it. After you've done so, press OK. Your password is now set.

Setting Up a New Checking or Savings Account

You need to create a new account for every bank account that you have whether it is a checking account, a savings account, or even a second checking or savings account.

To Do: Setting Up Your Checking Account

Nearly everyone has a checking account. You need one to pay the telephone bill and other basic expenses. To set up your checking account in Money 98, do the following:

1. From the Money 98 home screen, click the Accounts button. The Account Manager window shown in Figure 22.3 appears.

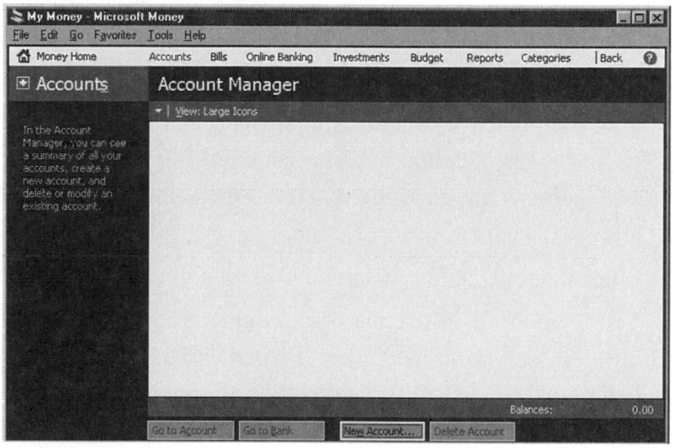

FIGURE 22.3.

This is the window you use to manage all your accounts after you define them.

2. Click the New Account button at the bottom of the screen. You're guided through a series of dialog boxes used to describe the account that you want to set up.

3. Enter the name of the bank or financial institution in which you hold the account, and press Next>.

> If you already hold an account at the institution, you may select its name by clicking the drop-down arrow next to the text box and selecting its name from the list. Note that this drop-down arrow only appears if you've already defined other accounts.

4. The next dialog box asks you to specify the type of account that you want to create. For the sake of this exercise, choose checking account. For future reference, you see a description of the other account types in this dialog box. Press Next> to continue.

> Setting up a savings account is identical to setting up a checking account, except, of course, that you specify savings instead of checking when you're prompted for the account type.

5. Next, enter a description of the account that helps to differentiate it from other accounts held at the same institution. For example, Wayne's Savings Account. This information also appears in the Account Manager window. Press Next>.

6. You are then asked to specify your purpose for creating the account. This information, used primarily for devising budgets and savings plans, can be classified one of four ways—Spending money for day-to-day expenses, a Short term savings/rainy day fund, Long term savings and investments, or Other. Press Next> after you've made your selection.

7. Enter the applicable account number, and click Next>.

8. You are then asked to enter the account's balance and type of currency. The second question may seem like a breeze compared to the first. If you don't know the exact ending balance, don't panic; you can always change it later. Press Next>.

9. The final dialog box asks whether you have other accounts at the same institution. If you select yes, you are led through another set of dialog boxes. If you said no, you can press Finish to complete the account's setup.

Setting Up Credit Card Accounts

If you're like many Americans, you probably have a credit card or two, maybe even more. Setting up a credit card or line of credit account is similar to setting up a checking account, with a few important differences.

To Do: Setting Up a Credit Card Account

With your account information in hand, follow these steps to set up your credit card account:

1. Select Accounts from the Money 98 Navigation bar to open the Account Manager window (refer to Figure 22.3).

2. Click New Account at the bottom of the Account manager window.

▼
3. Supply the name of the bank or financial institution that holds the account. Press Next> to proceed.

4. Select credit card from the kinds of accounts listed. Press Next>.

5. Next, you are asked to give the account a name. For example, your credit card for Target might have Retailer's National Bank for the name of the institution (the payee), but you know it as your Target card. This enables you to call it both. Click Next>.

6. You are then asked to tell Money 98 how much you owe on the account. If you don't know for sure, use the ending balance from your last statement; you can always back in the transactions when you get your next statement. (You learn more about this in Hour 23, "Investigating Online Banking.") Press Next>.

7. In the next dialog box, Money asks you whether the account is a credit card (an interest-charging account that you do not have to pay off every month) or a charge card (which you must pay off every month). You also have the option to tell Money that you want to pay the account's entire balance each month by checking the Always pay entire balance box. When you're finished, click Next>.

8. Supply the credit card's interest rate in the next dialog box. If an introductory rate is in effect, check the appropriate box, enter the introductory rate, the date it expires, and the permanent interest rate. Click Next> to continue.

9. Enter the account's credit limit, and then press Next>.

10. Tell Money whether you plan to keep track of all charges to the account or not, and then click Next>.

11. Finally, Money asks you whether you want to put the bill's due day on the Bill Calendar so that you are reminded that it's due on the money home screen. You must also provide the estimated monthly amount of the bill, its next due date, and the account from which you want to pay it (for example, checking). Click Finish to
▲ complete the setup.

Categorizing Your Money

Money 98 gives you dozens of ways to categorize your expenses. To see what they are, launch Money 98, and then click Categories on the Navigation bar. The Categories and Payees screen appears (see Figure 22.4).

FIGURE 22.4.

Money 98 gives you oodles of categories to start with.

Notice that the categories are arranged hierarchically. For example, Gasoline falls under Automobile. In this case, Automobile is the parent category—or simply category—and Gasoline is a subcategory.

You may be wondering why you should bother categorizing your income and expenses. Two words say it all—budget and IRS. These categorizations give you much better control over budgeting because you can see exactly where your money's going (and hopefully coming from). It can also simplify things greatly come tax time, though sadly use of some of the most powerful Money 98 tax features requires you to know your tax forms in excruciating detail. You can, however, still generate some terrific tax itemizations, which is a heck of a lot more than we may have had to begin with in most cases.

Recategorizing transactions after the fact can be a nightmare at best. I strongly urge you to take a few moments now to get acquainted with Money 98's existing categories and subcategories and how they work for your specific situation.

Chances are, you'll find at least a couple of categories and subcategories that you want to add.

To Do: Creating a New Category

Creating a new Money 98 category is as simple as following these few steps:

1. From within Money 98, click the Categories button on the Navigation bar. The Categories and Payees window you saw back in Figure 22.4 appears.

2. Click the New button found at the bottom of the screen. The New Category dialog box pops up. It asks whether you want to create a new category, or create a subcategory within an existing one. Click the New category radio button, and then click Next>.

22

3. Next, you are asked to give the new category a descriptive name. Specify whether it's an income or expense category. Make the appropriate selections, then click Next>.

4. Money then asks you to choose a concept for your new category. This enables the program to map your various expenses for tax purposes. Often Other expenses is as close as you come. Click Finish when you've made your selection.

Your new category appears with all the other categories in alphabetical order. But what if you want to create subcategories under the new category? We've got that covered, too.

To Do: Creating a New Subcategory

To create a subcategory under your new category (or under an existing one, for that matter), follow these steps:

1. From within Money 98, click Categories on the Navigation bar. The friendly Categories and Payees window appears again.

2. Click the category under which you want to create a subcategory to activate it.

3. Click the New button at the bottom of the screen. The dialog box in Figure 22.5 appears.

FIGURE 22.5.

Verify that the proper parent category is listed before moving on.

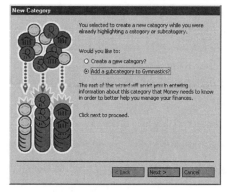

4. Verify that Money lists the correct parent category, select the Add a subcategory to radio button, and then click Next>.

5. Money asks you to name the subcategory. It also gives you a second chance to verify that the subcategory is being created under the proper parent. If it isn't, just click the arrow next to the Subcategory for drop-down box and select the desired category. Click Next>.

6. You can specify a mapping concept as you did above for budgeting and tax purposes. Click Finish after you've made your selection.

The new subcategory appears on the Categories and Payees window under the category that you specified.

Keeping Track of the Payees

As you see in the next hour when we finally put Money to work, Money 98 can remember some of the things that you tell it. For instance, when you enter the name of your mortgage company a second time, the mortgage company's name magically appears after you type just a few letters. Money 98, however, has much more to it than that. You can enter tons of data about a payee that you can access in a heartbeat.

What if you lose a credit card? You can have the issuer's toll-free number and the account number a click away without having to sift through a bunch of dusty old papers. Or what if you want to pay a bill in advance, but don't have a payment stub with the payee's address handy? By carefully collecting information on all your payees—or at least those that you deal with on a regular basis—you can save yourself a lot of aggravation and hassle in the long run.

To Do: Entering Information About a Payee

Because you're a beginning Money user and I haven't shown you how to log in transactions yet, I assume you haven't defined any payees yet. That means you have to create a payee before you can enter details about the payee.

This exercise goes a lot smoother if you have the necessary paperwork on your payees close at hand.

The following steps guide you through creating and providing details for a new payee:

1. From within Money, click the Categories button on the Navigation bar.

2. Click the Payees button on the left side of the screen. The Payees list appears, which is probably still empty in your case.

3. Press the New button at the bottom of the screen. A tiny dialog box appears.

4. Enter the name of the payee, and click OK. The payee's name appears in the Payees window.

5. Double-click the payee's name to begin entering data on it. The window in Figure 22.6 appears.

▼

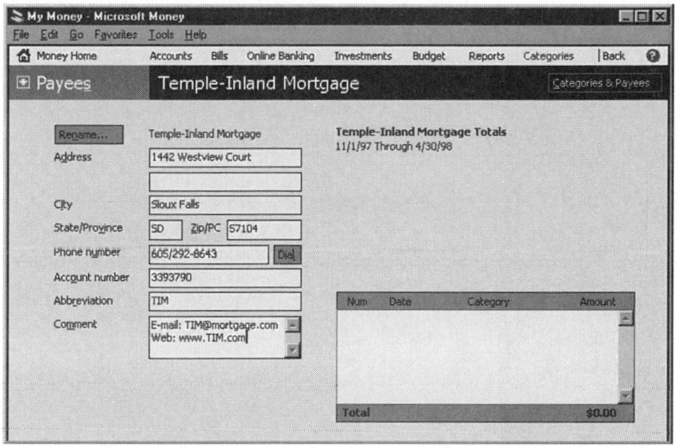

▼ **FIGURE 22.6.**

A comment box is even provided in which to squeeze information for which you are not prompted.

22

6. The fields in the payee's window are pretty self-explanatory. After you've finished entering the information that you want to have on hand, you can go about adding other payees. Money saves the data for you without doing anything else.

▲

Shutting Down Money 98

Money 98, like most other applications, can be shut down a variety of ways. You can select File, Exit, or simply double-click the x in the upper-right corner of the program window.

Because Microsoft believes that backing up financial files is vitally important, you are prompted to back up your files each time that you exit the program.

To Do: Backing Up Your Money Files Upon Exiting the Program

These steps show you how to back up your Money 98 files:

1. Exit Money 98 as described above. The Back Up dialog box appears.

Oddly, Money 98 automatically saves its backup to another file on the C drive, the very same drive that holds the original copy of the files. Let's face it, if something happens to the original that requires you to fall back to a backup, chances are it's because something happened to the hard drive. Do yourself a favor by backing up to a clearly labeled floppy disk.

▼

▼ 2. Insert a clearly labeled floppy disk into your machine.

3. Click the Browse button in the Back Up dialog box.

4. Click the arrow next to the drop-down Save in box, and select 3 ¹/₂ Floppy (A:) from the list as shown in Figure 22.7.

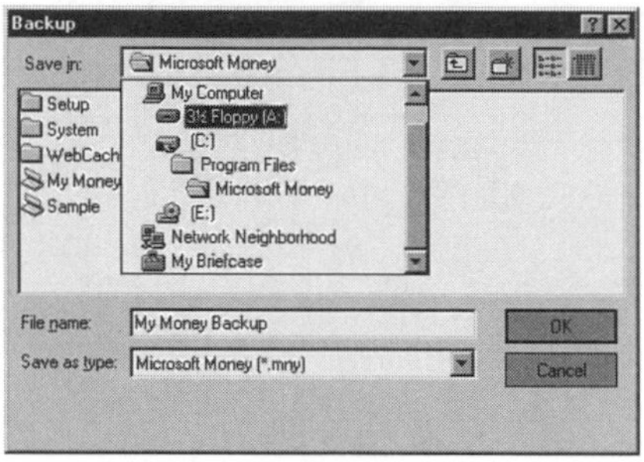

FIGURE 22.7.

Selecting Save in 3 1/2 Floppy assures that you have a useable backup copy of your files should you need it.

5. Click OK, and press the Back Up button. The floppy drive grinds away as it compresses your files.

6. You're done with the backup. Now take the disk out of your machine and put it in
▲   a safe place—preferably one that you'll remember!

Money 98's a smart little application; it remembers what you've told it. All you have to do in the future to create a backup copy of your files is place your money disk in the floppy drive, exit the program as usual, and press the Back Up button. The backup file is saved to the floppy disk just like before.

Recovering from Disaster

You thought it would never happen to you, but your luck runs out. One day without warning, your hard drive screeches to a halt. You can't do anything with the system except cringe over all those hours you spent keying in data. Luckily, you had the foresight to back up your Money 98 records, right?

After you've replaced the hard drive or had it repaired, you'll be happy to know that restoring your financial records is relatively painless.

To Do: Restoring Your Money Files from a Backup Copy

I hope you are never in this situation, but the following are the steps you need to follow just in case you ever have to restore your Money files from a backup copy:

1. Put the floppy with the backup copy of your Money files into your system's A drive.

▼   2. Launch Money 98, and select File, Restore. The file that you restore from the A
         drive should appear in the Restore file from list. If it doesn't, click the arrow by the
         Look in drop-down box and select the A drive.

      3. Click the Restore button. The Restore dialog box displays all your Money files, but
         as a precaution, it asks you to give the restored file a new name so as not to erase
         its original.

      4. Enter the new name of the file in the File name text box.

      5. Click OK. The new data file appears after a few moments. If you backed up the
         data the last time you used Money, you're in luck; you won't have to reenter any-
▲   thing.

You're back in business!

Printing Checks: Know What You're Getting Into

As you may have assumed, Money 98 is capable of printing your checks for you. The
question remains, however, do you really want it to?

For starters, you need a printer. You may or may not have bought one at the same time
you purchased your computer. Although printers have gotten increasingly more affordable, it may not be worth buying one right away just to print checks. If you plan to print
documents or Internet content, too, that's an entirely different matter.

Perhaps the biggest deterrent to having Money print your checks is the cost. Microsoft
charges around $50 for only 250 checks. Your bank might charge $15 for 500! Even
Microsoft as much as admits that you don't print checks with Money 98 to save money;
you do it to save time and keep yourself organized. Hey, it's in the Help file!

If you're still interested in having Money print checks, you want to launch Money and
select Help, ordering Checks to see just what they have available. When you've selected
your checks, you will want to call 1-800-432-1285 to order them so that you can begin
using Money 98 as soon as possible.

Summary

In this hour, you learned how to set up Money 98 by creating accounts, payee listings,
and categories. We also explored the pros and cons of printing your checks with this
powerful program.

Next hour, we finally put Money 98 to the task. We learn how to pay bills and reconcile
our accounts, along with a host of other interesting tidbits.

Workshop

The following workshop helps you solidify the skills you learned in this lesson.

Quiz

Take the following quiz to see how much you've learned.

Questions

1. What can you do to protect your Money 98 data?

   a. Create a password

   b. Create a backup file on a floppy disk

   c. Hire an armed guard

2. Which of the following cannot be found on the money home screen?

   a. A link to stock quotes

   b. A list of bills due in the near future

   c. The weather forecast

3. What should you do if your computer's hard drive dies?

   a. Lay down and cry.

   b. Make sure that you know where that Money 98 backup disk is!

   c. Shout obscenities and threats until the hard drive starts working again.

Answers

1. a., b. Although I guess an argument could be made for all three, a and b are definitely the most useful.

2. c. You can't have everything!

3. b. You'll be oh-so-grateful that you backed up your files. As for option c, it doesn't work—I've tried it myself!

Activity

Earlier in the hour, I went on and on about the importance of planning your financial categories and subcategories in advance. I'll bet you didn't do it, did you? Well I'm giving you a second chance. Sit down with a pen and paper, and jot down the types of spending that you want to track. When you've got a structure that makes sense given your financial situation, create the new categories before you forget them. You can thank me later.

HOUR 23

Using Money 98

Now that you're familiar with Money 98 enough to know your way around, it's time to get to the basics—the stuff you work with on a week-to-week (if not day-to-day) basis. Not only do you learn how to perform a variety of transactions, but you find the answers to these questions:

- How do I record monthly bills such as the cable bill?
- Do I have to record past transactions when I get started with Money 98?
- Why do I need to transfer funds from my checking to credit card accounts when paying a bill, instead of just recording a normal transaction?
- My paycheck is deposited directly to the bank. Can I schedule its appearance in the account?
- How do I reconcile my accounts?

Using the Checking and Saving Registers

After you've opened an account (review Hour 22, "Getting Started with Microsoft Money 98" if you need to refresh your memory about how to create an account), you can start recording transactions in its register. The register (see Figure 23.1) is where you record checks, deposits, charges, and withdrawals. The register in your checkbook has places for jotting down the transaction's check number and date, and for keeping a running total of the account's balance. Money 98's registers do the same thing (and presumably they're much more legible and free of mathematical errors than the records many of us keep).

FIGURE 23.1.

A Money 98 register looks exactly like the one in your checkbook.

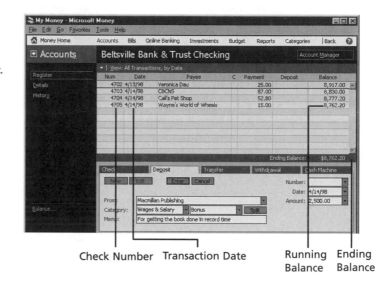

Check Number   Transaction Date   Running   Ending
                                                    Balance   Balance

In the sections that follow, we explore Money 98's checking and savings registers, how to get to them, and how to post transactions to them.

Getting There: Finding Your Way to the Desired Register

If you've learned nothing else from this book, you've probably figured out that Windows applications nearly always have multiple ways of doing things. Getting to the desired account's register is no exception. Opening an account's register is a two-step process. First, you must get to the Account Manager window shown in Figure 23.2. Next, you must choose the appropriate account.

FIGURE 23.2.

The Account Manager window is where you go to choose the account with which you want to work.

23

To get to the Account Manager, use any of these three commands:

- From the Money 98 menu bar, select Go, Accounts.
- Press Ctrl+Shift+A.
- From within another register, click the Account Manager button.

From the Account Manager window, you can open an account's register using any of these three methods:

- Double-click the account's icon.
- Click an icon, and then press the Go to Account button.
- Click the Accounts drop-down list (see Figure 23.3), and make your selection.

FIGURE 23.3.

The Accounts drop-down box is just one way to get to the desired account.

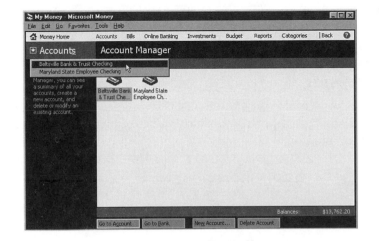

You know the chart of the day that appears on your Money 98 home screen? Well, if that chart reflects data about the account whose register you'd like to access, you should see the account's name listed below the chart. Run the mouse pointer over the account's name. If it turns into a pointing hand, click it, and you are instantly transported to the account's register.

Recording Transactions in the Register

After you've opened the desired account register, you can select the type of transaction you'd like to record. Do this by clicking the applicable tab at the bottom of the register window (see Figure 23.4).

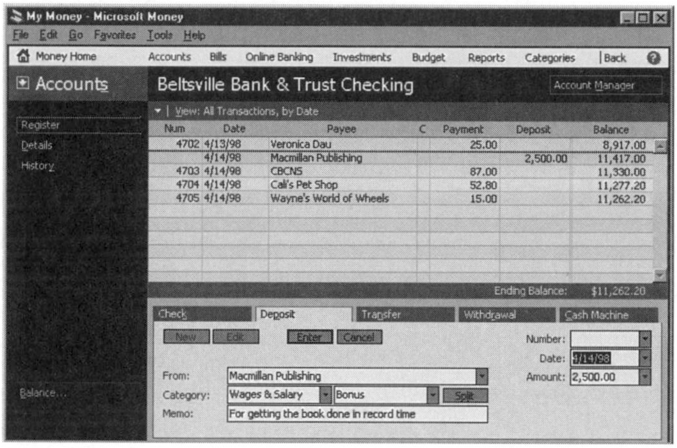

FIGURE 23.4.

In this example, a deposit is being recorded on the register.

You have five types of transaction tabs to choose from. From left to right, they are:

- *Check.* Enter the checks that you write under this tab.
- *Deposit.* Record any deposits made to the account under this tab. That includes those made via a cash machine.
- *Transfer.* Moving money from one account to another? Do it under this tab.

Believe it or not, checks written to a financial institution as payment for a credit card or line of credit must be treated as transfers from checking to the credit card's account, not as simple checks. This helps Money 98 keep track of the balances in both accounts.

- *Withdrawal.* Report any moneys withdrawn from the account on this tab (except for those withdrawn from a cash machine).

- *Cash Machine.* Cash machine withdrawals should be entered here.

To Do: Entering a Transaction on an Account Register

A lot of steps may be involved in entering a transaction, but the process is much quicker than it first appears. To record a transaction, follow these steps:

1. Open the register of the account with which you need to work, as previously instructed.

2. Click the tab that best describes the type of transaction that you want to record. (Remember Check, Deposit, Transfer, Withdrawal, and Cash Machine from the preceding section?)

3. Record the number of the check, if applicable, and press Tab to move to the next box on the form.

4. Enter the date of the transaction if it's a date other than the current date.

> If you're like me, you might sit down to write out bills twice a month, but you mail them as close to their due dates as you can. (Hey, I wanna hang on to that money as long as humanly possible!) You can enter a more accurate transaction date by clicking the drop-down arrow next to the Date text box. A little calendar pops up. Just click the desired date to enter it in the Date text box.

5. Enter the name of the party to whom the check must be made payable, or the source of the income being reported.

> If you put forth the effort to set up a payee's list (described in Hour 22 you need only type two or three letters of the payee's name before Money 98 fills in the rest. If you think that's cool, Money also assigns the same transaction amount, categories, and subcategories this time around, so you may have even less information to fill in!

6. Type the amount of the transaction. If it's an even dollar amount, you don't need to enter the decimal points and subsequent zeros; Money does it for you. (Now if only Money could raise the money to pay the bills....)

23

▼

7. Use the drop-down arrows next to the Category text boxes to select from the prede-fined categories. If you think of a better category or subcategory, type it, and Money fires off the New Category Wizard described in Hour 22.

8. Fill in the Memo box if you want to track any other details concerning the trans-action.

9. Click the Enter button or press the Enter key when you've finished entering all of the data.

▲

Suppose you started to record your paycheck in the checking account, but decided halfway through that you could afford to put it into savings instead. Before pressing the Account Manager button to move to the new account, be sure to press Cancel to clear the entry. Forgetting to do so could result in the transaction inadvertently being recorded in both accounts. Although the double record may temporarily give your finances a rosy appearance, the resulting overdraft notice and subsequent fines do not.

What Do I Have To Do To Get Started?

In the last hour, I promised to discuss just how much stuff you need to key in from the past to get up and running with Money 98. Although I'd like to say there's a simple answer to this question, I have to admit that there's not. A lot depends on what you're hoping to get from Money 98, how you entered the account's starting balance, and whether or not you hope to have Money help you with your taxes. If you're a meticulous bookkeeper and can provide up-to-the-minute balances for all your accounts, then you may get away with entering as little as a couple of key numbers from your next bank statement (such as interest earned, or checking fees).

If you fall somewhere in the middle like most of us, you probably followed Money's suggestion and entered the ending balance of your most recent bank statement. In that case, you need only to enter transactions that happened after the statement was processed. You can either do that by skimming through your checkbook and cash machine receipts, or you can simply wait until you get your next statement. That way, you see transactions that happened after the last statement through the transactions that you've already entered into Money.

Finally, are you expecting Money to help you gather tax data? If so, then you need to have transactions entered for the entire tax year in question. If it's January 15, backing data in for the previous two weeks may not be a big deal. If, however, it's November 15, you may want to hold off using Money data for tax help until next year, because it would take you longer to enter all the stuff than it would to pull all the paper documents and add it all up by hand.

Viewing an Account Register

Money 98 gives you a great deal of flexibility in viewing your registers. You can change the order in which transactions appear, filter which transactions appear, and even determine the amount of information that appears onscreen.

Your options for viewing your registers can be divided into four categories. You may choose one option from each of the four categories to get the display you want. To exercise these options, open the register that you want to view, click the Options drop-down box, and choose from the following options.

Transaction Order options:

- *By Date*. This default view displays transactions in order of the date that you supplied for the transaction.
- *By Number*. Choose this option when you need to track an item by its check number.
- *By Entry Date*. This view is good if you write a number of checks with a variety of dates at one time and you need to confirm that the check was written during your last bill-paying marathon.

Number of Transactions options:

- *All Transactions*. This option is self-explanatory. Choose it when you need to look through everything.
- *Unreconciled Transactions*. Balancing your virtual checkbook just got easier; you can weed out all the transactions that have already cleared the bank.

Amount of Detail options:

- *Top Line Only*. The default view in Money, the Top Line Only option cuts to the chase and gives you what you need to know and little more. Using this view also makes it possible for more entries to appear onscreen.
- *All Transaction Details*. Take a look at Figure 23.5 to see just how much information Money can display at once.

FIGURE 23.5.

The All Transaction Details view reveals all.

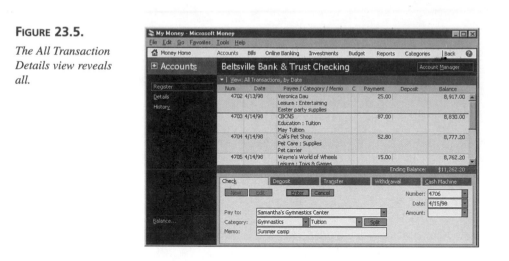

Transaction Forms option:

- *Transaction Forms*. Checked by default, this option automatically displays the transaction form when the register is open. If you want to see a larger chunk of the register at once, you can remove the check mark next to the option.

Working with Credit Cards and Lines of Credit

As mentioned earlier in this hour, there are a few subtle differences between recording a basic check and a credit card payment. The next few sections are devoted to exploring some of those subtleties.

To Do: Recording a Credit Card Charge

To record a charge in a credit card register, follow these steps:

1. Open the account register for the credit card to which you need to post the charge.

2. Click the Charge tab. Notice that it looks a whole lot like the check tab we worked through earlier in the hour.

3. Enter a reference number if you want, though this is also a good place to make note of an access check number.

4. Type the date of the charge. Again, the current date is supplied unless you tell Money otherwise.

5. Furnish the name of the business with whom you completed the transaction.

6. Enter the amount of the charge in the text box provided. Remember that you do not need to use the decimals and zeros if it's an even dollar amount.

7. You can also specify a category and subcategory for the charge if you want.

8. Describe the items included in the charge if you so choose. (This could come in handy at tax time.)

9. After you've verified that all of the data is correct, click the Enter button or press the Enter key to confirm the transaction.

Whatever you do, don't lose sight of the fact that credit card accounts track what you owe, not the amount of credit you have available. This can get confusing, especially when you look at your credit card account in context with the other accounts that clearly track your assets as opposed to liabilities.

Give Credit Where Credit is Due

If you purchase an item with a credit card and find that you need to return it, the odds are that the retailer credits your account rather than giving you cash back. So, how do you handle this with Money 98? It's much simpler than you may think. Just open the register of the credit card in question, click the Credit tab, and fill in the blanks as you do with every other type of entry. It's that simple.

To Do: Recording a Credit Card Payment

After you've figured out how much you can— and want—to pay the credit card company, follow these steps to log in your payment:

1. Open the account from which you plan to make the payment. It's probably your checking account.

2. At the bottom of the Account window, click the Transfer tab. You see the tab shown in Figure 23.6.

3. Supply the proper check number in the Number box.

4. Enter the date, or leave the text box alone if you want Money to supply the current date.

5. Specify the amount of the check to be written.

6. Click the drop-down arrow next to the To box, and select the credit card for which you want to send the check.

7. Type the name of the creditor, as it should appear on the check.

8. Enter a brief description of the transaction if you desire.

9. When you've typed everything, click the Enter button, or press the Enter key.

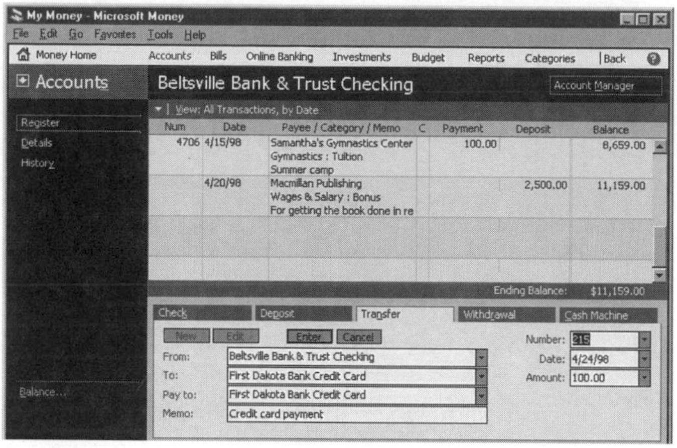

FIGURE 23.6.

The transfer tab enables you to shift money from one account to another.

The amount of your payment is subtracted from the amount you owe, and the resulting number is displayed at the bottom of the register.

Reconciling Bank Accounts

When you reconcile your accounts, you get a chance to take a second look at the records, verify that they're correct, and see that your register entries agree with what appears on the statement that you just received from the bank. This is your chance to tell Money which transactions cleared the bank, and to enter any bank fee that may be reflected on your statement.

To Do: Reconciling Your Checking or Savings Account

Reconciling an account is a two-step process. Before you can check off the transactions that have cleared the bank, you need to provide Money with some information from the new statement.

To balance an account, follow these steps:

1. Open the account that you want to balance using one of the methods presented earlier.

2. Click the Balance button that is located on the lower-left corner of the screen. The screen indicating why you should balance your accounts appears followed by the Balance dialog box (see Figure 23.7).

3. Type the date printed on the bank statement in the Statement date text box.

▼ 4. Money has filled in the starting balance, which is the account's balance reflected on your Money register for the account, but you must provide the balance presented on the bank statement in the Ending balance text box.

5. Next, you need to enter the amount of service charges that the bank charged you in the current statement. You need to scour the statement carefully for things like fees for ordered checks, ATM usage charges, and so on. Use the twin drop-down boxes underneath the Service charge box to categorize the expense.

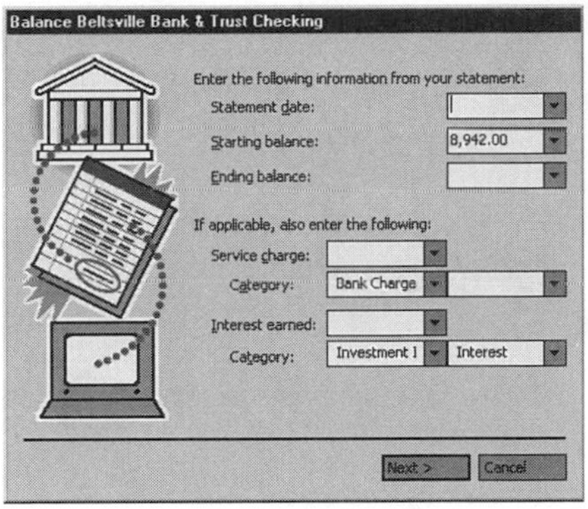

23

FIGURE 23.7.

Pressing the Balance button calls up a dialog box such as the one shown here.

Balance Beltsville Bank & Trust Checking

Enter the following information from your statement:
Statement date:
Starting balance: 8,942.00
Ending balance:

If applicable, also enter the following:
Service charge:
Category: Bank Charge
Interest earned:
Category: Investment I   Interest

Next >   Cancel

> Need to add up a bunch of stuff? No need to reach for the calculator or fire up a spreadsheet on your computer; just click the drop-down arrow next to the Service charge text box. A built-in calculator pops up, ready to accept the numbers you feed it.

6. If this is an interest-bearing account, you need to type the amount of interest earned on the statement in the Interest earned text box.

7. Press the Next> button to move to the Balance Account window (see Figure 23.8). You see only transactions that have not previously cleared the bank. If you entered amounts for service charges or interest earned, you see the items on the register with C (for cleared) already next to them.

8. Look over both your statement and register thoroughly. Click the C column next to the transactions that appear on both the register and your statement. The goal is to get the balance difference shown in the left windowpane to zero.

9. When the balance difference reaches zero, click the Next> button. You see a message congratulating you on reconciling your account.
▼

▼   10. After you've basked in your smooth account reconciliation, click the Finish button. All the Cs in the register turn to Rs to indicate that those accounts have been successfully reconciled.

FIGURE 23.8.

Uh-oh, it looks as though this account is missing some significant transactions!

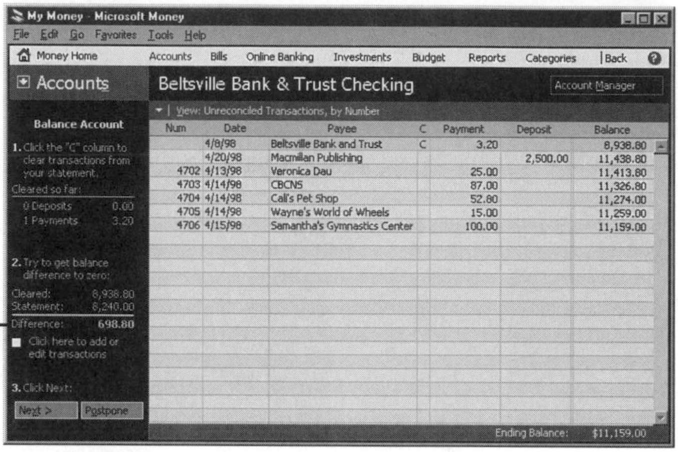

The difference between what you say that you have and what the bank says that you have

▲

Irreconcilable Differences

If entering the service charges and interest earned and marking all the transactions that have cleared still leaves you with a difference, try doing any or all the following to help reconcile the account:

- Is something missing? Skim over your statement to see whether there is a single transaction that's identical in amount to the difference shown. If there is, look at its check number and try to locate it in your Money register. If it's not there, enter it. If it is, try the next idea.

- If the amount of the difference agrees with something else you see in the register, verify that the transaction is not entered twice. If it is entered twice, you need to open the item's transaction window and delete it by pressing the Delete button.

- Grab that bank statement again and triple-check the service charges, interest earned, and so on, to be sure that the numbers have been entered into Money correctly.

- Anyone can make a mistake, especially if you're overly tired or distracted. Sometimes we mistype a number or even just flip-flop a couple of its numbers. This can be a tedious error to track down because you literally have to revisit each transaction and its corresponding statement listing, but it's mandatory in order to get that difference to zero.

Working with Scheduled Events in Money 98

With Money 98, you can schedule bill payment, have the program list bills due on the Money home screen, or have your direct-deposited paycheck appear in your records at a specified time.

To Do: Scheduling a Payment in the Bill Calendar

Follow these steps to schedule a payment in the Bill Calendar:

1. Click the Bills button on the Navigation toolbar. The Bill Calendar window appears.

2. Click the New Bill button to open the Create New Recurring Payment dialog box. This box presents you with a number of transaction choices.

3. The Bill button is already selected, so press Next> to move on.

> If your paycheck is automatically deposited into your checking account, select Deposit from the above list, and proceed with filling in all the blanks. Because this is an automatic deposit, however, you want to have Money automatically enter the transaction into your checking account register on a specified date. Do this by selecting Automatic entry from the Entry method drop-down list.

4. Microsoft goes into excruciating detail to explain what you're about to do. Just click Next> to continue scheduling the payment. The Edit Scheduled Withdrawal dialog box appears.

5. Use the Date text box to enter the date that the bill is due (or the date on which you want to mail the payment so that it won't be late).

6. Click the drop-down arrow next to the Frequency box to specify how often the payment should be made. Monthly is the most common option, although yearly is useful for things such as automobile club memberships, professional organization dues, and so forth.

7. Confirm that Manual entry appears in the Entry method box. You must use this option because you physically have to cut the check before it should be recorded in the register.

8. Use the Account drop-down list to specify which account should be tapped to cover the bill. Most likely your primary checking account is listed here.

9. In the Pay to box, enter the name of the party receiving the payment. If the payee is one with whom you deal regularly, you can select his or her name from the drop-down list.

23

10. If necessary, categorize the transaction in the drop-down boxes below the Pay to box.

11. Using the Amount text box, tell Money how much the creditor should be paid.

12. Click OK to confirm the entry. The newly scheduled bill appears in the Bill Calendar window with all the other bills.

Money indicates when scheduled bills are due by displaying the bill's name and amount on its home screen; however, before you think you can ignore the bills by not launching Money 98, think again.

You know the row of tool icons at the far right end of the Windows taskbar (the volume control icon, and so on)? Well, Money places its own glowing checkbook icon there to indicate that you have bills due. Sorry, there's no hiding from it!

To Do: Telling Money When to List Bills on the Home Screen

By default, Money gives you ten days warning to pay your bills. That should give you ample time to process and mail them; however, if you feel that's either too much or too little time, follow these steps to get the amount of time that you think works best for you:

1. Choose Tools, Options from the Money menu bar to launch the Options dialog box.

2. Click the Bills tab.

3. Use the Remind Me text box to enter the number of days ahead of time that you want to be warned. You can even tell Money to ignore weekends and holidays in that count by checking the respective option.

4. Click OK to confirm the chosen time.

Just because you scheduled a bill's payment doesn't mean that it gets paid by magic. You still have to pull out the checkbook, cut the check, and record it in the applicable register.

To Do: Recording a Scheduled Bill in a Register

The following are the steps that you use to record a scheduled payment in the appropriate register:

1. On the Money home screen, move the mouse pointer over one of the bills listed, and then click. The Bill Calendar window appears.

2. Select the bills that you want to pay by placing a check mark next to their listing.

Want to pay all bills due up through a certain date? Right-click the date on the calendar, and from the pop-up menu choose Check All Bills and Deposits Due Up To.

▼   3. Press the Enter Now button to reveal the Enter Recurring Withdrawal dialog box. It looks a lot like the Edit Scheduled Withdrawal dialog box that we saw earlier, doesn't it?

4. Locate the next available check number, and enter it in the Number box.

5. Enter the amount to be paid in the Amount text box. Note that if the bill is a recurring bill that remains the same month after month (such as a cable bill), you may not need to enter the amount due; Money does it for you.

6. Complete the transaction by pressing the Enter button or Enter key. If that was the only (or last) bill, you are returned to the Bill Calendar; otherwise, another Enter

▲   Recurring Withdrawal dialog box appears to lead you into the next bill due.

Summary

Are you ready to get all your finances in order? It's really not that hard to do with wizards and well-marked dialog boxes on your side. Additionally, many other features are buried within Money 98, but I feel that these two chapters go a long way toward getting you organized to work with Money 98.

Coming up next hour is a fun chapter about a greeting card maker, an encyclopedia, and a few fun puzzles.

Workshop

The following workshop helps you solidify the skills you learned in this lesson.

Quiz

Take the following quiz to see how much you've learned.

Questions

1. How much financial data do you have to back in to Money 98?

   a. Every transaction that you made since the day you opened the accounts.

   b. Only transactions that have been initiated after the last bank statement.

   c. It depends on how you entered your starting balance, and whether you want Money to help you with your taxes.

2. Which are valid ways that you can view a Money account register?

    a. By the transaction date

    b. By the dollar amount

    c. Grouped by category of spending

3. If you schedule a bill to be paid, what happens?

    a. When you boot your computer, a nagging voice says, "Pay those bills or else!"

    b. Bills due are listed on the Money home screen, and a glowing checkbook icon appears on the right end of the Windows taskbar.

    c. A graphic of Bill Gates dressed as Uncle Sam appears.

Answers

1. c. It really does depend on a variety of circumstances.

2. a. It is the only view you can select through the View menu.

3. b. Though C could bring a few chuckles...

Activity

So, which bills should you schedule for payment? Because listing every one of them would be downright depressing, I suggest that you schedule only bills, such as credit cards, that charge late fees.

Take a few minutes to go through your list of bills to see which creditors levy a late fee. When you have the list, schedule their payments so that you never get socked with another late fee again!

HOUR 24

Having Fun with Home Essentials

In this hour, you're introduced to the Microsoft Greetings Workshop, Microsoft Encarta Encyclopedia, Microsoft Entertainment Pack Puzzle Collection, and the Home Essentials Web site. The following questions are answered:

- What kinds of projects can I make with the Greetings Workshop?
- How can I deliver my Greetings Workshop creations?
- How do I find things with Encarta?
- Are there any fun games in the Entertainment Pack—Puzzle Collection?
- What do I find at the Home Essentials Web site?

Getting to Know the Microsoft Greetings Workshop

Microsoft teamed up with the Hallmark greeting card company to bring you a fantastically fun and useful greeting card design program. You can either take an existing card and modify its text to meet your needs or start with a blank project and add pictures and text where desired; however, the Greetings Workshop does much more than design cards. From the Greetings Workshop home screen (see Figure 24.1), you can create special calendars, award certificates, invitations, announcements, flyers, and stickers. You can browse through an Idea Book for tips on making milestone birthdays truly memorable. You can even have the program remind you about an upcoming special event before it happens (my favorite function) so that your card arrives on time.

FIGURE 24.1.

The Microsoft Greetings Workshop home screen acts as your creative project launch pad.

Designing a Card

As I mentioned earlier, you can either modify an existing card to meet your needs, or you can design one from scratch.

To Do: Creating a Greeting Card

To design a greeting card from a predesigned project, follow these steps:

1. Launch the Microsoft Greetings Workshop by clicking Start on the Windows taskbar, selecting Programs, Greetings Workshop, Greetings Workshop. The Sign In screen appears.

2. Click Guest to perform this walkthrough.

> You may add your name to the list of users by clicking Add a Name. The resulting screen prompts you for your first name. It also asks you to specify your level of computing experience. This information is used to customize the information that guides you through creating a project. When you're done, click OK. Your name now appears on the Sign In screen each time you launch the Greetings Workshop.

24

3. From the Greetings Workshop home screen, click the Cards icon. The How Do You Want to Get Started? box appears (see Figure 24.2).

FIGURE 24.2.

The Greetings Workshop assumes that you want to work with a predesigned project.

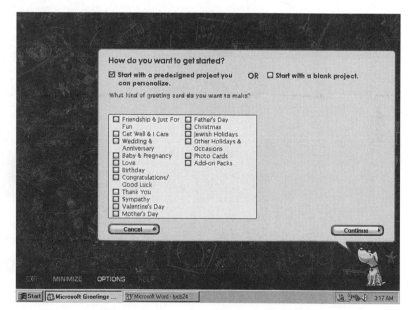

4. Confirm that the Start with a Predesigned Project You Can Personalize box is checked.

5. Choose the type of card that you want to create by clicking the box next to the desired category and clicking Continue when you're finished.

6. The Greetings Workshop asks you to choose a theme for your card. For instance, the Love category enables you to choose from General Love, Sentimental, Suggestive, New Romance, and so on. Click the desired check box and click OK.

> Don't like the choice you made? You can always click the Back button to revise your selection.

7. Now you are asked to choose a mood for your greeting—cute, funny, or serious. Check the desired box. A number of appropriate images appear in the design window.

8. Choose Browse the Designs Using the Scrollbars and click the one that you want. A Preview message box appears in the lower-left corner of the workspace (see Figure 24.3).

FIGURE 24.3.

Click the arrows next to the word Select to see other text options.

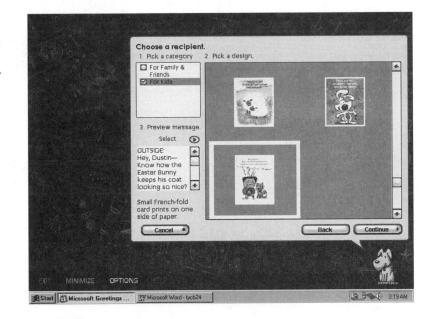

9. In the Preview message window, scroll through the card's text to see whether you like it. If an arrow appears next to the word Select, you may click it to see text alternatives.

10. When you've located the message you prefer, click Continue. The front page appears with the text highlighted.

> Not enough room for the text that you want to enter? Don't worry; the text box automatically expands to meet your needs.

11. Click inside the highlighted box and edit the text as necessary. Click Continue when you're done.

12. The inside of the card appears. Again, the text is highlighted, ready for you to edit. When you're finished, click Continue.

13. In the next screen, you get to personalize the electronic equivalent of the Hallmark seal. Just click inside the highlighted box to make your changes.

14. Your design is finished (see Figure 24.4). Save it by clicking the Save icon.

24

FIGURE 24.4.

Your project is finished and ready to send to that special someone.

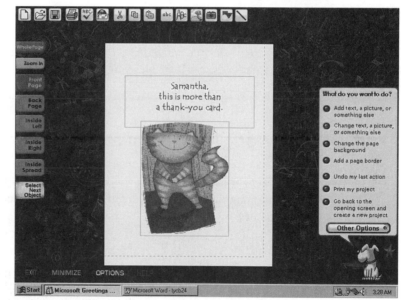

Although the preceding steps may look like a lot of work, the time really does pass quickly from the time you begin making your creation until you're ready to send it on to a friend. You follow similar steps to create other Greetings Workshop projects.

Greetings Workshop Views

On the final card screen (refer to Figure 24.4), you notice a lot of extra buttons. Down the left side of the screen is a set of View buttons. From top to bottom, they are:

- *Whole Page*. If you've zoomed in on a part of your card, use this button to return to whole page view.

- *Zoom In*. Click this button to get a closeup of your card. Because not all the enlarged card fits on the screen, Greetings Workshop gives you a set of scrollbars to help you get where you want to go.

- *Front Page*. This button returns you to the front page of your card in whole card view.

- *Back Page*. View your version of the Hallmark seal on the back of your project.

- *Inside Left*. This page is most commonly left blank; however, Greetings Workshop still makes it easy to access.

- *Inside Right*. Traditionally the panel on which the card's verse is held, the Inside Right view button is extremely useful for confirming that the card says what you want it to say.

- *Inside Spread*. If you wrote a long poem that required the use of both inner pages, this view is a must because it enables you to see both the inside left and right at the same time.

- *Select Next Object*. Click this button to highlight the next object box on the card.

Greetings Workshop Toolbars

When you activate a text box inside your project, you see two toolbars. Because the function of these icons is identical to the function of similar icons you've seen throughout this book, I just point out their location on the Greetings Workshop screens (shown in Figures 24.5 and 24.6).

Greetings Workshop's Context-Sensitive Help

Remember Clipper, the Office Assistant you met back in Hour 16? Well, the Greetings Workshop has its own mascot of sorts. Rocky, the adorable yellow dog, resides in the bottom-right corner of the screen to offer context-sensitive help geared to the level of computing experience that you specified in your sign-in profile.

Is Rocky a bit too annoying for your liking? Make him disappear by clicking the Options button and then clicking the No, Remove Him box. Click OK to exit the Settings box.

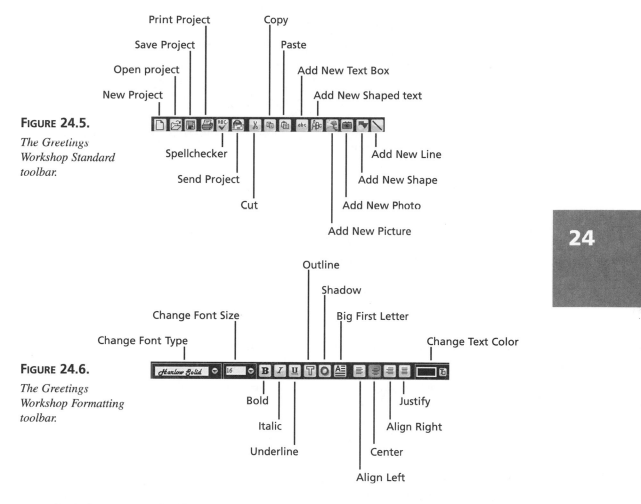

FIGURE 24.5.

The Greetings Workshop Standard toolbar.

FIGURE 24.6.

The Greetings Workshop Formatting toolbar.

Setting Reminders

If you're anything like me, you have enough trouble trying to remember the day of the week, let alone your best friend's birthday. Luckily, Greetings Workshop has a nifty reminder feature that may keep you out of the doghouse.

To Do: Setting Reminders for Special Occasions

To set reminders in Greetings Workshop, follow these steps:

1. Make sure that the Greetings Workshop home screen is visible. Either launch the program from Windows, or click the New Project icon if you're already working elsewhere inside the program.

▼ To Do

▼ 2. Click the Reminders icon. The What Do You Want to Do? box appears.

3. Click Set a Reminder for a Special Occasion. A text box appears.

4. Type the text that you want the program to display with your reminder, and then click Continue.

5. Click the appropriate month, day, and year, and then click Continue.

6. In the How Far in Advance Do You Want a Reminder Box, click the desired option. They range from one day to one month.

7. Click OK to move on.

8. The program confirms that your reminder has been set. Click OK to continue working in Greetings Workshop.

Printing Your Project

After you click the Print button, Greetings Workshop detects the default printer that you've specified in Windows. The program uses this information to guide you through a series of questions and printing tests. These vary depending on the type of printer you have configured. Don't worry; Rocky helps you through it!

Sending Your Project to Someone

In addition to printing your project, you have several other ways to format it for transmittal. You can email it, post it to the Greetings Workshop Web Post Office, or you can copy it to a floppy disk and send the project to someone via the U.S. Postal Service. Which method is best? That depends on what kind of computer equipment and Internet access the recipient has. Table 24.1 has some guidelines.

TABLE 24.1. BY WHICH METHOD SHOULD YOU SEND YOUR PROJECT?

If the Recipient Has This	Use This Method
No computer	Send printed projects by regular mail
Computer but no email	Send electronic version of printed projects on floppy disk by regular mail
Don't know what type of computer	Greetings Workshop Web Post Office
Macintosh	Greetings Workshop Web Post Office
Email on a Windows computer	Send via email
Email on other computer	Greetings Workshop Web Post Office

Earlier in the hour, you learned how Greetings Workshop prints your project. If you intend to use one of the other methods from Table 24.1, you need to click the Send button, and make the desired selection.

Using Encarta 98

What is Encarta 98? It's a multimedia encyclopedia contained on two CD-ROMS. Not only is Encarta much lighter in weight than its paper counterparts, it's far richer in content. In addition to reading about your chosen topic, you can listen to a flute, get a 360-degree view of one of the Natural Wonders, play educational games, and even link to the Web to family-friendly sites containing supporting content.

To open Encarta, click Start on the Windows taskbar, select Programs, Microsoft Reference, Encarta Encyclopedia. The home screen appears (see Figure 24.7).

24

FIGURE 24.7.

The Encarta 98 home screen.

Finding an Article in Encarta

Obviously, one of the most common things you do with Encarta is search for information. Encarta uses a tool called Pinpointer to home in on what you're looking for.

To Do: Using Pinpointer to Find Information

To find an entry using Pinpointer, follow these steps:

1. Start Encarta as described previously. The home screen appears (refer to Figure 24.7).
2. Click Encyclopedia Articles. The Pinpointer box appears (shown in Figure 24.8).

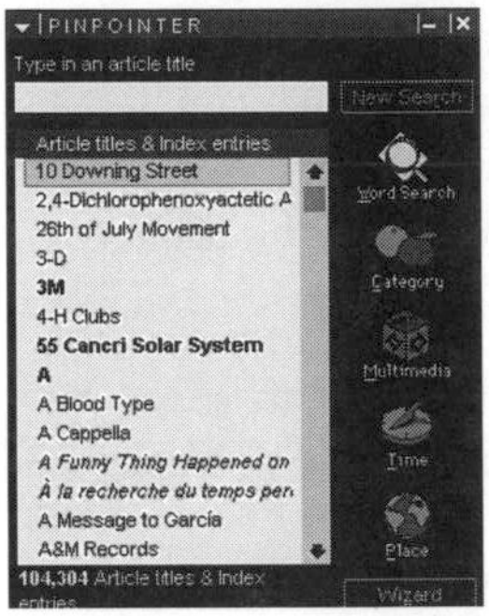

FIGURE 24.8.

The Pinpointer box is the starting point for all your encyclopedia searches.

3. Type the name of a subject into the text box. As each letter is typed, Pinpointer moves closer and closer to your desired topic.
4. When you see the subject that you want to research, click it. In many cases, you're taken to the item's entry in the encyclopedia. In other cases, you're given an outline from which to pick a narrower topic (see Figure 24.9).

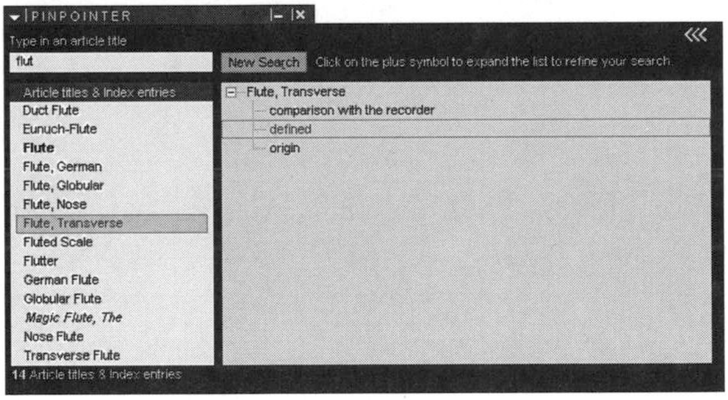

FIGURE 24.9.

Some larger entries present you with a mini-outline even before you get to the item's encyclopedia entry.

5. The desired entry appears, ready for you to browse its text, multimedia files, and any related Web links.

Interpreting the Encarta Article Screen

The Encarta Article Screen has three parts: the outline frame, the media frame, and the article frame (see Figure 24.10).

FIGURE 24.10.

The parts of the Encarta article screen.

Graphic Image   Article Frame

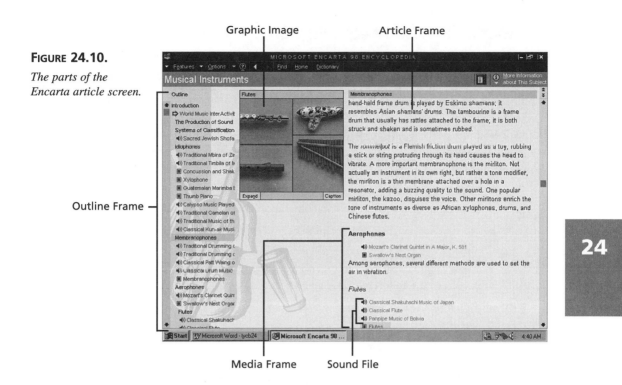

Outline Frame —

24

Media Frame   Sound File

The outline frame, as you might guess, houses an outline of the chosen article. You can click any topic listed and be taken directly to its section of the article, its media file, or whatever the case. This makes it extremely easy to find what you're looking for in Encarta.

The media frame holds the selected picture, drawing, or sound file and related caption. To play the sound file, click the purple right-pointing triangle underneath the media frame.

 As you scroll through an article, the graphic related to the section of text that you are reading is displayed automatically.

The article frame contains the text of the encyclopedia entry. You notice, however, that applicable sound and graphic icons are sprinkled throughout the text (refer to Figure 24.10).

Exploring the Media Features

Encarta's Media Gallery expands your knowledge by providing a host of innovative learning activities ranging from video tours to educational games. From the Encarta home screen, click Media Features. You see a list of Encarta's multimedia features, which include:

- *InterActivities*. Microsoft refers to InterActivities as mini-museums because they incorporate video and other multimedia technology to help you explore and experience more deeply a topic of interest.
- *Collages*. These content-rich collages incorporate essays and active screens to investigate both historical and contemporary topics.
- *Media Gallery*. This feature enables you to view the charts, graphs, sound files, videos, and every other multimedia resource in Encarta.
- *Topic Treks*. Encarta takes you on a variety of journeys. For instance, you can wind your way through the history of competitive sports.
- *Timeline*. This feature takes you through a chronology of events, their related multimedia files, and links to applicable encyclopedia entries and Web links.
- *World Maps*. You can start with the entire globe and work your way down to city maps with this intriguing Encarta feature. You can even jump from sites on a map to related Web sites and encyclopedia entries.

Need to access Pinpointer from within an article screen? Just click Find, and it appears in no time!

Having Fun with the Entertainment Pack Puzzle Collection

Whether you're looking for entertainment or merely want a diversion from a nasty case of writer's block, the Puzzle Collection may be just the thing for you! To access the Puzzle Collection, click Start on the Windows taskbar, select Programs, Microsoft Games, Puzzle Collection, Play the Puzzle Collection. The toolbar shown in Figure 24.11 appears.

To play a game, click its icon. The game launches along with a screen that presents the gist of the game along with a few basic how-tos. You also see three menu items at the top of each game window: a Game menu, which enables you to start a new game, gain access to game options such as sound effects and music, and view high scores;

a Play!/Pause! toggle button; and a Help menu, which enables you to access the game's content, index help functions, and activate or deactivate screen help tips that appear during play.

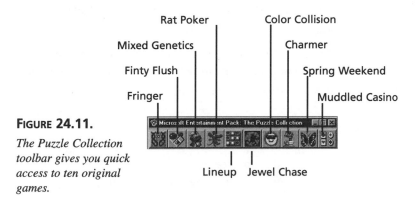

Rat Poker

Color Collision

Mixed Genetics

Charmer

Finty Flush

Spring Weekend

Fringer

Muddled Casino

FIGURE 24.11.

The Puzzle Collection toolbar gives you quick access to ten original games.

Lineup   Jewel Chase

To end a game, select Games, Exit.

Fringer

The object of Fringer is to eliminate ropes by untwisting knots. When a rope is completely untwisted, it disappears. After all the ropes are gone, you move to the next screen. The sliding bar pushes the knots down a hair with each pass. The game is over when a knot reaches the bottom.

To play Fringer, the basic commands you need to know include the following:

TABLE 24.2. FRINGER COMMANDS.

Do This	To Accomplish This
Left-/Right-arrow keys	Moves the frame from side to side
Spacebar/Up-arrow key	Untwists a knot

Finty Flush

If you like puzzles that require you to figure out what can fit where, you may like this one. The object of Finty Flush is to fill each empty grid with balls of one color. After you've filled three grids, you get a bonus point and can move to the next level. The game is over when the upper grid is full of columns.

Table 24.3 presents the keystrokes used to play Finty Flush.

TABLE 24.3. FINTY FLUSH COMMANDS.

Do This	*To Accomplish This*
Spacebar	To drop balls from the upper grid onto the lower grid
Left-/Right-arrow keys	To move the upper and lower grids
Enter or Backspace	To rotate the lower grid clockwise or counterclockwise
Up-/Down-arrow keys	To move between the upper and lower grids
Tab	To switch between the four lower grids
Insert	To add more columns to the upper grid

Mixed Genetics

Before you pull out this game, be aware that you need to give it your full attention. Mixed Genetics requires you to quickly pair certain element combinations.

To progress through the game, you must breed the mutant animals to produce pure offspring. You then rescue the pure offspring by moving them into the glass dome at the bottom of the screen. After you rescue the number of pure offspring specified on the glass beaker, you move to the next level.

> Click the Unmixed Genetics Guide in the lower-left corner to see what a pure animal should look like.

The game is over when the waiting area at the top of the screen is full.

Game play for Mixed Genetics is significantly different from the two games described previously. To play, keep the following in mind:

- Use the mouse to place three animals side by side in a test tube. Click the animal that you want to move, and move it where you want. Click again to release the animal.

- Right-click the middle animal (of the three you have arranged side by side) in the test tube to breed them.

> Offspring inherit any body parts that two or more parents have. Animals can breed three times before they disappear, though keep in mind that identical animals cannot breed together. Even if animals have different colored hearts, they are still considered identical and cannot breed with each other.

- Move any purebred animals to the glass dome at the bottom of the screen to rescue them.

- After you rescue the number of purebred animals specified on the glass beaker, you move to the next level.

- The game ends when the waiting area is full.

Rat Poker

This game is adorable! Furthermore, it's one of the easiest to get the hang of. In Rat Poker, the object is to line up a valid hand of rats to make them exit through the door at the bottom of the screen. When the number of rats listed on the exit counter reaches zero, you move to the next level.

The patterns of rats on the right side of the screen show the combinations of rats that can exit. The more complex the hand, the more points you earn.

The game ends when no more rats can enter the game field. So, how do you accomplish all this?

To Do: Playing Rat Poker

1. Trap and release rats to change their order by pressing the Spacebar. Press the Spacebar once to trap a rat, and press it a second time to swap the trapped rat with the one passing through the trap.

2. Arrange rats in patterns, or hands, such as those on the right side of the game screen to make them exit and to earn points. For example, on Level 1, when you line up three rats of the same color, you earn five points when they exit.

3. On certain levels, you can use the arms in the middle of the screen to move rats between traps. Press the Left- and Right-arrow keys to swing the arms.

4. On other levels, the arms don't move. You may need to change the active trap by pressing Tab.

5. When a valid hand reaches the bottom platform, the rats exit, thus freeing up room on the platform.

6. Move to the next level when the exit counter reaches zero.

7. The game is over when no more rats can enter the playing field (that is, when the platform is full of rats).

Lineup

Place a variety of sports balls in a solid line to make them disappear. Lineup challenges your spatial and organizational skills.

The object of this game is to connect opposite sides of the football field with a vertical or horizontal line of balls. You can use any combination of balls to form the line whether they're golf balls, soccer balls, or whatever. When you complete a line, all its balls disappear, giving you more space on the playing field. The game is over when the piece line on the right fills to the top.

Lineup's game screen consists of the bonus line, the piece line, game controls, and the field itself. The bottom box in the piece line shows the piece that you must place. To place it on the field, click where you want the white center of the piece to go. When a line becomes solid, those balls disappear, and you earn a number of points. Clearing a line enables you to place more pieces and continue the game.

Don't pack pieces onto the playing field. Instead, work on creating lines of balls. Enhance your score by placing pieces strategically. For example, surround a golf ball and earn a bonus. This bonus ball enables you to rotate the next piece that you must place, change the order of the piece line, or remove a piece from the playing field. Just click a piece to use a bonus ball.

Jewel Chase

This colorful path-finding game requires strategy and planning. The object of Jewel Chase is to use the arrow keys to move your thief (the yellow thief with the red hat) around the room and collect all the valuables. Your thief escapes through the red door to the next level. The game is over if the other thief escapes before you do.

Jewel Chase's game screen consists of game controls, an assortment of scattered valuables, locked doors and their keys, a thief, an opposing thief, and a red door.

Keep the following points in mind:

- Use the arrow keys to move the thief with the red hat around the room to collect valuables.
- You can only move to tiles that are the same color as the tile you are on. If a different color tile blocks you, you automatically jump to the next same-color tile.
- To move to a new color, go to a multicolored tile.
- If a locked door blocks you, collect a key, switch, or bomb to unlock it.

- After all the valuables are collected, escape through the red door. Don't let the opposing thief escape first. If you do, the game is over.

Color Collision

If you have good reflexes and can think quickly, Color Collision may be the game for you!

Use the arrow keys to make the collider hit circle rims or sticks that match the color of the collider. Each successful collision with a circle makes a green ball on the left side of the screen disappear. After all the green balls are gone, you move to the next level. If you hit a circle of the wrong color, it turns into a stick. If you hit a stick of the wrong color, you lose one of your three lives. The game is over when you lose all your lives.

To Do: Playing Color Collision

▼ To Do

The following task shows you how to play Color Collision:

1. Hit circle rims or sticks that match the color of the collider. The collider becomes the color of the inside of the circle that you just hit.

2. Now you have to match the new color to a new circle rim or stick.

3. For each successful collision with a circle, a green ball on the left side of the screen disappears. When all the green balls disappear from the left side of the screen, you go to the next level.

▲

> You collect any bonuses when you hit a circle of the same color as the collider. These bonuses appear at the bottom center of your screen. Should you collide with a mismatched circle, a stick appears on the playing field. Be careful! The more sticks that you have, the fewer points you can earn, and when you hit a stick of the wrong color, you lose a life! Obviously, the game ends when you lose your last life.

Charmer

The odds are that this game will live up to its title and charm your entire family (if they do not have a phobia of snakes, that is). The object of Charmer is to remove the colored pots by using a flute to charm the snakes up to the vine.

When a snake reaches the vine, its pot disappears and you earn points. The hearts on the left side of the screen show your nine lives.

Beware of falling lids! If a lid hits a pot, you lose a life. If you lose all your lives or if a stack of pots reaches the vine, the game is over.

Use the keys in Table 24.4 to play Charmer.

TABLE 24.4. CHARMER COMMANDS.

Do This	To Accomplish This
Left- and Right-arrow keys	Position a flute under a pot to charm a snake
Spacebar	Change to a different flute

Spring Weekend

This colorful mind teaser is similar to those slide puzzles that require you to unscramble the pieces to form them into a picture. Some might even say that it resembles a Rubik's cube where you can view only one side. Spring Weekend (one of my personal favorites from the Puzzle Collection), however, has a few differences.

The object of this puzzle is to make the set of figures on the left look like the model on the right. Click a figure with the right or left mouse button to rotate the ring of figures around it. Complete each puzzle in as few moves as possible to move to the next level. You have as much time as you need to think, but the game is over if the move counter reaches zero.

The more moves you use, the fewer points you earn.

Muddled Casino

If you want to do well at this game, you'd better know how to plan ahead and use your analytical skills! Don't expect this game to be a fluffy diversion from the chaos of whatever it is you're working on at the computer. The object of Muddled Casino is to remove all cards from the table in the order shown in the right column. The bottom card in the column indicates the first card to remove from the table.

After you've played through the Training levels, you bid against the house to win points. To break even, you need to remove six cards from each table. The game ends when you have fewer than 40 points to wager.

To play Muddled Casino, keep the following in mind:

- Remove all eight cards from the table in the order shown in the Sequence of Play column on the right. The bottom card in the column indicates the first card to remove from the table.

- Because the cards move in groups, positioning a group so that you can remove a particular card and determining a good bid are the keys to winning the game.

- Slide the cards to the exit in the lower-right corner of the screen. To choose the direction that you want to slide a group of cards, use the arrow keys.

- A box on each side of the table highlights to indicate the card group that can move in that direction.

- Each card on the table that can move in the selected group is highlighted with a blue arrow. To select a different card group, press the arrow key twice.

- To move the group of cards, press Spacebar. If you are stuck, press Tab to knock a card off the table.

> You can Tab a card off the table or into a black hole, but this costs you points. You lose the potential to earn back your chips each time that you Tab a card off the table or into a black hole. If you Tab more than two cards off the table, you won't break even.

- You cannot move a card toward another card within the same row. Even if the card is part of the group indicated by the box at the side of the table, it cannot be moved and it is not highlighted.

Summary

This hour mixed work with play by showing you how to create a personalized greeting card, how to locate information in Encarta, and how to escape from it all by playing any of the ten games in the Microsoft Entertainment Pack Puzzle Collection. As they say in the cartoons, "That's all, folks!" You now know a variety of ways to make your life more productive and fun using your new computer!

Workshop

The following workshop helps you solidify the skills you learned in this lesson.

Quiz

Take the following quiz to see how much you've learned.

Questions

1. What's the name of that perky yellow puppy who guides you through the Microsoft Greetings Workshop?

   a. Bullwinkle

   b. Rover

   c. Rocky

2. Which is not an element of the Encarta article screen?

   a. Text frame

   b. Media frame

   c. Article frame

3. What three menu items do all the games have in common?

   a. File, Edit, Help

   b. Game, End, Help

   c. Game, Play/Pause, Help

Answers

1. c. Rocky's the only dog you can get to obey with a click of the mouse!

2. a. The Text frame is not one of the frames included in the article window.

3. c. This is the correct choice for the Puzzle collection.

Activity

In an effort to help you keep your life in order long after you've finished reading this book, I recommend that you take the time right now to set greeting card reminders for all those special birthdays and anniversaries. Not only will that keep you out of trouble for forgetting to remember the occasion, but it can save you tons of money, too.

Have you noticed how much greeting cards cost lately? Even the cheesiest can eat the better part of $2. Make your own cards instead. It makes the recipient feel special, and it helps you tuck away some dough for that new computer game that you've been drooling over!

Appendix **A**

Installing Windows Applications

Whether you want to have the latest and greatest Web browser or to download a neat shareware program from the Internet, you want to know how to install (and yes, uninstall) software on your system. This appendix serves as your quick reference.

Installing Software

Most applications today come with their own installation programs, so installing software is a fairly simple process. Before you start, however, check these items:

- First, make sure that you exit any programs you might be running. Because most installation programs make changes to your system files, exiting your programs prevents any conflicts from occurring. In addition, you might need to restart your computer during the installation, so exiting your programs prevents any possible loss of data.

- If you're upgrading your software to a newer version, be sure to make copies of all your existing data, in case something happens to it during the upgrade process. Also, be aware that some programs (but certainly not the majority) require you to uninstall the previous version before upgrading. Most, however, enable you to simply upgrade over the existing software. Read the installation manual before proceeding.

Before you install any software on your PC, please read the instructions that come with it. Most software vendors provide complete installations that should be followed exactly. Sometimes these instructions may even be listed on the disk label. For the most part, all Windows programs follow these basic steps:

1. Insert the first installation disk (or the CD-ROM) into its drive.
2. Click the Start button and select Run.
3. Type the path and the filename of the installation program and click OK. For example, to install a program from drive A, you might type something like A:SETUP or A:INSTALL. (Check with the installation manual for the exact command that you need to type.) You can also open My Computer, open the drive containing the installation disk, and run the setup program.
4. At this point, the installation program prompts you to make whatever selections are needed. For example, you might be asked to select the drive and folder into which you want the program installed. If you're upgrading over a prior version, make sure that you select the directory in which it was originally installed. Continue to follow the onscreen prompts until the program is installed.

Many installations offer a choice of setup types that you can select. For example, you might be offered the choices Compact, Typical, and Custom. Compact in this case would offer you a slimmed-down version of the program (a good choice if you're short on hard disk space), while Typical installs all the basic options. Custom enables you to select the options that you want (and those that you don't want).

The installation program creates whatever folders are needed. After checking to make sure there is enough space, it then copies the contents of the installation disks or CD-ROM to your hard disk. It also adds a command for adding the program to your Start menu.

Uninstalling Software

If you've decided that you no longer need a particular program, you should remove it from the hard disk to make room for the programs that you do use. Follow these steps:

1. Click the Start button and select Settings. Then select Control Panel from the shortcut menu that appears.

2. Click (or double-click) the Add/Remove Programs icon. The Add/Remove Programs Properties dialog box appears (shown in Figure A.1).

FIGURE A.1.

Removing unwanted programs from the hard disk.

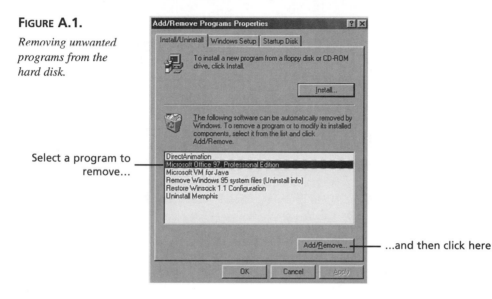

Select a program to remove...

...and then click here

3. Select the program that you want to delete and click Add/Remove.

4. You're prompted to insert the installation disk or CD-ROM for the program that you're removing. Do so, and then click OK.

5. Your application's uninstall program starts. Follow the onscreen prompts to remove the program from your hard disk.

Final Comments

If you find yourself frequently installing and uninstalling software on your computer, you may want to consider using one of the many Uninstaller programs on the market.

You can install software downloaded from the Internet by downloading it into a temporary folder and then running the downloaded program. This is a fairly straightforward process because much of the software on the Internet is presented in self-extracting files. Press the Start button, select Run, and then browse the directory in which you downloaded the file. Click the file to activate it, and then press OK.

Most software packages include a file on their installation disks called Readme.Doc or Readme.Txt. This file usually contains the latest information about the software and often includes the installation instructions. You can read this file by using a tool such as WordPad or Word.

INDEX